STATE RESPONSIBILITY
OF INVESTMENT

CW01501422

There is a wealth of material that shapes the law of State responsibility for breaches of investment contracts. First impressions of an unsettled or uncertain law have thus far gone unchallenged. But unchallenged first impressions point to the need for a detailed study that investigates and analyses the sources, the content, the characteristics and the evolution of this law. The argument at the heart of this monograph is that the law of State responsibility for breaches of investment contracts has carved a unique and distinct trajectory from the traditional route for the creation of international law, developing principally from arbitral awards, and mimicking, to a considerable extent, the general international law on the protection of aliens and alien property. This book unveils the remarkable journey of the law of State responsibility for breaches of investment contracts, from its origins, through its formation, to its arrival at the cusp of maturity.

DR JEAN HO, FCIArb, is Assistant Professor of Law at the National University of Singapore, where she lectures and supervises on diverse aspects of international investment law. Prior to academia, Dr Ho practiced in investor–State dispute settlement. Dr Ho is a member of the Investment Treaty Forum of the British Institute of International and Comparative Law, and an expert on the UNIDROIT Working Group on Land Agricultural Investment Contracts. Dr Ho is also a co-author of *International Investment Law and Arbitration: Commentary, Awards and Other Materials* (Cambridge University Press, 2018).

CAMBRIDGE STUDIES IN INTERNATIONAL AND COMPARATIVE LAW: 136

Established in 1946, this series produces high-quality, reflective and innovative scholarship in the field of public international law. It publishes works on international law that are of a theoretical, historical, cross-disciplinary or doctrinal nature. The series also welcomes books providing insights from private international law, comparative law and transnational studies which inform international legal thought and practice more generally.

The series seeks to publish views from diverse legal traditions and perspectives, and of any geographical origin. In this respect it invites studies offering regional perspectives on core *problématiques* of international law, and in the same vein, it appreciates contrasts and debates between diverging approaches. Accordingly, books offering new or less orthodox perspectives are very much welcome. Works of a generalist character are greatly valued and the series is also open to studies on specific areas, institutions or problems. Translations of the most outstanding works published in other languages are also considered.

After seventy years, Cambridge Studies in International and Comparative Law sets the standard for international legal scholarship and will continue to define the discipline as it evolves in the years to come.

Series Editors

Larissa van den Herik
Professor of Public International Law, Grotius Centre for International Legal Studies, Leiden University

Jean d'Aspremont
Professor of International Law, University of Manchester and Sciences Po Law School

A list of books in the series can be found at the end of this volume.

STATE RESPONSIBILITY FOR BREACHES OF INVESTMENT CONTRACTS

JEAN HO

National University of Singapore

CAMBRIDGE
UNIVERSITY PRESS

CAMBRIDGE
UNIVERSITY PRESS

University Printing House, Cambridge CB2 8BS, United Kingdom

One Liberty Plaza, 20th Floor, New York, NY 10006, USA

477 Williamstown Road, Port Melbourne, VIC 3207, Australia

314-321, 3rd Floor, Plot 3, Splendor Forum, Jasola District Centre, New Delhi - 110025, India

79 Anson Road, #06-04/06, Singapore 079906

Cambridge University Press is part of the University of Cambridge.

It furthers the University's mission by disseminating knowledge in the pursuit of education, learning and research at the highest international levels of excellence.

www.cambridge.org
Information on this title: www.cambridge.org/9781108402439
DOI: 10.1017/9781108235297

First published 2018
First paperback edition 2020

A catalogue record for this publication is available from the British Library

ISBN 978-1-108-41584-2 Hardback
ISBN 978-1-108-40243-9 Paperback

Cambridge University Press has no responsibility for the persistence or accuracy of URLs for external or third-party internet websites referred to in this publication, and does not guarantee that any content on such websites is, or will remain, accurate or appropriate.

For Sorna
sans changer

CONTENTS

vii

FOREWORD

For the last two decades, the focus in international investment law has been on *treaties*. At least for a while, it seemed like treaties were 'the only game in town'. Following Jan Paulsson's influential article in 1995 on 'Arbitration without Privity', the modality of consenting to arbitration by treaty moved centre stage. Yet the rise of arbitration without privity obscured the enduring importance of investments *contracts* in investment arbitration – as an alternative modality for investors and host states to agree to arbitration, as the legal instrument that governs nearly all cross-border investments and as part of the applicable law in investment treaty arbitration.

This focus on treaty, rather than contract, shaped the literature on the emerging investment treaty regime. Most authors have regarded investment contracts as a marginal phenomenon, not worthy of sustained attention – despite a long history of contract-based investment arbitration starting with *Suez Canal Co.* v. *Egypt* in 1864, as well as the continued importance of contract in the world of investment treaty arbitration. At the same time, this perception that the brave new world of investment treaty arbitration was all about treaties, rather than investment contracts, left a void regarding the core question in the law of state responsibility – whether and when breaches of (investment) contacts trigger the host state's responsibility.

In 1970, at a time when the question of state responsibility for contractual breaches was as important as it was controversial due to decolonization, waves of nationalizations and the New International Economic Order, ILC Special Rapporteur Robert Ago decided to exclude contractual breaches from the ILC's project of codifying state responsibility. Given the ILC's decision then to leave aside the topic, the rightly celebrated Articles on State Responsibility, that the ILC finalised in 2001, did not address the question of state responsibility for contractual breaches beyond the general principle in Article 3 that the characterisation as internationally unlawful is independent of domestic law, and vice versa.

Against the virtually blank canvas enters Dr Ho's timely monograph on the law of state responsibility with respect to contractual breaches. While the literature on investment arbitration has exploded over the last decade, making it harder and harder for PhD students and academics to find gaps worthy of book-length treatments in international investment law, Dr Ho has without doubt found such a gap.

Dr Ho reminds us that most investment disputes have their origin in contract, and marshals an impressive range of materials against the background cacophonous state practice in the nineteenth and early twentieth century. The book is part of an important strand of recent scholarship in international law that takes archival materials seriously, and makes productive use of them to complement published sources and scholarly writings.

States generally, and France, Great Britain and the Netherlands in particular, on whose archival records Dr Ho principally draws, were reluctant to exercise diplomatic protection in respect of contractual breaches. Yet mixed claims commissions in the first third of the twentieth century, and later investment tribunals, started to tailor the general rules on state responsibility for breaches of international obligations to breaches of contractual breaches. Thus, the major impetus for the development of this species of state responsibility came from arbitral awards, rather than state practice. The analysis of this rich corpus of arbitral practice, particularly under the main standards of protection in investment treaties, forms the book's core.

Dr Ho charts a middle course between absolute and inexistent contractual protection under international law. She challenges the common perception that state responsibility for contractual breaches, both under customary international law and under investment treaties, is exceptional, without going to the opposite extreme of absolute contractual protection. The school of absolute protection advocates state responsibility for contractual breaches as a matter of course, as reflected in theories of internationalisation that flourished at the time of the New International Economic Order, and in the contemporary investment regime in one view of umbrella clauses according to which these clauses transform contractual breaches automatically into breaches of international law. The opposing school holds that state responsibility for contractual breaches is triggered only in the most extreme circumstances.

In 1987, fittingly in a Festschrift dedicated to Roberto Ago, Stephen Schwebel concluded 'a State is responsible under international law if it commits not any breach, but an arbitrary breach, of a contract between that State and an alien. What is "arbitrary"? It is a breach "for governmental rather than commercial reasons".[1] To Dr Ho, by contrast, determining whether there is a breach of international law depending on a measure's sovereign or commercial character is 'artificial', and yields considerable uncertainty about the scope of contractual protection. Instead, she calls for a focus on the FET standard itself.

With her nuanced analysis of this and many other aspects of state responsibility for contractual breaches, Dr Ho's début dispels the uncertainties surrounding what the law on state responsibility for contractual breaches is and calls our attention to the emergence of a distinct, and well-settled body of rules on state responsibility for contractual breaches. She uncovers how this species of state responsibility developed, how FET became the most important standard in the contemporary investment treaty regime for the protection of contractual breaches, and looks ahead at its future. What is virtually certain is that state responsibility for contractual breaches will only grow in importance in the coming decades.

Dr Ho was my first PhD student at the University of Cambridge. We arrived in Cambridge at around the same time, and I had the pleasure of observing from up close the evolution of this work and her blossoming career as a scholar, as well as participating, modestly, in this endeavour. The supervisor's joy in seeing his former PhD student's book in print, especially of his very first PhD student, must be second only to the author herself. Here is wishing that my future PhD students bring similar scholarly abilities, personal qualities and passion to their PhD projects.

As her former supervisor of the PhD dissertation on which this book is based, I am not the most objective judge of this book's quality. It will be for the reader to judge its contribution. That said, this book will be of interest to a wide audience in academia and practice, and establishes Dr Ho as a leading scholar of investment law among the younger generation.

Michael Waibel
Lauterpacht Centre for International Law
University of Cambridge

---

[1] Stephen M. Schwebel, 'On Whether the Breach by a State of a Contract with an Alien is a Breach of International Law' in *Le Droit International à l'Heure de sa Codification: Etudes en l'Honneur des Roberto Ago* (Milan: Giuffrè, 1987).

PREFACE

I was intrigued by 'The Myth of International Contract Law'. Published in 1981, this article questions the existence of a body of international law dedicated to State breaches of contracts concluded with foreign investors. It also identifies the challenges and controversies associated with articulating and applying such a body of law. Scholarly deference over the next three decades to the findings in this article indicated acceptance of the myth as real. Yet, there is widespread acknowledgement that State responsibility may be engaged for a breach of contract. So long as there are internationally wrongful contractual breaches, there has to be a body of law, however rudimentary, incomplete, even unsatisfactory, from which to ascertain international wrongfulness. Can the myth be debunked? The article's author and my mentor, C. J. Koh Professor M. Sornarajah, stands his ground, but never stopped me from finding mine. After spending seven years pondering this question, I believe I have an answer.

This monograph is a substantially revised version of my doctoral thesis, which was written from October 2011 to October 2014 at the University of Cambridge. The thesis was supervised by Dr Michael Waibel, with advice from Professor John Bell. It was examined by Professor Christoph Schreuer and H. E. Judge James Crawford (then Whewell Chair in International Law at the University of Cambridge) in December 2014, and passed as is. Revisions to the thesis were undertaken from May 2016 to December 2017.

Video synopses of the monograph are available in English, French and Mandarin at the United Nations Audiovisual Library of International Law. My take on the law and its surrounding developments is informed by legal materials available up to 31 December 2017.

ACKNOWLEDGEMENTS

My former Dean, Professor Tan Cheng Han, my current Dean, Professor Simon Chesterman, and my mentors, C. J. Koh Professor M. Sornarajah and Professor Tan Yock Lin, encouraged me to pursue doctoral research at the University of Cambridge. The Faculty of Law at the National University of Singapore awarded me a full scholarship and relieved me of all teaching and administrative duties for the entire duration of my doctoral studies. The monograph was completed between May 2016 and December 2017 while I was on extended teaching relief. During this time, I held visiting appointments at Shearman & Sterling LLP in Paris, at WilmerHale in London, at the Lauterpacht Centre for International Law in Cambridge, and at the International Centre for the Settlement of Investment Disputes of the World Bank in Washington DC. This arrangement was made possible by my Vice-Dean for Academic Affairs, Associate Professor David Tan, my Vice-Dean for Research, Kwa Geok Choo Professor James Penner, and a grant from the Singapore Ministry of Education Academic Research Fund Tier 1 (WBS No. R-241-000-156-115). My stints in Paris, London, Cambridge and Washington DC were facilitated by Professor Emmanuel Gaillard, Professor Gary Born, Professor Eyal Benvenisti and Secretary-General Meg Kinnear.

Finola O'Sullivan, Elizabeth Spicer (until February 2017), Tom Randall (from April 2017) and the team at Cambridge University Press guided me throughout the publishing process. The monograph benefited from the comments of my examiners, Professor Schreuer and Judge Crawford, on my thesis, as well as the comments of two anonymous referees.

Archival research was conducted at various intervals from 2012 to 2017 at the Archives Diplomatiques at La Courneuve in Paris (France), the National Archives at Kew (United Kingdom), and the Nationaal Archief Den Haag at The Hague (Netherlands), where I was assisted by knowledgeable personnel.

Portions of the monograph were presented at Shearman & Sterling LLP in London, WilmerHale in London, l'Université de Paris II (Panthéon-Assas), the Investment Law and Policy Workshop at University College London, and at ICSID. The organisers and the participants gave feedback on my working drafts.

Yas Banifatemi, Emmanuel Gaillard, Kevin Gray, Thomas Hale, Ana Joubin-Bret, Meg Kinnear, Federico Ortino, James Penner, Lauge Poulsen, Margaret Ryan, Jeremy Sharpe, M. Sornarajah and Michael Waibel helped me refine my ideas.

Alastair Simon Chetty provided research assistance.

My loved ones soldiered on with me.

ABBREVIATIONS

Treaties and Other Instruments

ACIA	ASEAN Comprehensive Investment Agreement
CETA	EU-Canada Comprehensive Economic and Trade Agreement
ECT	Energy Charter Treaty
GATT	General Agreement on Tariffs and Trade
ICSID Convention	Convention on the Settlement of Investment Disputes between States and Nationals of Other States
NAFTA	North American Free Trade Agreement
New York Convention	Convention on the Recognition and Enforcement of Foreign Arbitral Awards
TPP	Trans-Pacific Partnership
UNCITRAL Rules	UNCITRAL Arbitration Rules
VCLT	Vienna Convention on the Law of Treaties

Bodies

ASEAN	Association of Southeast Asian Nations
ICC	International Chamber of Commerce
ICJ	International Court of Justice
ICSID	International Centre for Settlement of Investment Disputes
ILC	International Law Commission
OECD	Organisation for Economic Co-operation and Development
PCA	Permanent Court of Arbitration
PCIJ	Permanent Court of International Justice
SCC	Stockholm Chamber of Commerce
UN	United Nations
UNCITRAL	United Nations Commission on International Trade Law

| UNCTAD | United Nations Conference on Trade and Development |
| UNHRC | United Nations Human Rights Council |

Common Terms

BIT	bilateral investment treaty
FET	fair and equitable treatment
FTC	Free Trade Commission
IIA	International Investment Agreement
MFN	most favoured nation
MIT	multilateral investment treaty
MST	minimum standard of treatment
NIEO	New International Economic Order
NPM	non-precluded measures

Journals

AJIL	*American Journal of International Law*
BYIL	*British Yearbook of International Law*
EJIL	*European Journal of International Law*
ICLQ	*International & Comparative Law Quarterly*

Law Reports

ILR	*International Law Reports*
ILM	*International Legal Materials*
IUSCTR	*Iran-US Claims Tribunal Reports*
RIAA	*Reports of International Arbitral Awards*

Treaties and Other International Instruments

Abs-Shawcross Draft Convention on Investments Abroad, 1959.
Art. II
Accord entre la Confédération Suisse et la République Populaire Hongroise concernant la promotion et la protection réciproques des investissements, 5 October 1988.
Art. 1(2)(e)
Agreement between Japan and the State of Israel for the Liberalization, Promotion and Protection of Investment, 1 February 2017.
Agreement between the Government of Canada and the Government of the Republic of Ecuador for the Promotion and Reciprocal Protection of Investments, 29 April 1996 ('Canada-Ecuador investment treaty').
Art. XVIII(2)
Agreement between the Government of Great Britain, Northern Ireland and the Government of Malaysia, 21 May 1981.
Art. 1(1)(a)(v)
Art. 4(1)
Agreement between the Government of Japan and the Government of the Republic of Kenya for the Promotion and Protection of Investment, 28 August 2016.
Art. 5(1)
Agreement between the Government of the Islamic Republic of Pakistan and the Government of the Italian Republic on the Promotion and Protection of Investments, 19 July 1997.
Agreement between the Government of the United Kingdom of Great Britain and Northern Ireland and the Government of the Hungarian People's Republic for the Promotion and Reciprocal Protection of Investments, 9 March 1987 ('UK-Hungary investment treaty').
Art. 1(a)

United Nations Resolutions

National Legislation by Country

Australia

United Kingdom

Human Rights Act 1998.
  Art. 1
Petroleum and Submarine Pipe Lines Act 1975.
State Immunity Act 1978.
  Section 3

United States

Bill of Rights, Amendment V.
  Art. I
  Art. I(10)
US Federal Sovereign Immunities Act 1978.
  Section 1603

Arbitral Awards

Abaclat and Others *v.* Argentina, ICSID Case No. ARB/07/5. Decision on Jurisdiction and Admissibility, 4 August 2011 (Tercier, van den Berg, Abi-Saab (dissenting)).

Accession Mezzanine Capital and Ors *v.* Hungary, ICSID Case No. ARB/12/3. Award, 17 April 2015 (Rovine, Lalonde, Douglas).

ADC Affiliate Ltd. and Anor *v.* Hungary, ICSID Case No. ARB/03/16. Award of the Tribunal, 2 October 2006 (Kaplan, Brower, van den Berg).

AES Summit Generation Ltd. and Anor *v.* The Republic of Hungary, ICSID Case No. ARB/07/22. Award, 23 September 2010 (von Wobeser, Stern, Rowley).

Affaire Des Propriétés Religieuses (France, Royaume-Uni, Espagnole c Portugal) (1920) RIAA 7. Sentence, 4 September 1920 (Root, de Savornin Lohman, Lardy).

AGIP Spa *v.* The Government of the Popular Republic of the Congo, ICSID Case No. ARB/77/1 in 67 ILR 318. Award, 30 November 1979 (Trolle, Dupuy, Rouhani).

AHS Niger and Ors *v.* Republic of Niger, ICSID Case No. ARB/11/11. Award, 15 July 2013 (Mantilla-Serrano, Hubert, Kenfack-Douajni).

Alabama Claims (United States *v.* Great Britain) (1872) 29 RIAA 125.

Alex Genin, Eastern Credit Ltd. Inc. and Anor *v.* The Republic of Estonia, ICSID Case No. ARB/99/2. Award, 25 June 2001 (Fortier, Heith, van den Berg).

Chattin Claim (USA *v.* United Mexican States) (1927) 4 RIAA 282.

Cheek Claim (USA *v.* Siam) in H. L. Fontaine (ed.), *Pasicrisie Internationale: Histoire Documentaire des Arbitrages Internationaux* (Paris: Stampfli & Cie, 1902), p. 580. Award, 21 March 1898.

Claim of the George D. Emery Co. (USA *v.* Nicaragua) in US Department of State, *Papers Relating to the Foreign Relations of the United States* (Washington DC: Government Printing Office, 1909).

Claim of the Salvador Commercial Company (USA *v.* El Salvador) (1902) 15 RIAA 467.

CME Czech Republic B.V. *v.* Czech Republic, UNCITRAL. Partial Award, 13 September 2001 (Kühn, Schwebel, Hándl). Final Award, 14 March 2003 (Kühn, Schwebel, Brownlie).

CMS Gas Transmission Company *v.* The Argentine Republic, ICSID Case No. ARB/01/8. Award, 12 May 2005 (Orrego Vicuña, Lalonde, Rezek). Decision of the ad hoc Committee on the Application for Annulment of the Argentine Republic, 25 September 2007 (Guillaume, Elaraby, Crawford).

Compañia de Aguas del Aconquija S.A. and Vivendi Universal *v.* Argentine Republic, ICSID Case No. ARB/97/3. Decision on Annulment, 3 July 2002 (Fortier, Crawford, Fernández Rozas). Award, 20 August 2007 (Kaufmann-Kohler, Verea, Rowley).

Consortium RFCC c. Royaume du Maroc, Affaire CIRDI No. ARB/00/6. Sentence Arbitrale, 22 December 2003 (Briner, Cremades, Fadlallah).

Continental Casualty *v.* Argentina, ICSID Case No. ARB/03/9. Award, 5 September 2008 (Sacerdoti, Veeder, Nader).

Copper Mesa Mining Corp. *v.* The Republic of Ecuador, UNCITRAL-PCA Case No. 2012-2. Award (redacted), 15 March 2016 (Veeder, Cremades, Simma).

Dallah Real Estate and Tourism Holding Company *v.* The Ministry of Religious Affairs, Government of Pakistan, ICC Case No. (unknown). Final Award, 23 June 2006, unpublished, excerpted in [2010] UKSC 46.

Delagoa Bay Railway Arbitration (USA *v.* Portugal) in US Department of State, Papers Relating to the Foreign Relations of the United States (Washington DC: Government Printing Office, 1900).

Desert Line Projects LLC *v.* The Republic of Yemen, ICSID Case No. ARB/05/17. Award, 6 February 2008 (Tercier, Paulsson, El-Kosheri).

Deutsche Bank AG *v.* Democratic Socialist Republic of Sri Lanka, ICSID Case No. ARB/09/02. Award, 31 October 2012 (Hanotiau, Williams, Khan (dissenting)). Dissenting Opinion of Makhdoom Ali Khan, 31 October 2012.

H. G. Venable (USA *v.* United Mexican States) (1927) 4 RIAA 219.

Himpurna *v.* PT (Persero) in A. J. van den Berg (ed.), Yearbook Commercial Arbitration (The Hague: Kluwer Law International, 2000), vol. 15, p. 11. Award, 4 May 1999 (Paulsson, de Fina, Setiawan).

Hudson's Bay Company's Claim (Great Britain *v.* United States) in H. L. Fontaine (ed.), *Pasicrisie Internationale: Histoire Documentaire des Arbitrages Internationaux* (Paris: Stampfli & Cie, 1902), p. 44. Award, 1 July 1863.

Hulley Enterprises Ltd. *v.* Russia, PCA Case No. AA 226. Final Award, 18 July 2014 (Fortier, Poncet, Schwebel).

Illinois Central Railroad Company Case (USA *v.* United Mexican States) (1926) 4 RIAA 21.

Illinois Central Railroad Company Case (USA *v.* United Mexican States) (1926) 4 RIAA 134.

Impregilo SpA *v.* Argentine Republic, ICSID Case No. ARB/07/17. Award, 21 June 2011 (Danelius, Brower, Stern).

Impregilo SpA *v.* Islamic Republic of Pakistan, ICSID Case No. ARB/03/3. Decision on Jurisdiction, 22 April 2005 (Guillaume, Cremades, Landau).

Inmaris Perestroika Sailing Maritime Services GmbH and Others *v.* Ukraine, ICSID Case No. ARB/08/8. Excerpts of Award, 1 March 2012 (Alexandrov, Rubins, Cremades).

International Thunderbird Gaming Corp. *v.* Mexico, UNCITRAL-NAFTA. Arbitral Award, 26 January 2006 (van den Berg, Ariosa, Wälde).

International Fisheries Company Claim (USA *v.* United Mexican States) (1931) 4 RIAA 691.

Interoceanic Railway of Mexico (Acapulco to Veracruz) (Ltd.) and Ors Claim (Great Britain *v.* United Mexican States) (1931) 5 RIAA 178.

Ioannis Kardassopoulos and Ron Fuchs *v.* Georgia, ICSID Case Nos. ARB/05/18 and ARB/07/15. Award, 3 March 2010 (Fortier, Orrego Vicuña, Lowe).

Island of Palmas (United States *v.* The Netherlands) (1928) 2 RIAA 829. Award of the Tribunal, 4 April 1928 (Huber).

John B. Okie (USA *v.* United Mexican States) (1926) 4 RIAA 54.

Joy Mining Machinery Ltd. *v.* Egypt, ICSID Case No. ARB/03/11. Award on Jurisdiction, 6 August 2004 (Orrego Vicunã, Craig, Weeramantry).

Karaha Bodas *v.* Pertamina in (2001) 16 Mealey's International Arbitration Report C1. Final Award, 18 December 2000 (Derains, Bernadini, El Kosheri).

SGS Société Générale de Surveillance S.A. *v.* The Republic of Paraguay, ICSID Case No. ARB/07/29. Decision on Jurisdiction, 12 February 2010 (Alexandrov, Donovan, Mexía). Award, 10 February 2012 (Alexandrov, Donovan, Mexiá).

SGS Société Générale de Surveillance S.A. *v.* Republic of Philippines, ICSID Case No. ARB/02/6. Decision of the Tribunal on Objections to Jurisdiction, 29 January 2004 (El-Kosheri, Crawford, Crivellaro (partially dissenting)).

Shufeldt Claim (Guatemala *v.* USA) (1930) 2 RIAA 1079. Award, 24 July 1930 (Sisnett).

Siemens A.G. *v.* Argentina, ICSID Case No. ARB/02/8. Award, 6 February 2007 (Sureda, Brower, Janeiro).

Singer Sewing Machine Co. (USA *v.* United Mexican States) (1928) 4 RIAA 411.

Southern Pacific Properties (Middle East) Ltd. *v.* Arab Republic of Egypt, ICSID Case No. ARB/84/3. Award on the Merits, 20 May 1992 (Jiménez de Aréchaga, Pietrowski, El Mahdi (dissenting)).

Spanish Morocco Claims (Espagne *v.* Royaume-Uni) (1925) 2 RIAA 615.

Starrett Housing Corp. and Anor *v.* Iran and Ors, 85 ILR 350. Award, 14 August 1987 (Lagergren, Ameli, Holtzmann (concurring)).

Suez, Sociedad General de Aguas de Barcelona, S.A. and Anor *v.* Argentine Republic, ICSID Case No. ARB/03/17. Decision on Liability, 30 July 2010 (Salacuse, Kaufmann-Kohler, Nikken).

Talsud S.A. *v.* United Mexican States, ICSID Case No. ARB(AF)/04/4. Award, 16 June 2010 (Fortier, Gómez, Veeder).

Técnicas Medioambientales Tecmed S.A. *v.* The United Mexican States, ICSID Case No. ARB(AF)/00/2. Award, 29 May 2003 (Grigera Naón, Fernández Rozas, Bernam Verea).

Texaco Overseas Petroleum Company/California Asiatic Oil Company *v.* The Government of the Libyan Arab Republic, 53 ILR 389. Award on the Merits, 19 January 1977 (Dupuy).

The Sopron-Köszeg Local Company, (1930) 24 AJIL 164. Award, 18 June 1929.

Toto Costruzioni Generali S.p.A. *v.* The Republic of Lebanon, ICSID Case No. ARB/07/12. Decision on Jurisdiction, 11 September 2009 (van Houtte, Feliciani, Moghaizel). Award, 7 June 2012 (van Houtte, Schwebel, Moghaizel).

Turnbull Manoa Company and Anor Claim (United States *v.* Venezuela) (1903–5) 9 RIAA 261.

Union Bridge Company (USA *v.* Great Britain) (1024) 4 RIAA 138.

Arbitration Rules

International Cases

North Sea Continental Shelf Cases (Federal Republic of Germany *v.* Denmark; Federal Republic of Germany *v.* Netherlands) (Judgment) [1969] ICJ Rep 3.

Nottebohm Case (Liechtenstein *v.* Guatemala) [1953] ICJ Rep 111.

Payment of Various Serbian Loans Issued in France (France *v.* Yugoslavia) (12 July 1929) PCIJ, Series A, No. 20.

Van Marle and Ors *v.* The Netherlands in Report of the European Commission of Human Rights, App. Nos 8543/79, 8674/79, 8675/79 and 8685/79, 8 May 1984.

National Cases by Country

Australia

Attorney-General for the Northern Territory *v.* Chaffey and Anor [2007] 231 CLR 651.

In the Matter of the Commercial Arbitration Act 1990 and In the Matter of an Application Pursuant to Section 38 Thereof by the Independent State of Papua New Guinea *v.* Sandline International Inc. 117 ILR 565, Supreme Court of Queensland, 1999.

Mutual Pools and Staff Pte Ltd. *v.* Commonwealth of Australia [1994] 179 CLR 155.

Smith *v.* ANL Ltd. [2000] 204 CLR 493.

Smith-Kline and French Laboratories (Australia) Ltd. and Ors *v.* Secretary, Department of Community Services & Health [1990] 95 ALR 87.

Victoria Park Racing & Recreation Grounds Co. Ltd. *v.* Taylor [1937] 58 CLR 479.

France

L'arrêt Bianchi, Conseil d'Etat, CE n° 69336, 9 April 1993.

L'arrêt Perruche, Cour de Cassation, Ass. Plén. n° de pourvoi 99-13701, 17 November 2000.

L'arrêt Tanty, Conseil d'Etat, CE, 28 November 1924.

India

Achutan *v.* Kerala (1959) AIR (Supreme Court) 490.

Dwarkadas Shrinivas *v.* The Sholapur Spinning and Weaving Co. Ltd. and Others (1954) AIR (Supreme Court) 119.

Rabindra Kumar *v.* Forest Officer (1955) AIR (Manipur) 49.

Malaysia

Adong bin Kuwau and Ors *v.* Kerajaan Negeri Johor and Anor (1997) 1 MLJ 418.

Amit bin Salleh and Ors *v.* The Superintendent, Land & Survey Department Bintulu and Ors (2005) MLJ 258.

Government of Malaysia and Anor *v.* Selangor Pilot Association (1977) 1 MLJ 133.

Mohamad Rambli bin Kawi *v.* Superintendant of Lands Kuching and Anor (2010) 8 MLJ 441.

Selangor Pilot Association *v.* Malaysia (1975) 2 MLJ 66.

Station Hotels *v.* Malayan Railway Administration (1977) 1 MLJ 112.

Nigeria

Niger Delta Development Commission *v.* Nigeria Liquefied Natural Gas Company Ltd. (unpublished), commentary in B. Adaralegbe, 'Stabilizing Fiscal Regimes in Long-Term Contracts: Recent Developments from Nigeria' (2008) 1(3) *Journal of World Energy Law & Business* 239.

Singapore

GMR Malé International Airport Pte Ltd. *v.* The Republic of Maldives and Anor [2013] SGCA 16.

Government of the Lao People's Democratic Republic *v.* Sanum Investments Ltd. [2014] SGHC 15.

Sanum Investments Ltd. *v.* Government of the Lao People's Democratic Republic [2016] SGCA 57.

South Africa

Laugh It Off Promotions CC *v.* SAB International (Finance) B.V. t/a Sabmark International (Freedom of Expression Institute as amicus curiae) (2005) 8 BCLR 743.

Law Society of South Africa *v.* Minister for Transport (2011) 2 BCLR 150.

Phumelela Gaming & Leisure Ltd. *v.* Grndlingh and Ors (2006) 8 BCLR 883.

Port Elizabeth Municipality *v.* Various Occupiers (2005) 1 SA 217.

National Credit Regulator *v.* Opperman (2013) 2 BCLR 170.

Residents of the Joe Slovo Community, Western Cape *v.* Thubelisha Homes and Ors (2010) 3 SA 454.

United Kingdom

Council of Civil Service Unions and Ors *v.* Minister for the Civil Service [1965] AC 374.

Cugden Rutile (No. 2) Pty Ltd. and Anor *v.* Gordon William Wesley Chalk [1975] AC 520.

In re Malcolm [2004] EWCA Civ 1748.

Kahler *v.* Midland Bank Ltd. [1950] AC 24.

National Provincial Bank Ltd. *v.* Ainsworth [1965] AC 1175.

Playa Larga *v.* I Congreso del Partido [1981] 1 AC 244.

R *v.* Croydon London Borough Council and Anor Appeal [2009] UKSC 8.

R *v.* International Trustee for the Protection of Bondholders A/G (2) [1937] AC 500.

Rederiaktiebolaget Amphitrite *v.* The King [1921] KB 500.

Svenska Petroleum Exploration AB *v.* Government of the Republic of Lithuania [2007] QB 886.

The Commissioners for Her Majesty's Revenue and Customs *v.* John Richard Smith [2007] EWHC 488.

Thomas *v.* Sorrell [1973] Vaugh 330.

Tulk *v.* Moxhay [1848] 41 ER 1143.

Williams & Humbert *v.* W & H Trade Marks (Jersey) (1985), 75 ILR 268.

Wilson *v.* First County Trust Ltd. (No. 2) [2003] UKHL 40.

United States

Board of Education *v.* Vail, 466 US 377 (1984).

Bowen *v.* Public Agencies Opposed to Social Security Entrapment, 477 US 41 (1986).

City of El Paso *v.* Simmons, 379 US 497 (1965).

Eastern Enterprises *v.* Apfel, 524 US 498 (1998).

Fletcher *v.* Peck, 10 US (6 Cranch) 87 (1810).

Perry *v.* Sindermann, 408 US 593 (1972).

United States *v.* Juan Percheman, 32 US 51 (1833).

Vail *v.* Board of Education, 705 F 2d 1435 (7th Cir. 1983).

Diplomatic Correspondences by Country

France

L'Affaire Lapeyre (Autriche-Hongrie) (1914), Archives Diplomatiques La Courneuve, 140CPCOM/79.

National Archives Kew, FO 371/12738, A7606/7606/2 (Argentina), record discarded by the UK Foreign Office.

National Archives Kew, FO/371/4432, A1644/1644/6 (Brazil), record discarded by the UK Foreign Office.

National Archives Kew, FO 371/4445, A6211/2690/32 (Costa Rica), record discarded by the UK Foreign Office.

National Archives Kew, FO 371/11841, W1953/1953/17 (France), record discarded by the UK Foreign Office.

National Archives Kew, FO 371/12633, W2215/2215/17 (France), record discarded by the UK Foreign Office.

National Archives Kew, FO 371/6087, C347/347/19 (Greece), record discarded by the UK Foreign Office.

National Archives Kew, FO 371/9896, C12432/12432/19 (Greece), record discarded by the UK Foreign Office.

National Archives Kew, FO 371/9583, A3800/A5900/3800/35 (Peru), record discarded by the UK Foreign Office.

National Archives Kew, FO 371/9582, A3477/A3907/A6852/456/35 (Peru), record discarded by the UK Foreign Office.

National Archives Kew, FO 371/7106, W647/W1678/647/36 (Portugal), record discarded by the UK Foreign Office.

National Archives Kew, FO 371/11935, W8662/8662/36 (Portugal), record discarded by the UK Foreign Office.

National Archives Kew, FO 371/12702, W10280/116/36 (Portugal), record discarded by the UK Foreign Office.

United States

US Department of State, 'Letter from Mr Sickles to Mr Sagasta (8 January 1871)' in *Papers Relating to the Foreign Relations of the United States* (Washington DC: Government Printing Office 1871–2), p. 754.

Introduction

Investment contracts, generally understood as written agreements between foreign investors and host States or host State entities setting out their respective obligations in relation to a given venture, are the principal means by which foreign investment enters the territory of a host State. Common species of investment contracts include natural resource concessions, public service concessions, build-operate-and-transfer contracts and public–private partnerships.[1] Given how commonplace investment contracts are in begetting foreign capital inflow, the great majority of disputes between foreign investors and host States are contractual in origin. An important issue in investor-State disputes involving investment contracts is whether the breach of an investment contract by a State engages its responsibility under international law. Notwithstanding widespread acceptance that a breach of contract by a State may amount to an internationally wrongful act, the law of State responsibility for breaches of investment contracts seems unsettled.

A key reason for the uncertainty is the perception that the engagement of State responsibility for contractual breaches is exceptional. In 1970, the International Law Commission expunged the topic of contractual breaches for good from its codification project on State responsibility.[2] According to Special Rapporteur Roberto Ago, '[t]he violation by a State of a contractual obligation does not constitute, in and of itself, the objective element of an internationally wrongful act and is not at all capable of giving rise to State responsibility; the violation is subject to a different legal

---

[1] For an overview of the different types of investment contracts, see J. Ho, 'Investment Contracts and Internationalisation' in C. L. Lim, J. Ho and M. Paparinskis, *International Investment Law and Arbitration – Commentary, Awards and Other Materials* (Cambridge: Cambridge University Press, 2018) pp. 37, 52–4.

[2] R. Ago, 'First Report on State Responsibility' (7 May 1969–20 January 1970), UN Doc. A/CN.4/217, p. 137.

order, be it national law or some other law'.[3] Since this pronouncement, no detailed study has been undertaken to articulate what the law of State responsibility on contractual breaches is.

Inertia masks advancement. Legal development is evident in the case of investment contracts because foreign investors habitually invoke international law to protect their contractual rights. Early investors sought protection for their contractual rights from general international law on the treatment of aliens and alien property. Latter-day investors seek protection for their contractual rights from an array of investment treaty provisions conferring substantive protection on qualifying investments. Recurrent attempts to engage a host State's international responsibility for breaching an investment contract offered ample opportunity for this sub-field of the law of State responsibility to flourish.

There is a wealth of material that shapes the law of State responsibility for breaches of investment contracts. First impressions of an unsettled or uncertain law have thus far gone unchallenged. But unchallenged first impressions point to the need for a detailed study that investigates and analyses the sources, the content, the characteristics and the evolution of this law. The frequency which State responsibility for breaches of investment contracts arises for consideration in investor-State disputes, calls for a coherent and long overdue answer to the question of what the law of State responsibility for breaches of investment contracts *is*. This is the lacuna in the existing legal literature that this monograph has been written to address.[4]

The argument at the heart of this monograph is that the law of State responsibility for breaches of investment contracts has carved a unique and distinct trajectory from the traditional route for the creation of

---

[3] R. Ago, 'Fifth Report on State Responsibility to the ILC' (22 March 1976), UN Doc. A/CN.4/291, pp. 12–13. Author's translation from the original French.

[4] While various international law issues arising from investment contracts have been discussed in a series of influential articles by F. A. Mann, C. F. Amerasinghe, P. Weil, G. R. Delaume, G. Sacerdoti and V. V. Veeder, these articles date from the 1940s to the 1990s. Little has been written about investment contracts in the last three decades which have witnessed momentous developments. See F. A. Mann, 'The Law Governing State Contracts' (1944) 21 BYIL 11; same author, 'State Contracts and State Responsibility' (1960) 54 AJIL 572; C. F. Amerasinghe, 'State Breaches of Contracts with Aliens and International Law' (1964) 58 AJIL 881; P. Weil, 'Problèmes Relatifs aux Contrats Passés entre un Etat et un Particulier' (1969) 128(3) *Recueil des Cours* 95; G. R. Delaume, 'State Contracts and Transnational Arbitration' (1981) 75 AJIL 784; G. Sacerdoti, 'State Contracts and International Law: A Reappraisal' (1986–7) 7 *Italian Yearbook of International Law* 26; and V. V. Veeder, 'The Lena Goldfields Arbitration: The Historical Roots of Three Ideas' (1998) 47 ICLQ 747.

international law. Unlike the rest of the law of State responsibility which developed from the diplomatic and treaty practice of States, the law of State responsibility for breaches of investment contracts developed principally from arbitral awards. And despite the absence of a system of binding precedent in international arbitration, the law of State responsibility for breaches of investment contracts has managed to defy the odds and develop in a fairly stable manner. It mimics, to a considerable extent, the general international law on the protection of aliens and alien property. Characterising the law, as Ago once did, as one of exceptional application, understates the possibility of State responsibility being engaged for a breach of contract, and underestimates the role it has played and will continue to play in investment contract protection. The argument rests on a three-part structure, corresponding to a past-present-future framework of analysis. This chronological framework showcases the three critical and connected phases in the development of the law of State responsibility for breaches of investment contracts.

Phase 1 traces the historical context from which the law was borne. History is crucial to the setting out of the *lex lata* for three reasons.

First, it shows that the law of State responsibility on contractual breaches developed from arbitral awards not by chance, but by circumstance. States were often requested by their nationals to present contract claims to foreign States. Yet, despite many opportunities to explore the possibility of invoking international law in diplomatic correspondence and gravitate towards a shared body of rules, the treatment of contract claims differed from State to State and was rarely grounded in law (Chapter 1). This encouraged the perception that States were generally disinclined to bring contractual breaches within the purview of international law.

Second, this perceived disinclination, which only comes to light with a historical survey, has important ramifications for how the law of State responsibility for breaches of investment contracts will develop. Over time, arbitral *jurisprudence* revealed that conditions for the engagement of State responsibility for contractual breaches were mostly drawn from the well-established conditions found in the general international law on the treatment of aliens and alien property (see *Phase 2* below). The exception was 'internationalisation', which advocated the engagement of State responsibility for all contractual breaches. However, 'internationalisation' encountered and continues to encounter strong resistance from the arbitration community (see *Phase 2* below). The oft-canvassed reason for this resistance is deficiencies in the various theories of 'internationalisation'. But the more profound reason, and one which only recourse to history fleshes out, is because 'internationalisation' is too far removed from the perceived disinclination of States to frame contractual breaches as violations of international law, and from the baseline for investment contract protection found in general international law.

Third, the unusually prominent role arbitral awards play in articulating the law of State responsibility for breaches of investment contracts requires explanation. The absence of customary international law specific to contractual breaches, ambiguous treaty practice, and incomplete, aborted or shelved codification efforts gave rise to a unique set of circumstances which enabled arbitral awards to become a principal source of international law (Chapter 2). This phenomenon existed before the current age of investment treaty arbitration where arbitral awards are often taken for granted as the first port of call for research into international investment law. When viewed in its proper and illuminating historical context, there are good reasons why the law of State responsibility for breaches of investment contracts developed through arbitral awards. History thus provides a strong justification for why arbitral awards, despite being traditionally viewed as a subsidiary source of international law, can be instrumental in bringing about legal development and change.

Phase 2 investigates why the development of the law of State responsibility for breaches of investment contracts, despite being located in arbitral *jurisprudence*, has been more harmonious than haphazard. The most plausible explanation for this is the greater inclination of arbitral tribunals to adopt, adapt and apply established rules on the protection of aliens and alien property to contractual breaches. This is why arbitral *jurisprudence* on the core standard of treatment, which is derivative of the minimum standard of treatment of aliens and reflected in the treaty standard of Fair and Equitable Treatment (FET) of qualifying investments (Chapter 3), and the unlawful expropriation of contractual rights (Chapter 4), both under general international law and investment treaty law, possesses greater potential for coherent development. Anchoring a developing law to settled law is a promising recipe for legal certainty and stability. In contrast, radical theories espoused by a few arbitral tribunals to facilitate the engagement of State responsibility for investment contracts in the name of investment protection inevitably encounter resistance and rejection. The 'internationalisation' of investment contracts is a case in point because neither general international law nor umbrella clauses in investment treaties provides firm support for the conversion of contractual obligations into international obligations (Chapter 5). Irreconcilable rulings abound precisely because arbitral tribunals are unfettered by earlier arbitral awards advocating dubious uses of international law.

Phase 3 anticipates how the relationships between general international law and investment treaty law will shape future content of the emerging international law on investment contract protection, which will in turn influence future strategy on bringing international investment contract claims. Conditions for the engagement of State responsibility for contractual breaches, while ascertainable to date, are neither cast in stone nor a closed list. It is therefore necessary to explore how the law may evolve, and how this evolution may affect the prospects of international investment contract claims. The findings in *Phase 2* predict that the future of investment contract protection lies in moderation. Legal development will entrench and elaborate on qualified contractual protection, numbering the days of absolute contractual protection through 'internationalisation'. The reliability of this prediction is strengthened in two ways.

First, through the stabilising influence of the general international law on investment treaty law on the topic of investment contract protection (Chapter 6). General international law supplies the foundational content for investment treaty law and is relevant to the interpretation of investment treaty provisions invoked for investment contract protection. Content articulation or content development for investment treaty law attracts far less controversy when it preserves the position in general international law, than when it deviates significantly, in the absence of unambiguous treaty language authorising the deviation, from that position. Therefore, with the probable demise of absolute contractual protection which finds little to no support in general international law, future development of the law of State responsibility will likely be led by contractual breaches that violate the core standard of treatment or that amount to unlawful expropriations.

Second, through empirical evidence that FET claims, although better suited than unlawful expropriation and umbrella clause claims to investment contract protection, do not enjoy a higher success rate than the other two treaty claims (Chapter 7). The content of FET is grounded to the core standard of treatment, tempering the prospect that State responsibility for breaches of investment contracts will be casually engaged through a rapidly evolving and expansive definition of FET. That said, contract-based FET claims are poised to become a prominent category of international investment contract claims, given their undiluted focus on the manner of the host State's contractual breach and the relative predictability of the content of FET that is specific to investment contract protection.

Together, *Phases 1, 2* and *3* outlined here demonstrate why the law of State responsibility for breaches of investment contracts should no longer be deemed unsettled or uncertain. Its sources, content, characteristics and evolution are all capable of articulation and analysis in a detailed yet compact study. Contrary to earlier wisdom, there is an international law on investment contract protection. The following chapters unveil the remarkable journey of this law from its origins, to its formation, to its arrival at the cusp of maturity.

1

Power and Principle in the Origins
of Contractual Protection

Given the refusal of the ex-Sultan to honour his obligations and to repay what has been due for the last 10 years, not only for recent expenditures, but also for jewellery and money obtained on credit, I am forced to officially request the Dutch authorities at The Hague and in Riau to promptly reimburse Mr Sabatier, by whatever means they deem appropriate ...

We find ourselves, I admit, in the presence of a delicate question of international law, but it seems at first glance difficult to ask the protector nation of an indigenous Prince to assume his obligations and meet the debts that he contracted in his capacity as a sovereign.

Letter from the French Consul to the Dutch Consul General in Singapore,
28 March 1911[1]

[H]is Excellency the Governor General of the Dutch Indies, is of the opinion that the debt referred to in your letter cannot be considered as anything other than a debt of a purely private character, and for which the appeal by Mr Sabatier to the good offices of the [French] government does not appear justified.

Response from the Dutch Consul General to the French Consul in Singapore,
7 June 1911[2]

1.1 Introduction

When investors in the past were embroiled in contractual disputes with foreign States, they never quite knew what to expect. Like Mr Sabatier, the claimant may first submit a contract claim to its home State, requesting diplomatic support. Like Mr Sabatier, the claimant then awaits the discretionary decision of its home State to offer diplomatic support. And like Mr Sabatier, the supported claimant may eventually receive no satisfaction when the host State firmly denies the home State's demand for payment,

---

[1] Archives Diplomatiques La Courneuve, 138CPCOM/6. Author's translation from the original French.
[2] Ibid.

regardless of the factual or legal merits of the claim. If we fixate on the outcome of *Réclamation Sabatier*, which is typical of contract claims presented through diplomatic channels, the excerpt above is no more than a reproduction of a short-lived diplomatic exchange. A closer reading of *Réclamation Sabatier* reveals that it is actually a microcosm of the circumstances that led to the emergence of legal content on contractual protection, and where both power and principle converged in the making of international law.

Power is commonly understood as anything that establishes and maintains control and domination of a person by another person.[3] In inter-State relations, power can be asserted through a multitude of ways, ranging from a written demand to armed intervention, to procure a desired outcome. The content of asserted power in a given scenario may be one dimensional, such as the isolated pursuit of the desired outcome, or multidimensional, such as the concurrent pursuit of discrete objectives. The assertion of power by a claimant State may not procure a desired outcome if the respondent State neutralises the attempt at control and domination. *Réclamation Sabatier* involved the assertion and counter-assertion of power that did not bring about the desired outcome for the claimant State, France. In its written demand, France asserted the power to determine the outcome of the dispute (the satisfaction of the contract claim by the Netherlands), the power to determine the format of dispute settlement (the recourse to diplomacy) and the power to determine the legal content on contractual protection (the characterisation of a contractual breach as a question of international law). In its response, the Netherlands counter-asserted the power to reject all the French stipulations, attempting to neutralise the French attempt at domination and control. France's decision not to press the claim, for reasons that have never been made known, enabled the Dutch counter-assertion of power to prevail.

---

[3] H. Morgenthau, *Politics among Nations: The Struggle for Power and Peace* (revised by K. W. Thompson and W. D. Clinton), 7th edn (New York, NY: McGraw-Hill, 2006), p. 11. Although Morgenthau's definition of power has been criticised (see for instance K. J. Holsti, 'The Concept of Power in the Study of International Relations' (1964) 7(4) *International Studies Quarterly* 179), it has withstood significant revision in seven editions of the leading treatise on international relations. In the first edition of *Politics among Nations* (New York, NY: A. A. Knopf, 1948), p. 13, power was defined as 'man's control over the minds and actions of other men'. Its ability to capture and adapt to evolving inter-State dynamics over nearly six decades, in contexts ranging from the aftermath of World War II, to the Cold War, and to the ongoing war against terror, attests to it applicability to a wide variety of settings, including the present one on contractual protection.

The three-pronged content of power in *Réclamation Sabatier*, namely, the power to determine the outcome of the dispute, the power to determine the format of dispute settlement, and the power to determine the legal content on contractual protection, is present to varying degrees in three sequential periods in history that housed different approaches of the principal trading nations of France, the Netherlands, the United Kingdom and the United States to contractual protection. The first period is the early 1800s to the early 1900s where contract claims were presented through diplomatic channels, and where the power to determine the outcome of the dispute was the dominant, and often solitary, theme in diplomatic missives. The second period is the early 1900s to the 1920s where home States asserted the power to determine the format of contract claim resolution. Instead of taking the usual diplomatic route, they persuaded a number of host States to have outstanding claims decided by standing bodies with State-appointed commissioners. These bodies, also known as Mixed Claims Commissions, are formally tasked by their founding States with the impartial adjudication of claims in accordance with principles of law. The power to determine the legal content on contractual protection and the outcome of the dispute was delegated to the Commissions.[4] The third period is the 1920s to the 1990s where States and private actors began asserting the power to determine the legal content on contractual protection through codification projects on international law. Some States and private actors further asserted the power to determine the outcome of future disputes, by inserting or attempting to insert a clause equating every breach of contract by a host State to an international wrong in model investment protection codes. Such a clause prohibits any interference with a concluded contract and advocates absolute contractual protection.

---

[4] The establishment of Mixed Claims Commissions is the extension of ancient practice, where States agree to settle their disputes peacefully by submitting these disputes to a tribunal comprising distinguished individuals, or to a court, whose decision is binding on the disputing States. The earliest recorded example of the pacific settlement of a dispute through third-party adjudication dates back to 750 BC. It involved the city-State of Lacedaemon (later known as Sparta) and the autonomous region of Messenia, both territories being part of modern-day Greece. The dispute, which arose from the murder of Lacedonians by a Messenian and the subsequent refusal of Messenia to commit its citizen to trial in Lacedaemon, was eventually submitted to a court in Athens for resolution. A fuller account of this dispute and its aftermath is found in Pausanias, *Description of Greece* (translated by W. H. S. Jones), revd edn (Cambridge, MA: Harvard University Press, 1918), Book IV, paras. 4.4.5–4.5.9. Other early examples of inter-State arbitrations are reviewed in W. L. Westermann, 'Interstate Arbitration in Antiquity' (1907) 2(5) *The Classical Journal* 197.

Legal content on contractual protection emerged in the second and third periods, where the power to determine such content was regularly asserted, be it by Mixed Claims Commissions exercising a delegated power, or by the launch of codification projects. Yet, the principles of law that were identified and applied by the Commissions to determine the outcome of contractual disputes grew authoritative over time, while the prospect of absolute contractual protection in certain model codes was and remains controversial. The different fates that different principles on contractual protection experienced suggest that States and other actors in international law have been more willing to affirm principles enunciated in certain circumstances than in others. It may therefore be said that although the power to determine legal content was asserted in both the awards of the Mixed Claims Commissions and in the model clauses presented by codifiers as restatements of international law, the principles on contractual protection that emerged in the former context exerted a stronger compliance pull than the principle of absolute contractual protection that was advocated in the latter.[5]

This chapter argues that while the frequent assertion of the power to determine the legal content on the international responsibility of States towards contractual protection enables the emergence of such content, it is the assertion of this power in circumstances that inhibit content crafting to the obvious benefit of one State or a select group of States, that elevates the compliance pull of articulated content.[6] These circumstances were present

---

[5] T. M. Franck, *The Power of Legitimacy among Nations* (Oxford: Oxford University Press, 2010), pp. 24–6. Franck identifies 'legitimacy' as the variable that determines the strength of a rule's compliance pull, and defines it as 'a property of a rule or rule-making institution which itself exerts a pull toward compliance on those addressed normatively because those addressed believe that the rule or institution has come into being an operates in accordance with generally accepted principles of right process'. This chapter does not challenge Franck's proposed nexus between a rule's legitimacy and its compliance pull. It eschews the label of 'legitimacy' with the open-endedness of circumstances surrounding the emergence of principles of contractual protection, because the latter already explains the difference in compliance pull across principles, without the additional assignment of degrees of 'legitimacy' to different principles.

[6] The use of power in this chapter to explain the legal origins of contractual protection is analogous to the use of power to explain the rise of arbitration as a mode of international commercial dispute settlement. In T. Hale, *Between Interests and Law: The Politics of Transnational Commercial Disputes* (Cambridge: Cambridge University Press, 2015), p. 10, Hale argues that arbitration was popularised through 'market power'. This is animated by a firm's 'demand' for a particular dispute resolution institution, whose success vis-à-vis firms with conflicting 'demands' is 'determined by the attendant constellation of power and interests, which [in turn] determines the "supply" of institutional outcomes'; see also pp. 58–61. In this chapter, the power to determine the mode of dispute settlement is asserted by States

when Mixed Claims Commissions deciding contract claims against States asserted the delegated powers of legal content-determination and outcome-determination. Despite the fact that these Commissions were usually the product of a creditor home State successfully imposing its chosen format of dispute settlement on a debtor host State, the Commissions' duty to adjudicate submitted claims impartially turned out to be an important safeguard against the engineering of principles on contractual protection that invariably favour the satisfaction of claims presented by the home State. And having invoked rule by law to bind host States to unfavourable decisions by Mixed Claims Commissions, home States were similarly constrained when they were on the receiving end of unfavourable rulings. The resulting capacity of Mixed Claims Commissions to elaborate principles on contractual protection with a strong compliance pull portended the capacity of later arbitral tribunals, operating within similar circumstances of imposed and delegated powers, to achieve the same. The early, compelling normative contribution of the Mixed Claims Commissions to contractual protection is the first step to understanding why the law of State responsibility for breaches of investment contracts developed primarily through arbitral awards.

1.2   The Early 1800s to the Early 1900s: Contractual Protection through Diplomacy

When contractual protection was effected through diplomacy, States appeared to be more concerned with asserting the power to determine the outcome of a presented claim than with redirecting claims to a different forum for settlement, or with locating the factual or legal justifications for satisfying or denying a claim. *Réclamation Sabatier* stands out in the sea of diplomatic exchanges on contract claims because it underscores how State preoccupation with outcome limited the potential for States to debate and develop legal content on contractual protection during the period of diplomacy. Relying on original archival research into the diplomatic practice of France, the Netherlands and the United Kingdom, and the annotated diplomatic practice of the United States,[7] this section demonstrates

---

against other States, while in *Between Interests and Law* this power is asserted by private firms against other private firms.

[7] E. M. Borchard, 'Contractual Claims in International Law' (1913) 13(6) *Columbia Law Review* 457 at 466–70; same author, *The Diplomatic Protection of Citizens Abroad; or, The Law of International Claims* (Cleveland, OH: Banks Law Publishing, 1915), pp. 280–95; C. Eagleton, *The Responsibility of States in International Law* (New York, NY: New York

the evident preoccupation of both home and host States with the outcome of a contract claim, almost always to the exclusion of other concerns.

Home States rarely proffered detailed reasons for supporting or dismissing contract claims. Many claims received no support whatsoever,[8] while other claims were deemed to warrant presentation to the supposedly defaulting host State. Archival records rarely reveal any articulated or observable basis for why some claims are supported but others are not, or why some claims are pursued more aggressively than others. As a result, while the presentation of a claim with a demand for satisfaction is an assertion of power by the home State to determine the outcome of the claim, it does not necessarily establish the veracity of the claim, nor serve as a predictor of outcome. It is not uncommon for home States to receive inflated and unmeritorious contract claims. Diplomatic correspondence shows that the United Kingdom and France do investigate the veracity of contract claims, adjusting those that appear inflated,[9] and discarding those that appear unmeritorious.[10] The Netherlands, on the other hand, has presented a claim to the UK Foreign Office in the wake of the surrender of the Transvaal Republic, on the word of its national and without

---

University Press, 1928), chap. 7; and C. C. Hyde, *International Law Chiefly as Interpreted and Applied by the United States*, 2nd revd edn (Boston, MA: Little, Brown and Company, 1945), vol. II, Section 303. Detailed study of US diplomatic practice on contract claims was made possible by the periodic compilation and publication of US diplomatic correspondence. The leading digests that included sections on contract claims were compiled by J. B. Moore (*A Digest of International Law in Six Volumes* (Washington, DC: Government Printing Press, 1906)) and F. Wharton, (*A Digest of the International Law of the United States in Three Volumes* (Washington, DC: Government Printing Press, 1886)) with extensive reproductions of and references to diplomatic documents published by the US Department of State in yearly editions of *Papers Relating to the Foreign Relations of the United States* (Washington, DC: Government Printing Office, 1861). These papers have been digitised by the University of Wisconsin in a free, searchable database: see University of Wisconsin-Madison Libraries, 'Foreign Relations of the United States', online: https://digital.library .wisc.edu/1711.dl/FRUS (accessed 31 December 2017).

[8] See, for instance, *Claim by NV Chemische Fabriek v/h Dr A Haagen against Italy* (30 November 1935), Nationaal Archief Den Haag, 2.05.26/982.

[9] UK: *Claim of Patent Lighting Company against the Government of Paraguay* (1930), National Archives Kew, FO 371/14250, A92/A707/A2218/92/33.

[10] France: *Réclamation Gautreau* (Pérou), Archives Diplomatiques La Courneuve, 190CPCOM/22, 190CPCOM/23; *L'Affaire Lapeyre* (Autriche-Hongrie) (1914), Archives Diplomatiques La Courneuve, 140CPCOM/79; and *Réclamation Société d'Entreprises de Dragages* (Brésil) (1916), Archives Diplomatiques La Courneuve, 144CPCOM/106.

UK: Claim by Anglo-French company against the Government of Italy (1920) (National Archives Kew, FO 371/4890, C189/189/22); and Claim of Anglo-Roumanian Produce Company against Government of Roumania (1928), National Archives Kew, FO 371/12965, C53/53/37.

any supporting documentation. The Foreign Office replied that it was not prepared to entertain the claim as 'no trace can be found, either in the office of the Military Governor at Pretoria, or in that of the Assistant Inspector of Remounts, Johannesburg, that any horse was commandeered from Mr Rijss'.[11] It is uncertain whether all submitted claims were carefully scrutinised, if at all, by home States. The United Kingdom, for example, viewed diplomatic intervention for contract claims as 'entirely a question of discretion',[12] and it seems likely that the Netherlands may have too.

When home States decide to diplomatically support a contract claim, the power to determine the outcome of the claim is normally asserted through a written demand or several written demands, and occasionally in conjunction with other means to encourage satisfaction of the claim by host States. *Réclamation Sabatier* is an example of the unsuccessful assertion of power through written demand by a home State to determine the outcome of a contract claim. Examples of successful assertion through written demand can be found in Dutch diplomatic practice.[13] One such example involved claims by a flower merchant, La Maison Jean Barth Bos, against the municipality of Catania in Italy. Here, La Maison Bos sought outstanding payment of 199 French francs (worth approximately 750 euros today)[14] for a quantity of blooms supplied to the public gardens in Cantania. The Dutch vice-consul at Cantania intervened after repeated

---

[11] Letter from the Foreign Office to Count de Rechteren Limpurg Almelo (13 September 1902), Nationaal Archief Den Haag, 2.05.44/520.

[12] Circular addressed by Viscount Palmerston to Her Majesty's Representatives in Foreign States, respecting the Debts due by Foreign States to British Subjects (January 1848), reproduced in D. C. M. Platt, *Finance, Trade, and Politics in British Foreign Policy 1815–1914* (Gloucestershire: Clarendon Press, 1968), Appendix II; see also Mann, 'The Law Governing State Contracts', at 14.

[13] See also *Réclamation des employés du chemin de fer du Lunghai* (Chine) (31 March 1927, 28 May 1927), Notes au Wai Chiao Pou des Représentants de la Belgique, de la France et des Pays-Bas, Nationaal Archief Den Haag, 2.05.37/3736; *Achteratallig salaris door China verschuldigd aan den heer Ir.v.d.Veen* (Chine) (1929), Nationaal Archief Den Haag, 2.05.37/3736; and *Claim of the Transvaal Warehouse Company against the Government of the Late South African Republic* (UK) (1903), Nationaal Archief Den Haag, 2.05.44/520. The Dutch government has even intervened in contract claims against foreign nationals, see *Claim of Mr Kehlenbrink against H. Ruttonjee & Son* (Hong Kong) (1913), Nationaal Archief Den Haag, 2.05.27.01/96; *Claim of Ho Bee & Co against Ong Ang Tjim* (Hong Kong) (1916), Nationaal Archief Den Haag, 2.05.27.01/96; *Réclamation Snyders* (Italie) (1916), Nationaal Archief Den Haag, 2.05.26/783; and *Réclamation Anonima Astrea* (Italie) (1935), Nationaal Archief Den Haag, 2.05.26/986.

[14] Historical exchange rate obtained from Historical Statistics, 'Historical Currency Converter', online: www.historicalstatistics.org/Currencyconverter.html (accessed 31 December 2017).

POWER AND PRINCIPLE

requests by La Maison Bos for payment went unanswered.[15] The mayor
of Cantania responded to the vice-consul's written request for payment,
arguing that payment to La Maison Bos was withheld because the blooms
delivered did not conform to contractual stipulations. The vice-consul
sent several more written demands, and the consul at Messine wrote to the
mayor as well.[16] Persistence paid off as payment was eventually made to La
Maison Bos from the national treasury.[17]

   Although unsuccessful in *Réclamation Sabatier*, France had a reputation
for 'extraordinary tenacity' in its support for contract claims,[18] and a more
aggressive pursuit may involve written and verbal demands, as well as
close monitoring of the actions taken by the host State to satisfy the claim.
This tenacity was seen in *Réclamation Decauville*, and in *Réclamation de
la Société des Abbatoirs de Para*. The former claim involved non-payment
for railway construction materials purchased by the Guatemalan government from a French supplier. After sending two requests for payment
that met with silence, the French consul in Guatemala decided to seek an
audience with President Estrada Cabrera to present the claim in person.
He managed to secure two meetings, a month apart, with the president
to discuss the claim and was assured by the president on both occasions
that payment for the materials will be made. The French consul then
asked to speak with the Guatemalan minister for foreign affairs as well,
and extracted further assurances that the claim will be satisfied as soon as
possible.[19] Within months, the French claimant received the outstanding
payment from the Guatemalan government.[20] In the latter claim, the local

[15] *Lettre du Consulat des Pays-Bas de Messine provisoirement à Palerme à Son Excellence Ministre Plenipotentiaire des Pays-Bas à Rome* (19 January 1912), Nationaal Archief Den Haag, 2.05.26/781.
[16] *Lettre du Consulat des Pays-Bas de Messine provisoirement à Palerme à Son Excellence Ministre Plenipotentiaire des Pays-Bas à Rome* (27 January 1912), Nationaal Archief Den Haag, 2.05.26/781.
[17] *Lettres du Consulat des Pays-Bas de Messine provisoirement à Palerme à Son Excellence Ministre Plenipotentiaire des Pays-Bas à Rome* (5 February 1912, 23 February 1912, 26 February 1912, 5 March 1912), Nationaal Archief Den Haag, 2.05.26/781.
[18] *Lettre de la Légation du Pérou au Chile au Monsieur le Ministre des Affaires Etrangères* (9 October 1886), Archives Diplomatiques La Courneuve, 190CPCOM/20 (author's trans-lation from the original French). See also *Note pour le Président du Conseil des Ministres* (23 October 1912), Archives Diplomatiques La Courneuve, 166CPCOM/39.
[19] *Lettre de la Légation de la République Française au Centre-Amérique à Son Excellence Monsieur Pichon, Ministre des Affaires Etrangères* (23 January 1911), Archives Diplomatiques La Courneuve, 166CPCOM/39.
[20] *Lettre de l'Administrateur Délégué de la Société Nouvelle des Etablissements Decauville Ainé à Monsieur le Ministre des Affaires Etrangères – Direction Sud-Amérique* (9 September 1911), Archives Diplomatiques La Courneuve, 166CPCOM/39.

government in Brazil terminated the concession of a French company to operate a slaughterhouse.[21] The French government obtained an impressive compensation settlement for the claimant and proceeded to track every move of the impoverished local government as it scrambled to get a loan. The Brazilian press condemned the episode as a 'grave humiliation which has been imposed on Brazil by foreigners'.[22]

When host States accede to home States' demands for satisfaction, such as Guatemala to France in *Réclamation Decauville*, and Brazil to France in *Réclamation de la Société des Abbatoirs de Para*, the home State successfully asserts the power to determine the outcome of the contract claim.[23] Host States are in a position to counter-assert the power to determine the same by denying the satisfaction demanded. Counter-assertion often assumes one of two forms. The first is silence when presented with a contract claim, and the second is written denial of the claim. Silence and communicated denial amount to successful counter-assertions of power to determine the outcome of the claim when the home State does not follow up on the first written demand,[24] or abandons the claim after repeated demands for satisfaction are ignored. A memorable illustration of silence as successful counter-assertion involved a number of contract claims submitted by a Dutch national, Mr Bakels, regarding the operation of mining concessions in Tianjin, China and Mongolia. The Tianjin concession awaited the final authorisation of the viceroy of the Province of Zhili (where Tianjin is located), Yuan Shih-Kai, while the Mongolian concession which was awarded by the Mongol Prince Ka-La-Sin required further confirmation

---

[21] *Lettre de la Légation de France au Brésil au Monsieur Stephen Pichon, Ministre des Affaires Etrangères* (12 May 1913), Archives Diplomatiques La Courneuve, 144CPCOM/104.

[22] *Lettre de la Légation de France au Brésil au Monsieur Pichon, Ministre des Affaires Etrangères* (26 July 1913), Archives Diplomatiques La Courneuve, 144CPCOM/104 (author's translation from the French translation of the original Portuguese).

[23] See also *Claim of AG Tyler against the Government of Austria/United States* (1925), National Archives Kew, FO 371/10662, C5707/5707/3, C11422/5707/3, C12515/5707/3; and *Claim of Salvador Railway Company against the Government of El Salvador* (1921), National Archives Kew, FO 371/5551, A7522/7522/8.

[24] *Réclamation Pemarchan, Lettre du Consulat Général de France au Vénézuéla à Monsieur le Ministre des Affaires Etrangères* (4 December 1869), Archives Diplomatiques La Courneuve, 752SUP/476; *Réclamation Derbès, Note Interne du Ministère des Affaires Etrangères* (26 April 1911), Archives Diplomatiques La Courneuve, 144CPCOM/103; *Réclamation Buisson, Lettre du Ministre de France au Brésil à Son Excellence Monsieur le Ministre des Affaires Etrangères* (22 December 1913), Archives Diplomatiques La Courneuve, 144CPCOM/104; and *Réclamation Taximètre (Argentine), Note Interne du Ministère des Affaires Etrangères* (17 November 1917), Archives Diplomatiques La Courneuve, 137CPCOM/42.

from the imperial Qing government before Mr Bakels could start work.[25] Mr Bakels' interest in Chinese mines coincided with the ascent of Yuan Shih-Kai, an autocratic general and trusted advisor of the Qing government, who later declared himself the first president of the Republic of China.[26] Yuan had hoped that foreign investment in Zhili's mines would generate jobs and wealth. But mining concessions previously awarded to foreigners did not bring about the desired outcome.[27] Deeply sceptical of the concrete benefits China enjoys from mining concessions held by foreign investors, Yuan and the Qing government remained silent in the face of repeated presentations of Mr Bakels' claims by the Dutch Chargé d'Affairs in Beijing.[28] The claims were eventually abandoned.

When host States respond to written demands from home States to satisfy a contract claim with a simple denial, this usually suffices for a successful counter-assertion of power to determine the outcome of the claim.[29] An example where a written denial by the host State resulted in non-satisfaction of the presented contract claim is, of course, *Réclamation*

---

[25] *Letter from Mr Bakels to the Dutch Minister [for Foreign Affairs]* (16 December 1905), Nationaal Archief Den Haag, 2.05.90/483.

[26] J. Chen, *Yuan Shih-k'ai*, 2nd revd edn (Stanford, CA: Stanford University Press, 1972), chaps. 3 and 5.

[27] Dietring, 'Tientsin Trade Report for the Year 1902', Nationaal Archief Den Haag, 2.05.90/483.

[28] *Letter from the Légation des Pays-Bas to His Excellency Yuan* (22 October 1902), Nationaal Archief Den Haag, 2.05.90/483; and *Letter from Mr Bakels to Viceroy Yuan Shih-Kai* (14 July 1903), Nationaal Archief Den Haag, 2.05.90/483.

[29] See also *Réclamation Moktar (Maroc), Lettre de la Chambre des Députés à Monsieur le Ministre des Affaires Etrangères* (4 March 1909), Archives Diplomatiques La Courneuve, 179CPCOM/412; *Réclamation Lanadis, Lettre du Ministre de France en Haïti à Monsieur le Ministre des Affaires Etrangères* (8 May 1910), Archives Diplomatiques La Courneuve, 166CPCOM/39; *Réclamation Lefébure, Lettre du Ministre de France au Perou à Son Excellence Monsieur Pichon Ministre des Affaires Etrangères* (5 December 1910), Archives Diplomatiques La Courneuve, 190CPCOM/25; *Réclamation Sibrie et Bertin, Lettre du Ministre de France en Haïti à Monsieur le Ministre des Affaires Etrangères* (6 June 1911), Archives Diplomatiques La Courneuve, 166CPCOM/39; *Réclamation Rémant, Lettre du Ministre de France au Perou à Son Excellence Monsieur de Selves, Ministre des Affaires Etrangères* (25 August 1911), Archives Diplomatiques La Courneuve, 190CPCOM/25; *Réclamation Fould, Lettre du Ministre de France en Haïti à Son Excellence Monsieur le Ministre des Affaires Etrangères* (1 March 1913), Archives Diplomatiques La Courneuve, 166CPCOM/40; *Réclamation St Chamond, Lettre de la Légation de France au Mexique au Monsieur le Ministre des Affaires Etrangères* (25 November 1913), Archives Diplomatiques La Courneuve, 181CPCOM/57; and *Réclamation Guilhou, Lettre du Ministre de France en Haïti à Son Excellence Monsieur le Ministre des Affaires Etrangères* (18 October 1916), Archives Diplomatiques La Courneuve, 166CPCOM/41. One exception is the claim presented by the Dutch government on behalf of La Maison Jean Barth Bos against the Italian municipality of Catania, discussed earlier.

Sabatier. Another example is the *Claim of Boulton and Company (in Liquidation) against the Yugoslav Government.*[30] Here, a UK bank in receivership sought unpaid interest on a loan extended to the government of Montenegro in 1909. Montenegro, along with Bosnia and Herzigovina, Croatia, Macedonia, Serbia and Slovenia, made up the Socialist Federal Republic of Yugoslavia until the Republic's dissolution in 1992. The liquidator repeatedly sought satisfaction of the claim amounting to £3,686, 1s, 7d (worth approximately £221,035.21 today)[31] from the Yugoslav Minister of Finance in Belgrade to pay the bank's creditors, to no avail. The liquidator then approached the Foreign Office to support the claim, appending a statement of accounts which detailed the amounts of interest owed over an eighteen-year period. The United Kingdom agreed to intervene diplomatically. The Foreign Office then sent an official to 'mention[] this matter privately to the Yugoslav Minister of Finance'.[32] The Yugoslav government responded tersely, seemingly foreclosing further discussion of the matter:[33]

> We refer to the note (no. 126/6) of the Legation of Great Britain concerning the new claim of Messrs Boulton Brothers and company. The Royal Ministry of Foreign Affairs is honoured to refer the matter to the competent Ministry for its attention. According to that Ministry, the claim of the aforementioned bank, which was subject to a minute examination, is unfounded. All claims by the bank against the former Montenegrin government have been settled by the payment of the sum of £6,120 on 22 January 1924.

The liquidator's flagging enthusiasm for the claim as time wore on without any genuine prospect of satisfaction was taken into consideration by the Foreign Office before verbal inquiries were made. However, archival records strongly suggest the United Kingdom's decision to withdraw its support after the initial overture was mainly driven by Yugoslavia's denial of the claim, because no external or internal diplomatic correspondence appeared after the Yugoslav response.

---

[30] *Claim of Boulton and Company (in Liquidation) against the Yugoslav Government* (1931), National Archives Kew, FO 371/15274, C6325/C9178/6325/92.

[31] Historical exchange rate obtained from This Is Money, 'Historic Inflation Calculator: How the Value of Money Has Changed since 1900', online: www.thisismoney.co.uk/money/bills/article-1633409/Historic-inflation-calculator-value-money-changed-1900.html (accessed 31 December 2017).

[32] *Letter from Neville Henderson to Sir John Simon* (3 December 1931), see fn. 30.

[33] *Letter from the Ministry of Foreign Affairs of Yugoslavia to the Legation of Her Britannique Majesty in Belgrade* (3 December 26, November 1932), ibid., Author's translation from the original French.

This section concludes the discussion on the period of diplomacy with a few observations on studies positing that the United Kingdom and the United States also asserted the power to determine the outcome of contract claims over unpaid sovereign loans against South American host States through the use of force.[34] A closer examination of the circumstances surrounding the UK-led offensive against Venezuela in 1902–3,[35] and the US-led, French-endorsed offensive against Haiti in 1915,[36] reveals that support for contract claims was not the sole or overriding objective of gunboat diplomacy.[37] The costly risk of ineffective coercion, both financial and political, discourages home States from resorting to militarised diplomatic intervention at the slightest provocation.[38] Moreover, archived records already show that the power of outcome-determination for contract claims was asserted by the United Kingdom and the United States, if at all, through written means.[39] It is likelier that force was used by the

---

[34] These include C. K. Hobson, *The Export of Capital* (New York, NY: Macmillan, 1914), p. xxii; P. S. Dunn, *The Protection of Nationals: A Study in the Application of International Law* (Baltimore, MD: The Johns Hopkins Press, 1932), pp. 54–7; L. Whitehead, 'Latin American Debt: An International Bargaining Perspective' (1989) 15(3) *Review of International Studies* 231 at 234; C. Marichal, *A Century of Debt Crises in Latin America: From Independence to the Great Depression, 1820–1930* (Princeton, NJ: Princeton University Press, 1989), p. 121; M. Hilaire, *International Law and the United States Military Intervention in the Western Hemisphere* (Boston, MA: Kluwer Law International, 1997), p. 11; P. F. Diehl and G. Goertz, *War and Peace in International Rivalry* (Ann Arbor, MI: University of Michigan Press, 2000), p. 25; R. Dornbusch, *Keys to Prosperity: Free Markets, Sound Money, and a Bit of Luck* (Cambridge, MA: MIT Press, 2000), p. 9; F. Fukuyama, *State-Building: Governance and the World Order in the 21st Century* (Ithaca, NY: Cornell University Press, 2004), p. 36; and M. Finnemore, *The Purpose of Intervention: Changing Beliefs about the Use of Force* (Ithaca, NY: Cornell University Press, 2004), p. 24; cf. M. Waibel, *Sovereign Defaults before International Courts and Tribunals* (Cambridge: Cambridge University Press, 2011), pp. 29–30.

[35] M. Tomz, *Reputation and International Cooperation: Sovereign Debt across Three Centuries* (Princeton, NJ: Princeton University Press, 2007), pp. 135–40; and Platt, *Finance, Trade, and Politics*, pp. 339–46.

[36] N. Maurer, *The Empire Trap* (Princeton, NJ: Princeton University Press, 2013), pp. 90–7; and Hon. C. E. Hughes, 'Observations on the Monroe Doctrine' (1923) 17 AJIL 611 at 621–2.

[37] Cf. Dunn, *The Protection of Nationals*, pp. 53–7.

[38] C. Lipson, *Standing Guard: Protecting Foreign Capital in the Nineteenth and Twentieth Centuries* (Berkeley, CA: University of California Press, 1985), pp. 47–50. Tomz points out that, in addition to the Netherlands, significant creditor nations such as Belgium and Switzerland never used force to recover unpaid debts, *Reputation and International Cooperation*, pp. 147–52.

[39] The United Kingdom has handled so many contract claims that not all records could be preserved. Examples of contract claims handled by the Foreign Office but whose records were subsequently discarded include: National Archives Kew, FO 371/12738, A7606/7606/2 (Argentina); National Archives Kew, FO/371/4432, A1644/1644/6 (Brazil);

United Kingdom in response to the injuries inflicted on British nationals and their property by local armed forces during the 1900–2 Venezuelan civil war, and to a series of unprovoked attacks on British vessels by the Venezuelan navy from 1901 to 1902.[40] The US military intervention in Haiti in 1915, and its military occupation of Santo Domingo in 1916, were driven in part by the desire to check European imperialism,[41] and in part by the desire to prevent further default on sovereign loans made by US lenders.[42] That said, the US government tried its best to avoid forceful pursuit of contract claims, which promised unwanted entanglement in local politics and governance.[43] As US President Herbert Hoover declared to an assembly of journalists in 1929, 'it never has been and ought not to be the policy of the United States to intervene by force to secure or maintain contracts between our citizens and foreign states or their citizens'.[44]

1.3   The Early 1900s to the 1920s: Contractual Protection through International Adjudication

The establishment of Mixed Claims Commissions for the final settlement of contract claims has been likened to an 'appeal to general rules and principles of law'.[45] However, as Mixed Claims Commissions are often

---

National Archives Kew, FO 371/4445, A6211/2690/32 (Costa Rica); National Archives Kew, FO 371/11841, W1953/1953/17 (France); National Archives Kew, FO 371/12633, W2215/2215/17 (France); National Archives Kew, FO 371/6087, C347/347/19 (Greece); National Archives Kew, FO 371/9896, C12432/12432/19 (Greece); National Archives Kew, FO 371/9583, A3800/A5900/3800/35 (Peru); National Archives Kew, FO 371/9582, A3477/A3907/A6852/456/35 (Peru); National Archives Kew, FO 371/7106, W647/W1678/647/36 (Portugal); National Archives Kew, FO 371/11935, W8662/8662/36 (Portugal); and National Archives Kew, FO 371/12702, W10280/116/36 (Portugal). The sheer volume of claims which stretches available resources, and the long-standing tolerance by the United Kingdom for Venezuela's default on its sovereign bonds (Tomz, *Reputation and International Cooperation*, pp. 135–6) makes the suggestion of the United Kingdom's belated fervour for contractual protection, manifested by an abrupt turn from conciliatory to confrontational diplomacy in 1902 (H. Feis, *Europe, The World's Banker, 1870–1914* (New Haven, CT: Yale University Press, 1930), p. 109), too convenient to be persuasive.

[40] Tomz, *Reputation and International Cooperation*, pp. 136–7; and Platt, *Finance, Trade, and Politics*, p. 346, where the author observes that '[b]ondholder grievances, whatever the provocation, never became a determining factor in British policy in Latin America'.

[41] Hughes, 'Observations on the Monroe Doctrine', pp. 621–2.

[42] Maurer, *The Empire Trap*, pp. 90–7.

[43] Ibid., pp. 148–87.

[44] H. Hoover, 'Address to the Gridiron Club (13 April 1929)' in H. Hoover, *1929: Containing the Public Messages, Speeches, and Statements of the President, March 4 to December 31, 1929* (Ann Arbor, MI: University of Michigan Library Press, 2005), p. 70.

[45] Dunn, *The Protection of Nationals*, p. 58.

imposed on the debtor-host by the creditor-home State, sceptics contend that 'principles of law' familiar only to select Western States, are being disguised as widely accepted principles by Mixed Claims Commissions.[46] This implies a disadvantage for the host State, whose conduct with respect to submitted contract claims is measured against exotic 'principles of law'.

This section refutes the depiction of Mixed Claims Commissions as partial adjudicatory bodies by demonstrating that principles on contractual protection that can be traced back to Commission awards actually emerged in circumstances which curbed their partiality towards home States. To this end, this section first examines the context surrounding the creation of three well-known Mixed Claims Commissions (Section 1.3.1), followed by how the power to determine the legal content of contractual protection and outcome of a contract claim was delegated to and exercised by the three profiled Commissions (Section 1.3.2). Building on the findings in Sections 1.3.1 and 1.3.2, the remainder of this section distils three principles on contractual protection, and discusses how their compliance pull is enhanced by their origins and by their appearance in the awards of modern-day international tribunals (Section 1.3.3).

1.3.1 Three Case Studies on the Assertion of Power by Home States to Determine the Format of Dispute Settlement

As institutions 'often constituted in a situation where the investor's home [S]tate possessed much greater diplomatic power than the host [S]tate',[47] Mixed Claims Commissions may be regarded as symbols of home State power. The power to determine the format of dispute settlement may be asserted by a single home State, or collectively by a group of home States. One example of collective assertion is the Allied blockade of Venezuela in 1902–3, which was lifted upon the establishment of Mixed Claims Commissions to hear outstanding claims between United Kingdom, German and Italian nationals, and Venezuela.[48] Another example of collective assertion is the

---

[46] T. A. Nissel, 'A History of State Responsibility: The Struggle for International Standards (1870–1960)', PhD thesis, University of Helsinki (2016), pp. 143–53 and 181–8.

[47] T. G. Nelson, '"History Ain't Changed": Why Investor-State Arbitration Will Survive the "New Revolution"' in M. Waibel et al. (eds.), The Backlash against Investment Arbitration (Alphen aan den Rijn: Kluwer Law International, 2010), pp. 555, 568.

[48] Collective pressure, led by the United States, was also behind the establishment of an international arbitral commission to hear claims against the Dominican Republic, San Domingo Improvement Company Claims (Dominican Republic v. United States) (1904) 11 RIAA 25. For an account of the rise of US influence in the Dominican Republic, see C. Veeser, A World Safe for Capitalism (New York, NY: Columbia University Press, 2007), pp. 126–42.

United Kingdom orchestrating a joint campaign against Mexico several years later, in the immediate aftermath of the Mexican civil war of 1914–7. The United Kingdom rallied States whose nationals had outstanding contract claims against Mexico, including France and the United States, into rejecting the Mexican government's offer to establish an independent commission to hear those claims. The United Kingdom considered the offer a ruse to stave off diplomatic intervention, and urged other home States not to act 'without previously consulting His Majesty's Government'.[49] The impasse ended only when the incumbent Mexican government was overthrown, and the new government concluded treaties establishing Mixed Claims Commissions.[50] As host States, for varying reasons, did not challenge the establishment of Mixed Claims Commissions, the assertion of power by home States, in various forms, to submit contract claims to international adjudication was largely successful. The creation of the Italy-Venezuela Claims Commission (Section 1.3.1.1), the US-Mexico Claims Commission (Section 1.3.1.2) and the US-Guatemala Claim Commission (Section 1.3.1.3), are illustrative.

1.3.1.1   The Italy-Venezuela Claims Commission

The Italy-Venezuela Claims Commission was established by the Protocol of 13 February 1903, in exchange for the lifting of the Allied blockade against Venezuela. Although the offer to submit to arbitration came from Venezuela,[51] one objective of the Allied blockade was to 'force the settlement of an accumulation of claims'.[52] Venezuela was cornered into arbitration on Allied terms, making its offer to arbitrate an irony of its predicament, rather than a product of free choice. As the subsequent UK-led campaign against Mexico showed, a mere offer by the debtor State to establish a commission to hear outstanding contract claims with foreign nationals may not satisfy the home States of these nationals. The only way for such a Commission to meet the expectations of home States is if it is a creature of the home States. The different Mexican Claims Commissions passed muster because they were borne from the stipulations of the more powerful State. Likewise, the Italy-Venezuela Claims Commission,

---

[49] *Letter from M Balfour, No. 23321/26/A* (12 February 1918), Archives Diplomatiques La Courneuve, 181CPCOM/55.
[50] Abraham Howard Feller, *The Mexican Claims Commissions, 1923-1934; a study in the law and procedure of international tribunals* (New York: The Macmillan Company 1935) pp. 19–20.
[51] Dunn, *The Protection of Nationals*, p. 58.
[52] Platt, *Finance, Trade, and Politics*, p. 340.

an Allied creation, was imposed by a stronger Italy, successfully asserting its power to determine the format of dispute settlement on a weaker
Venezuela.

1.3.1.2   The US-Mexico Claims Commission

The US-Mexico Claims Commission was established by the General
Claims Convention of 8 September 1923.[53] Given the scale of US investments in Mexico, especially in mining and oil, the United States maintained
an active interest, and occasionally a military presence, in Mexico.[54] Long
before the United Kingdom tried to impose Mixed Claims Commissions
on Mexico through collective pressure, the United States had already settled many claims with Mexico through international arbitration.[55] The
US official policy of resolving disputes with its South American neighbours using 'good offices', turned out to be a by-word for the 'imposition of arbitrations'.[56] In Mexico's case, its reasons for accepting a Mixed
Claims Commission asserted by the United States were very different from
those that motivated Venezuela to accede to the Commission asserted by
Italy. The overhanging threat of US military intervention, reinforced by
warships patrolling the coastlines,[57] nudged Mexico towards accepting
a Mixed Claims Commission largely fashioned on US terms. But force
was not the principal push factor. The newly formed post-revolutionary
government sought political recognition from the United States, and saw
acceptance of a Mixed Claims Commission as a good way to secure it.[58]
Closely tied to the desire for political recognition was the conviction held
by liberal-minded South American politicians that an appreciation of and
adherence to international law will boost a government's standing among
States[59] and attractiveness to foreign investors.[60] For Mexico, a country that
was 'too big to invade',[61] agreeing to the establishment of the US-Mexico

---

[53] US Senate, *Treaties, Conventions, International Acts, Protocols, and Agreements between the USA and Other Powers* (Washington, DC: Government Printing Office, 1938), p. 4441.
[54] Maurer, *The Empire Trap*, pp. 137–47.
[55] Nissel, 'A History of State Responsibility', p. 75.
[56] Ibid., p. 70.
[57] B. Loveman, *No Higher Law: American Foreign Policy and the Western Hemisphere since 1776* (Chapel Hill, NC: University of North Carolina, 2010), p. 153.
[58] Nissel, 'A History of State Responsibility', p. 73.
[59] A. B. Lorca, *Mestizo International Law: A Global Intellectual History 1842–1933* (Cambridge: Cambridge University Press, 2014), pp. 65–72.
[60] Nissel, 'A History of State Responsibility', p. 74; also Dunn, *The Protection of Nationals*, pp. 57–8.
[61] Maurer, *The Empire Trap*, p. 137.

Claims Commission was probably due in larger part to the potential for reputational benefits, than to the constraint of averting imminent military occupation by the United States.

1.3.1.3   The US-Guatemala Claim Commission

The US-Guatemala Claim Commission was established by a Special Agreement of 2 November 1929.[62] In an Exchange of Notes between the United States and Guatemala, the two countries agreed to submit the claim of Mr P. W. Shufeldt against the Government of Guatemala to arbitration before Sir Herbert Sisnett, the chief justice of British Honduras. The 1920s was a period of great unrest in Guatemala. After President Estrada Cabrera was overthrown by the National Assembly in 1920, military hostilities between warring political factions broke out. In the next decade, Guatemala underwent seven presidencies, two military coups, sporadic rebellions and bouts of election-related violence.[63] Additionally, the Guatemalan economy, like the rest of South America, was heavily dependent on sovereign loans and imports from the United States. As the US economy inched towards recession, finally going into freefall with the onset of the Great Depression in October 1929, Guatemala's economy was brought to the brink of collapse. Throughout the 1920s and the early 1930s, the United States kept a close political and economic watch over Guatemala. It intervened on several occasions to facilitate negotiations between political opponents, and to check the escalation of hostilities and civil unrest.[64] It also deployed agents to assume fiscal administration of Guatemala should the country default on its sovereign loans.[65] Although never formally acknowledged as such, Guatemala was a *de facto* US protectorate, reliant on US patronage.[66] Guatemala's special relationship with the United States deflected challenge to the US policy of arbitrating disputes with its South American neighbours, and fostered ready acceptance of US assertion of power to submit Mr Shufeldt's claim to the US-Guatemala Claim Commission for settlement.

---

[62] *Shufeldt Claim* (*Guatemala v. USA*) (1930) 2 RIAA 1079, Award, 24 July 1930 (Sisnett), pp. 1081–2.

[63] F. Lehoucq, *The Politics of Modern Central America: Civil War, Democratization, and Underdevelopment* (New York, NY: Cambridge University Press, 2012), pp. 21–8.

[64] E. Torres-Rivas, *History and Society in Central America* (translated by D. Sullivan-González) (Austin, TX: University of Texas Press, 1993), chap. 4.

[65] Maurer, *The Empire Trap*, p. 203.

[66] Ibid.

1.3.2   Three Case Studies on the Assertion of Delegated Power by Mixed Claims Commissions to Determine the Legal Content of Contractual Protection and the Outcome of the Dispute

Whether a host State agreed to have outstanding claims submitted to a Mixed Claims Commission for adjudication to exit a naval blockade imposed by the home State, to further its reputational standing in the eyes of the home State or to continue receiving patronage from the home State, the Commission's terms of establishment nonetheless committed both host and home States to an impartial, binding legal process. This process usually entailed the appointment of one commissioner each by the host and home States to make a joint decision on claims, equal opportunity for host and home State agents to plead and present evidence on the claims, and an obligation on the part of the Commission to render mutually binding decisions that are even-handed and juridically sound. The commitment to an impartial, binding legal process is discernible from the founding documents of the Italy-Venezuela Claims Commission, the US-Mexico Claims Commission, and the US-Guatemala Claim Commission.

The relevant provisions in the Protocol of 13 February 1903 and in the Protocol of 7 May 1903 establishing the Italy-Venezuela Claims Commission read:

Protocol of 13 February 1903

Article VI

The Mixed Commission shall consist of one Italian member and one Venezuelan member. In each case, where they come to an agreement their decision shall be final. In cases of disagreement, the claims shall be referred to the decision of an umpire nominated by the President of the United States of America.

Protocol of 7 May 1903

Article II

Before assuming the functions of their office the umpire and both the commissioners shall make solemn oath or declaration carefully to examine and impartially to decide according to the principles of justice and the provisions of the Protocol of the 13th of February, 1903, and of the present agreement, all claims submitted to them; the oath or declaration so made shall be embodied in the record of their proceedings ...

Article III

... The commissioners shall be bound before reaching a decision, to receive and carefully examine all evidence presented to them by the Government of Venezuela and the Royal Italian Legation at Caracas, as well as oral or written arguments submitted by the agent of the Government or of the Legation ...

The relevant provisions in the General Claims Convention of 8 September 1923, establishing the US-Mexico Claims Commission read:

Article I

All claims (except those arising from acts incident to the recent revolutions) against Mexico of citizens of the United States, whether corporations, companies, associations, partnerships or individuals, for losses or damages suffered by persons or by their properties, and all claims against the United States of America by citizens of Mexico, whether corporations, companies, associations, partnerships or individuals, for losses or damages suffered by persons or by their properties ... shall be submitted to a Commission consisting of three members for decision in accordance with the principles of international law, justice, and equity.

Such Commission shall be constituted as follows: one member shall be appointed by the President of the United States; one by the President of the United Mexican States; and the third, who shall preside over the Commission, shall be selected by mutual agreement between the two Governments ...

Article II

The Commissioners so named shall meet at Washington for organization within six months after the exchange of the ratifications of this Convention, and each member of the Commission, before entering upon his duties, shall make and subscribe a solemn declaration stating that he will carefully and impartially examine and decide, according to the best of his judgment and in accordance with the principles of international law, justice and equity, all claims presented for decision, and such declaration shall be entered upon the record of the proceedings of the Commission ...

Article VIII

The High Contracting Parties agree to consider the decision of the Commission as final and conclusive upon each claim decided, and to give full effect to such decisions ...

The relevant provisions in the Protocol of Arbitration of 2 November 1929, establishing the US-Guatemala Claim Commission read:

Article 2

Each Government shall appoint one or more representatives who shall have the authority necessary to appear before the Arbitrator and to represent it.

Article 4

The representatives of the parties shall submit to the Arbitrator a written statement which shall comprise their respective points of view in the relation of the facts, the statements of the juridic point upon which their cause is based and all the proofs which they may wish to present as basis for their claims.

Article 11

The decision of the Tribunal ... when made, shall be forthwith communicated to the Governments at Guatemala and Washington. It shall be
accepted as final and binding upon the two Governments.

Mixed Claims Commissions are created and exist for the specific
purpose of deciding fixed categories of claims between nationals of one
Contracting State and the other Contracting State. Their mandates are tai-
lored by the Contracting States for that purpose and expire once that purpose is met. As Contracting States are in no way bound to consult or adopt
the mandate of a different Commission, mandates vary across Mixed
Claims Commissions. For example, whether a Mixed Claims Commission
can exercise jurisdiction over contract claims depends on whether it is
authorised to do so by the Contracting States in the terms of its establishment.[67] Therefore, whatever powers a Mixed Claims Commission can
exercise is delegated by its founding States. To enable Commissions to discharge the task of conducting an impartial legal process to which contract
claims will be submitted for final settlement, founding States delegated the
power to determine the legal content of contractual protection, and the
power to determine the outcome of a contract claim, to the Commissions.

The power of the Italy-Venezuela Claims Commission to determine the
legal content of contractual protection is delegated through Article II of the
Protocol of 7 May 1903, which obliges the Commission to decide claims
'according to the principles of justice'. The same power is delegated to the
US-Mexico Claims Commission through Articles I and II of the General
Claims Convention of 8 September 1923, and to the US-Guatemala
Claim Commission through Article 4 of the Protocol of Arbitration of 2
November 1929. The power of the Italy-Venezuela Claims Commission
to determine the outcome of a contract claim is delegated through Article
VI of the Protocol of 13 February 1903 which provides that the decision
of the Commission shall be 'final'. The same power is delegated to the US-
Mexico Claims Commission through Article VIII of the General Claims
Convention, and to the US-Guatemala Claim Commission through Article
11 of the Protocol of Arbitration. Additionally, both the delegated power
to determine legal content and outcome must be exercised impartially by
the Commission. The duty of the Italy-Venezuela Claims Commission to
decide impartially is stated expressly in Article II of the Protocol of 7 May
1903 and implied in Article III of the Protocol of 7 May 1903, while the

---

[67] *Illinois Central Railroad Co. Case* (*USA v. Mexico*) (1926) 4 RIAA 21, para. 4.

impartiality of the US-Mexico Claims Commission is stipulated in Article II of the General Claims Convention. An impartial legal process is implied in the terms of establishment of the US-Guatemala Claim Commission through the appointment of a national of a non-Contracting State as sole arbitrator, and the equal opportunity for both Contracting States to present their respective cases before the arbitrator pursuant to Article 2 of the Protocol of Arbitration.

Sceptics may dismiss the duty of Mixed Claims Commissions to exercise the power to determine the legal content of contractual protection and the outcome of submitted contract claims in an impartial manner, as a veneer for what is arguably a dictated claims settlement mechanism. The reality, though, is more reassuring. Mixed Claims Commissions have taken the duty to adjudicate impartially seriously, scrutinising, adjusting, and even dismissing claims presented by the more dominant of their founding States. The reasoned decisions of the Commissions do not reveal a tendency to craft legal content on contractual protection or the outcome for a contract claim to favour the State which successfully asserted the power to determine the format of dispute settlement. The capacity of Mixed Claims Commissions to act impartially in determining the legal content of contractual protection and the outcome of a contract claim, is displayed in three awards rendered by the Commissions profiled in Section 1.3.1. The first is the award in the *Martini Case,* which was decided by the Italy-Venezuela Claims Commission (Section 1.3.2.1),[68] the second is the award in the *North American Dredging Company of Texas Claim,* which was decided by the US-Mexico Claims Commission (Section 1.3.2.2)[69] and the third is the award in the *Shufeldt Claim,* which was decided by the US-Guatemala Claim Commission (Section 1.3.2.3).[70]

1.3.2.1   The Martini Case

In the *Martini Case,* an Italian company sought more than 9 million bolivars (worth approximately USD 33 million today)[71] from the Venezuelan government for the breach and failure to ensure the peaceful enjoyment

---

[68] *Martini Case (Italy v. Venezuela)* (1903) 10 RIAA 644.
[69] *North American Dredging Company of Texas Claim (USA v. United Mexican States)* (21 March 1926) 4 RIAA 26.
[70] *Shufeldt Claim (Guatemala v. USA)* (24 July 1930) 2 RIAA 1079.
[71] Calculated using the 1930 pegged conversion rate of 3.914 bolivars to 1 USD: OANDA, 'Venezuelan Bolivar', online: www.oanda.com/currency/iso-currency-codes/VEF (accessed 31 December 2017); and the Consumer Price Inflation Calculator: Bureau of Labor Statistics, 'CPI Inflation Calculator', online: https://data.bls.gov/cgi-bin/cpicalc.pl (accessed 31 December 2017).

of a contract. The contract provided that disputes arising from the execution of the contract should be submitted to Venezuelan courts, applying
Venezuelan law, for settlement. No provision is made for the submission of
claims to international adjudication. The claim alleged that Venezuela's forcible recruiting of the company's employees for the ongoing civil war, and the
blockading of a port, violated the terms of a concession for the operation of
railways, mines and other enterprises. The claim also alleged that Venezuela
was liable for the damage inflicted on the company's properties by revolutionary troops. After hearing the arguments and evidence presented by the
State agents, as well as witness testimonies, the Italian Commissioner took
the view that the claim should be allowed with a reduction in quantum.[72]
The Venezuelan Commissioner was in favour of dismissal, on the basis that
the forum selection clause in the contract deprived the Commission of jurisdiction over the claim.[73] Because the Italian and Venezuelan commissioners were unable to agree, the claim was then referred to the US-appointed
umpire, prominent lawyer and counsel to the United States, Jackson H.
Ralston,[74] in accordance with Article VI of the Protocol of 13 February 1903.

Umpire Ralston first addressed the issue of the Commission's jurisdiction over the claim. In his view, the forum selection clause in the contract
did not bar the Commission from exercising jurisdiction over the Italian
company's contract claim against Venezuela, because Venezuela's obligation pursuant to the 1903 Protocols to submit outstanding claims to
international adjudication superseded any earlier contractual promise to
litigate before domestic courts. By recommending reliance on treaty language to resolve a conflict between a State's treaty and contractual choice
of forum for the settlement of contract claims, Umpire Ralston articulated
legal content on contractual protection:[75]

> Italy and Venezuela, by their respective Governments, have agreed to sub-
> mit to the determination of this Mixed Commission the claims of Italian

---

[72] See fn. 68, p. 656.
[73] Ibid., p. 660.
[74] Umpire Ralston lectured at Stanford Law School from 1929 to 1933. After his death in
1945, his widow established the Jackson H. Ralston Prize in International Law which is
'intended to recognize original and distinguished contributions by a man or woman to
the development of the role of law in international relations': Stanford Law School, 'The
Jackson H. Ralston Prize in International Law', online: https://law.stanford.edu/about/his-
tory/the-ralston-prize/ (accessed 31 December 2017). Previous recipients of the Ralston
Prize include Louise Arbor (2008), formerly Justice of the Supreme Court of Canada
and currently UN Special Representative for International Migration, and Tommy Koh
(1985), formerly Singapore's ambassador to the United States and currently Singapore's
ambassador-at-large.
[75] See fn. 68, pp. 663–4 (footnote omitted).

citizens against Venezuela. The right of a sovereign power to enter into an agreement of this kind is entirely superior to that of the subject to contract it away. It was, in the judgment of the umpire, entirely beyond the power of an Italian subject to extinguish the superior right of his nation, and it is not to be presumed that Venezuela understood that he had done so. But aside from this, Venezuela and Italy have agreed that there shall be substituted for national forums, which, with or without contract between the parties, may have had jurisdiction over the subject-matter, an international forum, to whose determination they fully agree to bow. To say now that this claim must be rejected for lack of jurisdiction in the Mixed Commission would be equivalent to claiming that not all Italian claims were referred to it, but only such Italian claims as have not been contracted about previously, and in this manner and to this extent only the protocol could be maintained. The umpire cannot accept an interpretation that by indirection would change the plain language of the protocol under which he acts and cause him to reject claims legally well-founded.

Umpire Ralston then reviewed the various heads of claim submitted by the Italian company, and found that 'the same items have been repeated several times, and that properly analysed the claim should amount to about one-third of the above'.[76] He held that the Venezuelan government was in breach of the contract, and calculated damages in accordance with 'the legal principle stated in the American and English Encyclopedia of Law', which records that 'the usual practice is to assess the damages up to the rendition of the decree, in order to prevent further litigation'.[77] Guided by national laws, including Venezuelan law, in determining the outcome of the claim, Umpire Ralston was unwilling to hold the Venezuelan government accountable for the full sum of damages for breach, or for losses occasioned by revolutionary activities:[78]

Many of the other claims for damage rest upon the existence of war, for which Venezuela cannot be specially charged, however regrettable the facts in themselves may be. It is strongly urged upon the umpire that large damages should be awarded under the head of lack of pacific enjoyment of the thing rented, and aid is invoked of the principle embodied in section 1575 of the Italian, and section 1529 of the Venezuelan Civil Code, making it the duty under any contract of the owner renting property to maintain the lessee in the peaceful enjoyment of the thing rented during the time of the contract. This simply means that such enjoyment shall be preserved as against the owner and others claiming title, but is no covenant against the action of trespassers. As far, therefore, as the Government may thus be

---

[76] Ibid., p. 662.
[77] Ibid., p. 667.
[78] Ibid., p. 668.

legally responsible, the umpire has, in this opinion, sought to hold it to such
responsibility.

The final amount of damages awarded to the Italian company was
439,673.16 bolivars,[79] less than 5 per cent of the original claim.[80]

1.3.2.2   The North American Dredging
Company of Texas Claim

Unlike the Italy-Venezuela Claims Commission where the umpire stepped
in only in the event of disagreement between the two commissioners, the
US-Mexico Claims Commission functioned as a collegial three-member
panel. It comprised one US-appointed commissioner, one Mexico-
appointed commissioner and a presiding commissioner jointly selected
by the United States and Mexico.[81] The US-Mexico Claims Commission
could exercise jurisdiction over claims involving losses or damage to persons or properties, but not claims arising from revolutionary activities.[82]

In the *North American Dredging Company of Texas Claim*, a US company
sought the recovery of USD 233,523.30 plus interest from the Mexican

---

[79] Ibid., pp. 668–9.
[80] There is a postscript to the *Martini Case*. Several months after the award was issued, the
procurator general of Venezuela brought an action against the Italian company before the
Federal Court of Cassation in Caracas, claiming unpaid rent and mining royalties pursuant
to the terms of the concession. The Court granted the pecuniary relief sought by the procurator general. The orders for payment seemed to contradict the Ralston award, and sparked
a flurry of diplomatic exchanges between Italy and Venezuela. Both governments eventually agreed to arbitrate the question of whether the Court's decision constituted a denial of
justice to the Italian company, or a violation of an 1861 treaty between Venezuela and Italy
(*Arbitral Award in the Martini Case (3 May 1930)* (translated by Ö. Undén), (1931) 25 AJIL
544). The three-member tribunal found by a majority that there was no treaty violation, and
unanimously that the Court's orders for payment flouted the Ralston award. Venezuela's
conduct was a denial of justice because '[a]ccording to the admitted rules on the responsibility of states, Venezuela is, therefore, responsible if the attitude of a Venezuelan court is
incompatible with an international arbitral award rendered in accordance with an international treaty to which Venezuela is one of the contracting parties' (p. 577). The issue before
the *Martini* tribunal was whether the Venezuelan judiciary complied with international law
(p. 564), whereas the issue before the *Martini* Commission, and one issue before the Federal
Court of Cassation, was whether the Venezuelan government was in breach of contract.
Therefore, although the award of the *Martini* tribunal is credited as the 'leading case' for the
proposition that a State's breach of contract *per se* is not a breach of international law (see,
for example, Amerasinghe, 'State Breaches of Contracts' 881 at 891–2), the tribunal's findings were tangential to contractual protection under international law.
[81] General Claims Convention of 8 September 1923, see fn. 69, p. 12 (Art. I).
[82] General Claims Convention of 8 September 1923, Ibid., p. 11 (Art. I).

government for breaching a dredging contract. The contract contained the following clause:[83]

> The contractor and all persons who, as employees or in any other capacity, may be engaged in the execution of the work under this contract either directly or indirectly, shall be considered as Mexicans in all matters, within the Republic of Mexico, concerning the execution of such work and the fulfilment of this contract. They shall not claim, nor shall they have, with regard to the interests and the business connected with this contract, any other rights or means to enforce the same than those granted by the laws of the Republic to Mexicans, nor shall they enjoy any other rights than those established in favor of Mexicans. They are consequently deprived of any rights as aliens, and under no conditions shall the intervention of foreign diplomatic agents be permitted, in any matter related to this contract.

This clause is also known as a Calvo clause. It is named after Argentinian jurist Carlos Calvo, who argued that international law guarantees the right of every State to freedom from interference by foreign States, and demands the absolute equality of treatment between nationals and foreigners.[84] The two tenets of Calvo's doctrine unite to preclude home States from intervening diplomatically to protect their nationals against host States. Calvo's doctrine was developed to resist, in the name of international law, frequent intervention in South America by the United States and European States. Yet, by leaving the foreigner at the mercy of the host State, it largely failed to convert United States and European international lawyers to whom it was addressed.[85] As a manifestation of Calvo's doctrine, the Calvo clause raises 'a highly controversial issue of contemporary international law and policy',[86] and whose validity is, to many, 'a highly controversial matter'.[87]

The Mexican agent submitted that the presence of a Calvo clause in the contract removes the claim from the Commission's otherwise broad jurisdictional competence, and asked the Commission to dismiss the claim. In a unanimous decision, the Dutch presiding commissioner and the United States and Mexican commissioners agreed that the Calvo clause deprives the Commission of jurisdiction over the claim. The Commission's analysis on the effect and reach of a Calvo clause in international law, which is a clear

---

[83] Ibid., pp. 26–7.
[84] D. R. Shea, *The Calvo Clause: A Problem of Inter-American and International Law and Diplomacy* (Minneapolis, MN: University of Minnesota Press, 1955), pp. 19–20.
[85] Ibid., p. 20.
[86] Ibid., p. 28.
[87] Ibid., p. 31.

assertion of power to determine the legal content of contractual protection, merits reproduction in full:[88]

> What, therefore, are the rights which claimant waived and those which he did not waive in subscribing to [the Calvo clause] of the contract? (a) He waived his right to conduct himself as if no competent authorities existed in Mexico; as if he were engaged in fulfilling a contract in an inferior country subject to a system of capitulations; and as if the only real remedies available to him in the fulfilment, construction, and enforcement of this contract were international remedies. All these he waived and had a right to waive, (b) He did not waive any right which he possessed as an American citizen as to any matter not connected with the fulfilment, execution, or enforcement of this contract as such, (c) He did not waive his undoubted right as an American citizen to apply to his Government for protection against the violation of international law (internationally illegal acts) whether growing out of this contract or out of other situations, (d) He did not and could not affect the right of his Government to extend to him its protection in general or to extend to him its protection against breaches of international law. But he did frankly and unreservedly agree that in consideration of the Government of Mexico awarding him this contract, he did not need and would not invoke or accept the assistance of his Government with respect to the fulfilment and interpretation of his contract and the execution of his work thereunder. The conception that a citizen in doing so impinges upon a sovereign, inalienable, unlimited right of his government belongs to those ages and countries which prohibited the giving up of his citizenship by a citizen or allowed him to relinquish it only with the special permission of his government.

Critics pointed out that the Commission's construction of the Calvo clause in the *North American Dredging Company of Texas Claim* allows diplomatic intervention in cases where the host State breaches international law, when Calvo clauses are meant to serve as blanket prohibitions to diplomatic intervention.[89] Contested interpretation aside, the Commission's upholding of the Calvo clause, which led to the dismissal of the claim for lack of jurisdiction, is highly significant at a time when the validity of Calvo clauses was debated in international legal doctrine. It swung the debate in general favour of Calvo's supporters.

The Commission subsequently upheld, by a majority, the Calvo clause in the *International Fisheries Company Claim*.[90] Noting that the US agent petitioned the Commission to reconsider its decision in the

---

[88] Ibid., pp. 30–1.
[89] P. S. Dunn, *The Diplomatic Protection of Americans in Mexico* (New York, NY: Columbia University Press, 1933), pp. 409–12; and Feller, pp. 188–9.
[90] *International Fisheries Company Claim* (*USA v. United Mexican States*) (1931) 4 RIAA 691.

North American Dredging Company of Texas Claim,[91] the presiding commissioner nonetheless held that '[t]he instant case is included in the principles fixed by the Commission in the decision of the case of the *North
American Dredging Company*, and is not therefore within the jurisdiction
of the Commission'.[92] Adherence by the US-Mexico Claims Commission
to the *Dredging* decision on Calvo clauses,[93] despite the doctrinal controversy surrounding Calvo clauses, the protests of the US agent after
the *North American Dredging Company of Texas Claim*, and the lengthy
dissent of the US commissioner in the *International Fisheries Company
Claim*,[94] attests to the capacity of Mixed Claims Commissions to act
impartially when determining the legal content of contractual protection and the outcome of a contract claim. Having delegated the power of
decision-making 'in accordance with the principles of international law,
justice, and equity' to the US-Mexico Claims Commission in Article I of
the General Claims Convention, and having pledged to 'give full effect' to
the decisions of the Commission in Article VIII, the United States eventually accepted the *Dredging* decision as final and did not mount further
challenges. The determination of the US-Mexico Claims Commission to
defend the validity of Calvo clauses, in defiance of the position taken by its
dominant founding State, cultivated perception of the *Dredging* decision
as a quality decision:[95]

> The nuanced manner in which the award in *North American Dredging*
> upheld the relevant Calvo clause was so successful in terms of articulating a
> viable distinction [between claims based on an alleged violation of interna-
> tional law and claims not so based] that it may be described as a watershed.
> From 1926 onward, it became exceedingly difficult for foreigners to deny
> the validity of a Calvo Clause, and equally difficult for the local government
> to insist that its scope extended to alleged violations of international law.

---

[91] Ibid., p. 692.

[92] Ibid., pp. 701–2.

[93] Further support for the Dredging decision can be found in the *Mexican Union Railway
(Ltd.) Claim (Great Britain v. United Mexican States)* (1930) 5 RIAA 115, p. 166; see also
the *Ornato Pitol Claim (Italy v. United Mexican States)* (1927) (unpublished), excerpted
in Feller, pp. 196–8 and critiqued in Shea, *The Calvo Clause*, pp. 254–5; the *Interoceanic
Railway of Mexico (Acapulco to Veracruz) (Ltd.) and Ors Claim (Great Britain v. United
Mexican States)* (1931) 5 RIAA 178, pp. 126–9; the *El Oro Mining and Railway Company
(Ltd.) Claim (Great Britain v. United Mexican States)* (1931) 5 RIAA 223, pp. 149–50; and
the *Veracruz (Mexico) Railways (Ltd.) Claim (Great Britain v. United Mexican States)* (1931)
5 RIAA 221, pp. 207–10.

[94] See fn. 92, pp. 703–46.

[95] J. Paulsson, *Denial of Justice in International Law* (Cambridge: Cambridge University Press,
2005), p. 31.

1.3.2.3   The Shufeldt Claim

In the *Shufeldt Claim*, the issue before sole Arbitrator Sisnett was the validity of a Guatemalan legislative decree cancelling a chicle extraction contract, and the corresponding right of the affected concessionaire, Mr Shufeldt, to indemnification. For six years, Mr Shufeldt performed a contract that was concluded with the executive and approved by the Guatemalan Legislative Assembly, until its cancellation by the Legislative Assembly in 1928.

Arbitrator Sisnett prefaced his decision with the assurance that he had 'given all the evidence put before me and all the points raised my most careful consideration with the hope of arriving at a just, fair and impartial decision'.[96] His commitment to thoroughness and objectivity could be seen in his finding that the cancellation was invalid and entitled Mr Shufeldt to indemnification. The analysis struck a difficult balance between deference for Guatemala's sovereign prerogatives and tangible contractual protection for the US investor in international law:[97]

> This decree was approved of by the President and published in the *El Guatemalteco* of 7th July 1928. This brought the contract summarily to an end, thus depriving Shufeldt of all his rights under the contract.
>
> The grounds on which the decree is based are three:
>
> (1) harmful to national interests,
> (2) in violation of dispositions and prohibitions defined under the laws of the Republic and especially those contained in articles 653, 1458, 1459 of the Fiscal Code,
> (3) that it is within legislative attributes to approve or disapprove of such contracts.
>
> As to (1) and (3), it is perfectly competent for the Government of Guatemala to enact any decree they like and for any reasons they see fit, and such reasons are no concern of this Tribunal. But this Tribunal is only concerned where such a decree, passed even on the best of grounds, works injustice to an alien subject, in which case the Government ought to make compensation for the injury inflicted and can not invoke any municipal law to justify their refusal to do so.
>
> As to (2), the provisions of the Fiscal Code referred to relate solely to leases of national forests and leases of national real property. Article 653 is found in title 6 of the Fiscal Code in the same title and chapter that article 650 referred to before is found, and on a consideration of the two articles under same title and chapter I come to the conclusion that article 653 refers to leases by the Jefe Politico and not to contracts celebrated by the Executive

---

[96] Ibid., p. 1083.
[97] Ibid., pp. 1095 and 1098.

for the exploitation of national forests as provided by article 650. Articles 1458 and 1459 deal with the alienation of national property.

...

The Guatemala Government contend further that the decree of the 22nd May 1928 was the constitutional act of a sovereign State exercised by the National Assembly in due form according to the Constitution of the Republic and that such decree has the form and power of law and is not subject to review by any judicial authority. This may be quite true from a national point of view but not from an international point of view, for 'it is a settled principle of international law that a sovereign can not be permitted to set up one of his own municipal laws as a bar to a claim by a sovereign for a wrong done to the latter's subject'.

Having dealt with all the points of any importance urged for and against the right of Shufeldt to claim pecuniary indemnification I come to the conclusion and find that he has such a right.

As Arbitrator Sisnett did not refer to any authorities, it is unclear on what basis he labels the 'principle of international law that a sovereign can not be permitted to set up one of his own municipal laws as a bar to a claim by a sovereign for a wrong done to the latter's subject', as 'settled'.[98] He may have preferred to frame a known legal proposition as a 'settled principle' of contractual protection to highlight the incongruity of a host State evading its contractual obligations simply by changing its own laws. By calling for compensation when the use of sovereign prerogatives to cancel a contract 'work injustice to an alien subject', Arbitrator Sisnett asserted the delegated power to determine legal content on contractual protection.

Arbitrator Sisnett then located the standard of indemnification in Guatemalan law, the governing law of the contract.[99] Accordingly, 'whoever concludes a contract is bound not only to fulfil it but also to recoup or compensate (the other party) for damages and prejudice which result directly or indirectly from the nonfulfilment or infringement by default or fraud of the party concerned and that such compensation includes both damage suffered and profits lost: *damnum emergens et lucrum cessans*'.[100]

---

[98] The earliest endorsement for the principle, which predates the *Shufeldt Claim*, came from the first judgment of the PCIJ in 1923, the *Case of the SS Wimbledon* (*United Kingdom* v. *Japan*) (17 August 1923) PCIJ, Series A, No. 1, para. 48. Other endorsements from the PCIJ, the ICJ and international arbitral tribunals, postdate the *Shufeldt Claim*. They are reviewed in the official commentary to Art. 3 of the Articles on State Responsibility: see ILC, 'Draft Articles on Responsibility of States for Internationally Wrongful Acts, with Commentaries' (2001), *Yearbook of the International Law Commission*, vol. II, part 2, pp. 36–7. The principle was applied for the first time in the context of contractual protection in the *Shufeldt Claim*.

[99] See fn. 62, p. 1085.

[100] Ibid., p. 1099.

Guided by the reminder that '*damnum emergens* is always recoverable, but the *lucrum cessans* must be the direct fruit of the contract and not too remote or speculative', Arbitrator Sisnett reviewed all the heads of claim, allowing some, reducing some and disallowing others.[101] Guatemala's liability for indemnification amounted to USD 225,468.38.[102]

The application of Guatemalan law in the *Shufeldt Claim* to quantify Mr Shufeldt's injured contractual rights stood out from contemporary distrust of the protection afforded by developing host State laws to foreign contractors.[103] Like the US-Mexico Claims Commission which upheld the validity of controversial Calvo clauses, Arbitrator Sisnett, a British national, avoided adopting the partisan rhetoric employed by jurists from developed States.[104] Although the Guatemalan government could not avoid contractual liability by changing national law, this was not construed as a criticism of Guatemalan law, which makes adequate provision for contractual protection. Arbitrator Sisnett may have allowed Mr Shufeldt's contract claim against Guatemala, but the reasoning behind the power to determine the outcome conveyed a decision that was 'just, fair and impartial'.

1.3.3   The Emergence of Three General Principles on Contractual Protection

The impartiality of Mixed Claims Commissions when exercising their delegated power to determine the legal content of contractual protection and the outcome of contract claims generated a credible body of arbitral awards from which principles on contractual protection could be distilled. Two factors enhance the compliance pull of distilled principles. The first, located in their origins, is the willingness of home and host States, especially the State whose position the arbitral award does not favour, to respect the binding finality of Commission rulings. The second, located in their future, is the tendency of other international tribunals, conferred with different mandates and dealing with different fact patterns, to adopt these principles and apply them to the dispute at hand. Together, the double-barrelled endorsement imparts authoritativeness to Commission

---

[101]   Ibid., pp. 1100–1.

[102]   Ibid., p. 1102.

[103]   *Petroleum Development Ltd.* v. *The Sheikh of Abu Dhabi*, 18 ILR 144, Award, September 1951 (Asquith), p. 149; and *Ruler of Qatar* v. *International Marine Oil Co.*, 20 ILR 534, Award, June 1953 (Bucknill), pp. 544–5.

[104]   See, for instance, A. McNair, 'The General Principles of Law Recognized by Civilized Nations' (1957) 33 BYIL 1 at 4.

rulings, paying some otherwise bespoke principles the compliment of general applicability.[105]

For the Contracting States to those agreements that established the Italy-Venezuela, US-Mexico and US-Guatemala Claims Commissions, compliance with the decisions rendered by the Commissions is one of the terms of establishment. That said, a State dissatisfied with the legal content articulated or outcome reached by a Commission may renege on its promise to treat the Commission's decisions as final and binding.[106] This did not happen. One possible reason why Contracting States complied with the decisions of Mixed Claims Commissions is reciprocity. Although the agreements establishing the Italy-Venezuela and US-Mexico Commissions envisaged the mutual presentation of claims, the bulk of the claims were presented by Italy against Venezuela, and by the United States against Mexico. The US-Guatemala Claim Commission was established to hear one claim presented by the United States against Guatemala. To impress upon host States that a decision based on law ordering the satisfaction of a contract claim must be observed, home States must, by example, accord the same level of respect to Commission decisions that order the dismissal of a presented contract claim. Another possible reason for compliance is reputation. As noted in Section 1.3.1.2, Mexico agreed to the establishment of the US-Mexico Claims Commission to improve its standing in the eyes of

---

[105] ILC, 'Draft Articles on Responsibility of States', pp. 32–3, 35, 37–8, 40–1, 45–7, 49–53, 55, 57–8, 62, 69, 73, 75, 77, 81, 89, 92, 96–7, 99, 101–2, 106–7, 122 and 140.

[106] Occasionally, States consent to arbitrate disputes arising from an investment contract with a foreign national, only to later boycott arbitral proceedings initiated by the foreigner. Arbitral awards rendered without the participation of the respondent State include *Lena Goldfields* v. *USSR*, *The Times*, 3 September 1930; *Texaco Overseas Petroleum Company/ California Asiatic Oil Company* v. *The Government of the Libyan Arab Republic*, 53 ILR 389, Award on the Merits (Dupuy), 19 January 1977; *Dallah Real Estate and Tourism Holding Company* v. *The Ministry of Religious Affairs, Government of Pakistan*, ICC Case No. (unknown), Final Award, 23 June 2006, unpublished, excerpted in [2010] UKSC 46; and, most recently, in the still-pending *Limited Liability Company Lugzor and Ors* v. *The Russian Federation* (see PCA Press Release, 'Arbitration between Limited Liability Company Lugzor and Four Others as Claimants and the Russian Federation as Respondent (13 December 2017)', online: www.pcacases.com/web/sendAttach/2262 (accessed 31 December 2017)). Notably, the United States, having previously accepted the compulsory jurisdiction of the ICJ in a declaration made in accordance with Art. 36(2) of the ICJ Statute, withdrew from the proceedings in the *Case Concerning Military and Paramilitary Activities in and against Nicaragua (Nicaragua* v. *United States of America)*. The United States claimed that the ICJ lacked 'jurisdiction and competence' over the dispute: US Department of State, 'US Withdrawal from the Proceedings Initiated by Nicaragua in the ICJ', Department Statement, 18 January 1985, Department State Bulletin, No. 2096 (March 1985), p. 64. Shortly after its withdrawal, the United States notified the UN of the termination of its Art. 36(2) declaration.

the United States and the rest of the world. Acceptance of the Commission's jurisdiction over listed categories of claims can be manifested by ready compliance with the Commission's decisions on those claims. For home States like Italy and the United States, the imposition of Mixed Claims Commissions on host States such as Venezuela, Mexico and Guatemala marked a turn to law in the formulation of foreign policy. Complying with Commission decisions, both favourable and unfavourable, reinforced the noble pursuit of a foreign policy that promotes the rule of law. Finally, the ability of Mixed Claims Commissions to adjudicate claims impartially in reasoned decisions engender respect for, and ultimately encourage compliance by, Contracting States with Commission awards.

The compliance pull of principles on contractual protection distilled from awards of Mixed Claims Commissions is further enhanced when they are assimilated to general principles by other international arbitral tribunals.[107] Due to the absence of binding precedent in international arbitration, later tribunals are not obliged to adopt principles on contractual protection enunciated by earlier tribunals. When later tribunals nonetheless gravitate towards a handful of principles and adopt them, these principles receive a stamp of approval. The higher a principle's approval rating, whether as a result of its teleological appeal or the frequency of its subsequent application, the more likely it will be adopted by future tribunals looking to base their decisions on established authority. The remainder of this section identifies three principles on contractual protection that have found express or implied purchase with modern-day international arbitral tribunals tasked with the resolution of investor–State disputes that are contractual in origin.[108]

---

[107] Within Mixed Claims Commissions, the *Dredging* interpretation of Calvo clauses has been deemed authoritative by the US-Mexico Claims Commission in the *International Fisheries Company Claim*, the UK-Mexico Claims Commission in the *Mexican Union Railway (Ltd.) Claim*, and the Italy-Mexico Claims Commission in the *Ornato Pitol Claim*: see Feller, fn. 50, pp. 196–8 and Shea, *The Calvo Clause*, pp. 254–5.

[108] Having already considered the possible reasons for State compliance with the awards of Mixed Claims Commissions, the remainder of Section 1.3.3 examines the compliance pull of distilled principles on contractual protection through the optic of principle adoption by modern-day investor–State arbitral tribunals, instead of the optic of State compliance with the decisions of those modern-day tribunals. It suffices to note that in the post-Mixed Claims Commissions landscape, voluntary compliance by respondent States with awards of international arbitral tribunals whose jurisdictions they accept, whether by consenting to arbitrate in a treaty or in a contract, is the norm. Examples of non-compliance, sometimes involving impecunious host States facing a large damages award, exist, but are too far and few to destabilise the climate of compliance. It is therefore possible, without revisiting the reasons underlying the compliance pull on States of principles on contractual protection

1.3.3.1 Principle 1: Contractual Forum Selection Clauses Are Not Jurisdictional Bars to International Claims

One principle distilled from the *Martini Case* and the *North American Dredging Company of Texas Claim* is the inability of forum selection clauses to completely preclude investors from bringing international claims when State breaches of contracts are simultaneously governed by conventional or customary international law. In the *Martini Case*, Arbitrator Ralston found that a clause directing the parties to submit disputes arising from the meaning and execution of the contract to the Venezuelan courts applying Venezuelan law was overridden by the terms of the Protocols establishing the mandate of the Italy-Venezuela Claims Commission to hear contract claims of Italian nationals against Venezuela.[109] In the *North American Dredging Company of Texas Claim*, the Commission found that an investor signing a contract containing a Calvo clause does not waive his right to seek diplomatic protection from his home State when the host State violates international law.[110] As a result, forum selection clauses, of which Calvo clauses are among the most emphatic, are not jurisdictional bars to international tribunals tasked with assessing a State's breach of contract in accordance with its international obligations.

Nearly eighty years after the *Martini* and *Dredging* decisions, an arbitral tribunal was constituted pursuant to the 1997 Agreement between the Republic of the Philippines and the Swiss Confederation on the Promotion and Reciprocal Protection of Investments[111] to consider the legal effect of a forum selection clause directing the parties to submit disputes arising from a customs services inspection contract to the Filipino courts. Guided by the relevant findings in the *Martini Case* and the *North American Dredging Company of Texas Claim*, the tribunal in *SGS Société Générale de Surveillance S.A.* v. *Republic of Philippines* held that it had jurisdiction over contract claims against the Philippines pursuant to Article VIII(2) of the

---

that emerged from Mixed Claims Commissions, to partially attribute an enhanced compliance pull for States to the adoption of these principles by modern-day international arbitral tribunals.

[109] See fn. 68, pp. 661 and 663–4; see also the *Orinoco Steamship Company Claim* (*United States* v. *Venezuela*) (1903–5) 9 RIAA 180, p. 181; the *Rudloff Claim* (*United States* v. *Venezuela*) (1903–5) 9 RIAA 244, p. 244; the *Turnbull Manoa Company and Anor Claim* (*United States* v. *Venezuela*) (1903–5) 9 RIAA 261, p. 261; and the *Selwyn Claim* (*United States* v. *Venezuela*) (1903) 9 RIAA 380, p. 380.

[110] See fn. 69, pp. 30–1.

[111] Signed 31 March 1997, entered into force 23 April 1999.

Philippine–Swiss investment treaty,[112] but such claims were only admissible after they have been heard by the Filipino courts:[113]

> 151. The United States-Mexico General Claims Commission took a similar approach in the *North American Dredging Company of Texas* case. The Commission said:
>
> 'each case involving the application of a valid clause partaking of the nature of the Calvo Clause will be considered and decided on its merits. Where a claim is based on an alleged violation of any rule or principle of international law, the Commission will take jurisdiction notwithstanding the existence of such a clause in a contract subscribed by such claimant. But where a claimant has expressly agreed in writing, attested by his signature, that in all matters pertaining to the execution, fulfilment, and interpretation of the contract he will have resort to local tribunals, remedies, and authorities, and then wilfully ignores them by applying in such matters to his government, he will be held bound by his contract and the Commission will not take jurisdiction of such claim.'
>
> 152. It is true that there are decisions apparently to the opposite effect, but mostly these depend on the existence of a provision overriding contractual forum clauses. For example, the Italian-Venezuelan Protocol of 13 February 1903 contained two salient provisions: in Article I, Venezuela expressly recognized 'in principle the justice of the [Italian] claims' – this amounted in effect to an acknowledgement of indebtedness. Secondly, the Protocol was concerned with a defined class of existing claims; after dealing with certain of these specifically, it referred 'all the remaining Italian claims, without exception' to the Mixed Commission. In the *Martini* case, Arbitrator Ralston was able to rely on 'the plain language of the protocol' in dismissing arguments based on a local forum clause.
>
> ...
>
> 154. In the Tribunal's view, this principle is one concerning the admissibility of the claim, not jurisdiction in the strict sense. The jurisdiction of the Tribunal is determined by the combination of the BIT and the ICSID Convention. It is, to say the least, doubtful that a private party can by contract waive rights or dispense with the performance of obligations imposed on the States parties to those treaties under international law. Although under modern international law, treaties may confer rights, substantive and procedural, on individuals, they will normally do so in order to achieve some public interest. Thus the question is not whether the Tribunal has

---

[112] Article VIII(2) provides in relevant part: 'If these consultations do not result in a solution within six months from the date of request for consultations, the investor may submit the dispute either to the national jurisdiction of the Contracting Party in whose territory the investment has been made or to international arbitration.'

[113] ICSID Case No. ARB/02/6, Decision of the Tribunal on Objections to Jurisdiction, 29 January 2004 (El-Kosheri, Crawford, Crivellaro (partially dissenting)), paras. 151–2 and 154 (footnotes omitted).

jurisdiction: unless otherwise expressly provided, treaty jurisdiction is not abrogated by contract. The question is whether a party should be allowed to rely on a contract as the basis of its claim when the contract itself refers that claim exclusively to another forum. In the Tribunal's view the answer is that it should not be allowed to do so, unless there are good reasons, such as force majeure, preventing the claimant from complying with its contract. This impediment, based as it is on the principle that a party to a contract cannot claim on that contract without itself complying with it, is more naturally considered as a matter of admissibility than jurisdiction.

1.3.3.2   Principle 2: Contractual Breaches *per se* Are Not Violations of International Law

Another principle that has been traced back to scions of the *Martini Case* and the *North American Dredging Company of Texas Claim*, namely, the *Martini Award* and the *International Fisheries Company Claim*, rules out contractual breaches *per se* by States as violations of international law. The tribunal in the *Martini Award* hinted at the principle by requiring proof of 'incontestable validity' that a Venezuelan court's finding that the Venezuelan government did not commit a breach of contract was 'manifestly unjust'.[114] In other words, a breach of contract must be so blatant that for a court to rule otherwise is a denial of justice. The US-Mexico Claims Commission in the *International Fisheries Company Claim* was more explicit. It held that when a State cancels a contract, '[t]his is the situation which is always being aired by private parties before courts having jurisdiction, and no reason is seen why the same fact, for the sole reason that one of the parties to the contract is a government, can constitute an international delinquency'.[115]

The principle that a breach of contract *per se* is not a breach of international law receives widespread support. Scholarly efforts linking the principle to its possible sources have not been challenged.[116] It appears to be so embedded in legal consciousness and parlance that some modern-day international arbitral tribunals adopting it readily assume its general

---

[114] See fn. 68, pp. 571–2; see also Amerasinghe, 'State Breaches of Contracts', pp. 891–2.

[115] See fn. 90, p. 700.

[116] Hyde, '*International Law Chiefly as Interpreted*', Section 303; Mann, 'State Contracts and State Responsibility' 572 at 574 and 580–1; R. Y. Jennings, 'State Contracts in International Law' (1961) 37 BYIL 156 at 165–8; Amerasinghe, 'State Breaches of Contracts', p. 897; H. Pazarci, 'La Responsabilité Internationale des Etats à l'Occasion des Contrats Conclus Entre Etats et Personnes Privées Etrangères' (1975) 79 *Revue Générale de Droit International Public* 354 at 371–2; Delaume, 'State Contracts and Transnational Arbitration' 784 at 806; and Sacerdoti, 'State Contracts and International Law', 26 at 46.

applicability. Although its source was not identified by the tribunal in *SGS Société Générale de Surveillance S.A.* v. *Islamic Republic of Pakistan*,[117] the principle conditioned the interpretation of Article 11 of the 1995 Agreement between the Swiss Confederation and the Islamic Republic of Pakistan on the Promotion and Reciprocal Protection of Investments:[118]

163. Article 11 of the BIT states:

Either Contracting Party shall constantly guarantee the observance of the commitments it has entered into with respect to the investments of the investors of the other Contracting Party.

As noted earlier, during the hearing on the Respondent's Objections to Jurisdiction, counsel for the Claimant characterized this clause as an 'elevator' or 'mirror effect' clause that takes breaches of contract under municipal law and elevates them immediately to the level of a breach of an international treaty. Counsel for the Claimant freely acknowledged that this interpretation was 'far-reaching', but asserted that nevertheless this is what the article means and that the Claimant's view of its meaning was supported by the commentary on articles of this type found in other bilateral investment treaties.

164. It appears that this is the first international arbitral tribunal that has had to examine the legal effect of a clause such as Article 11 of the BIT. We have not been directed to the award of any ICSID or other tribunal in this regard, and so it appears we have here a case of first impression. We begin, as we commonly do, by examining the words actually used in Article 11 of the BIT, ascribing to them their ordinary meaning in their context and in the light of the object and purpose of Article 11 of the Swiss-Pakistan Treaty and of that Treaty as a whole.

...

167. Considering the widely accepted principle with which we started, namely, that under general international law, a violation of a contract entered into by a State with an investor of another State, is not, by itself, a violation of international law, and considering further that the legal consequences that the Claimant would have us attribute to Article 11 of the BIT are so far-reaching in scope, and so automatic and unqualified and sweeping in their operation, so burdensome in their potential impact upon

---

[117] ICSID Case No. ARB/01/13, Decision of the Tribunal on Objections to Jurisdiction, 6 August 2003 (Feliciano, Faurès, Thomas).

[118] Signed 11 July 1995, entered into force 6 May 1996. Decision of the Tribunal on Objections to Jurisdiction, ibid., paras. 163–4 and 167 (footnotes omitted). Notably, the Swiss government objected to the tribunal's interpretation of Art. 11 on the basis that select categories of contractual breaches by the host State, such as the revocation of promises which induced the investment, amount to a violation of Art. 11. But Switzerland neither challenged the adoption of a general principle of contractual protection by the tribunal, nor the outcome of the dispute arrived at by the tribunal as a result of that adoption: see Letter from the Swiss Secretariat for Economic Affairs to the ICSID Secretary-General, 'Umbrella Clauses in Bilateral Investment Agreements', 1 October 2003, 19 *Mealey's International Arbitration Reports* E1.

a Contracting Party, we believe that clear and convincing evidence must be adduced by the Claimant. Clear and convincing evidence of what? Clear and convincing evidence that such was indeed the shared intent of the Contracting Parties to the Swiss-Pakistan Investment Protection Treaty in incorporating Article 11 in the BIT. We do not find such evidence in the text itself of Article 11. We have not been pointed to any other evidence of the putative common intent of the Contracting Parties by the Claimant.

1.3.3.3 Principle 3: Only Contractual Breaches *Iure Imperii* Are Potential Violations of International Law

A third principle, articulated in the *Shufeldt Claim*, limits violations of international law to contractual breaches carried out in a State's sovereign capacity. The dispute in the *Shufeldt Claim* arose from the cancellation of a chicle extraction contract by legislative decree of the Guatemalan government, a sovereign act. Rejecting Guatemala's argument that sovereign acts are exempt from any form of judicial review, Arbitrator Sisnett called the ultimate supervision of sovereign acts by international law, regardless of their legality under national law, a 'principle of international law'.[119] Judge Hersch Lauterpacht held that this principle was a principle of contractual protection in his Separate Opinion in the *Certain Norwegian Loans Case* before the International Court of Justice (ICJ).[120] Judge Stephen M. Schwebel, a former president of the ICJ, also approved the application of this principle to contracts. In an influential chapter on contractual protection in international law, Judge Schwebel identifies the *Shufeldt Claim* as the key award in a string of twelve arbitral awards from which the principle emerged.[121]

The clarity of Arbitrator Sisnett's decision, coupled with later support from ICJ judges for his findings, persuaded modern-day international

---

[119] See fn. 62, p. 1098.

[120] *Certain Norwegian Loans Case* (*France* v. *Norway*) (Preliminary Objections) [1957] ICJ Rep 9, p. 37:

> The question of conformity of national legislation with international law, is a matter of international law. The notion that if a matter is governed by national law it is for that reason at the same time outside the sphere of international law is both novel and, if accepted, subversive of international law. It is not enough for a State to bring a matter under the protective umbrella of its legislation, possibly of a predatory character, in order to shelter it effectively from any control by international law. There may be little difference between a Government breaking unlawfully a contract with an alien and a Government causing legislation to be enacted which makes it impossible for it to comply with the contract.

[121] S. M. Schwebel, 'On Whether the Breach by a State of a Contract with an Alien is a Breach of International Law' in S. M. Schwebel (ed.), *Justice in International Law: Selected Writings of Stephen M. Schwebel* (Cambridge: Grotius, 1994), pp. 425, 431–3.

ribunals that the *Shufeldt Claim* is the progenitor of this 'principle of international law'. The tribunal in *Bankswitch Ghana Ltd.* v. *The Republic of Ghana Acting as the Government of Ghana* credited the *Shufeldt Claim* as the sole authority for this principle of contractual protection:[122]

> ... the Tribunal adheres to the principle that, if a State repudiates or violates its obligations under a contract with a foreign entity, it is responsible for such a violation if its breach is discriminatory or is akin to an expropriation in that the contract is repudiated or breached for governmental rather than commercial reasons. Such a breach is considered to be 'arbitrary' and subjects the breach to international standards. The action or inaction by a State vis-à-vis a foreign entity may be perfectly lawful in terms of its municipal law, but may still engage its international responsibility. For example, the breach of a commercial contract by a State in ordinary commercial intercourse may not be a violation of international law, but the use of its sovereign authority, contrary to the expectations of the parties, to abrogate or violate a contract with a foreign entity is a violation of international law.
>
> A case that is quite on point here is the *United States of America on Behalf of P. W. Shufeldt* v. *The Republic of Guatemala* in which the arbitrator held that Guatemala's action in recognition of the validity of the contract precluded it from denying its validity under principles of international law. In the *Shufeldt Case*, as here, Guatemala did not take steps to cancel the contract or refer the dispute to arbitration, but rather continued to treat the contract as valid and enforceable, acting pursuant to it. It might be true that the Ghanaian government is able to act in such a manner to

---

[122] UNCITRAL, Award Save as to Costs, 11 April 2014 (Hwang, Schwebel, Born), paras. 11.68–11.69 (footnotes omitted). See *Impregilo SpA* v. *Islamic Republic of Pakistan*, ICSID Case No. ARB/03/3, Decision on Jurisdiction, 22 April 2005 (Guillaume, Cremades, Landau), para. 260 (fn. 118), where the tribunal referenced 'the review of jurisprudence in Stephen M. Schwebel "*Justice in International Law*" (Grotius / Cambridge University Press), chap. 26: "*On Whether the Breach by a State of a Contract with an Alien Is a Breach of International Law*'" (original emphasis), and concluded that

> [o]nly the State in the exercise of its sovereign authority ('*puissance publique*'), and not as a contracting party, may breach the obligations assumed under the BIT. In other words, the investment protection treaty only provides a remedy to the investor where the investor proves that the alleged damages were a consequence of the behaviour of the Host State acting in breach of the obligations it had assumed under the treaty. (original emphasis)

The tribunal in *Sempra Energy International* v. *Argentine Republic*, ICSID Case No. ARB/02/16, Award, 28 September 2007 (Orrego Vicuña, Lalonde, Morelli Rico), para. 310 (fn. 112), also accepted the general applicability of Principle 3; but cf. *Duke Energy Electroquil Partners and Anor* v. *Ecuador*, ICSID Case No. ARB/04/19, Award, 18 August 2008 (Kaufmann-Kohler, Pinzón, van den Berg), para. 320: 'Another open question is whether sovereign interference is needed to constitute a breach of an umbrella clause. While, as indicated by Respondent, language to that effect appears in some cases ... a majority of decisions do not formulate such distinction.'

the detriment of its nationals, but when a foreign entity is involved and the agreement in question is an 'international' one, it is a settled principle of international law that a sovereign cannot be permitted to set up one of its own municipal laws as a bar to a claim for a wrong done to the foreign entity. While a State may act in contravention of its private obligations when such a decision is for the benefit of the 'public good', because a foreign entity is, by definition, not a part of the national public whose welfare the State is promoting, the State is obligated under international law as well as in equity to repair the resultant situation, whether by payment of compensation or the restitution of its contract.

The propriety of ruling out contractual breaches carried out in a non-sovereign capacity as breaches of open-ended treaty obligations to observe all commitments entered into with respect to protected investors and investments[123] is contested.[124] As explained by Judge James Crawford, the fourth and final Special Rapporteur of the ILC's work on State responsibility, the engagement of a State's responsibility under international law 'do[es] not, generally speaking, rest on a distinction between conduct *iure imperii* and conduct *iure gestionis*'.[125] For those who remain persuaded that the distinction has a role to play in determining a State's international responsibility for contractual breaches, the *Shufeldt Claim* stands for a general principle of contractual protection.

1.4   The 1920s to the 1990s: Contractual Protection through Codification

In addition to the contribution of Mixed Claims Commissions, States and private actors also asserted the power to determine legal content on contractual protection through projects on the codification of international law. The six most significant codification projects during the 1920s to the 1990s were the 1930 Hague Codification Conference, the 1959 Abs-Shawcross Draft Convention on Investments Abroad,[126] the 1961 Harvard Draft Convention on the Responsibility of States for Injuries to the Economic

---

123   See discussion at Chapter 5, Section 5.3.3.1.
124   J. Crawford, 'Treaty and Contract in Investment Arbitration' (2008) 24(3) *Arbitration International* 351 at 368.
125   J. Crawford, 'Revising the Draft Articles on State Responsibility' (1999) 10 EJIL 435 at 440; see also C. Chinkin, 'A Critique of the Public/Private Dimension' (1999) 10 EJIL 387 at 392.
126   UNCTAD, 'International Investment Instruments: A Compendium, Volume V (Regional Integration, Bilateral and Non-governmental Instruments)', online: http://unctad.org/en/Docs/dite2vol5_en.pdf (accessed 31 December 2017).

Interests of Aliens,[127] the 1967 OECD Draft Convention on the Protection of Private Foreign Investment,[128] the 1956–70 ILC project on State responsibility and the 1995 Multilateral Agreement on Investment (MAI). The Hague Conference, OECD Draft Convention, the ILC project and MAI were undertaken by States, while the Abs-Shawcross Draft Convention and the Harvard Draft Convention were undertaken by private actors.[129]

Two principles on contractual protection emerged from these codification efforts. The first is the principle of absolute contractual protection presented in the OECD Draft Convention and the Abs-Shawcross Draft Convention. States and individuals who favoured the characterisation of every breach of contract by a host State as a violation of an international obligation also asserted the power to determine the outcome of a contractual dispute by foreclosing any discussion on the legal consequences of a breach of contract by the host State. The second principle, which calls for the engagement of State responsibility only when a host State arbitrarily breaches a contract, appeared in the Harvard Draft Convention. The OECD Draft Convention, the Abs-Shawcross Draft Convention and the Harvard Draft Convention were never tabled for signature and ratification by States. The principle of absolute contractual protection has attracted many critics, while the principle prohibiting arbitrary conduct has attracted little attention. Neither principle, when identified as part of a draft convention, appears to share the compliance pull of principles which emerged from the awards of Mixed Claims Commissions.

This section posits that the noticeably weaker compliance pull of principles on contractual protection identified in codification efforts is attributable to the partisan circumstances, real or perceived, of their emergence. To this end, it examines the different sets of circumstances surrounding the four codification projects undertaken by States (Section 1.4.1) and those surrounding the two codification projects undertaken by private actors (Section 1.4.2).

1.4.1   State Codifications

The first codification project on contractual protection in international law was undertaken during the 1930 Hague Codification Conference.

---

[127] L. B. Sohn and R. R. Baxter, 'Responsibility of States for Injuries to the Economic Interests of Aliens' (1961) 55 AJIL 545.

[128] Signed 12 October 1967, not yet in force, C(67)102, p. 14. For a list of other private codification efforts, see Ago, 'First Report on State Responsibility', pp. 141–56.

[129] For a list of other private codification efforts, see Ago, 'First Report on State Responsibility', pp. 141–56.

It revealed profound disagreement among States on the engagement of State responsibility for contractual breaches. In the questionnaire drafted by the Committee of Experts, one of the questions asked of States was whether international responsibility could be engaged for the unilateral abrogation of contractual engagements with foreigners.[130] Six different responses were collated from the replies submitted by twenty-six countries. Nine countries were against a finding of State responsibility,[131] nine declined to comment on the relevance of international law,[132] three were in favour of a finding of State responsibility,[133] two were undecided if international responsibility should be engaged,[134] two believed that the topic was inappropriate for codification[135] and one recommended its reappraisal at a future date.[136] France completed the entire questionnaire by referring only to French law. It withheld comment on the international responsibility of States for contractual breaches, claiming that 'it will be indispensable, before endeavouring to regulate the responsibility of the State in a convention, to obtain accurate information concerning the rules followed by the various bodies of national law in this respect'.[137] Like France, most of the States that responded to the questionnaire were reluctant to propose rules that might curtail sovereign prerogatives. According to the United Kingdom, 'the sovereign authority of the State, its power to terminate by appropriate means any such concession or contract on grounds of public policy i.e., that the interests of the State require it, must be recognized'.[138]

---

[130] The questionnaire as well as the text of replies from governments are reproduced in S. Rosenne (ed.), *Conference for the Codification of International Law [1930]* (New York, NY: Oceana Publications, 1975), vol. II, pp. 160–251.

[131] Letter of 30 October 1928 (Austria), p. 180; Telegram of 3 November 1928 (New Zealand), p. 217; Letter of 5 November 1928 (Denmark), p. 189; Letter of 14 November 1928 (Great Britain), p. 205; Letter of 4 December 1928 (India), p. 209; Letter of 11 December 1928 (South Africa), p. 165; Letter of 9 January 1929 (Australia), p. 175; Letter of 21 January 1929 (Czechoslovakia), p. 250; and Letter of 12 March 1929 (Belgium), p. 182.

[132] Letter of 23 August 1928 (Chile), pp. 183–4; Letter of 26 October 1928 (Siam), p. 236; Letter of 3 November 1928 (Irish Free State), p. 210; Letter of 19 November 1928 (Italy), p. 211; Letter of 19 November 1928 (Sweden), p. 237; Letter of 26 November 1928 (Roumania), pp. 235–6; Letter of 29 November 1928 (Japan), p. 213; Letter of 7 December 1928 (France), pp. 197–200; and Letter of 27 January 1929 (Bulgaria), p. 183.

[133] Letter of 31 October 1928 (Finland), p. 195; Letter of 10 December 1928 (Netherlands), p. 223; and Letter of 25 January 1929 (Switzerland), p. 244.

[134] Letter of 29 October 1928 (Hungary), p. 209; and Letter of 8 December 1928 (Norway), pp. 216–7.

[135] Letter of 28 July 1928 (Egypt), p. 192; and Letter of 3 January 1929 (Poland), p. 234.

[136] Letter of 13 December 1928 (Germany), p. 171.

[137] Letter of 7 December 1928 (France), p. 197.

[138] Letter of 14 November 1928 (Great Britain), p. 205.

Due to the disparateness of submitted views, this inaugural codification project was abandoned.

The second State codification project, where contractual protection was one of several foreign investment-related concerns, was undertaken by Member States of the OECD and culminated in the 1967 OECD Draft Convention. The OECD was established in 1961 by eighteen European nations, Canada and the United States. Its mission was to promote economic development throughout the world.[139] The founding members of the OECD were mostly developed States whose nationals invested in States with developing economies, but who rarely hosted investments from nationals of developing States. Their common status as traditional capital-exporting nations facilitated the pursuit of a common agenda on investment protection in general, and on contractual protection in particular, against traditional capital-importing nations. Part of this agenda was securing maximum protection for their nationals who had entered into contracts with foreign States. For Austria, Belgium, Canada, Denmark, France, Germany, Greece, Iceland, Ireland, Italy, Japan, Luxembourg, Netherlands, Norway, Portugal, Spain, Sweden, Turkey, the United Kingdom and the United States, investment contracts should be protected in the manner stipulated in Article 2 of the 1967 OECD Draft Convention:

> Each Party shall at all times ensure the observance of undertakings given by it in relation to property of nationals of any other Party.

The commentary to Article 2 exalts *pacta sunt servanda* as 'the basic norm of any system of law relating to agreements'.[140] Accordingly, an undertaking given by States in 'agreements between States and foreign nationals … gives rise to an *international* right that the [State] Party of the nationals concerned or of his successor in title is entitled to protect'.[141] Article 2 thus lays down the rule that 'States [a]re not entitled unilaterally to modify or abrogate such agreements'.[142] To do so is to violate international law. If States cannot interfere with investment contracts without attracting sanction by international law, contractual protection is absolute. Article 2 is remarkable not only because it advocates the principle of absolute contractual protection, but because it arouses suspicions of a partisan agenda. Apart from the Netherlands, none of the OECD States who participated in the

---

[139] As of 31 December 2017, the OECD has 35 Member States: OECD, 'Members and Partners', online: www.oecd.org/about/membersandpartners (accessed 31 December 2017).

[140] See fn. 128, p. 14.

[141] Ibid. (original emphasis).

[142] Ibid.

1930 Hague Codification Conference supported the engagement of State responsibility for the unilateral abrogation of contractual engagements. On the contrary, States like France, Italy and the United Kingdom were disinclined to equate a breach of contract by a State to a violation of international law.

The impression that Article 2 of the 1967 OECD Draft Convention targets interference by developing States, and not OECD States, with investment contracts, is validated by a series of important UN resolutions where developing States pressed for the submission of investment contracts to the default protection of host State laws.[143] The divide between developing and OECD States is borne out in the voting pattern for the Charter of Economic Rights and Duties of States, tabled on the heels of the establishment of the New International Economic Order (NIEO). The NIEO marked the transition from a world economy driven by colonialism to one defined by the sovereign equality of States. Notably, the 1974 Charter, which sets out the rights and duties of all States in the NIEO, makes no mention of international law. According to the roll call vote, 120 States voted in favour of the Charter, while 16 States voted against.[144] All of the sixteen 'No' votes came from OECD States,[145] who, just a few years ago, asserted that international law confers absolute protection on investment contracts in the 1967 OECD Draft Convention.

Given its partisan overtone and implicit rejection by the vast majority of States, the principle of absolute contractual protection found in Article 2 of the 1967 OECD Draft Convention did not gain traction in subsequent State codification efforts. The third significant State codification project was undertaken by the ILC, within the broader rubric of State responsibility. The first Special Rapporteur on State responsibility and President of the ILC, Francisco García-Amador, experienced great difficulty in proposing acceptable rules to the thirty-four elected members of the ILC in

---

[143] Permanent Sovereignty Over Natural Resources, UNGA Res. 1803 (XVIII) (14 December 1962), GAOR Supp. 17, p. 15; Declaration on the Establishment of a New International Economic Order, UNGA Res. A/Res/3201 (S-VI) (9 May 1974); Programme of Action on the Establishment of a New International Economic Order, UNGA Res. A/Res/3202 (S-VI) (15 May 1974); and UN General Assembly Resolution on a Charter of Economic Rights and Duties of States, UNGA Res. A/Res/3281 (XXIX) (12 December 1974), see especially Report of the Working Party of the Trade and Development Board, TD/B/AC.12/4 partially reproduced in J. Kuusi, *The Host State and the Transnational Corporation* (London: Saxon House, 1976), pp. 131–5.

[144] (1975) 16 ILM 263.

[145] These States are: Austria, Belgium, Canada, Denmark, France, Germany, Ireland, Italy, Japan, Luxembourg, Netherlands, Norway, Spain, Sweden, United Kingdom and United States.

1956. His First Report, which submitted that the non-performance of a contract by a State could 'give rise to international responsibility on the part of the State',[146] provoked so much opposition that his Second Report in 1957 posited that 'the non-performance of contractual obligations of this type does not *per se* constitute an international wrong'.[147] Despite the major adjustments made by García-Amador to his earlier report to accommodate the different views of the ILC members, there was no consensus on the horizon. The impasse came to an end in 1970, during the term of its second Special Rapporteur and future ICJ Judge, Roberto Ago, when the topic of contractual breaches was expunged for good from the agenda of the ILC.[148] Unlike García-Amador, Ago was doubtful that contractual protection in international law merited codification. Ago reasoned that since contracts concluded between States and individuals are 'normally governed by the juridical order of the contracting State', it was unnecessary to reopen the debate over the engagement of State responsibility for contractual breaches. Ago added that '[t]he violation by a State of a contractual obligation does not constitute, in and of itself, the objective element of an internationally wrongful act and is not at all capable of giving rise to State responsibility; the violation is subject to a different legal order, be it national law or some other law'.[149]

For more than two decades after the ILC excluded contractual protection from its codification project on State responsibility, no other significant State codification projects were undertaken. Instead, States concluded a large number of BITs,[150] some of which expressly confer treaty protection on contractual rights. For instance, the 1991 US-Argentina investment treaty provides that 'any right conferred by ... contract' qualifies as a protected investment.[151] In particular, Article II(2)(c) obliges each contracting

---

[146] 'State Responsibility' (20 January 1956), UN Doc. A/CN.4/96, p. 182.
[147] 'Responsibility of the State for Injuries Caused in its Territory to the Person or Property of Aliens (Part I: Acts and Omissions)' (15 February 1957), UN Doc. A/CN.4/106, p. 117. One commentator has called the Second Report 'a pale shadow of the first': P. Allot, *State Responsibility: A Dangerous Fiction* (London: British Institute of International and Comparative Law, 1987), p. 29.
[148] Ago, 'First Report on State Responsibility', p. 137.
[149] Ago, 'Fifth Report on State Responsibility to the ILC', pp. 11–13.
[150] According to the BIT database maintained by the UNCTAD, 1758 out of 2782 BITs, or nearly two-thirds of the BITs in existence, were concluded between 1980 and 1999: UNCTAD, 'International Investment Agreements Navigator', online: https://investmentpolicyhub.unctad.org/IIA (accessed 31 December 2017).
[151] Treaty between United States of America and The Argentine Republic Concerning the Reciprocal Encouragement and Protection of Investment. Signed 14 November 1991, entered into force 20 October 1994.

State to 'observe any obligation it may have entered into with regard to investments'. Although Article II(2)(c) resembles Article 2 of the 1967 OECD Draft Convention, there is little agreement on whether Article II(2)(c) stands for the principle of absolute contractual protection.[152] The appearance of treaty provisions like Article II(2)(c) revives the issue of whether a breach of contract by a State warrants sanction by international law. The topic that the ILC dismissed as inapposite for codification in 1970, retained its relevance to the law of State responsibility throughout the 1980s and 1990s in an ever-growing network of BITs.

The fourth and final State codification project was undertaken, once again by the OECD, in 1995. OECD States decided that the time was ripe to negotiate an MAI. The objective of the MAI was 'to provide a broad multilateral framework for international investment with high standards for the liberalisation of investment regimes and investment protection and with effective dispute settlement procedures'.[153] The mass of bilateral agreements on contractual protection did not pave the way for a multilateral agreement. One delegation proposed the inclusion of a 'respect clause', a replica of Article 2 of the 1967 OECD Draft Convention, in the text of the MAI:[154]

> Each Contracting Party shall observe any obligation it has entered into with regard to a specific investment of an investor of another Contracting Party.

Despite the ability of OECD States to agree on a principle of absolute contractual protection in 1967, the appeal of such a principle appears to have diminished by 1995. The proposal did not receive sufficient support from other OECD State delegations and no 'respect clause' appeared in any draft versions of the MAI or in commentaries on the MAI. The rift of opinions over other proposed clauses in the MAI ran so deep that negotiations were discontinued in 1998, barely three years after they started.[155]

Of the four State codification projects discussed above, only one – the 1967 OECD Draft Convention – asserted legal content on contractual

---

[152] The interpretation of investment treaty provisions like Art. II(2)(c) is discussed in detail in Chapter 5, Section 5.3.3.3.

[153] OECD, 'Multilateral Agreement on Investment', online: www.oecd.org/investment/internationalinvestmentagreements/multilateralagreementoninvestment.htm (accessed 31 December 2017).

[154] OECD, 'The Multilateral Agreement on Investment Draft Consolidated Text, 22 April 1998, DAFFE/MAI(98)7/REV1', online: www.oecd.org/daf/mai/pdf/ng/ng987r1e.pdf (accessed 31 December 2017), p. 116. There are no records in publicly available documents on which country proposed the 'respect clause'.

[155] For a pithy account of the negotiating history of the MAI, see P. Muchlinski, 'The Rise and Fall of the Multilateral Agreement on Investment: Where Now?' (2000) 34 *International Lawyer* 1033.

protection in its completed form. The inaugural attempt at codifying contractual protection in international law during 1930 Hague Codification Conference and the most recent attempt to do so during negotiations for the MAI were abandoned for lack of consensus. ILC Members did not object when Special Rapporteur Ago recommended dropping the topic of contractual protection from the ILC's codification agenda on State responsibility. The principle of absolute contractual protection was asserted in Article 2 of the 1967 OECD Draft Convention as a restatement of international law. Even so, its advancement by OECD States to the obvious disadvantage of developing host States, and its fundamental incompatibility with the tenet of sovereign equality in the NIEO, greatly weakened its compliance pull. Even if the principle of absolute contractual protection was once endorsed by twenty OECD States, the MAI negotiations show that over time, many OECD States withdrew open support for such a principle.

1.4.2 Private Codifications

The first significant private codification project that addressed contractual protection was the 1959 Abs-Shawcross Draft Convention. It was completed in two years under the stewardship of then chairman of Deutsche Bank, Hermann Abs, and former UK Attorney-General, Lord Hartley Shawcross.

  Abs was a renowned banker, and during his tenure as chairman, Deutsche Bank was the second largest bank in Europe. Even before he became chairman, Abs' banking prowess was already well-known during the Third Reich, and he became a reliable and trusted ally of the Nazi leaders.[156] Abs assisted the Nazi government with fending off creditors seeking repayment of loans made to Germany after World War I. Abs was also instrumental in getting Deutsche Bank to fund armed conquests of European nations by Nazi forces during World War II, reaping substantial profits from the seized economies in the process, and multiplying the wealth of the Bank and its Nazi associates. When the war ended, the US government pressed for Abs' arrest and prosecution before the International Military Tribunal at Nuremberg for suspected war crimes. The UK government, on the other hand, had other plans for Abs. It wanted him to help rebuild the German banking system in order to relaunch the German economy. Abs was arrested in January 1946 but released after three months upon the intervention of the UK government. And despite the surfacing of a report in 1947 implicating Abs in war crimes, Abs was never

---

[156] R. S. Wistrich, *Who's Who in Nazi Germany* (London: Routledge, 2002), pp. 1–2.

prosecuted at Nuremberg. The chief prosecutor for the United Kingdom at Nuremberg was the then Attorney-General, Sir Hartley Shawcross, later Lord Shawcross.

Lord Shawcross returned to private practice after stepping down as Attorney-General in April 1951. One of his notable clients was the Anglo-Iranian Oil Company, later renamed the British Petroleum Company.[157] For several years, the UK company was the focus of discontent in Iran after it transpired that the terms of a concession that it had been awarded entitled Iran to only a small percentage of profits made from the mining and sale of Iranian oil. In March 1951, the Iranian parliament voted to nationalise the Anglo-Iranian Oil Company. And in May 1951, just weeks after Lord Shawcross stepped down as Attorney-General, the United Kingdom espoused the claim of the Anglo-Iranian Oil Company against Iran before the ICJ.[158] A clause in the terminated concession provided that the 'Concession shall not be annulled by the [Iranian] Government and the terms therein contained shall not be altered either by general or special legislation in the future, or by administrative measures or any other acts whatever of the executive authorities'.[159] This clause, according to the United Kingdom, imposed 'an international obligation upon a State to observe the terms of a concession granted to a foreigner – an obligation towards the State of which the latter is a national – and the international responsibility of the grantor State is engaged, if there is a breach of this obligation and if municipal remedies have been exhausted without success'.[160] The ICJ did not comment on the UK's legal position on contractual protection as the claim was dismissed on jurisdictional grounds.[161]

---

[157] L. Dingle, 'Conversations with Professor Sir Elihu Lauterpacht, Second Interview (7 March 2008): USA (1940–44) and Career to 1962', online: www.squire.law.cam.ac.uk/eminent-scholars-archiveprofessor-sir-elihu-lauterpacht/conversations-professor-sir-eli-lauter-pacht (accessed 31 December 2017), Transcript, p. 7.

[158] *Anglo-Iranian Oil Co. (United Kingdom v. Iran)* (Preliminary Objection) [1952] ICJ Rep 93.

[159] Memorial Submitted by the Government of the United Kingdom of Great Britain and Northern Ireland, Ibid., p. 86.

[160] Memorial Submitted by the Government of the United Kingdom of Great Britain and Northern Ireland, Ibid., 79. Holding Iran to the letter of its bargain with a UK investor appears strategic in light of the United Kingdom's own unwillingness to be bound rigidly to contracts it concluded with foreign investors, see D. W. Bowett, 'State Contracts with Aliens: Contemporary Developments on Compensation for Termination or Breach' (1988) 58 BYIL 49 at 58–9 (fn. 40).

[161] *Anglo-Iranian Oil Co. (United Kingdom v. Iran)* (Preliminary Objection) [1952] ICJ Rep 93, pp. 111–5. Five other contract claims were espoused by home States before the PCIJ and the ICJ, but only one, the *Mavrommatis Jerusalem Concessions Case (Greece v. UK)* (26 March 1925) PCIJ, Series A, No. 5, attained final resolution. As the dispute arose in the unique

Subsequently, Lord Shawcross became part of a contingent of lawyers negotiating a joint concession on behalf of eight oil companies, including the Anglo-Iranian Oil Company, with the Iranian government.[162] Another lawyer retained by the Anglo-Iranian Oil Company for the negotiations with Iran was the young Sir Elihu Lauterpacht. He proposed that the investor would be better protected if, in addition to a non-interference clause like the one found in the terminated concession, Iran's contractual obligations were incorporated by reference into a treaty between the United Kingdom and Iran.[163] This proposal is designed to minimise, if not preclude, host State interference with investment contracts, because every breach of contract 'shall be *ipso facto* deemed to be a breach of the treaty',[164] exposing the host State to sanction by international law. Although Sir Lauterpacht's proposal was not adopted, the then novel way of using international law to secure absolute contractual protection will probably have made an impression on those who were acquainted with his proposal, including Lord Shawcross.

Abs' proven aptitude for protecting German investments abroad, and Lord Shawcross' experience with advising a UK investor trying to shield its concessionary rights from host State interference, offered common ground on the matter of contractual protection. However, an understandably investor-oriented approach, like the one taken by the OECD States in their 1967 Draft Convention, is also partisan because any articulated principle on contractual protection reflects sectarian interests. Unsurprisingly, Article II of the 1959 Abs-Shawcross Draft Convention advocated absolute contractual protection, with a possible nod to Sir Lauterpacht's advice to the Anglo-Iranian Oil Company:

> Each Party shall at all times ensure the observance of any undertakings, which it may have given in relation to investments made by nationals of any other Party.

---

historical context of the Mandate of Palestine, there was little in the PCIJ's ruling from which general principles on contractual protection could be distilled, see E. M. Borchard, 'The Mavrommatis Concessions Cases' (1925) 19 AJIL 728 at 738. The *Payment of Various Serbian Loans Issued in France (France v. Yugoslavia)* (12 July 1929) PCIJ, Series A, No. 20 and the *Losinger & Co. (Switzerland v. Yugoslavia)* (27 June 1936) PCIJ, Series A/B, No. 67 cases settled, while the *Ambatielos (Greece v. United Kingdom)* (Merits: Obligation to Arbitrate) [1953] ICJ Rep 10, pp. 19–22, and the *Certain Norwegian Loans Case (France v. Norway)* (Preliminary Objections) [1957] ICJ Rep 9, pp. 22–7, cases were dismissed, like the *Anglo-Iranian Oil Company Case*, on jurisdictional grounds.

[162] L. Dingle, 'Conversations with Professor Sir Elihu Lauterpacht, Second Interview (7 March 2008)' p. 7.

[163] A. Sinclair, 'The Origins of the Umbrella Clause in the International Law of Investment Protection' (2004) 20(4) *Arbitration International* 411 at 414–7.

[164] E. Lauterpacht, 'Anglo-Iranian Oil Company Ltd Persian Settlement – Opinion', 20 January 1954, p. 4, quoted in Sinclair, ibid., p. 415.

According to the official commentary to the 1959 Abs-Shawcross Draft Convention, Article II represented one of the 'fundamental principles of international law regarding the treatment of the property, rights, and interests of aliens' whereby no distinction was drawn 'between the rule [of *pacta sunt servanda*] applicable to treaties and that applicable to contracts with aliens'.[165] Commentators were divided on whether Article II merely repeated a general principle on contractual protection or was in fact a creation of the drafters. One commentator stated that '[t]he purpose of [Article II] is to dispel whatever doubts may possibly exist as to whether a unilateral violation of a concession contract is an international wrong',[166] while another challenged the drafters' depiction of Article II as a restatement of international law.[167] A third commentator alluded to the duplicity of presenting innovation as 'a restatement of principles of conduct relating to foreign investments',[168] with the observation that 'if conditions were such that promulgation of the code would be possible, it could be said then that there would be no real need for it'.[169] The appearance of the principle of absolute contractual protection in a codification project helmed by individuals with partisan leanings, like OECD States proposing rules of State conduct that affect mainly non-OECD States, explains its limited appeal and weaker compliance pull. As noted in the introduction to Section 1.4, the 1959 Abs-Shawcross Draft Convention was never tabled for signature and ratification by States.

The second significant private codification project that addressed contractual protection was the 1961 Harvard Draft Convention. It grew from a suggestion made by the then Secretary of the ILC, Dr Yuen-Li Liang, for the Harvard Law School (HLS) to revise a draft convention which was prepared in 1929 for the Harvard Research in International Law (HRIL).[170] The HRIL was an initiative of Manley O. Hudson, a professor of international law at HLS and a judge on the PCIJ, which produced conventions on

[165] H. Abs and Lord H. Shawcross, 'The Proposed Convention to Protect Private Foreign Investment' (1960) 9 *Journal of Public Law* 115 at 119–20; also Lord H. Shawcross, 'The Problems of Foreign Investment in International Law' (1961) 102 *Recueil des Cours* 335 at 351–5. *Pacta sunt servanda* means agreements must be kept.

[166] I. Seidl-Hohenveldern, 'The Abs-Shawcross Draft Convention to Protect Private Foreign Investment: Comments on the Round Table' (1961) 10 *Journal of Public Law* 100 at 104.

[167] S. D. Metzger, 'Multilateral Conventions for the Protection of Private Foreign Investment' (1960) 9 *Journal of Public Law* 133 at 137.

[168] See fn. 128, Preamble.

[169] A. S. Miller, 'Protection of Private Foreign Investment by Multilateral Convention' (1959) 53 AJIL 371 at, p. 377.

[170] Sohn and Baxter, 'Responsibility of States for Injuries', 545 at 545.

different topics of international law drafted by various advisory boards.[171]
One such convention was the 1929 Draft Convention on Responsibility
of States for Damage Done on Their Territory to the Person or Property
of Foreigners.[172] HLS entrusted the revision of the 1929 Draft Convention
to two of its professors, Louis Bruno Sohn and Richard Reeve Baxter.
Professors Sohn and Baxter then assembled an advisory committee comprising nine US experts on international law, most of whom came from
academia.[173]

The provision on contractual protection in the 1929 Draft Convention,
Article 8(a), reads:[174]

> A [S]tate is responsible if an injury to an alien results from its non-
> performance of a contractual obligation which it owes to the alien, if local
> remedies have been exhausted without adequate redress.

Its revision appeared as Article 12(1) of the 1961 Harvard Draft
Convention, which reads:

> The violation through an arbitrary action of the State of a contract or con-
> cession to which the central government of that State and an alien are par-
> ties is wrongful.

Although the official commentary on Article 12(1) did not explain the
grounds for the revision of Article 8(a) in the 1929 Draft Convention,
it is apparent from a simple textual comparison of the two provisions
that, unlike Article 8(a), Article 12(1) does not permit, under any circumstances, the assimilation of every contractual breach to a violation
of international law. Under Article 12(1), the breach has to be 'arbitrary'
in order for it to be considered 'wrongful'. Notably, the official commentary to Article 12(1) downplayed the usefulness of *pacta sunt servanda* as
a guiding principle which the drafters of the 1959 Abs-Shawcross Draft
Convention found illuminating. The drafters of Article 12(1) countered
that while '[p]*acta sunt servanda* is undoubtedly the basic norm of any system of law dealing with agreements[,] the principle speaks on such a high

---

[171] HeinOnline, 'Harvard Research in International Law', online: heinonline.org/HeinDocs/
HarvardResearchbrochure.pdf (accessed 31 December 2017).
[172] The 1929 Draft Convention was prepared by Professor Edwin Montefiore Borchard of the
Yale Law School.
[173] The committee counted Professor Philip C. Jessup as a member, until his election to the
ICJ. For the full list of committee members, see Sohn and Baxter, 'Responsibility of States
for Injuries', p. 546 (fn. 6).
[174] Harvard Draft Convention on the Responsibility of States for Injuries to the Economic
Interests of Aliens, (1929) 23 AJIL Special Supplement 133 at 134.

level of abstraction that it affords little or no guidance in the resolution of concrete legal disputes relating to agreements'.[175] They consciously avoided the extremes where 'every violation ... of a contract or concession between a State and an alien were to be regarded as engaging State responsibility', and where the contract was 'governed exclusively by the municipal law of the contracting State' such that the State possessed '[a]bsolute freedom to perform or not to perform'.[176] Article 12(1) was therefore a 'middle course' where State responsibility for contractual breaches is only engaged in the event of 'a "denial of justice" in litigation in the courts of the respondent State respecting an alleged breach of the contract and [in] cases in which the breach of the contract or concession has been characterized as "arbitrary" or "tortious"'.[177]

By laying down a moderate principle of qualified contractual protection, Article 12(1) of the 1961 Harvard Draft Convention was poised to command wider acceptance than the radical principle of absolute contractual protection in Article II of the 1959 Abs-Shawcross Draft Convention. Moreover, the identification of arbitrariness as a marker of internationally wrongful State conduct finds support in the *Martini Award*,[178] and the *International Fisheries Company Claim* discussed in Section 1.3.2.[179] However, Article 12(1) has not been cited by modern-day international tribunals for the principle of non-arbitrariness in contractual protection.[180]

One possible reason for the neglect of Article 12(1) is the fact that the 1961 Harvard Draft Convention is a product of a handful of US international lawyers that has never been ratified by any State. For a code that targets State conduct towards aliens, *ex post* endorsement from its target audience is necessary for turning principles conceived by academics without the input of States, into principles that States are nonetheless willing to comply with. Even the principle of absolute contractual protection, with

---

[175] See fn. 127, p. 569.

[176] Ibid., pp. 569–70.

[177] Ibid., p. 570.

[178] Ibid., pp. 571–2.

[179] Ibid., p. 699. There is also some support among scholars that arbitrariness can amount to a violation of customary international law, see for example C. Schreuer, 'Protection against Arbitrary or Discriminatory Measures' in C. A. Rogers and R. P. Alford (eds.), *The Future of Investment Arbitration* (Oxford: Oxford University Press, 2009), pp. 188–9.

[180] The omission is significant, given how non-arbitrariness forms part of the content of the core standard of treatment that investment contracts attract under international law, see discussion at Chapter 3, Sections 3.2.1 and 3.3.

all its partisan underpinnings in the unratified 1959 Abs-Shawcross Draft Convention, reappeared as Article 2 of the 1967 OECD Draft Convention with the support of 20 OECD States.

A second possible reason for the marginalisation of Article 12(1) is the refusal of the ILC to utilise the 1961 Harvard Draft Convention while codifying the law of State responsibility. Up until 1970, contractual protection was still officially on the ILC's codification agenda. Principles identified in HLS-led codifications can exert a strong compliance pull when they are consulted and relied upon by the ILC for the latter's codification projects.[181] The first Special Rapporteur on State responsibility, García-Amador, was guided by Article 8(a) of the 1929 Draft Convention when proposing his vision of contractual protection to the ILC members.[182] The prospect of absolute contractual protection, which Article 8(a) permitted, provoked so much opposition that García-Amador had to forego his initial vision, as well as reliance on Article 8(a). An earlier version of the 1961 Harvard Draft Convention was not well-received by ILC members who 'seriously questioned whether the existing law could be regarded as providing corroboration of the principles upheld by the Harvard jurists'.[183] García-Amador made no mention of Article 12(1) in his later reports. His successor, Ago, had even less reason to rely on Article 12(1), since one of his earliest decisions as the second Special Rapporteur was to expunge the topic of contractual protection from the ILC's codification agenda.

Although the principle prohibiting arbitrary conduct, unlike the principle of absolute contractual protection, does not favour a small group of States at the expense of other States, its advancement by a small group of Harvard jurists in the 1961 Harvard Draft Convention nonetheless lent it a partisan flavour. States were simply not prepared to endorse the views of a few academics during the divisive and protracted ILC negotiations on the codification of the law of State responsibility.[184]

---

[181] One example is the 1932 Harvard Draft Convention on Diplomatic Privileges and Immunities ((1932) 26(1) AJIL Special Supplement 15), which the ILC referred to as an 'important draft' and reviewed with approval in its work on diplomatic intercourse and immunities (ILC, 'Diplomatic Intercourse and Immunities – Memorandum Prepared by the Secretariat' (21 February 1956), UN Doc. A/CN.4/98, pp. 149–52), and which culminated in the Vienna Convention on Diplomatic Relations. Signed 18 April 1961, entered into force 24 April 1964, 500 UNTS 95.
[182] F. V. García-Amador, 'State Responsibility' (20 January 1956), UN Doc. A/CN.4/96, pp. 176, 180, and 205–6.
[183] Ago, 'First Report on State Responsibility', p. 135.
[184] Notably, a number of investment treaties offer protection against arbitrary measures for all qualifying investments, and not just contracts, by the host State (see for instance

1.5   Conclusion

The history of contractual protection in international law tells a story of legal principles emerging from exhibitions of power.

The power to determine the outcome of a contract claim, the power to determine the mode of settling a contract claim and the power to determine the legal content of contractual protection, have been asserted by States, arbitral tribunals and private actors at three different junctures over the course of nearly 200 years. During the age of diplomacy, the power to determine the outcome of a contract claim was regularly asserted by home and host States, but not the power to determine the mode of dispute settlement, nor the power to determine the legal content of contractual protection. As a result, claims were satisfied or dismissed for reasons seldom made known in diplomatic correspondence, but which were probably unrelated to their legal merit. During the age of international adjudication, States asserted, or acceded to, the power to determine the mode of dispute settlement, by establishing Mixed Claims Commissions to hear contract claims between nationals of one founding State against the other founding State. The power to determine the legal content of contractual protection, and the power to determine the outcome of a claim, were delegated by the founding States to the Commissions, who asserted them regularly during adjudication. And during the age of codification, the power to determine the legal content of contractual protection was asserted by States and private actors to a greater extent than the power to determine the mode of dispute settlement or the power to determine the outcome of a contract claim.

Whichever configuration the content of asserted power takes, this chapter sought to show that the legal contours of contractual protection only emerged when one objective of asserted power was the advancement of a legal position. This was realised through the assertion of power to determine the legal content of contractual protection, which was far more noticeable during the periods of international adjudication and codification, than during the period of diplomacy. As a result, the period of diplomacy presented little opportunity to distil principles on contractual protection. In contrast, the period of international adjudication proffered three principles to help ascertain when interference by a host State with a contract invites sanction by international law. The first is that contractual forum selection

---

Treaty Between the United States of America and the Czech and Slovak Federal Republic Concerning the Reciprocal Encouragement and Protection of Investments. Signed 22 October 1991, entered into force 19 December 1992, Art. II(2)(b)). No connection has ever been made between these provisions and Art. 12(1) of the 1961 Harvard Draft Convention.

clauses are not jurisdictional bars to international claims; the second is that contractual breaches *per se* are not violations of international law; and the third is that only contractual breaches *iure imperii* potentially violate international law. The period of codification proffered two additional principles, namely, the principle of absolute contractual protection, and the principle prohibiting arbitrary host State interference with contracts.

Principles on contractual protection that emerged from projects on the codification of international law have been rejected or sidelined by a large number of States, while those articulated by Mixed Claims Commissions were honoured by their founding States, and continue to be applied by modern-day international arbitral tribunals constituted to hear investment contract claims against host States. In other words, principles on contractual protection that emerged in the former context appear to be less persuasive, and exert a weaker compliance pull, than principles that emerged in the latter context. This chapter then sought to show that a principle's weaker compliance pull is attributable to the partisan circumstances of its emergence. The State and private codification efforts that generated principles on contractual protection are the 1967 OECD Draft Convention, the 1959 Abs-Shawcross Draft Convention and the 1961 Harvard Draft Convention. Each of these codifications projects, as their names imply, reflected the particular agenda of a select group of States or individuals. Principles on contractual protection that emerged in circumstances where real or perceived sectarian interests are upsold as universal interests bear the taint of partiality that necessarily diminishes their broader appeal. In comparison, principles on contractual protection articulated by Mixed Claims Commissions are less likely to attract allegations of partiality. This is because Mixed Claims Commission, as illustrated for instance by the US-Mexico Claims Commission's defence of Calvo clauses in the *North American Dredging Company of Texas Claim*, have demonstrated the capacity to adjudicate claims impartially. In standing and substantiating their ground, even if this meant dismissing the claim presented by or rejecting the legal position of the dominant founding State, Mixed Claims Commissions produced awards recording independent, quality legal analysis.

The willingness of founding States to comply, for better or for worse, with the awards of Mixed Claims Commissions, enhanced the compliance pull of principles on contractual protection contained in these awards. As the earliest source of general principles on contractual protection in international law, the awards of Mixed Claims Commissions foreshadowed the exceptional importance of arbitral awards to the development of the law of State responsibility for breaches of investment contracts – the subject of Chapter 2.

Arbitral Awards and the Generation
of International Law

2.1 Introduction

The content of the law of State responsibility is said to derive from the practice of States.[1] This observation holds true whenever there is sufficient State practice gravitating towards common parameters governing the engagement of State responsibility. When relevant State practice is largely non-existent, the content of the law of State responsibility must be located elsewhere. Contractual protection is an area where the content of the law of State responsibility did not emerge from State practice. As shown in Chapter 1, diplomatic correspondence revealed that States rarely attempted to resolve contractual disputes between foreign nationals and host States by invoking international law. Instead, home States simply demanded satisfaction of a contract claim, which host States then ignored or complied with as they saw fit.[2] Legal content on the international responsibility of host States for interfering with contracts concluded with foreign nationals began emerging in the arbitral awards rendered by Mixed Claims Commissions.[3] This signalled the uniquely prominent role that arbitral awards have played and continue to play in generating an international law on contractual protection.

The idea that arbitral awards are capable of generating international law has struggled for acceptance. It was once greeted with scepticism because developing host States suspected that arbitral tribunals were partial to foreign investor interests,[4] making any generated law a partisan law.

---

[1] P. Reuter, 'Principes de Droit International Public' (1961) 103 *Recueil des Cours* 425 at 585.

[2] See discussion at Chapter 1, Section 1.2.

[3] See discussion at Chapter 1, Section 1.3.3.

[4] See generally M. Sornarajah, 'The Myth of International Contract Law' (1981) 15 *Journal of World Trade Law* 187; also A. A. Fatouros, 'International Law and the Internationalized Contract' (1980) 74 AJIL 134 at 137 and 139; and J. Paulsson, 'Third World Participation in International Investment Arbitration' (1987) 2 *ICSID Review – Foreign Investment Law Journal* 19 at 19–20. A concrete example is the president of the Russian delegation to the 1922 Hague Conference, M. Litvinoff, announcing that his government did not believe

Suspicions alone are inconclusive. The proven ability of Mixed Claims Commissions to arrive at decisions that do not favour the claim presented by the more dominant and developed founding State undermined suspicions regarding the partiality of these arbitral tribunals.[5] Empirical evidence on the decisional patterns of modern-day arbitral tribunals deciding investment disputes suggests that these tribunals do not routinely favour investor claims.[6] Over time, doubts over the capacity of arbitral awards to generate international law subsided.[7] The authors of arbitral awards are now regarded as 'important agents, whether of regression, stabilization or change' in international law.[8] In the context of foreign investment protection, of which contractual protection forms a part, there appears to be greater acceptance of the capacity of arbitral awards to make and shape international law.[9]

---

that an impartial arbitral tribunal could be found to hear disputes with foreign creditors, going as far as to say that 'only an angel could be unbiased in judging Russian affairs', see Netherlands Department of Foreign Affairs, *Conference at The Hague (June 26–July 20, 1922) – Minutes and Documents* (The Hague: Government Printing Office, 1922), pp. 31–2, 123 and 126. Russia subsequently boycotted the *Lena Goldfields* v. *USSR* arbitration (*The Times*, 3 September 1930), which concerned a claim that Russia had terminated a gold mining concession without compensating the UK investor.

[5] See discussion at Chapter 1, Section 1.3.2. Mixed Claims Commissions, which were prevalent in the 1800s to the early 1900s, were established by bilateral treaties to adjudicate agreed categories of claims, such as contract claims, between nationals of a State party and the other State party.

[6] S. D. Franck and L. E. Wylie, 'Predicting Outcomes in Investment Treaty Arbitration' (2015) 65 *Duke Law Journal* 459 at 487–518.

[7] Discomfort, for some, persists. After examining interpretation trends from a dataset of more than a hundred publicly available arbitral awards rendered in investment treaty disputes, G. Van Harten suggests that arbitral tribunals may be biased in favour of claimants from Western capital-exporting States, 'Arbitrator Behaviour in Asymmetrical Adjudication: An Empirical Study of Investment Treaty Arbitration' (2012) 50(1) *Osgoode Hall Law Journal* 211 at 240–5.

[8] W. M. Reisman, 'The Future of International Investment Law and Arbitration' in A. Cassese (ed.), *Realizing Utopia the Future of International Law* (Oxford: Oxford University Press, 2012), pp. 275, 286.

[9] J. Paulsson, 'International Arbitration and the Generation of Legal Norms: Treaty Arbitration and International Law' in A. J. van den Berg (ed.), *International Arbitration 2006: Back to Basics? ICCA Congress Series* (The Hague: Kluwer Law International, 2007), vol. 13, pp. 879, 881; G. Kaufmann-Kohler, 'Arbitral Precedent: Dream, Necessity or Excuse?' (2006) 23(3) *Arbitration International* 357 at 375; A. Reinisch, 'The Role of Precedent in ICSID Arbitration' (2008) 2 *Austrian Arbitration Yearbook* 495 at 497; see also C. McLachlan, 'Investment Treaties and General International Law' (2008) 57(2) ICLQ 361 at 391–2 and 400 where the author argues that 'investment arbitral awards can only serve as an elucidation of the law, not as a binding source of it'; cf. G. Guillaume, 'The Use of Precedent by International Judges and Arbitrators' (2011) 2(1) *Journal of International Dispute Settlement* 5 at 23.

This chapter argues that not only do arbitral awards generate international law, they are a principal source of international law on contractual protection (Section 2.2). Arbitral awards are only binding on the parties to the dispute and not on future tribunals. The freedom of arbitral tribunals to reject legal content on contractual protection proposed by earlier tribunals, and create different legal content, makes arbitral awards a potentially disorderly source of law (Section 2.3). When a principal source of law is also potentially disorderly, ascertaining the content of international law on contractual protection can be challenging. In practice though, arbitral tribunals consult and adopt the legal content generated by earlier arbitral awards. This chapter then examines two possible motivations for the voluntary adherence by arbitral tribunals with earlier arbitral awards. The first is the process of natural selection, which positions highly regarded arbitral awards as leading content generators. The second is the presence of a prevailing answer to a common problem, which identifies sizeable clusters of arbitral awards as collective content generators (Section 2.4). Despite the potential for legal content to develop in a haphazard manner, the combination of natural selection and a prevailing approach promotes convergence of legal content across arbitral awards, thereby enabling reliance on arbitral awards as a principal source of international law on contractual protection.

2.2   How Arbitral Awards Became a Principal Source of International Law on Contractual Protection

Arbitration is a popular mode of settling contractual disputes between foreign investors and host States. Whether arbitration is provided for in an arbitration clause in an investment contract or in an investment treaty, the replacement of local remedies with an international tribunal constituted by the disputing parties is a concession many States are willing to make to attract foreign investment. Many claims submitted to arbitration raise the issue of the host State's international responsibility for interfering with an investor's contractual rights. This has resulted in a large number of arbitral awards dealing with State responsibility for breaches of investment contracts.[10]

Sheer numbers make arbitral awards a likely reference point when formulating the content of international law, but they do not fully explain the uniquely prominent status of arbitral awards as a source of law. This

---

[10]   These awards form the backbone of Chapters 3, 4 and 5.

section identifies and discusses three factors which unite to transform arbitral awards from a promising into a principal source of international law on contractual protection. The first factor is the capacity of arbitral awards to generate binding legal content on the parties to the dispute (Section 2.2.1), and the second is the presence of a lacuna or ambiguity in what would otherwise be the international law on contractual protection (Section 2.2.2). The third factor is the publication of arbitral awards, which gave later arbitral tribunals the opportunity to be acquainted with and to adopt legal content generated by earlier arbitral awards (Section 2.2.3).

2.2.1   *The Capacity of Arbitral Awards to Generate Binding Legal Content on Disputing Parties*

Some of the earliest arbitral awards enunciating principles on contractual protection under international law were issued by Mixed Claims Commissions. As explained in Chapter 1, the terms of establishment agreed upon by the founding States gave Commissions the power to determine the legal content of contractual protection and obliged the founding States to treat Commission awards as final and binding.[11] In practice, States complied with Commission awards, even when the ruling was unfavourable. Whether they did so in the interest of reciprocity, to uphold the rule of law, or out of conviction in the cogency of the Commission's decision, compliance expressed a willingness to be bound by the legal content generated in Commission awards.[12]

The rationale for the constitution of modern-day arbitral tribunals differs from the Mixed Claims Commissions of the past. Yet, certain features of establishment, like the delegation of power from the disputing parties to the arbitral tribunal to determine the legal content of contractual protection, and the obligation of the disputing parties to treat an award of the arbitral tribunal as final and binding remain the same. Many investment contracts record the consent of the contracting parties to submit any future disputes between them to arbitration. The contract usually stipulates the governing law which the arbitral tribunal is expected to apply to the merits of the dispute, implying the delegated power of the tribunal to generate legal content. The contract may also provide for the binding finality of any resulting arbitral award. More unusually, a contract may provide for the enforcement of an arbitral award, in the event that the party against whom

---

[11] See discussion at Chapter 1, Section 1.3.2.
[12] See discussion at Chapter 1, Section 1.3.3.

the award is made does not comply with it voluntarily. And when one of the contracting parties is a State, enforcement can be better assured by an express waiver of sovereign immunity from the execution of the award against State-owned assets. There are several factors, including reputational standing among foreign investors and the dissatisfaction of domestic investors, that can motivate States either to comply with or to repudiate an arbitral award in favour of a foreign investor's claim.[13] Barring a handful of instances of non-compliance due to host State impecuniosity,[14] compliance, which demonstrates a strong commitment to foreign investment protection, remains the norm.[15]

One example of an investment contract that underscores the capacity of an arbitral tribunal to generate binding legal content on the disputing parties, even in the absence of voluntary compliance with the arbitral award by the losing party, is a contract for the exploration and production of hydrocarbons concluded by a US-owned investor with the Ministry of Energy and Mineral Resources of the Republic of Kazakhstan:[16]

> Applicable Law
> Clause 26.1 This Contract and other agreements signed on the basis of this Contract shall be governed by the law of the State unless stated otherwise by the international treaties to which the State is a party.
> ...

---

[13] C. M. Ryan, 'Discerning the Compliance Calculus: Why States Comply with International Investment Law' (2009) 38 *Georgia Journal of International and Comparative Law* 63 at 81–94.

[14] Argentina's failure to pay the damages awarded to US investors in *CMS Gas Transmission Company* v. *The Argentine Republic*, ICSID Case No. ARB/01/8, Award, 12 May 2005 (Orrego Vicuña, Lalonde, Rezek) and *Azurix Corp.* v. *The Argentine Republic*, ICSID Case No. ARB/01/12, Award, 14 July 2006 (Rigo Sureda, Lalonde, Martins) led the United States to suspend its preferential trading status, see The White House Office of the Press Secretary, 'Presidential Proclamation – To Modify Duty-Free Treatment under the Generalized System of Preferences and for Other Purposes (26 March 2012)', online: obamawhitehouse .archives.gov/the-press-office/2012/03/26/presidential-proclamation-modify-duty-free-treatment-under-generalized-s (accessed 31 December 2017), para. 2.

[15] See for instance the high regard in which Switzerland holds arbitral awards interpreting substantive protection provisions in investment treaties, Letter from the Swiss Secretariat for Economic Affairs to the ICSID Secretary-General, 'Umbrella Clauses in Bilateral Investment Agreements', 1 October 2003, 19 *Mealey's International Arbitration Reports* E1, cover letter: 'An issue that we follow carefully are the decisions of various arbitral tribunals on selected aspects of BITs. Such decisions, and in particular those by ICSID tribunals take on a great importance and are not only observed by the professionals in the field but also by the public at large and politicians.'

[16] Signed 27 May 2002, excerpted in *Caratube International Oil Company LLP and Anor.* v. *Republic of Kazakhstan*, ICSID Case No. ARB/13/13, Award, 27 September 2017 (Lévy, Aynès, Salès), pp. 8–10.

Procedure for Dispute Resolution

...

27.2 **Referral to Arbitration**. In the event that any dispute cannot be resolved by amicable settlement within sixty (60) days after notice in writing of such by one Party to the other Party, the Parties agree that their exclusive means of dispute resolution shall be (a) to submit the matter to arbitration for final settlement in accordance with the then current Rules of Conciliation and Arbitration of the International Centre for Settlement of Investment Disputes ('ICSID') if the Competent Authority has become a party to the ICSID Convention at the time a proceeding is instituted, or (b) to submit the dispute for resolution according to the Arbitration (Additional Facility) Rules of ICSID if the Competent Authority has not become a party to the ICSID Convention at the time when any proceeding is instituted. Any arbitral tribunal constituted pursuant to this Contract shall consist of three arbitrators, one appointed by the Contractor and one appointed by the Competent Authority, and a third arbitrator, who shall be president of the Tribunal and shall not be a resident of Kazakhstan, appointed by agreement of the Parties, or failing such agreement, by the Chairman of the Administrative Council of ICSID. In the event that the Contractor or the Competent Authority fails to appoint an arbitrator within ninety (90) calendar days after the notice of registration of a request for arbitration has been sent the remaining arbitrators shall be appointed in accordance with the Rules under ICSID.

...

27.5 **Arbitral Award**. Any arbitral award made in respect of any matter submitted to arbitration pursuant to Section 27.2 shall be final and binding upon the Parties ... Within three (3) months from the date determined by the arbitrators, full payment of any arbitral award shall be made ...

...

27.7 **Enforcement and Consent**. Each of the Parties hereby consents to submit to ICSID any dispute, controversy or claim arising out of or in connection with this Contact. Each of the Parties agrees that any judgement rendered by the arbitrators against it and entered in any court of record in London, England or any other competent court, may be executed against its assets in any jurisdiction. The Parties consent to being sued for enforcement of the award and any costs, fees or other charges for which they may be liable under this Article. Each of the Parties hereby agrees that all of the transactions contemplated by this Contract shall constitute and shall be deemed to constitute an investment within the jurisdiction of ICSID. The Competent Authority warrants that it is a structural subdivision and agent of the Government of the Republic of Kazakhstan.

...

27.9 **Waiver of Immunity**. Each of the Parties expressly and irrevocably waives any claim to immunity (including, but not limited to, sovereign immunity, immunity from service of process, immunity of property from award) from suit, execution, set-off, attachment or other legal process under any applicable law or in respect of any arbitral award rendered.

The submission of a contractual dispute to arbitration may also begin with an offer by the State contracting party to arbitrate a defined category of future disputes with protected investors in an applicable investment treaty. Consent is perfected when a protected investor accepts the State's offer to arbitrate by filing a request for arbitration. Like investment contracts, investment treaties also delegate the power to generate legal content to arbitral tribunals constituted pursuant to treaty terms and procure the binding finality of arbitral awards.[17] These provisions are present in the Treaty between the United States of America and the Republic of Kazakhstan Concerning the Encouragement and Reciprocal Protection of Investment:[18]

Article VI

(4) Each Party hereby consents to the submission of any investment dispute[19] for settlement by binding arbitration in accordance with the choice specified in the written consent of the national or company under paragraph 3. Such consent, together with the written consent of the national or company when given under paragraph 3 shall satisfy the requirement for:

   (a) written consent of the parties to the dispute for purposes of Chapter II of the ICSID Convention (Jurisdiction of the Centre) and for purposes of the Additional Facility Rules; and

   (b) an 'agreement in writing,' for purposes of Article II of the United Nations Convention on the Recognition and Enforcement of Foreign Arbitral Awards, done at New York, June 10, 1958 ('New York Convention').

   ...

---

[17] Unlike investment contracts where only one contracting party is a State or State entity, investment treaties can only be concluded between States. The distinction matters if one takes the position that only States have the power to determine the content of international law, and therefore only States can delegate this power to arbitral tribunals. Legal content on contractual protection generated in an arbitral award rendered by an arbitral tribunal constituted pursuant to an investment contract amounts at best to a unilateral declaration of the current state of international law by the State party to the contract. The distinction melts away if one accepts that both States and private actors assert the power to determine the content of contractual protection under international law (see Chapter 1, Section 1.4.2), and that States can agree to be bound by content developed by private actors.

[18] Signed 19 May 1992, entered into force 12 January 1994.

[19] Investment dispute is defined in Art. VI(1) as:

   For purposes of this Article, an investment dispute is a dispute between a Party and a national or company of the other Party arising out of or relating to (a) an investment agreement between that Party and such national or company; (b) an investment authorization granted by that Party's foreign investment authority to such national or company; or (c) an alleged breach of any right conferred or created by this Treaty with respect to an investment.

(6) Any arbitral award rendered pursuant to this Article shall be final and binding on the parties to the dispute. Each Party undertakes to carry out without delay the provisions of any such award and to provide in its territory for its enforcement.

2.2.2   Lacuna or Ambiguity in the Law

A traditional point of departure for identifying the sources of international law is Article 38(1) of the Statute of the International Court of Justice.[20] Article 38(1) enumerates the law applicable by the ICJ, 'whose function is to decide in accordance with international law such disputes as are submitted to it'. Article 38(1) presents a hierarchy of sources: Articles 38(1)(a) to (c) mandate the application of treaty, customary and general principles of law, while Article 38(1)(d) identifies 'judicial decisions … as a subsidiary means for the determination of rules of law'. Although Article 38(1) makes no mention of arbitral awards, it is generally accepted that arbitral awards occupy the same rung on the hierarchy of sources as judicial decisions.[21] The formal subsidiarity of arbitral awards as a source of international law ceases to matter when 'international law knows no norm at all but a lacuna'.[22] In an entirely unregulated field, arbitral awards, by being first in time to proffer guidance, generate legal content 'if only because there is not much else at which to look'.[23] By default and in substance, arbitral awards become a principal source of international law.

---

[20] Signed 26 June 1945, entered into force 24 October 1945, (1945) 39 AJIL Supplement 215. R. Y. Jennings did not directly contest the general applicability of Art. 38(1) when he wrote that 'it is an open question whether [Art. 38(1)] is now of itself a sufficient guide to the content of modern international law'; see 'What Is International Law and How Do We Tell It When We See It?' (1981) 37 *Swiss Yearbook of International Law* 59, reprinted in R. Y. Jennings, *Collected Writings of Sir Robert Jennings* (The Hague: Kluwer Law International, 1998), pp. 730, 732.

[21] H. Lauterpacht, *The Development of International Law by the International Court* (London: Stevens & Sons, 1958), pp. 13–23; W. Friedmann, *The Changing Structure of International Law* (London: Stevens & Sons, 1964), pp. 120 and 141–6; and M. Virally, 'The Sources of International Law' in M. Sørensen (ed.), *Manual of Public International Law* (London: Macmillan, 1968), pp. 116 and 149–52.

[22] P. Weil, 'Towards Relative Normativity in International Law' (1983) 77 AJIL 413 at 414.

[23] R. B. Lillich and D. B. Magraw (eds.), *The Iran–United States Claims Tribunal: Its Contribution to the Law of State Responsibility* (New York, NY: Transnational Publishers, 1998), p. 23; see also J. Crawford, 'The ILC's Articles on Responsibility of States for Internationally Wrongful Acts: A Retrospect' (2002) 96 AJIL 874 at 886; and more generally A. T. Guzman, *How International Law Works* (Oxford: Oxford University Press, 2008) where game theory is used to explain how international tribunals which 'serve to establish or clarify the substantive rules of international law' on State responsibility induce compliance by States with their decisions, pp. 49–55.

As demonstrated in Chapter 1, the awards of Mixed Claims Commissions became the earliest generators of legal content on contractual protection because there was no State practice in diplomatic correspondence on contract claims from which customary rules could be deduced.[24] After Mixed Claims Commissions exhausted their mandates and were no longer established by States to settle outstanding claims, other arbitral tribunals exercising the delegated power to generate legal content on contractual protection continued to fill the lacuna.

The subsequent appearance and proliferation of investment treaties, many of which explicitly protect an investor's rights arising from a contract, questions the characterisation of arbitral awards as a principal source of international law. After all, treaty law precedes arbitral awards in the formal hierarchy established by Article 38(1).[25] However, the following remark by a leading arbitrator for investment disputes, Gabrielle Kaufmann-Kohler, suggests that the prominence of arbitral awards as a source of international law is not diminished by the existence of investment treaties:[26]

> When arbitrators apply a body of rules that is less developed and is still in the process of being formed, their role with respect to the establishment of predictable rules is much more important. This is so today in sports law and investment law.

Kaufmann-Kohler's observation that 'investment law' is 'a body of rules that is less developed and is still in the process of being formed' strongly suggests ambiguity in the content of treaty law.[27] As one commentator puts it, although investment treaties may be regarded as the 'basic building block[s] of this emerging regime for investment [protection]', they are 'breathtaking in their generality, vagueness, and lack of specificity'.[28] In order to ascertain the character of protection that investment treaties

---

[24] See discussion at Chapter 1, Sections 1.2 and 1.3.
[25] For a criticism on how formalism can distort the actual contribution of a source to the development of international law, see J. E. Alvarez, 'The Public International Law Regime Governing International Investment' (2009) 344 *Recueil des Cours* 193 at 357. For a plea for the replacement of Art. 38(1) formalism in the identification of law-generating sources with 'written linguistic indicators' which are present in, for instance, the published awards of arbitral tribunals, see J. d'Aspremont, *Formalism and the Sources of International Law: A Theory of the Ascertainment of Legal Rules* (Oxford: Oxford University Press, 2011), pp. 142–51, 186–9 and 206.
[26] Kaufmann-Kohler, 'Arbitral Precedent', p. 375.
[27] Alvarez, 'The Public International Law Regime Governing International Investment', pp. 354–64 and 480–1.
[28] J. W. Salacuse, *The Law of Investment Treaties* (Oxford: Oxford University Press, 2010), pp. 3–16.

confer on investment contracts, arbitral tribunals exercise their delegated power to generate legal content by interpreting open-textured treaty provisions.[29] A treaty that has never been subject to interpretation by an international tribunal remains a stand-alone source of international law, whatever its ambiguities. When it has, international law is an amalgamation of the treaty provisions and the arbitral award which interprets those provisions. Therefore, the status of arbitral awards as a principal source of international law is not necessarily compromised by the presence of treaty law.[30] Investment treaties and arbitral awards interpreting them are intertwined and equally important sources of international law.

2.2.3   Access to and Adoption of Legal Content Found in Earlier Arbitral Awards

It is a common misconception that arbitral awards are always kept confidential and therefore inaccessible. As arbitration is a consensual form of dispute settlement, confidentiality over the proceedings and of the resulting award is maintained to the extent agreed upon by the disputing parties. Arbitral awards are publicly accessible so long as the parties to the awards consent to their publication. Disputes involving States can and often touch on the propriety of exercise of sovereign powers, giving rise to 'many most interesting questions of international law'.[31] Therefore such disputes have a strong public dimension that disputes between private parties lack. Although consent to publish has to be freely given by the disputing parties, the public importance of disputes involving States urges parties to consent to the publication of arbitral awards. As a result, published arbitral awards are more commonplace in inter- or investor–State disputes[32] than in private commercial disputes.

---

[29] The canons of treaty interpretation, which arbitral tribunals are expected to apply, are found in Arts. 31 and 32 of the Vienna Convention on the Law of Treaties, signed 23 May 1969, entered into force 27 January 1980, 1155 UNTS 331.

[30] The awards of earlier panels of the Iran–United States Claims Tribunal interpreting provisions of the Treaty of Amity, Economic Relations, and Consular Rights between the United States of America and Iran, signed 15 August 1955, entered into force 16 June 1957, 284 UNTS 93, are a case in point, see Lillich and Magraw, *The Iran–United States Claims Tribunal,* pp. 23–37. The same is true for the awards of the dispute settlement panels of the World Trade Organization, interpreting provisions of the 1994 General Agreement on Tariffs and Trade, signed 15 April 1994, entered into force 1 January 1995, 1867 UNTS 187; see D. Palmeter and P. C. Mavroidis, 'The WTO Legal System: Sources of Law' (1998) 92 AJIL 398 at 400–6.

[31] J. H. Ralston, *Venezuelan Arbitrations of 1903* (Washington, DC: Government Printing Office, 1904), 'Preface', p. iii.

[32] The publication of arbitral awards is one facet of the movement towards greater transparency in investor–State dispute settlement proceedings. This movement has culminated in

In the late 1800s to the early 1900s, arbitral awards involving State parties were published either in a volume of awards compiled on private initiative, under the direction of one of the State parties, or individually in academic journals like the *American Journal of International Law* or the *Revue Générale de Droit International Public*. Certain arbitral awards predating 1900 were compiled for francophones in two volumes edited by French academics Albert Geouffre de Lapradelle and Nicolas Politis.[33] The awards of the various Venezuelan Mixed Claims Commissions seated at Caracas in 1902–3 were published in English in two volumes under the direction of the US Senate with the consent of the Venezuelan and all other participating governments.[34] In 1948, the UN decided to undertake a systematic compilation of all published arbitral awards settling disputes between States. This entailed reproducing post-1900 awards, and in due course pre-1900 awards, in chronological volumes of the *Reports of International Arbitral Awards*. The objective of the compilation was to facilitate research into the legal content of arbitral awards in the interest of the 'progressive development of international law'.[35]

Today, technological advancement has greatly enhanced accessibility to arbitral awards. Whereas published awards were once consulted from hard copies of books or journals in libraries, the mass digitisation of print materials permits anyone with a computer and an internet connection and the relevant database access to peruse soft copies of arbitral awards from anywhere in the world.[36] The publication of arbitral awards is a key step to

---

the UN Convention on Transparency in Treaty-Based Investor–State Arbitration, signed 10 December 2014, entered into force 18 October 2017; 'Mauritius Convention', UN Doc. A/RES/69/116, Annex, which adopted the UNCITRAL Rules on Transparency in Treaty-Based Investor–State Arbitration, UNCITRAL, 'UNCITRAL Rules on Transparency in Treaty-Based Investor–State Arbitration (effective date: 1 April 2014)', online: www .uncitral.org/uncitral/en/uncitral_texts/arbitration/2014Transparency.html (accessed 31 December 2017) ('UNCITRAL Rules')). According to Art. 3(1) of the UNCITRAL Rules, arbitral awards 'shall be made available to the public'. In the interest of greater transparency, publication of arbitral awards is by default, rather than by consent. At the time of writing, the Mauritius Convention has twenty-two signatories, three of whom (Canada, Mauritius and Switzerland) have ratified it.

[33] A. de Lapradelle and N. Politis, *Recueil des Arbitrages Internationaux* (Paris: Pedone, 1905), vols. I and II.

[34] Ralston, *Venezuelan Arbitrations of 1903*, p. iii; and J. H. Ralston, *Report of French–Venezuelan Mixed Claims Commission of 1902* (Washington, DC: Government Printing Press, 1906), p. iii.

[35] UN Office of Legal Affairs (Codification Division), 'Reports of International Arbitral Awards', online: https://legal.un.org/riaa/ (accessed 31 December 2017).

[36] Technological advancement is bolstered by free access to a large number of arbitral awards online. The bulk of published investor–State arbitral awards are freely accessible on ITA

these awards 'releas[ing] their full precedential force'.[37] While the findings, including legal findings, in an arbitral award are only formally binding on the disputing parties, it is a fact that later arbitral tribunals as well as parties' counsel consult the legal content generated in earlier arbitral awards for guidance. The legal principle proposed in an earlier arbitral award may be adopted by a later arbitral tribunal, sometimes on the recommendation of parties' counsel, hearing a dispute involving different parties and a different fact pattern. Chapter 1 identified three principles on contractual protection that emerged in the awards of Mixed Claims Commissions and that were later adopted by arbitral tribunals, some of which credited the Commission award or awards as the exclusive source of the legal principle.[38] Given the lacuna or ambiguity in the international law on contractual protection, the earlier, published arbitral award is elevated to a principal source of international law, and its legal content adopted to bind disputing parties other than the original disputing parties.

2.3   A (Dis)orderly Source of International Law

There is no formal system of binding precedent in international arbitration, requiring arbitral tribunals to follow the decisions of earlier tribunals. Such a system exists in countries belonging to the common law tradition such as the United Kingdom and Australia, and binds lower courts to the rulings of higher courts.[39] In theory, every arbitral tribunal can decide a dispute without consulting, much less adopting, the legal principles found in earlier, published arbitral awards. At a disorderly extreme, there can be as many legal propositions as there are arbitral awards. In practice, however, later arbitral tribunals consult earlier arbitral awards and adopt the legal principles articulated therein. This was how, over time, legal principles on contractual protection that emerged in awards rendered by Mixed Claims Commissions became general principles on contractual protection.[40] Voluntary adherence to earlier arbitral awards has been likened to *jurisprudence constante*, which is a feature of countries belonging to the civil law

---

Law, online: www.italaw.com (accessed 31 December 2017), a website maintained by Canadian academic A. Newcombe from the University of Victoria.

[37] M. Shahabuddeen, *Precedent in the World Court* (Cambridge: Cambridge University Press, 1996), p. 32.

[38] See discussion at Chapter 1, Section 1.3.3.

[39] P. H. Glenn, *Legal Traditions of the World: Sustainable Diversity in Law*, 5th edn (Oxford: Oxford University Press, 2014), pp. 236–86.

[40] See discussion at Chapter 1, Section 1.3.3.

tradition such as France and Belgium.[41] Unlike the system of binding judicial precedent found in common law countries, *jurisprudence constante* refers to the accretion of similar rulings when decisions of higher courts are not formally binding on lower courts, but are nonetheless highly persuasive and often followed. If voluntary adherence to earlier arbitral awards is *jurisprudence constante*, then, despite the absence of binding precedent, arbitral awards will converge on legal content. This section first elaborates on the difficulty posed by the absence of a system of binding precedent on the identification of legal content from arbitral awards (Section 2.3.1), before evaluating the strength of the analogy between voluntary adherence to arbitral awards and *jurisprudence constante* (Section 2.3.2).

2.3.1   The Absence of a Formal System of Binding Precedent for Arbitral Awards

The main concern with the freedom of arbitral tribunals to depart at will from the legal findings in earlier arbitral awards is inconsistency in the content of international law. What is endorsed as a legal principle on a given subject matter by one arbitral tribunal may be ignored or rejected by another deciding the same subject matter. As all arbitral awards are capable of generating legal content, a law that is largely reliant on arbitral awards to supply its content may find itself in a disorderly state. The difficulty of locating a consistent view on what the content of international law on a given issue is has long been regarded as the inconvenient consequence of relying on arbitral awards as a source of law.

In 1944, Manley Hudson pointed out the inconsistency inherent in arbitral awards supplying content to the law of State responsibility:[42]

> Claims made by individuals or private companies against States have long been fruitful of international litigation. Numerous international tribunals have been created to deal directly or indirectly with such claims and their jurisprudence has had a formative influence on the development of international law with respect to State responsibility ... It has supplied many precedents to serve as guides for the future, but it has not developed a consistent body of case law.

---

[41] J. H. Merryman and R. Pérez-Perdomo, *The Civil Law Tradition: An Introduction to the Legal Systems of Europe and Latin America*, 3rd edn (Stanford, CA: Stanford University Press, 2007), pp. 34–60.

[42] M. Hudson, *International Tribunals Past and Future* (New Haven, CT: Rumford, 1944), p. 197; also Shahabuddeen, *Precedent in the World Court*, p. 44, where it was observed that '[t]he transient nature of arbitral awards has however worked against the emergence of a smooth process of development'.

In 1968, Charles de Visscher attributed the reluctance of the ICJ to refer to arbitral awards in its judgments to inconsistencies in legal findings across different arbitral awards:

> [R]eferences to arbitral awards are rare in the decisions of the International Court of Justice as they were in those of its predecessor ... The rarity of such references is a matter of prudence; the Court is careful not to introduce into its decisions elements whose heterogeneous character might escape it[s] vigilance.

In 1990, Christine Gray concluded, after studying arbitral awards for the purpose of distilling common trends in the award of remedies by tribunals in international claims, that:

> A study of the large arbitral practice that followed is still vital for a proper understanding of judicial remedies and their award by more recent tribunals ... a brief description that is nevertheless full enough to show clearly the problems involved in any attempt to derive coherent rules on judicial remedies from arbitral practice.

Although the absence of a formal system of binding precedent for arbitral awards precipitated inconsistent rulings by arbitral tribunals on similar or identical issues of international law, neither Hudson, nor Visscher, nor Gray discount the importance of arbitral awards as a source of international law. Nor is it necessarily the case that a greater degree of consistency across arbitral awards on certain areas of international law is unattainable. James Crawford urged arbitral tribunals to heed the opinions of earlier arbitral tribunals, so that arbitral awards can converge on the content of international law, and become *jurisprudence constante*:[43]

> The doctrine of precedent in the English legal system is a doctrine of the centralization of authority. It seeks to prevent lower courts going off on frolics of their own, and centralizes law-making authority in the highest court ... A more sensible approach which this common lawyer finds is the principle of *jurisprudence constante* – the general sense of the way decisions should be made in relation to similarly formulated provisions ... The only way we are going to get it ... is for arbitrators to pay decent regard to the opinions of other investment arbitrators. Let us pay decent regard to what other people say. One may have to disagree, but if so it is better to say one is disagreeing and to make it clear why, than simply to ignore contrary decisions, as has happened in a number of cases ... let us hope that the strategies of unification which international law has, which are quite different from the strategies of unification of the common law, may in time prevail.

---

[43] J. Crawford, 'Similarity of Issues in Disputes Arising under the Same or Similarly Drafted Investment Treaties' in E. Gaillard and Y. Banifatemi (eds.), *Precedent in International Arbitration* (New York, NY: Juris Publishing, 2007), pp. 97, 102–3.

2.3.2   *The Analogy between Voluntary Adherence to*
Earlier Arbitral Awards and Jurisprudence Constante

Like precedent,[44] *jurisprudence constante* is a legal term of art.[45] As Crawford pointed out, precedent refers to the centralisation of law-making authority. In common law countries such as England, this centralised authority is the highest court of the land. As there is no hierarchy among arbitral tribunals, there is no centralised law-making arbitral tribunal. Therefore, although unobjectionable when understood in the lay sense of the word, it is imprecise, as Crawford implies, to label earlier arbitral awards that are followed by later tribunals as 'arbitral precedent'. The alternative legal label that Crawford proposes, and one which some tribunals and scholars also favour,[46] is *jurisprudence constante*. As noted above, *jurisprudence constante* refers to the accumulation of similar judicial decisions on a point of law in a setting where lower courts are not bound to but for the most part obey the rulings of higher courts.

The analogy between voluntary adherence to earlier arbitral awards, which does not occur in a judicial setting that fosters *jurisprudence constante*, and *jurisprudence constante* is not self-evident. Yet, supporters of the analogy rarely provide justification for their stance. The notable exception, whose justification merits discussion, is Andrea Bjorklund. She defends

---

[44] J. Law and E. A. Martin, in J. Law (ed.), *A Dictionary of Law*, 8th edn (Oxford: Oxford University Press, 2015), define 'precedent' in English law as '[a] judgment or decision of a court, normally recorded in a law report, used as an authority for reaching the same decision in subsequent cases.'

[45] According to S. Guinchard and T. Debard, in *Lexique des Termes Juridiques 2017–2018* (Paris: Broché, 2017), p. 656, '*jurisprudence*' is defined as 'propositions contained in decisions of superior tribunals, and which give the appearance of being norms, given their general and abstract formulation', author's translation from the original French.

[46] See, for instance, in the conjoined arbitrations *Gemplus SA* et al. v. *United a Mexican States* (ICSID Case No. ARB(AF)/04/3) and *Talsud SA* v. *United Mexican States* (ICSID Case No. ARB(AF)/04/4), Award, 16 June 2010 (Fortier, Gómez, Veeder), paras. 6–26 and 16–27; *RosInvestCo UK Ltd.* v. *Russia*, SCC Arbitration V 079/2005, Final Award, 12 September 2010 (Veeder, Hobér, Eliasson), para. 653; T. Wälde, 'The Specific Nature of Investment Arbitration' in P. Kahn and T. Wälde (eds.), *New Aspects of International Investment Law* (The Hague: Martinus Nijhoff, 2007), p. 118; Alvarez, 'The Public International Law Regime Governing International Investment', pp. 355–6, 449 and 504; A. R. Sureda, *Investment Treaty Arbitration – Judging under Uncertainty* (Cambridge: Cambridge University Press, 2012), pp. 124–5; cf. C. Kessedjian, 'To Give or Not to Give Precedential Value to Investment Arbitration Awards?' in C. A. Rogers and R. P. Alford (eds.), *The Future of Investment Arbitration* (Oxford: Oxford University Press, 2009), pp. 43, 49–50.

the analogy, in the context of arbitral awards rendered by tribunals consti-tuted to interpret investment treaties, in the following manner:[47]

> *Jurisprudence constante* is an appealing analogy. In the French tradition, the starting point for any analysis is the language of the code, but judi-cial decisions construing the code will have an influence on other courts as representing an accepted interpretation of the same. Similarly, in an investment treaty case, the starting point for tribunal analysis should be the language of the treaty in question. Secondarily, but not insignifi-cantly, tribunals would next turn to the decisions of other tribunals con-struing identical or similar treaty language. Also, in France, precedent is used with two different meanings: it refers to the decision of a higher court which, while not binding, for practical purposes ought to be fol-lowed by lower courts; and it refers to the decision of even a lower or equal court which, while not binding, can serve as a positive (or nega-tive) model for the case under consideration. This latter description fits most neatly within the investment treaty context of dispersed tribunals of equal authority. Thus, decisions of other tribunals construing identical or similar treaty provisions would be viewed as persuasive to the extent they were well reasoned.

Bjorklund's justification comprises two limbs. First, followed arbitral awards are akin to *jurisprudence constante* because prior decisions condi-tion, rather than dictate, the interpretation of codified treaty provisions. Second, as arbitral tribunals are in a non-hierarchical relationship vis-à-vis each other, arbitral awards resemble the version of French *jurispru-dence* which gives judges a choice over which earlier decisions to follow. Neither limb successfully captures how *jurisprudence* becomes *constante* in France. This is key if the purpose of drawing an analogy between fol-lowed arbitral awards and *jurisprudence constante* is to augur greater con-sistency in legal content across arbitral awards.

Traditionally, in order for there to be consistency in the interpretation and application of the law, there must be a 'unifying element in a legal system characterized by centrifugal forces'.[48] The presence of 'a unify-ing element' is the linchpin of *jurisprudence constante* in France. This is seen in French administrative law where the landmark decisions of the Conseil d'Etat, accompanied by case notes of immense scientific value, have guided and moulded the decisions of administrative tribunals into

---

[47] A. Bjorklund, 'Investment Treaty Arbitral Decisions as Jurisprudence Constante' in C. B. Picker, I. D. Bunn, and D. W. Arner (eds.), *International Economic Law: The State and Future of the Discipline* (Oxford and Portland, OR: Hart, 2008), pp. 265, 272 (footnotes omitted).

[48] T. Koopmans, 'Stare Decisis in European Law' in D. O'Keeffe and H. G. Schermers (eds.), *Essays in European Law and Integration* (Deventer: Kluwer, 1982), p. 11.

jurisprudence constante.[49] This is also the case in the French law of obligations where, according to the leading treatise on the subject, decisions of the Cour de Cassation have led, developed and regulated judicial interpretation of the antiquated provisions in the French Civil Code through 'policy-oriented adjudication'.[50] The 'unifying' force of the supreme adjudicatory bodies like the Conseil d'Etat and the Cour de Cassation is acutely felt even by the French Parliament. It has legislated at times to complement a welcome *jurisprudence constante*,[51] and at times to counteract the probable emergence of an unwanted *jurisprudence constante.*[52] Absent 'centrifugal forces' in the form of the Conseil d'Etat and the Cour de Cassation, it seems improbable that judicial decisions in France can coalesce into *jurisprudence constante.*

With the paper exception of the Appellate Tribunal which was established to correct 'any errors in the application of interpretation of applicable law' in the EU–Canada Comprehensive Economic and Trade Agreement (CETA),[53] and the possible exception of the Free Trade Commission (FTC), which was established to resolve any disputes arising from the interpretation of the North American Free Trade Agreement (NAFTA),[54] there is no other institutionalised 'centrifugal force' in the landscape of investor–State arbitral awards. At the time of writing, the effectiveness of the CETA Appellate Tribunal as a 'centrifugal force' remains untested, and the interpretive notes issued by the NAFTA FTC, which purportedly lay

---

[49] R. Cassin and M. Waline, 'Préface' in M. Long et al. (eds.), *Les Grands Arrêts de la Jurisprudence Administrative*, 21st edn (Paris: Dalloz, 2017), pp. vi–vii.

[50] M. Fabre-Magnan, *Droit des Obligations 1 – Contrat et Engagement Unilatéral*, 4th edn (Paris: Presses Universitaires de France, 2016), pp. 80–1, author's translation from the original French; and *Droit des Obligations 2 – Responsabilité Civile et Quasi-Contrats*, 3rd edn (Paris: Presses Universitaires de France, 2013), pp. 207–13.

[51] See loi n° 3258, 12 February 2002, in Assembleé Nationale, 'Projet de loi n° 3258, texte adopté n° 785', online: www.assemblee-nationale.fr/11/pdf/ta/ta0785.pdf (accessed 31 December 2017), where proposed amendments to the Code de la santé publique followed the recommendations in *l'arrêt Bianchi*, a decision of the Conseil d'Etat, CE n° 69336, 9 April 1993.

[52] See loi n° 2002-303, 4 March 2002, Art. 1, which was promulgated to overturn the decision of the Cour de Cassation creating a category of no-fault compensation for infants born with congenital defects in *l'arrêt Perruche* (Ass. Plén. n° de pourvoi 99-13701, 17 November 2000). Loi n° 2002-303, 4 March 2002, Art. 1. is also called 'loi anti-*Perruche*'.

[53] Signed 30 October 2016, provisionally entered into force 21 September 2017, Art. 8.28(2) (a). See also Art. 8.29, where the CETA Contracting Parties – the EU and Canada – pledge to 'pursue with other trading partners the establishment of a multilateral investment tribunal and appellate mechanism for the resolution of investment disputes.'

[54] The FTC has since issued several clarifications to guide tribunals interpreting NAFTA provisions; see US Department of State, 'Interpretation of Certain Chapter 11 Provisions'; 'Statement on Non-Disputing Party Participation'; and 'Statement on Notices of Intent to Submit a Claim to Arbitration', online: www.state.gov/s/l/c3439.htm (accessed 31 December 2017).

down the correct interpretation of NAFTA provisions, are disregarded by some NAFTA tribunals.[55]

Some may consider the annulment mechanism set out in Article 52 of the Convention on the Settlement of Disputes between States and Nationals of Other States (ICSID Convention) the next best thing to a centrifugal force.[56] According to Article 52(1), either party to an arbitral award issued by an arbitral tribunal constituted in accordance with the ICSID Convention[57] may request its annulment because

> (a) ... the Tribunal was not properly constituted; (b) ... the tribunal has manifestly exceeded its powers; (c) ... there was corruption on the part of a member of the Tribunal; (d) ... there has been a serious departure from a fundamental rule of procedure; or (e) ... the award has failed to state the reasons on which it is based.

Given the large number of arbitral awards issued by ICSID tribunals over five decades,[58] the process of review and annulment, which checks wayward arbitral awards, may bring about the coherent development of the law. Unlike the CETA Appellate Tribunal, Article 52(1) does not empower an ICSID ad hoc committee hearing an application for annulment to annul an arbitral award for errors of law. Moreover, the infrequency of annulments being sought, in comparison to the number of arbitral awards issued, gives rise to serious doubts over the ability of annulment committees to exercise supervisory control over arbitral

---

[55] The patchy record of adherence to FTC interpretive notes by NAFTA tribunals is discussed in A. Roberts, 'Power and Persuasion in Investment Treaty Interpretation: The Dual Role of States' (2010) 104(2) AJIL 179 at 180–1, 194 and 216 (fn. 170).

[56] Signed 18 March 1965, entered into force 14 October 1966, 575 UNTS 159.

[57] The choice of ICSID arbitration may be made in an investment contract or in an investment treaty. An example of an investment contract referring the disputing parties to ICSID arbitration is the contract for the Exploration and Production of Hydrocarbons underlying the dispute in *Caratube International Oil Company LLP & Anor. v. Republic of Kazakhstan*, ICSID Case No. ARB/13/13, Award, 27 September 2017 (Lévy, Aynès, Salès) Clause 27.2. One of many investment treaties giving disputing parties the option of submitting to ICSID arbitration is the US–Kazakhstan investment treaty, op. cit., Art. VI(3)(a)(i). When both the home State of the investor and the host State are parties to the ICSID Convention, the arbitration will be conducted in accordance with the ICSID Rules of Procedure for Arbitration Proceedings (Arbitration Rules) (in effect from 10 April 2006, reprinted in ICSID, *ICSID Convention, Regulations and Rules* (Washington: ICSID, 2006)). If one of the States is not a party to the ICSID Convention, the arbitration will be conducted in accordance with the ICSID Additional Facility Rules (in effect from 10 April 2006) ('ICSID Additional Facility Rules'), Art. 2.

[58] At the date of writing, there are 261 arbitral awards rendered under the ICSID Convention, see ICSID, 'The ICSID Caseload – Statistics (Issue 2017-2)', online: https://icsid.worldbank.org/en/Documents/resources/ICSID%20Web%20Stats%202017-2%20(English)%20Final.pdf (accessed 31 December 2017), p. 18.

tribunals in the way that higher courts constantly guide the legal find-ings of lower courts.[59] Several annulment committees have since clari-fied that they should not be held responsible for the harmonisation of legal content across arbitral awards.[60]

Although 'arbitral precedent' and *jurisprudence constante* are com-mon terms in existing literature on international law, both tend to obscure the real motivations for later tribunals to follow earlier arbitral awards. The absence of a centrifugal force in international arbitration not only accounts for the absence of a system of binding precedent among arbi-tral awards, it also discredits the analogy between voluntary adherence to earlier arbitral awards and *jurisprudence constante*. Stripped of inaccurate labels that carry the promise of consistency in legal content and coherence in legal development, the odds are in favour of arbitral awards being a dis-orderly source of international law on contractual protection. Yet, despite the odds, arbitral awards can and do converge on legal content. The fol-lowing section investigates this phenomenon.

2.4 Why Arbitral Awards Converge on the Content of International Law

If voluntary adherence to arbitral awards is neither explained by arbitral precedent nor by *jurisprudence constante*, the motivations for adherence lie elsewhere. There are two possible reasons why later arbitral tribunals voluntarily adopt the content of international law generated in earlier arbi-tral awards. The first is the operation of the 'Darwinian imperative', where only the fittest awards survive.[61] Accordingly, arbitral awards exhibiting

---

[59] Over the course of five decades, fifty-five decisions on applications for annulment have been issued, 'The ICSID Caseload – Statistics (Issue 2017-2)', p. 18. On average, there is one application for annulment for every five arbitral awards. See also T. Wälde, 'Comments and Discussion' in Gaillard and Banifatemi, *Precedent in International Arbitration*, 149, p. 153, who opined that 'the ICSID annulment committee construction is highly dysfunctional and produces enormous lack of coherence'.

[60] *MCI Power Group LC and New Turbine Inc.* v. *Ecuador*, ICSID Case No. ARB/03/6, Decision on Annulment, 19 October 2009 (Hascher, Danelius, Tomka), para. 24; *Enron Creditors Recovery Corp. and Anor* v. *Argentina*, ICSID Case No. ARB/01/3, Decision on the Application for Annulment of the Argentine Republic, 30 July 2010 (Griffith, Robinson, Tresselt), para. 340.

[61] Paulsson, 'International Arbitration and the Generation of Legal Norms', p. 881; also A. Pellet, 'Article 38' in A. Zimmerman et al. (eds.), *The Statute of the International Court of Justice – A Commentary*, 2nd edn (Oxford: Oxford University Press, 2012), p. 731, quoting Paulsson with approval at p. 856: '[E]xactly as "there are awards and awards, some des-tined to become ever brighter beacons, others to flicker and die near-instant deaths", there are judgments and judgments. Central to the question is the persuasiveness of the legal

hallmarks of superior quality will be prized by later tribunals above arbitral awards that do not, and will be followed as authorities for the legal propositions they advance. The second reason is the availability of an existing legal solution to a common legal problem. When the same solution has already been adopted by several, or even many, arbitral tribunals dealing with an identical or very similar legal problem, later arbitral tribunals may be more inclined to adopt a prevailing solution than to develop their own from scratch. This section explores how the process of natural selection (Section 2.4.1) and the existence of a prevailing answer to a common question (Section 2.4.2) foster the convergence of legal content found in arbitral awards on international law.

2.4.1   The Natural Selection of Arbitral Awards

A number of arbitral awards have received such firm endorsement from the ICJ, whose decisions are 'a powerful tool of consolidation and of evolution of international law',[62] that it places their fitness as content generators of international law beyond challenge. One often cited example is the *Alabama Claims* award of 1872.[63] This award of the US–UK Mixed Claims Commission, was credited by the ICJ in the *Nottebohm* case as the source for the legal principle that 'in the absence of any agreement to the contrary, an international tribunal has the right to decide as to its own jurisdiction and has the power to interpret for this purpose the instruments which govern that jurisdiction.'[64] Another example is the decision of the Spain–UK Mixed Claims Commission on the *Ziat, Ben Kiran* claim, which forms part of the *Spanish Morocco Claims* award of 1925.[65] The award has been cited by Judges Fitzmaurice and Jessup in their Separate Opinions to the *Barcelona Traction* case for the proposition that the grant or refusal of

---

reasoning[.]'; J. P. Commission, 'Precedent in Investment Treaty Arbitration – A Citation Analysis of a Developing Jurisprudence' (2007) 24(2) *Journal of International Arbitration* 129 at 156; Guillaume, 'The Use of Precedent by International Judges and Arbitrators', p. 2; also McLachlan, 'Investment Treaties and General International Law', p. 392: 'The extent to which any particular tribunal decision deserves currency as a precedent depends on whether it correctly expounds international law, and not upon any *a priori* weight to be attached to the decision *per se*.'

[62] Pellet, 'Article 38', p. 862.
[63] *United States* v. *Great Britain* (1872) 29 RIAA 125.
[64] *Liechtenstein* v. *Guatemala* [1953] ICJ Rep 111, at p. 119. For other instances in which arbitral awards have been relied on by the ICJ as a source of international law, see Lauterpacht, *The Development of International Law by the International Court*, pp. 15–18; Shahabuddeen, *Precedent in the World Court*, pp. 36–8; and Pellet, 'Article 38', p. 859.
[65] *Espagne* v. *Royaume-Uni* (1925) 2 RIAA 615, p. 729.

diplomatic protection by a home State should be tempered by equitable considerations.[66]

Apart from endorsement by the ICJ, commentators have also weighed in on the fitness of certain arbitral awards. The legal analysis of Max Huber, who was then the newly elected president of the PCIJ, in the *Spanish Morocco Claims* award has been praised by Lord McNair, a former president of the ICJ, as 'a leading exposition of the principles of State responsibility'.[67] The well-known *Lena Goldfields* award, which generated legal content on contractual protection, was lauded by Wolfgang Friedmann as an 'important decision ... which first articulated the principle of unjust enrichment in international law'.[68] Additionally, V. V. Veeder considered the *Lena Goldfields* award the supplier of 'several innovative and hugely important ideas' to international arbitration.[69] More recently, the decision of the ad hoc committee in *Compañia de Aguas del Aconquija S.A. and Vivendi Universal* v. *Argentine Republic* established that a breach of an investment contract is judged in accordance with the contractual proper law, while the breach of an investment treaty is a question for international law.[70] During his 2007 Annual Freshfields Lecture, Crawford often referred to the *Vivendi* annulment decision, calling it 'still the leading case on the contract/treaty distinction'.[71]

Although compliments are routinely paid to a handful of arbitral awards, regular condemnation of a particular arbitral award is unusual. This makes it difficult to ascertain which arbitral awards are destined to be shunned by future arbitral tribunals. The improbability of an arbitral award being wholly devoid of merit limits the ability of the process of natural selection to distinguish arbitral awards that are worthy of adherence from those that are not. Arbitral awards of doubtful merit for some may present redeeming qualities for others,[72] thereby enabling them to survive

---

[66] *Belgium* v. *Spain* (Second Phase) [1970] ICJ Rep 3; Separate Opinion of Judge Fitzmaurice, p. 85; and Separate Opinion of Judge Jessup, p. 199.

[67] A. McNair, *International Law Opinions* (Cambridge: Cambridge University Press, 1956), p. 199.

[68] Friedmann, *The Changing Structure of International Law*, p. 146.

[69] V. V. Veeder, 'The Lena Goldfields Arbitration: The Historical Roots of Three Ideas' (1998) 47 ICLQ 747 at 747–8.

[70] ICSID Case No. ARB/97/3, Decision on Annulment, 3 July 2002 (Fortier, Crawford, Fernández Rozas), paras. 95–6.

[71] Crawford, 'Treaty and Contract in Investment Arbitration', p. 351 at 358. It is worth noting that Crawford was a member of the ad hoc committee that rendered the *Vivendi* annulment decision.

[72] M. Sornarajah, *International Commercial Arbitration: The Problem of State Contracts* (Singapore: Longman, 1990), p. 192.

alongside their so-called fitter counterparts. One example of an arbitral award that defies neat categorisation as fit or unfit is the award in *Sandline International Inc.* v. *The Independent State of Papua New Guinea*.[73] The dispute arose from a breach of contract for the supply of military and security services to a UK firm by Papua New Guinea. The contract stipulated that the contractual proper law was English law. The tribunal nonetheless held that it was bound to apply the rules on contractual protection found in international law because it was an 'international arbitral tribunal':[74]

> The rules of international law in this case are clearly established and their application causes no difficulty … An agreement between a private party and a State is an international, not a domestic, contract. *This Tribunal is an international, not a domestic, arbitral tribunal and is bound to apply the rules of international law.* Those rules are not excluded from, but form part of, English law, which is the law chosen by the parties to govern their contract.

The tribunal ruled in favour of Sandline's claim and ordered damages to be paid by Papua New Guinea. After the application to set aside the award was refused by the Supreme Court of Queensland,[75] the Papuan government agreed to satisfy the claim.[76] Commentators appear divided on the fitness of the legal content generated by the *Sandline* award. Notwithstanding indirect support in older academic writing for the conviction of the *Sandline* arbitral tribunal that an international arbitral tribunal should be applying international law to the dispute,[77] some contemporary commenters remain unimpressed. They argue that '[t]he unsatisfactory outcome of the Supreme Court decision in this case is exaggerated by the fact that the original decision of the Arbitral Tribunal is arguably unsustainable in law'.[78] The legal content generated by the *Sandline* arbitral award was construed as an unwarranted departure from 'a long and consistent line of compelling authority … [that contained] no example of an arbitral tribunal applying international law in the face of a clear and exclusive choice

---

[73] Interim Award, 9 October 1998, 117 ILR 552.

[74] Ibid., para. 10.1 (emphasis added).

[75] *In the Matter of the Commercial Arbitration Act 1990 and In the Matter of an Application Pursuant to Section 38 Thereof by the Independent State of Papua New Guinea* v. *Sandline International Inc.*, 117 ILR 565, Supreme Court of Queensland, 1999.

[76] *BBC News*, 'PNG Pays Up to Mercenaries (1 May 1999)', online: http://news.bbc.co.uk/2/hi/asia-pacific/333234.stm (accessed 31 December 2017).

[77] T. Meron, 'Repudiation of Ultra Vires State Contracts and the International Responsibility of States' (1957) 6 ICLQ 273 at 275 where it is argued that, '[c]onfronted with a question of contract, an international tribunal, whose normal function is to administer international law, may find it necessary to apply a certain domestic law.'

[78] D. Sturzaker and C. Cawood, 'The Sandline Affair: Illegality and International Law' (1999) *Australian International Law Journal* 214 at 215.

of domestic law'.[79] Christine Chinkin, in contrast, was far less critical of the *Sandline* arbitral award. She used it to illustrate how 'there is no guarantee of consistency between different tribunals in their treatment of the relationship between international and national law'.[80] Chinkin may have had doubts over the cogency of the reasoning in the arbitral award, since she pointed out that 'none of [the arbitrators] were primarily international lawyers'.[81] Yet, even if her assessment of the *Sandline* arbitral award was not entirely positive, it was passably neutral. She did not disapprove of the tribunal 'drawing upon international and national law as each best served their objective and by collapsing boundaries between them' in generating legal content on contractual protection.[82] Whatever its deficiencies, the *Sandline* arbitral award did not perish. It was cited in argument nearly a decade later before the English Court of Appeal in *Svenska v. Lithuania*.[83]

The objective of natural selection is to identify fit arbitral awards that are worthy of adherence as the leading content generators of international law on contractual protection. Hallmarks of fit arbitral awards referenced at the start of this section include, but are not limited to, the eminence of the tribunal rendering the award, the ability of the award to propose or articulate generally acceptable rules in an important, but unsettled or novel area of law, and the ability of the award to secure the endorsement of the ICJ or eminent scholars.[84] While many published arbitral awards may not benefit from eminent authorship or endorsement, reasoned approval for the legal content they generate, whether in later arbitral awards or academic writings or both, may also indicate fitness. Even so, the projected binary consequence of natural selection, where fit arbitral awards survive and unfit awards perish, remains a hypothetical, simplistic ideal. While certain arbitral awards have been recognised as fit, others in the vast and growing repository of arbitral awards are not necessarily unfit. Some may

---

[79] Ibid., p. 219.
[80] C. Chinkin, 'Monism and Dualism: The Impact of Private Authority on the Dichotomy between National and International Law' in J. Nijman and A. Nollkaemper (eds.), *New Perspectives on the Divide between National and International Law* (Oxford: Oxford University Press, 2007), pp. 135, 155–7.
[81] Ibid., p. 156.
[82] Ibid., p. 157.
[83] *Svenska Petroleum Exploration AB* v. *Government of the Republic of Lithuania* [2007] QB 886, p. 889.
[84] Fit arbitral awards are awards with what I. Venzke calls 'semantic authority'. Fit arbitral awards possess the 'capacity to influence and shape meanings as well as the ability to establish its communications as authoritative reference points in legal discourse'. *How Interpretation Makes International Law – On Semantic Change and Normative Twists* (Oxford: Oxford University Press, 2012), p. 63.

be controversial, and some may be overlooked. Given the resilience of the *Sandline* arbitral award, controversial awards may not actually perish. In a similar vein, previously overlooked awards may one day enter the spotlight. The legal content that controversial and overlooked awards generate remains available for adoption. Although natural selection in practice does not disqualify any arbitral award from being a content generator, it promotes convergence of legal content on international law by drawing the attention of later arbitral tribunals to recognisably authoritative earlier arbitral awards and implicitly warning tribunals to approach the legal content found in controversial or overlooked awards with caution.

2.4.2   A Prevailing Answer to a Common Question among Arbitral Awards

In 1904, French Nobel Laureate and international lawyer Louis Renault observed that convergence in legal content across arbitral awards is possible when different arbitral tribunals gravitate towards the same solution to a common legal problem:[85]

> When a controversial question has been answered in the same way by several arbitral tribunals, we are assured of the authoritativeness of a solution that has been repeatedly arrived at by independent and esteemed judges of different nationalities. We cannot reach the same solution by taking a myopic view of things, by lacking impartiality or by prioritizing national interests. This solution becomes a part of international law by virtue of being a written response to the needs of justice and the broader interests of humanity.

There are several plausible explanations why an arbitral tribunal adopts a solution to a controversial legal problem formulated by an earlier tribunal instead of crafting its own. The first explanation is the cogency or adaptability of the solution to the legal problem at hand. This is seen in the interpretation given by the US–Mexico Claims Commission in the *North American Dredging Company of Texas Claim* to a Calvo clause, which prohibits contracting parties from submitting disputes to international adjudication.[86] Without wanting to deny the validity of a Calvo clause which the contracting parties agreed to, but without wanting to deprive the private contracting party of access to international adjudication, the Commission held that a Calvo clause cannot preclude diplomatic intervention in cases where a breach of contract by a host State is simultaneously a breach of

---

[85]   L. Renault, 'Préface', de Lapradelle and Politis, *Recueil des Arbitrages Internationaux*, vol. I, p. vii, author's translation from the original French.
[86]   *USA v. United Mexican States* (1926) 4 RIAA 26.

international law.[87] The 'watershed' solution[88] has been adopted by arbitral tribunals interpreting contractual forum selection clauses, not just Calvo clauses that do not provide for access to international adjudication.[89] The second explanation is the fitness of the arbitral award containing the solution. As discussed in the preceding section, a cogent solution formulated by eminent arbitrators can, by virtue of its perceived superior quality, attract the attention and adherence of later tribunals. One example of a fit arbitral award is the *Vivendi* annulment decision, which solved the distinction between contract claims and treaty claims. It was rendered by a tribunal comprising L. Yves Fortier, a leading international arbitrator and former Canadian ambassador to the UN; H. E. James Crawford, then Whewell Chair of International Law at the University of Cambridge and later judge on the ICJ; and José Carlos Fernández Rozas, a professor of private international law in Spain. Repeated adoption by later tribunals confers the solution it proposed with authority.[90] Third and finally, is a sizeable number of published arbitral tribunals that have already adopted an existing solution, such solution conveying the accumulated wisdom and approval of the arbitrators who have dealt with the same problem. Unless there are compelling reasons for departing from a tried-and-tested solution, later arbitral tribunals are likely to follow in the known footsteps of earlier arbitral tribunals.[91]

---

[87] Ibid., pp. 30–1.
[88] J. Paulsson, *Denial of Justice in International Law* (Cambridge: Cambridge University Press, 2005), p. 31.
[89] See discussion at Chapter 1, Section 1.3.2.2.
[90] *SGS Société Générale de Surveillance SA* v. *Islamic Republic of Pakistan*, ICSID Case No. ARB/01/13, Decision of the Tribunal on Objections to Jurisdiction, 6 August 2003 (Feliciano, Faurès, Thomas), paras. 147–8; *SGS Société Générale de Surveillance SA* v. *Republic of Philippines*, ICSID Case No. ARB/02/6, Decision of the Tribunal on Objections to Jurisdiction, 29 January 2004 (El-Kosheri, Crawford, Crivellaro (partially dissenting)), para. 153; *SGS Société Générale de Surveillance SA* v. *The Republic of Paraguay*, ICSID Case No. ARB/07/29, Decision on Jurisdiction, 12 February 2010 (Alexandrov, Donovan, Mexía), paras. 130–2.
[91] Fidelity to the solutions found in earlier arbitral awards has been referred to as 'path dependency', whereby the 'accumulation of identical or similar solutions ... generate[s] a phenomenon of imitation', see A. Mourre, 'The Case for the Publication of Arbitral Awards' in A. Malatesta and R. Sali (eds.), *The Rise of Transparency in International Arbitration* (New York, NY: Juris Publishing, 2013), pp. 53, 60. Fidelity is also considered a virtue by some arbitral tribunals who expressly disclaim the binding force of earlier arbitral awards, see *Saipem S.p.A.* v. *The People's Republic of Bangladesh*, ICSID Case No. ABR/05/07, Decision on Jurisdiction and Recommendation on Provisional Measures, 21 March 2007 (Kaufmann-Kohler, Schreuer, Otton), para. 67 (footnotes omitted):

> The Tribunal considers that it is not bound by previous decisions. At the same time, it is of the opinion that it must pay due consideration to earlier decisions of

When a controversial question is answered in the exact same way by arbitral tribunals, it undoubtedly fosters convergence in legal content across arbitral awards. But a question is controversial precisely because it evokes different reactions and responses. This can result in arbitral tribunals developing different answers to the same question. When later arbitral tribunals have a choice of several solutions, there is a chance that the more popular solution may not be the better solution. One question pertaining to the law of State responsibility that has engendered two different answers from arbitral tribunals is the correlation between the taking of non-precluded measures (NPM) by a host State under an investment treaty[92] and the invocation by a host State of the defence of necessity under Article 25 of the International Law Commission's Articles on State Responsibility.[93] The first answer posits that when an NPM clause applies, the substantive obligations in the treaty do not apply to the State, and Article 25 of the Articles on State Responsibility cannot be activated

---

international tribunals. It believes that, subject to compelling contrary grounds, it has a duty to adopt solutions established in a series of consistent cases. It also believes that, subject to the specifics of a given treaty and of the circumstances of the actual case, it has a duty to seek to contribute to the harmonious development of investment law and thereby to meet the legitimate expectations of the community of States and investors towards certainty of the rule of law.

[92] An example of an NPM clause is Art. XI of the Treaty between the United States of America and the Argentine Republic concerning the Reciprocal Encouragement and Protection of Investment, signed 14 November 1991, entered into force 20 October 1994: 'This Treaty shall not preclude the application by either Party of measures necessary for the maintenance of public order, the fulfillment of its obligations with respect to the maintenance or restoration of international peace or security, or the Protection of its own essential security interests.'

[93] ILC, 'Draft Articles on Responsibility of States for Internationally Wrongful Acts, with Commentaries' (2001), Yearbook of the International Law Commission, vol. II, Part Two. Art. 25 provides:

(1) Necessity may not be invoked by a State as a ground for precluding the wrongfulness of an act not in conformity with an international obligation of that State unless the act:
   (a) is the only way for the State to safeguard an essential interest against a grave and imminent peril; and
   (b) does not seriously impair an essential interest of the State or States towards which the obligation exists, or of the international community as a whole.
(2) In any case, necessity may not be invoked by a State as a ground for precluding wrongfulness if:
   (a) the international obligation in question excludes the possibility of invoking necessity; or
   (b) the State has contributed to the situation of necessity.

in the absence of a breach by a State of its substantive treaty obligations.[94] The second answer calls for an NPM clause to be interpreted in light of Article 25 of the Articles on State Responsibility, whereby the host State must show that its measures meet the standard of necessity in Article 25 of the Articles on State Responsibility if it wants to be excused for any treaty violations.[95]

The dichotomy between primary and secondary rules governing the law of State responsibility which is Hartian in origin[96] supplies a conceptual framework for State responsibility.[97] The primary rules establish the international obligations of States, whereas the secondary rules apply after international responsibility is engaged. Whether a host State's international responsibility is engaged is determined by reference to the primary rules which are found in treaties and in customary international law. Thereafter may secondary rules, such as Article 25 of the Articles on State Responsibility, be invoked to justify or excuse a violation of international law. In other words, Article 25 of the Articles on State Responsibility does not bear upon whether there has been a treaty violation. To the extent that the difference between primary and secondary rules in international law is not disputed, recognising the correspondingly different spheres of their application is essential to a proper understanding of the law of State responsibility as presented in the Articles on State Responsibility. Of the

---

[94] *CMS Gas Transmission Company v. The Argentine Republic*, ICSID Case No. ARB/01/8, Decision of the ad hoc committee on the Application for Annulment of the Argentine Republic, 25 September 2007 (Guillaume, Elaraby, Crawford), para. 129; *Sempra Energy International v. Argentina*, ICSID Case No. ARB/02/16, Decision on the Argentine Republic's Application for Annulment of the Award, 29 June 2010 (Söderlund, Edward, Jacovides), para. 200.

[95] *CMS Gas Transmission Company v. The Argentine Republic*, paras. 357 and 373–4; *LG & E Energy Corp. v. Argentina*, ICSID Case No. ARB/02/1, Decision on Liability, 3 October 2006 (de Maekelt, Rezek, van den Berg), para. 245; *Enron Corporation and Ponderosa Assets LP v. Argentina*, ICSID Case No. ARB/01/3, Award, 22 May 2007 (Orrego Vicuña, van den Berg, Tschanz), para. 333; *Sempra Energy International v. Argentina*, ICSID Case No. ARB/02/16, Award, 28 September 2007 (Orrego Vicuña, Lalonde, Morelli Rico), para. 375; *Continental Casualty v. Argentina*, ICSID Case No. ARB/03/9, Award, 5 September 2008 (Sacerdoti, Veeder, Nader), para. 167 (fn. 242) and 168; *El Paso Energy International Company v. Argentina*, ICSID Case No. ARB/03/15, Award, 31 October 2011 (Caflisch, Bernadini, Stern), para. 613.

[96] H. L. A. Hart, *The Concept of Law* (Oxford: Clarendon Press, 1983), pp. 79–99.

[97] It would have surprised Hart that his theory exerted such a profound influence on the study of State responsibility by the ILC since he was of the opinion that 'international law not only lacks the secondary rules of change and adjudication which provide for legislature and courts, but also a unifying rule of recognition specifying "sources" of law and providing general criteria for the identification of its rules', Hart, *The Concept of Law*, p. 214.

two answers to the correlation between an NPM clause in an investment treaty and Article 25 of the Articles on State Responsibility, the first answer, which resists conflation of the two provisions, reflects a firmer grasp of the conceptual framework relied upon by the ILC for its codification of the law of State responsibility. Yet, it is the second answer, which calls for the interpretation of an NPM clause in light of Article 25 of the Articles on State Responsibility, that has been adopted by more arbitral tribunals. While it is impossible to predict if a future tribunal grappling with the same question will adopt the first or the second answer, the fact that more arbitral tribunals favour the second answer is a pull factor. Therefore, the price of convergence on a prevailing answer may be the better answer.

2.5   Conclusion

When arbitral awards are a principal source of law, identifying the content of international law that they generate is not a straightforward exercise. The absence of a centralised law-generating authority, such as an apex court in legal systems with binding judicial precedent or with *jurisprudence constante*, promises a permanent state of divergent views on what the content of international law is or should be. There are no hard and fast rules governing the adoption of legal content found in earlier arbitral awards by later arbitral tribunals. If a later arbitral tribunal decides to adopt, it does so voluntarily. Voluntary adherence to earlier arbitral awards is the means by which legal content across arbitral awards converges, but this renders uncertain the prospect of convergence.

Despite the odds being in favour of non-convergence, arbitral tribunals are motivated in practice to consult and adopt the legal content found in earlier arbitral awards. When arbitral tribunals review existing awards to see how earlier tribunals addressed the same legal problem, awards that stand out for adoption are fit awards and clusters of awards that advocate a common answer. The former category of awards is obtained by applying the process of natural selection, whereby awards authored by eminent tribunals, proposing cogent principles in an unsettled or novel area of law and endorsed for their quality, are deemed to possess high normative value and are worthy of adherence. The latter category of awards is obtained by observing whether a solution, or which solution if there is a choice of several, attracts a high or higher quantity of adherents. Quality awards and popular solutions are persuasive motivations for later arbitral tribunals to take the legal content generated in earlier arbitral awards seriously. However, neither quality nor quantity, without more, ensures the systematic convergence of legal content across arbitral awards, so that an identifiable body of international law on contractual protection can take root, and not just be a catalogue of discrete legal principles. The process of natural selection does not disqualify any arbitral award from future adoption, while a prevailing answer may not be founded on a keen appreciation of existing law. Arbitral tribunals still run the risk of being overwhelmed or misguided by earlier arbitral awards.

The lacuna in the law of State responsibility pertaining to contractual protection supplied the opening for arbitral awards to step up as a principal source of international law. But given the propensity for arbitral awards to be a disorderly source of law, the stable development of the law of State responsibility for breaches of investment contracts needs weightier, more determinate anchors than fit awards and popular solutions to impel adherence. These anchors are the international core standard of treatment of aliens, the subject of Chapter 3, and the international law on the protection of alien property, the subject of Chapter 4. Neither the core standard of treatment of aliens nor the legal protection of alien property recognises absolute protection. Therefore, the doctrine of internationalisation, which advocates absolute contractual protection, which has no weightier anchor than some like-minded arbitral tribunals and academic commentators, and which forms the subject of Chapter 5, is a magnet for controversy. That said, the potent combination of weighty and determinate anchors, fit awards and popular solutions, do not change the fact that arbitral tribunals are still free to depart from the legal content found in earlier arbitral awards. Therefore, the depiction of the substantive content of the law of State responsibility for breaches of investment contacts in the following chapters will showcase considerable convergence, but not absolute consistency, in legal content across arbitration awards. When arbitral awards are a principal source of international law, the body of law they generate inevitably contains a margin of differentiation.

3

State Responsibility and the Core Standard of Treatment

3.1 Introduction

State responsibility for the breach of an investment contract is engaged when that breach violates the standard of treatment that contracts are entitled to under international law. While there is little difficulty identifying some principles of contractual protection,[1] no bespoke standard of treatment for contracts comes immediately to mind. The two most well-known standards of treatment in international law are the minimum standard of treatment (MST) of aliens and the more recent fair and equitable treatment (FET) of protected foreign investments. MST is a customary standard, while FET is a standard found in a vast number of investment treaties. Much attention has been paid to how FET correlates to MST in the context of foreign investment protection, and the meticulous findings chronicled elsewhere need not be reproduced here.[2] In contrast, little has been said about whether and how MST and FET establish the international responsibility threshold for contractual breaches.[3] The sizeable number of contract-based FET claims attests to the relevance and importance of FET

---

[1] See discussion at Chapter 1, Section 1.3.3.; Section 1.4.2.

[2] The leading works in chronological order are S. Vasciannie, 'The Fair and Equitable Treatment Standard in International Investment Law and Practice' (1999) 70(1) BYIL 99; J. C. Thomas, 'Reflections on Article 1105 of NAFTA: History, State Practice and the Influence of Commentators' (2002) 17(1) *ICSID Review – Foreign Investment Law Journal* 21; C. Schreuer, 'Fair and Equitable Treatment in Arbitral Practice' (2005) 6(3) *Journal of World Investment and Trade* 357; I. Tudor, *The Fair and Equitable Treatment Standard in the International Law of Foreign Investment* (Oxford: Oxford University Press, 2008); R. Kläger, *Fair and Equitable Treatment International Investment Law* (Cambridge: Cambridge University Press, 2011); A. Diehl, *The Core Standard of International Investment Protection: Fair and Equitable Treatment* (The Hague: Kluwer Law International, 2012); M. Paparinskis, *The International Minimum Standard and Fair and Equitable Treatment* (Oxford: Oxford University Press, 2013).

[3] Vasciannie was one the first to accept that an FET clause extends to host State contractual undertakings, 'The Fair and Equitable Treatment Standard in International Investment Law and Practice', p. 131.

as a standard of treatment for contracts.[4] But examining FET in isolation throws no light on the relevance or importance of the older MST to contracts. And since contractual protection under international law predates investment treaties, a thorough inquiry into the existence and contours of the standard of treatment for contracts must predate contract-based FET claims.

This chapter argues that there exists a core standard of treatment for investment contracts. Given the lacuna in international law on contractual protection,[5] the contours of a standard of treatment for contracts derived from the standard for alien protection – MST. These contours were largely maintained by arbitral tribunals interpreting and imparting content to FET when deciding contract-based FET claims. The alignment of the content on contractual protection derived from MST, and deduced from FET, establishes a core standard of treatment for investment contracts. When there exists a meaningful core standard against which host State breaches of investment contracts can be measured for international wrongfulness, the law of State responsibility on the topic of contracts is no longer unknown. This is a law that can be articulated and analysed. To this end, this chapter first explains how a core standard for contractual protection derived from the minimum standard for alien protection (Section 3.2), before demonstrating how the content of this core standard was maintained through the application of FET to contractual breaches (Section 3.3). This chapter then considers five different categories of contractual breaches by host States that potentially violate the core standard of treatment (Section 3.4).

3.2   The Derivation of a Core Standard for Contractual Protection from the Minimum Standard for Alien Protection

There is precedent for the notion that an articulated standard for alien protection can set the standard for contractual protection. A prominent example is the derivation of a Calvo clause, a contractual clause, from the Calvo standard of treatment of aliens.[6] As noted in Chapter 1, Calvo clauses reflect the teachings of Argentinian jurist Carlos Calvo, who argued that

---

[4] R. Dolzer and C. Schreuer, *Principles of International Investment Law*, 2nd edn (Oxford: Oxford University Press, 2012), pp. 152–4.

[5] See discussion at Chapter 1, Section 1.2; Chapter 2, Section 2.2.2.

[6] G. H. Hackworth, *Digest of International Law* (Washington, DC: Government Printing Office, 1943), vol. 5, 471, pp. 635, 636–9.

aliens should be subject to the same standard of treatment as nationals.[7] Inserted with the objective of precluding foreign diplomatic intervention in the event of a dispute, Calvo clauses limit foreign contracting parties to the avenues of redress available to domestic contracting parties. The Calvo standard could not become the minimum standard for alien protection partly because it did not set out what exactly alien protection entailed. By identifying any national standard as the ruling standard, the Calvo standard honoured subjectivity, envisaging as many ruling standards as there are national standards. More importantly, the Calvo standard offered no objective benchmark against which the adequacy of a national standard could be assessed. Key trading nations were unconvinced that leaving their nationals at the mercy of the host State was synonymous with adequate minimum protection for aliens in foreign lands.[8]

It is generally accepted that the minimum standard for alien protection, or MST, was expressed by the US-Mexico Claims Commission in the *Neer Claim*:[9]

> Without attempting to announce a precise formula, it is in the opinion of the Commission possible ... to hold (first) that the propriety of governmental acts should be put to the test of international standards, and (second) that the treatment of an alien, in order to constitute an international delinquency, should amount to an outrage, to bad faith, to wilful neglect of duty, or to an insufficiency of governmental action so far short of international standards that every reasonable and impartial man would readily recognize its insufficiency.

The *Neer Claim* was presented by the United States on behalf of the widow of a mine superintendent who was shot and killed by a group of armed men while on his way home in the village of Guanacevi. The deceased's widow was an eyewitness to the murder but was unable to provide helpful information on the perpetrators to the Mexican authorities.[10] The Mexican authorities took steps to investigate the murder, such as arresting suspects and interviewing witnesses, but the real perpetrators were never apprehended. The charge brought against the Mexican

---

[7] See discussion at Chapter 1, Section 1.3.2.2. A modern defence of the Calvo doctrine, mounted against the backdrop of arbitral tribunals ruling on State compliance with investment treaty obligations and imposing constraints on sovereignty in the process, can be found in S. Montt, *State Liability in Investment Treaty Arbitration: Global Constitutional and Administrative Law in the BIT Generation* (Oxford: Hart, 2009).

[8] D. R. Shea, *The Calvo Clause – A Problem of Inter-American and International Law and Diplomacy* (Minneapolis, MN: University of Minnesota Press, 1955), p. 20.

[9] *USA* v. *United Mexican States* (1926) 4 RIAA 60, p. 61.

[10] Ibid., pp. 61 and 63.

authorities was the denial of justice occasioned by 'an unwarrantable lack of diligence or an unwarrantable lack of intelligent investigation of the culprits'.[11] Although the Commission conceded that the Mexican authorities could have employed 'better methods' for the murder investigation,[12] it rejected the claim that justice had been denied and that Mexico was obliged to pay damages.

Given the factual background of the *Neer Claim* from which MST emerged, it may not be apparent how the minimum standard for alien protection can be adapted for contractual protection. While it is possible to envisage contractual breaches being committed in 'bad faith', it stretches the imagination to construe contractual interference by the host State as an 'outrage', a 'wilful neglect of duty', or a gross 'insufficiency of governmental action'. The last three criteria are apposite markers of State responsibility when the life or liberty of an alien is at stake but are not representative of conduct in situations where a breach of contract by the host State amounts to an international wrong. Moreover, a finding of bad faith is not necessary for the engagement of State responsibility. One commentator surmises that 'so crude a standard has little relevance to questions arising from modern commercial contracts and concessions'.[13] This criticism underestimates the adaptability of a 'crude standard'. The *Neer Claim* drew the baseline for the standard of treatment that aliens were entitled to receive from a host State at a denial of justice.[14] The oft-quoted passage on MST is preceded by the important clarification that the Commission was responding to observations that it will be 'impracticable to lay down in advance precise and unyielding formulas by which the question of a denial of justice may in every instance be determined', and that 'the evasive and complex character (*le caractère fuyant et complexe*) of a denial of justice seems to defy definition'.[15] As a baseline, denial of justice is sufficiently 'crude' that it can be moulded to suit different contexts. In the context of alien protection, denial of justice is the MST bearing the components identified in the *Neer Claim*. In the context of contractual protection, the *Neer Claim* supplied a baseline for the core standard of treatment for contracts, but it is mainly the arbitral awards that dealt with or touched on contract claims that supplied the components of that core standard. In other words,

---

[11] Ibid., p. 61.
[12] Ibid., pp. 62 and 66.
[13] R. Y. Jennings, 'State Contracts in International Law' (1961) 37 BYIL 156 at 180.
[14] Denial of justice is understood in its broadest sense, where it applies to acts of the executive, the legislature, and the judiciary.
[15] *USA v. United Mexican States* (1926), p. 61.

denial of justice as MST is context-neutral, but the components of denial of justice as MST are context-specific.

The application of denial of justice as MST to contractual protection was considered in the *Chattin Claim* by the same Commission that decided the *Neer Claim*.[16] The presiding commissioner held that only State conduct that indirectly brings about the injury complained of needs to be measured against MST as defined in the *Neer Claim*. The 'non-execution of private contracts' is an example of indirect liability.[17] In contrast, 'governmental acts … in the form of breach of government contracts made with private foreigners … are at once recognized as acts involving direct liability'.[18] '[T]he non-performance of government contracts', according to the presiding commissioner, citing the *Illinois Central Railroad Company* case in support, engages a State's international responsibility 'even where none of the aggravating circumstances' pointing to a denial of justice is present.[19] The proposed ease with which 'governmental acts involving direct liability' engage State responsibility did not appeal to the US and Mexican commissioners. The US commissioner declined to commit to the application of MST only to cases involving indirect liability,[20] while the Mexican commissioner was strongly against the creation of double standards. In his view, the distinction between direct and indirect liability is immaterial to the engagement of State responsibility. Preserving denial of justice as MST as articulated in the *Neer Claim*,[21] the Mexican commissioner held that what matters for a finding of State responsibility 'is *whether there exists an injury*, and whether the act which causes it violates *any rule of international law*, regardless of whether the act was intentional or not'.[22]

Notwithstanding the divergence of views among the commissioners, the *Chattin Claim*, read in conjunction with the *Neer Claim*, supports the adoption of denial of justice as the core standard for contractual protection.[23] In the same way that mistreatment of an alien, in and of itself, does not amount to a violation of international law, a breach of contract, in and

---

[16]   *USA* v. *United Mexican States* (1927) 4 RIAA 282.
[17]   Ibid., p. 286.
[18]   Ibid., p. 286.
[19]   Ibid., p. 287.
[20]   Ibid., p. 295.
[21]   Ibid., p. 311.
[22]   Ibid., p. 310 (original emphasis); see also *George W. Cook* (*USA* v. *United Mexican States*) (1927) 4 RIAA 213, pp. 215–16.
[23]   In *Robert R. Brown* (*USA* v. *Great Britain*) (1923) 4 RIAA 120, pp. 128–9, the Commission held that the cancellation of a public tender for mining licenses by the Transvaal government after the bids were submitted deprived the claimant of his right to a mining license.

of itself, is insufficient to engage State responsibility.[24] The presiding commissioner's reliance on the *Illinois Central Railroad Company* case is misplaced. The Commission there specified that while claims falling within the Commission's jurisdiction had to be 'claims of an international character', this did not in any way mean that 'they must be claims entailing international responsibility of governments'.[25] Mexico admitted liability to make payment under a contract for the purchase of locomotives from the Illinois Central Railroad Company, but its international responsibility was not in issue.[26] Moreover, other awards cited by the presiding commissioner for the engagement of State responsibility in the absence of aggravating circumstances either did not involve any consideration of the defaulting State's international responsibility[27] or involved State conduct that fell short of one of the *Neer* components for MST.[28] Finally, to illustrate how an alien may suffer a denial of justice when neither life nor liberty is at stake, the *Neer* Commission opined that

> [i]f a foreigner, in the pursuit of his private interests, needs a document, which can only be delivered by one of the administrative authorities in the country where he transacts his affairs, and if this document is improperly withheld or delivered too late to be of any use, this will again constitute the same breach of international law, without any judicial authority being blameable.[29]

The unjustified withholding of necessary permits and licenses by the host State who is also a contracting party can cause loss to foreign investors who are unable to perform their end of the contractual bargain and generate revenue from their investment. And according to the *Neer* Commission, this withholding must be improper for State conduct to fall short of MST. The proposal by the presiding commissioner in the *Chattin Claim* that a breach of contract by a host State in the absence of aggravating circumstances is

---

This deprivation, achieved by '[a]ll three branches of the Government conspir[ing] to ruin his enterprise', was 'a denial of justice within the settled principles of international law'.

[24] See also discussion at Chapter 1, Section 1.3.3.2.

[25] *USA v. United Mexican States* (1926) 4 RIAA 21, p. 23.

[26] *USA v. United Mexican States* (1926) 4 RIAA 134, p. 135.

[27] *John B. Okie* (*USA v. United Mexican States*) (1926) 4 RIAA 54, p. 56.

[28] Both *Union Bridge Company* (*USA v. Great Britain*) (1024) 4 RIAA 138, pp. 141–2, which concerned the accidental confiscation of neutral property during wartime without compensation, and *H.G. Venable* (*USA v. United Mexican States*) (1927) 4 RIAA 219, p. 229, where court and railway officials stood idly by while thieves dismantled and stole property impounded by court order, showcased 'an insufficiency of governmental action so far short of international standards that every reasonable and impartial man would readily recognize its insufficiency'.

[29] *USA v. Mexico* (1926) 4 RIAA 60, Opinions of the Commissioners.

a violation of international law contravenes the intended application of MST in the *Neer Claim*. It should therefore be rejected. Aggravating circumstances may not take the form of 'an outrage', or 'bad faith', or 'wilful neglect of duty', or 'an insufficiency of governmental action so far short of international standards that every reasonable and impartial man would readily recognize its insufficiency' as stipulated in the *Neer Claim*. They must nonetheless be present in one form or another for a breach of contract by a host State to amount to a violation of international law.

A review of arbitral awards involving or illuminating contract claims uncovers two aggravating circumstances that turn a breach of contract by a host State into a violation of international law. The first is arbitrariness, where the facts strongly suggest that a contract was breached or terminated on a whim, or without defensible grounds that may justify the breach or termination (3.2.1).[30] The second is the use of sovereign powers to interfere with a contract without providing compensation for injury caused, or avenues through which the foreign private contracting party can seek redress (3.2.2).[31]

3.2.1   Arbitrariness

It is a known policy of the US government to offer diplomatic protection only for 'matters of contract ... [where] it is manifest that such gross misconduct has been committed as amounts to a denial of justice'.[32] In presented contract claims, the breach or termination is often framed as a denial of justice, and one basis for such denial is arbitrary interference with the contract by the host State. In the *Claim of the Salvador Commercial Company*, the US claimant obtained an exclusive, long-term concession to trade from the port of El Triunfo in El Salvador.[33] Through the industry of the claimant and its US investors and managers, the profitability of the concession, once secured, was assured for the remainder of the duration of the concession. The El Salvador government suddenly issued an edict closing the port of El Triunfo, as a result of which the 'concession [was]

---

[30] Jennings, 'State Contracts in International Law', p. 165.

[31] Ibid., p. 168.

[32] US Department of State, 'Letter from Mr Sickles to Mr Sagasta (8 January 1871)' in *Papers Relating to the Foreign Relations of the United States* (Washington, DC: Government Printing Office 1871-2) 754, p. 755. For contract claims that did not allege a 'flagrant violation of international law', the use of 'good offices' sufficed, see E. M. Borchard, *The Diplomatic Protection of Citizens Abroad or The Law of International Claims* (Cleveland, OH: Banks Law Publishing, 1915), p. 284.

[33] *USA v. El Salvador* (1902) 15 RIAA 467.

stricken down and practically cancelled and destroyed'.[34] Ignoring the appeal of the US claimant to lift the edict, the government proceeded to grant trading concessions to its own nationals on terms previously granted to the US claimant. Citing with approval the view that the United States should intervene to protect US nationals abroad 'when the foreign government itself becomes itself a party to important contracts, and then not only fails to fulfil them, but capriciously annuls them',[35] the arbitral tribunal held by a majority that the *de facto* cancellation of the concession by the El Salvador government was a denial of justice.[36] Identifying arbitrariness as an aggravating circumstance that gives rise to a denial of justice in contractual disputes, the two arbitrators added that '[i]t is abhorrent to the sense of justice to say that one party to a contract, whether such party be a private individual, a monarch, or a government of any kind, may arbitrarily, without hearing and without impartial procedure of any sort, arrogate the right to condemn the other party to the contract'.[37]

Post-*Neer* arbitral awards which acknowledge that proof of arbitrariness in the breach or cancellation of a contract by the host State validates a claim for denial of justice include the *International Fisheries Company Case*[38] and the *Mexican Union Railway (Ltd.) Claim*.[39] The underlying contract in both disputes contained a Calvo clause, directing a claimant to seek redress from domestic courts and waiving its right to bring an international claim. Although the Commissions arrived at different interpretations of Calvo clauses, with the US-Mexico Claims Commission in *International Fisheries* holding that a Calvo clause is deactivated when there is a denial of justice *latu sensu*, and a majority of the UK-Mexico Claims Commission in *Mexican Union Railway* holding that a Calvo clause is only deactivated when there is a denial of justice by domestic courts, both Commissions accepted that an arbitrary breach of contract amounts to a violation of international law. The Commission in *International Fisheries* rejected the US claim that the cancellation of a concession by the Mexican government for non-performance by the US concessionaire amounted to a denial of justice. According to the Commission, the cancellation 'was not an arbitrary act ... which in itself might be considered as a violation

---

[34] Ibid., p. 476.
[35] Ibid., p. 477.
[36] Ibid., pp. 476–8. The third arbitrator, an El Salvadoran national, dissented. No dissenting opinion appears to have been published.
[37] Ibid., p. 478.
[38] *USA* v. *United Mexican States* (1931) 4 RIAA 691, pp. 698–9.
[39] *Great Britain* v. *United Mexican States* (1930) 5 RIAA 115.

of some rule or principle of international law, requisites to be established in order that the Commission might take jurisdiction, notwithstanding the existence of a clause partaking of the nature of the Calvo clause in a contract subscribed by a claimant'.[40] The majority of the Commission in *Mexican Union Railway* held that the claimant who was bound by a Calvo clause must first seek redress from Mexican courts.[41] Unless and until it has done so, a denial of justice claim cannot ripen even if the devaluation of a railway concession by a catalogue of haphazard State activities ranging from failure to protect the railway from constant attacks by revolutionaries, to ordering repairs on the railway, to threats of cancelling the concession, 'constitute a breach of international law'.[42] The dissenting UK commissioner held that 'arbitrary proceedings of public authorities' constitute a breach of international law, thereby entitling a home State to intervene diplomatically, even if there is no denial of justice by domestic courts.[43] Maintaining that the claim pleads aggravating circumstances that turn contractual interference by a host State into international wrong, he concluded that 'the British Government is entitled to present it to the Commission and the latter has jurisdiction to determine it, provided the losses claimed do not arise solely from the fulfilment or interpretation of the contract or the execution of the work there under'.[44]

3.2.2   Contractual Breaches Iure Imperii without Compensation for Injury Suffered or Prospect of Redress

States have a duty under international law to provide redress for causing injury to an alien.[45] Redress can take the form of an offer of compensation or access to effective local remedies. When an injury is caused without an offer of compensation or satisfaction through the pursuit of local remedies, the injured alien possesses a right to redress that is cognisable in international law. Contractual breaches *iure imperii* expose the imbalance in the relationship between a foreign investor and its host State contracting party. Just like how only a State has the sovereign power to arrest and detain an alien, only a State has the sovereign power to unilaterally

---

[40] *USA* v. *United Mexican States* (1931), p. 699.
[41] Ibid., pp. 118–21.
[42] Ibid., pp. 116–7 and 122.
[43] Ibid., p. 127.
[44] Ibid., p. 128.
[45] M. Huber, *Réclamations britanniques dans la zone espagnole du Maroc* (The Hague: Publisher not identified, 1925), p. 57.

terminate a contract by legislative or executive decree. Therefore, the duty of States to provide redress where contractual breaches *iure imperii* cause injury to aliens,[46] is a subset of the broader duty to provide redress when conduct involving the exercise of sovereign prerogatives and causing injury to aliens amounts to a denial of justice as MST. Two arbitral awards serve to illustrate.

In the *Shufeldt Claim*, a chicle concession contract was cancelled by legislative decree without an offer of compensation by the Guatemalan government.[47] The United States and Guatemala agreed to submit the claim to arbitration. The key issue before the sole arbitrator was whether the US concessionaire had 'the right to claim a pecuniary indemnification for damages and injuries' caused by the promulgation of the legislative decree declaring his concession null and void.[48] Although it is not apparent from the text of award if the United States couched the claim of Mr Shufeldt in the language of a denial of justice, the policy of the United States to intervene diplomatically only when contractual interference is accompanied by aggravating circumstances giving rise to a violation of international law should be borne in mind. Furthermore, the sole arbitrator found that the contentions of the United States on behalf of Mr Shufeldt were 'sound and in keeping with the principles of international law'.[49] The sole arbitrator then examined the legislative decree terminating the concession and held that Mr Shufeldt had the right to be indemnified for the losses suffered as a result of the cancellation. According to the sole arbitrator, 'where such a decree, passed even on the best of grounds, works injustice to an alien subject, in which case the Government ought to make compensation for the injury inflicted and can not invoke any municipal law to justify their refusal to do so'.[50] By the reasoning of the sole arbitrator, injustice is not worked when there is simply a breach of contract *iure*

---

[46] *Delagoa Bay Railway Arbitration* (*USA v. Portugal*) in US Department of State, *Papers Relating to the Foreign Relations of the United States* (Washington, DC: Government Printing Office, 1900), p. 903, and *Papers Relating to the Foreign Relations of the United States* (Washington, DC: Government Printing Office, 1902), pp. 848–52; also *Cheek Claim* (*USA v. Siam*), Award, 21 March 1898 in H. L. Fontaine (ed.), *Pasicrisie Internationale: Histoire Documentaire des Arbitrages Internationaux* (Paris: Stampfli & Cie, 1902) p. 580; and tangentially *Claim of the George D. Emery Co.* (*USA v. Nicaragua*) in US Department of State, *Papers Relating to the Foreign Relations of the United States* (Washington, DC: Government Printing Office, 1909), pp. 460–7.

[47] *Guatemala v. USA* (24 July 1930) 2 RIAA 1079. See also discussion at Chapter 1, Section 1.3.2.3.

[48] Ibid., p. 1083.

[49] Ibid., p. 1094.

[50] Ibid., p. 1095.

imperii, but rather, when this breach *iure imperii* caused injury which was not compensated. The aggravating circumstance that puts a State in violation of the core standard for contractual protection is therefore a combination of the existence of a contractual breach *iure imperii*, the existence of an injury that was caused by the breach, and the failure of the injuring State to compensate the injured alien.

In the *Brown Claim*, a public tender for gold mining licenses was withdrawn by executive decree of the Transvaal government after bids, including one drawn up by US national Mr Brown for 1,200 licenses, were submitted.[51] Brown then brought a claim against the government in the High Court of the Transvaal Republic, demanding the issuance of licences on the basis that he had already pegged them at the mining site.[52] Several days after the claim was filed, one of the two legislative chambers of the Transvaal Republic adopted a resolution approving of the executive decree withdrawing the public tender and declaring that no one who has suffered damage as a result of the withdrawal shall be entitled to compensation. The High Court found for Brown and ordered the relevant personnel to issue the mining licenses. This led to 'an amazing controversy between the Court and the Executive', which culminated in the promulgation of new laws on the subordination of the judiciary to the executive.[53] Brown was left in legal limbo as it was unclear if the earlier favourable judgment will be enforced under the new regime, or if bringing a new claim before courts that are answerable to the executive would lead to redress. Although Brown was never formally issued the licenses that he sought, the High Court declared Brown a *de facto* licensee. Therefore, Brown's predicament in the Transvaal Republic is akin to a foreign investor who is obstructed, by the exercise of sovereign prerogatives, from performing a contract concluded with the host State. According to the arbitral tribunal, '[a]ll three branches of the Government conspired to ruin his enterprise', and even '[t]he judiciary, at first recalcitrant, was at length reduced to submission and brought into line with a determined policy of the Executive to reach the desired result regardless of Constitutional guarantees and inhibitions'.[54] Not only was there no offer of compensation for what was essentially a contractual breach *iure imperii* causing financial injury, the prospect of redress through the pursuit of local remedies was illusory. The arbitral tribunal

---

[51] *Robert R. Brown* (*USA* v. *Great Britain*) (1923) 6 RIAA 120.
[52] Ibid., p. 122.
[53] Ibid., pp. 124–6.
[54] Ibid., p. 129.

concluded that Brown had 'acquired rights of a substantial character, the improper deprivation of which did constitute a denial of justice'.[55]

3.3 The Preservation of the Core Standard of Treatment for Investment Contracts

As States gradually replaced diplomatic intervention on behalf of injured nationals investing abroad with investment treaties empowering injured nationals to bring a claim directly against the host State, the legal basis underlying a contractual breach that engages State responsibility also changed. While home States once sought arbitral rulings of host State international responsibility on the basis that a breach of contract amounted to a denial of justice as MST, injured investors now seek arbitral rulings of host State international responsibility on the basis that a breach of contract amount to a denial of FET. Virtually all investment treaties oblige host States to accord protected investments, which includes contractual rights, FET. The ubiquity of the FET standard, coupled with the notable success rate of FET claims, fuels perception of FET as the most investment-friendly, and by association contract-friendly, treaty standard of protection.[56] This may explain why a large number of FET claims originate in a breach of contract by the host State. The volume of contract-based FET claims has necessitated many attempts by arbitral tribunals to interpret and impart content to FET. Although there is currently no universally agreed definition of FET, the preferred approach for interpreting FET in the context of contractual breaches imparts content that approximates the content of denial of justice as MST (3.3.1). The core standard of treatment for investment contracts is further preserved by the growing trend in investment treaty practice, where FET is expressly pegged to MST (3.3.2). This obliges arbitral tribunals tasked with adjudicating contract-based FET claims to first ascertain what the MST for investment contracts is, and to then assimilate FET to that core standard.

---

[55] Ibid., p. 129. Although the United Kingdom annexed the Transvaal Republic, the tribunal took the view that the authority exerted by the United Kingdom over this annexed territory 'fell far short of what would be required to make her responsible for the wrong inflicted on Brown', p. 130. Therefore, the claim presented by the United States to the United Kingdom was dismissed.

[56] C. Schreuer, 'Fair and Equitable Treatment' in A. K. Hoffman (ed.), *Protection of Foreign Investments through Modern Treaty Arbitration – Diversity and Harmonisation* (Geneva: Association Suisse de l'arbitrage, 2010) 125, p. 125.

3.3.1   *The Turn to Fair and Equitable Treatment*

In 1999, Vasciannie observed that the imprecise content of FET stemmed from 'the fact that the words "fair and equitable treatment", in their plain meaning, do not refer to an established body of law or to existing legal precedents'.[57] Today, numerous investor–State arbitral awards interpreting the FET standard constitute a principal source of law on the content of FET,[58] thereby alleviating to some extent the problem of imprecision. Arbitral *jurisprudence* proffers two approaches. The first counsels that the FET standard is geared towards the protection of an investor's legitimate expectations, thus paring down the content of FET to a single component (Section 3.3.1.1). The second counsels that the FET standard addresses various concerns, including arbitrariness, lack of due process, and possibly investor reliance on host State representations, without any particular concern taking precedence over the rest (Section 3.3.1.2). According to the first approach, FET is exclusive to legitimate expectations, whereas according to the second approach, FET is inclusive of several discrete concerns, which may include legitimate expectations. Despite calls by some commentators to accord greater prominence to legitimate expectations when imparting content to FET in relation to host State contractual undertakings, the majority of arbitral tribunals hearing contract-based FET claims adopt the second approach. The possible reasons for this preference will be discussed (Section 3.3.1.3).

3.3.1.1   Approach 1: FET Has a Single Component

The tribunal in *Técnicas Medioambientales Tecmed S.A.* v. *The United Mexican States* was one of the first to define FET in terms of investor expectations:[59]

> The Arbitral Tribunal finds that the commitment of fair and equitable treatment included in Article 4(1) of the Agreement is an expression and part of the bona fide principle recognized in international law ... The Arbitral Tribunal considers that this provision of the Agreement, in light of the good faith principle established by international law, requires the Contracting Parties to provide to international investments treatment that does not affect the basic expectations that were taken into account by the foreign investor to make the investment.

---

[57] 'The Fair and Equitable Treatment Standard in International Investment Law and Practice', p. 103.

[58] See discussion at Chapter 2, Section 2.2, and especially Section 2.2.2.

[59] ICSID Case No. ARB(AF)/00/2, Award, 29 May 2003 (Grigera Naón, Fernández Rozas, Bernam Verea), paras. 153–4.

Among these 'basic expectations', added the tribunal, are the host State's commitment to 'act in a consistent manner, free from ambiguity and totally transparently in its relations with the foreign investor, so that it may know beforehand any and all rules and regulations that will govern its investments, as well as the goals of the relevant policies and administrative practices or directives, to be able to plan its investment and comply with such regulations'.[60]

The tribunal in *Saluka Investments B. V.* v. *The Czech Republic* went even further in exalting the central importance of investor expectations to FET:[61]

> An investor's decision to make an investment is based on an assessment of the state of the law and the totality of the business environment at the time of the investment as well as on the investor expectation that the conduct of the host State subsequent to the investment will be fair and equitable. The standard of 'fair and equitable treatment' is therefore closely tied to the notion of legitimate expectations which is the dominant element of that standard. By virtue of the 'fair and equitable treatment' standard included in Article 3.1 the Czech Republic must therefore be regarded as having assumed an obligation to treat foreign investors so as to avoid the frustration of investors' legitimate and reasonable expectations.

According to the *Saluka* tribunal, expectations formed in the absence of specific host State assurances to a certain investor or a certain investment, can qualify as legitimate expectations. If taken to the extreme, this approach treats virtually any expectation that the investor may entertain for the investment from its point of entry as a legitimate expectation. Under domestic law, legitimate expectations are created by the express conferral of rights on an individual by the State.[62] Similarly, under international law, legitimate expectations must arise from specific undertakings given by States, and do not develop in the abstract.[63]

Fietta criticises the expansive reading of legitimate expectations by the *Saluka* tribunal as 'extend[ing] far beyond any previous authority on the relevance of legitimate expectations to the fair and equitable standard'.[64]

---

[60] Award, ibid., para. 154.

[61] UNCITRAL, Partial Award, 17 March 2006 (Watts, Fortier, Behrens), paras. 301–2.

[62] For a summary on how legitimate expectations are understood in various legal systems, see E. Snodgrass, 'Protecting Investors' Legitimate Expectations: Recognizing and Delimiting a General Principle' (2006) 21(1) *ICSID Review – Foreign Investment Law Journal* 1 at 25–30.

[63] B. Cheng, *General Principles of Law as Applied by International Courts and Tribunals* (Cambridge: Grotius Publications, 1953), pp. 137–40.

[64] S. Fietta, 'Expropriation and the "Fair and Equitable" Standard: The Developing Role of Investors' "Expectations" in International Investment Arbitration' (2006) 23(5) *Journal of International Arbitration* 375 at 397.

Notably, the tribunals in *Metalpar S.A. and Buen Aire S.A.* v. *The Argentine Republic*,[65] and *Glamis Gold Ltd.* v. *The United States of America*,[66] both of which post-date *Saluka*, held that legitimate expectations can only arise when the host State makes specific commitments towards the investor.

3.3.1.2   Approach 2: FET Has Several Components

Other tribunals take the view that the content of FET comprises discrete categories of State actions or omissions, each of which is capable of triggering the international responsibility of the State for denying FET. The tribunal in *Alex Genin, Eastern Credit Limited Inc. and Anor* v. *The Republic of Estonia* was one of the first to identify the different components of FET:[67]

> Article II(3)(a) of the [US-Estonia] BIT requires the signatory governments to treat foreign investment in a 'fair and equitable' way. Under international law, this requirement is generally understood to 'provide a basic and general standard which is detached from the host State's domestic law.' While the exact content of this standard is not clear, the Tribunal understands it to require an 'international minimum standard' that is separate from domestic law, but that is, indeed, a minimum standard. Acts that would violate this minimum standard would include acts showing a wilful neglect of duty, an insufficiency of action falling far below international standards, or even subjective bad faith.

Article II(3)(a) of the US-Estonia investment treaty provides that protected investments 'shall at all times be accorded fair and equitable treatment ... and shall in no case be accorded treatment less than required by international law'.[68] As Article II(3)(a) only prohibits treatment 'less than that required by international law', but imposes no ceiling on the treatment that protected investments can receive, it does not instruct arbitral tribunals to equate 'fair and equitable treatment' to 'treatment [no] less than required by international law'. It is therefore remarkable that the *Genin* tribunal likened the FET standard to an 'international minimum standard'. And although the *Genin* tribunal did not refer to the *Neer Claim*, the components it identified as the content of FET, namely, 'a wilful neglect of duty, an insufficiency of action falling far below international standards, or even

---

[65] ICSID Case No. ARB/03/5, Award on the Merits, 6 June 2008 (Blanco, Cameron, Chabaneix), paras. 185–6.

[66] NAFTA-UNCITRAL, Award, 8 June 2009 (Young, Caron, Hubbard), paras. 766–7.

[67] ICSID Case No. ARB/99/2, Award, 25 June 2001 (Fortier, Heith, van den Berg), para. 367 (footnotes omitted).

[68] Treaty Between the Government of the United States of America and the Government of the Republic of Estonia for the Encouragement and Reciprocal Protection of Investment (signed 19 April 1994, entered into force 16 February 1997).

subjective bad faith', mirrors the components identified by the US-Mexico Claims Commission for denying justice to an alien in the *Neer Claim*. The likelihood that the *Genin* tribunal adopted the minimum standard for alien protection for FET is irresistible when one recalls the *Neer* formulation that State conduct violates MST when it amounts 'to bad faith, to wilful neglect of duty, or to an insufficiency of governmental action so far short of international standards'.[69]

Over time, as more tribunals applied the FET standard to a variety of fact patterns, the content of FET benefitted from further reflection. The tribunal in *Waste Management Inc. v. United Mexican States (No. 2)* formulated a more elaborate definition of FET:[70]

> [F]air and equitable treatment is infringed by conduct attributable to the State and harmful to the claimant if the conduct is arbitrary, grossly unfair, unjust or idiosyncratic, is discriminatory and exposes the claimant to sectional or racial prejudice, or involves a lack of due process leading to an outcome which offends judicial propriety – as might be the case with a manifest failure of natural justice in judicial proceedings or a complete lack of transparency and candour in an administrative process. In applying this standard it is relevant that the treatment is in breach of representations made by the host State which were reasonably relied on by the claimant.

The *Waste Management (No. 2)* tribunal was interpreting Article 1105 of the North American Free Trade Agreement. Article 1105 is titled 'Minimum Standard of Treatment' and directs Contracting Parties to 'accord to investments of investors of another Party treatment in accordance with international law, including fair and equitable treatment'.[71] Notably the *Waste Management (No. 2)* tribunal, unlike the *Genin* tribunal, did not replicate the *Neer* formulation of denial of justice as MST when interpreting FET. Instead, by referring to 'arbitrary, grossly unfair, unjust or idiosyncratic ... [and] discriminatory' conduct and 'lack of due process ... as might be the case with a manifest failure of natural justice in judicial proceedings or a complete lack of transparency and candour in an administrative process', the *Waste Management (No. 2)* tribunal is likely to agree that arbitrariness and contractual breaches *iure imperii* without compensation for injury suffered or prospect of redress are aggravating circumstances that turn a contractual breach into a violation of FET. The *Waste Management (No. 2)* formulation of FET as MST appears to preserve the core standard

---

[69] *USA v. United Mexican States* (1926), p. 61.
[70] ICSID Case No. ARB(AF)/00/3, Award, 30 April 2004 (Crawford, Civiletti, Gómez), para. 98.
[71] Signed 17 December 1992, entered into force 1 January 1994, (1993) 32 ILM 289, p. 605, Art. 1105(1).

of treatment for contractual protection outlined in Section 3.2, and where frustrated investor expectations is not a known aggravating circumstance.

The *Waste Management (No. 2)* tribunal acknowledged that investor expectations can inform the content of FET, but it did not include investor expectations in the list of host State conduct that could breach FET. Therefore, treatment 'in breach of representations made by the host State which were reasonably relied on', unlike 'arbitrariness' and 'lack of due process' will not constitute, in and of itself, a violation of FET.[72] It is likelier that frustrated investor expectations, if any, will assist the tribunal in determining if the alleged misconduct was 'arbitrary … or involves a lack of due process'.[73] According to the tribunal in *Waste Management (No. 2)* therefore, the protection of legitimate expectations, unlike non-arbitrariness and due process, is not a main component of the content of FET.

Outside NAFTA Chapter 11, the text of applicable investment treaties do not always link FET to MST. One such example is the Kazakhstan-Turkey BIT whose Preamble contains the bare statement that 'fair and equitable treatment of investment is desirable'.[74] Yet, when imparting content to the FET standard in the Kazakhstan-Turkey BIT, the tribunal in *Rumeli Telekom A. S. and Anor v. Republic of Kazakhstan* implicitly relegated legitimate expectations to a subsidiary component.[75] Repeating the formulation for the content of FET as MST laid down by the *Waste Management (No. 2)* tribunal, the *Rumeli Telekom* tribunal identified State conduct that is 'arbitrary, grossly unfair, unjust, idiosyncratic, discriminatory, or lacking in due process' as 'concrete principles' of FET.[76] The *Rumeli Telekom* tribunal supplemented this finding with the remark that 'to comply with the [FET] standard, the State must respect the investor's reasonable and legitimate expectations'.[77] A violation of FET was found on the facts but on combined grounds of arbitrariness, absence of transparency, due process,

---

[72] *Mobil Investments Canada Inc. and Anor v. Canada*, ICSID Case No. ARB(AF)/07/4, Decision on Liability and on Principles of Quantum (redacted), 22 May 2012 (van Houtte, Janow, Sands), paras. 152–3.

[73] P. Dumberry, 'The Protection of Investors' Legitimate Expectations and the Fair and Equitable Treatment Standard under NAFTA Article 1105' (2014) 31(1) *Journal of International Arbitration* 47 at 62.

[74] Agreement between the Republic of Turkey and the Republic of Kazakhstan concerning the Reciprocal Promotion and Protection of Investments, signed 1 May 1992, entered into force 10 August 1995.

[75] ICSID Case No. ARB/05/16, Award, 29 July 2008 (Hanotiau, Boyd, Lalonde).

[76] Award, ibid., para. 610.

[77] Award, ibid., para. 610.

and breached legitimate expectations.[78] It is doubtful if the claimants' FET claim in *Rumeli* v. *Kazakhstan* would have succeeded if only its legitimate expectations had been breached.

Some arbitral tribunals hearing contract-based FET claims attach greater importance to frustrated investor expectations than the *Waste Management (No. 2)* and *Rumeli Telekom* tribunals. For example, although the tribunal in *MTD Equity Sdn. Bhd. and Anor* v. *Republic of Chile* did not expressly include legitimate expectations in its multi-component formulation of FET,[79] it proceeded to quote and endorse the defining passage from *Tecmed* v. *Mexico* where the tribunal there interpreted FET to mean the exclusive protection of investor expectations.[80] The ad hoc Committee in MTD's application for annulment chided the tribunal for doing do.[81] A tribunal that defines FET solely with reference to investor expectations, the ad hoc Committee warned, risks acting in manifest excess of its powers because '[t]he obligations of the host State towards foreign investors derive from the terms of the applicable investment treaty and not from any set of expectations investors may have or claim to have'.[82] In this case though, the tribunal's discussion of MTD's expectations vis-à-vis Chile was not a manifest excess of its powers as those expectations arose from specific undertakings given in investment contracts concluded with a Chilean State entity, and had potential bearing on MTD's FET claim.[83]

A number of tribunals list legitimate expectations as one of the key components of FET, and a frustration of the investor's legitimate expectations alone suffices to violate FET. The tribunal in *Parkerings-Compagniet AS* v. *Republic of Lithuania* held that in addition to 'unfair and discriminatory conduct' and 'arbitrary conduct', the investor's legitimate expectations are a separate ground for assessing the breach of FET.[84] The tribunal in *Biwater Gauff (Tanzania) Ltd.* v. *United Republic of Tanzania* identified 'protection of legitimate expectations', 'good faith' and 'transparency, consistency, non-discrimination' as the three main components of FET.[85] The tribunal

---

[78] Award, ibid., paras. 612–9.
[79] ICSID Case No. ARB/01/7, Award, 25 May 2004 (Sureda, Lalonde, Blanco), para. 113.
[80] Award, ibid., para. 114.
[81] *MTD Equity Sdn Bhd and Anor* v. *Chile*, ICSID Case No. ARB/01/7, Decision on Annulment, 21 March 2007 (Guillaume, Crawford, Ordóñez Noriega), para. 67.
[82] Decision on Annulment, ibid., para. 67.
[83] Decision on Annulment, ibid., 69.
[84] ICSID Case No. ARB/05/8, Award, 11 September 2007 (Lévy, Lew, Lalonde), para. 279.
[85] ICSID Case No. ARB/05/22, Award, 24 July 2008 (Hanotiau, Born, Landau), para. 602. This formulation was adopted in *Walter Bau* v. *Thailand*, UNCITRAL, Award, 1 July 2009 (Barker, Lalonde, Bunnag), para. 11.5.

clarified that in order for investor expectations to be protected by the FET standard, they had to be 'reasonable and legitimate', and 'have been relied upon by the investor to make the investment'.[86] A more recent award where legitimate expectations were listed as a main component of FET is *Deutsche Bank AG* v. *Democratic Socialist Republic of Sri Lanka*. Using earlier formulations of FET as a template, the tribunal further elaborated on the content of FET:[87]

> [T]he Tribunal notes that the standard has been rightly – although not exhaustively – defined in the Waste Management II case, quoted above. Accordingly, its components may be distilled as follows: [i] protection of legitimate and reasonable expectations which have been relied upon by the investor to make the investment; [ii] good faith conduct although bad faith on the part of the State is not required for its violation; [iii] conduct that is transparent, consistent and not discriminatory, that is, not based on unjustifiable distinctions or arbitrary; [iv] conduct that does not offend judicial propriety, that complies with due process and the right to be heard[.]

In identifying legitimate expectations as one of the key components of FET, the content of FET according to the *Deutsche Bank* tribunal differs from the formulation in the *Waste Management (No. 2)* v. *Mexico* award. The earlier tribunal did not consider a breach of an investor's legitimate expectations as capable of amounting to a violation of FET. Therefore, although the *Deutsche Bank* tribunal endeavoured to follow in the footsteps of the *Waste Management (No. 2)* tribunal, the two tribunals actually disagree on the role and weight of legitimate expectations in the formulation of FET.

To recap, components of FET which are frequently listed under the second approach include non-arbitrariness, non-discrimination, administrative and judicial due process, transparency, even-handedness and stability. Transparency and even-handedness are the antithesis to arbitrary conduct, while non-discrimination, administrative and judicial candour and fairness, as well as stability, are hallmarks of due process. Therefore, the more widely accepted and broad brush aggravating circumstances for a violation of FET are arbitrariness and lack of due process.[88] These are the same aggravating circumstances that ought to be present for a breach of contract

---

[86]   Award, ibid., para. 602.
[87]   ICSID Case No. ARB/09/02, Award, 31 October 2012 (Hanotiau, Williams, Khan (dissenting)), para. 420. The dissenting arbitrator did not take issue with the majority's formulation of FET.
[88]   It has been said that 'the fair and equitable standard gives modern expression to a *general principle of due process* in its application to the treatment of investors', and 'requires the application of fundamental rule-of-law values in decision-making: predictability, accessibility; impartiality; and natural justice, as contrasted with arbitrary action', C. McLachlan,

by a host State to amount to a denial of justice and a violation of MST. Less frequently listed components of FET include bad faith and legitimate expectations. Arbitral tribunals seldom identify bad faith as a trigger for the violation of FET, probably because conclusive evidence of bad faith is hard to come by.[89] Arbitral tribunals are divided on labelling legitimate expectations as a component of FET. While the *MTD*, *Parkerings*, *Biwater Gauff* and *Deutsche Bank* tribunals are receptive to legitimate expectations as a discrete ground for violating FET, the *Waste Management (No. 2)* and *Rumeli Telekom* tribunals, and the *MTD* v. *Chile* ad hoc Committee exhibit reservations about placing legitimate expectations at the heart of FET. Disagreement over whether the frustration of investor expectations, in and of itself, violates FET, injects a margin of differentiation into arbitral *jurisprudence* interpreting FET according to the second approach.[90] As the second approach also identifies conduct that is arbitrary and lacking in due process as components of FET, it aligns the content of FET with the content of denial of justice as MST. To the extent that the second approach is the prevailing approach for interpreting FET in contract-based FET claims, the core standard for contractual protection, derived from the minimum standard for alien protection, is duly preserved.

3.3.1.3   The Preferred Approach for Contractual Breaches

Given how investment contracts embody obligations owed by a State or State entity to an investor, which are in turn capable of generating

---

'Investment Treaties and General International Law' (2008) 57(2) ICLQ 361 at 381 and 400 (original emphasis).

[89] Despite one commentator's insistence that tribunals should be more robust in labelling host State conduct as bad faith conduct when hearing FET claims, see D. Dragiuev, 'Bad Faith Conduct of States in Violation of the "Fair and Equitable Treatment" Standard in International Investment Law and Arbitration' (2014) 5(2) *Journal of International Dispute Settlement* 273, this is easier said than done. The three-member tribunal in *Deutsche Bank AG* v. *Democratic Socialist Republic of Sri Lanka* was sharply divided on whether the Sri Lankan Supreme Court violated the FET clause in the Germany-Sri Lanka investment treaty by issuing a stop payment order in relation to a debt owed by the State-owned Ceylon Petroleum Corporation to Deutsche Bank under a hedging agreement. The dissenting arbitrator strongly objected to what he perceived as the majority's insinuation that the Supreme Court had, by issuing the order on an *ex parte* urgent basis, acted in bad faith; see Dissenting Opinion of Makhdoom Ali Khan, paras. 106–13. To be fair, the majority called the Supreme Court's conduct a 'due process violation' (para. 478), but its belief that the order was issued for 'political reasons' (para. 479) also hinted at bad faith. The forcefulness of the dissent in *Deutsche Bank* v. *Sri Lanka* cautions against assuming that bad faith conduct is self-evident.

[90] See the discussion in Chapter 2, Section 2.4, on why having arbitral awards as a principal source of law can nonetheless engender broad convergence, but not absolute consistency, on legal content.

expectations for the investor, legitimate expectations arising from specific representations can feature in contract-based FET claims. Schreuer argues that legitimate expectations play a key role in the assessment of host State compliance with the FET standard in a contractual setting.[91] Unlike the *Saluka* tribunal though, Schreuer is more discerning about which investor expectations may trigger a violation of FET. Citing the *Tecmed* tribunal's list of 'basic expectations' with approval, Schreuer condenses these investor expectations into the overarching expectation of 'a transparent and stable legal framework'.[92] Therefore, even if 'an important aspect of the protection of the investor's legitimate expectations is the observance of obligations arising from contracts with the host State', not every breach of contract breaches a legitimate expectation which in turn violates FET.[93] Only those contractual breaches that imperil 'a transparent and stable legal framework' frustrate legitimate expectations that are protected by an FET clause:[94]

> A more relevant test for the violation of the FET standard with respect to contracts would be whether the investor's *legitimate expectations regarding a secure and stable legal framework are affected*. Not every violation of a contract would trigger a finding to this effect.

Other commentators who, like Schreuer, acknowledge the importance of legitimate expectations to the content of FET, do not advocate that tribunals take only legitimate expectations into account when deciding FET claims. Douglas urges tribunals to refer to 'the principle of estoppel or legitimate expectations to give content to the fair and equitable treatment standard', instead of 'preambular statements' in investment treaties on the desire of contracting States to achieve greater economic cooperation.[95]

---

[91] C. Schreuer, 'Fair and Equitable Treatment (FET): Interactions with Other Standards' in G. Coop and C. Ribeiro (eds.), *Investment Protection and the Energy Charter Treaty* (New York: JurisNet, 2008) 63, pp. 89–93.

[92] Ibid., p. 89.

[93] Ibid., pp. 89–90.

[94] Ibid., p. 93 (emphasis added).

[95] Z. Douglas, *The International Law on Investment Claims* (Cambridge: Cambridge University Press, 2012), p. 84. The principle of estoppel in international law requires a State to be 'consistent in its attitude to a given factual or legal situation', I. C. MacGibbon, 'Estoppel in International Law' (1958) 7 ICLQ 468 at 468; also A. McNair, 'The Legality of the Occupation of the Ruhr' (1924) 5 BYIL 17, p. 35; *Case Concerning the Temple of Preah Vihear* (*Cambodia* v. *Thailand*) (Merits) [1962] ICJ Rep 6, Dissenting Opinion of Sir Percy Spender 101, pp. 143–4. In the context of FET, a host State that has given various assurances to induce an investor to invest, which the investor relies on to its detriment, is estopped from denying that those assurances were made. For tribunals that recognise legitimate expectations as a main component of FET, host States are estopped from reneging on assurances that give rise to legitimate expectations. Therefore, whether the investor invokes the

As most tribunals accept that legitimate expectations are relevant to the content of FET, even if they disagree on whether legitimate expectations should be considered a main component of FET, Douglas' appeal to an established legal doctrine over vague economic policy when defining FET underlines what tribunals are already doing. Fietta notes that while 'the fair and equitable standard simpliciter has evolved over recent years so as to embrace a central role for the legitimate expectations principle', FET encompasses a 'broad range of mistreatment' which is not limited to 'specific state acts, decisions or assurances that are fundamental to the investor's decision to invest'.[96] Therefore, legitimate expectations may be crucial to a finding of whether there has been a breach of FET in some situations, but it cannot, as a general rule, be the only component of FET.

The reluctance of commentators to completely reduce FET to a byword for the protection of legitimate expectations is shared by tribunals hearing contract-based FET claims. Most of these tribunals define FET with a list of components which may or may not include legitimate expectations. There are three possible reasons for this.

First, as pointed out by the ad hoc Committee in *MTD* v. *Chile*, a tribunal's duty is to interpret the applicable investment treaty. FET clauses are not worded identically and on occasion, the applicable FET clause may be more specific, and less open-ended, on what the content of FET is.[97] One example is NAFTA Article 1105(1) where FET refers to 'treatment in accordance with international law'. The Federal Trade Commission issued an Interpretive Note in 2001, clarifying what 'treatment in accordance with international law' means. In the view of the FTC, FET for NAFTA members does not require 'treatment in addition to or beyond that which is required by the customary international law minimum standard of treatment of aliens'.[98] According to a recent study, most NAFTA tribunals do not regard legitimate expectations as a main component of FET because the protection of legitimate expectations is not recognised

---

principle of estoppel or pleads the frustration of its legitimate expectations in its FET claim, the same objection is raised: inconsistent host State conduct that causes prejudice to the investor.

[96] Fietta, 'Expropriation and the "Fair and Equitable" Standard', p. 389.

[97] Schreuer, 'Fair and Equitable Treatment in Arbitral Practice', p. 364: 'The meaning of a clause providing for fair and equitable treatment will ultimately depend on its specific wording'.

[98] NAFTA Law, 'Interpretive Note of the NAFTA Free Trade Commission on Article 1105 – Minimum Standard of Treatment in Accordance with International Law (31 July 2001)', online: www.naftalaw.org/commission.htm (accessed 31 December 2017).

under customary international law.[99] The formulation of FET provided by the *Waste Management (No. 2)* tribunal, excerpted previously, reflects this trend. Another example is Article 3 of the Oman-Yemen investment treaty[100], which was invoked in *Desert Line Projects LLC v. The Republic of Yemen*. FET under Article 3 has to be interpreted in light of an undertaking 'not to subject in any way to discriminatory or legally unjustified measures the management, maintenance, use, transfer, enjoyment, assignment of an investment mad by the investors of one of the two Contracting Parties in the territory of the other Contracting Party, as well as companies and projects in which such investments have been made.'[101] As the *Desert Line* tribunal did not attempt to define FET when applying Article 3 to the facts,[102] it must have accepted the list of undertakings as the list of components that FET under Article 3 of the Oman-Yemen investment treaty comprises. And since Article 3 does not refer to legitimate expectations, neither did the tribunal throughout the award. Therefore, the second approach which allows tribunals to tailor the content of FET to restrictive or unique treaty language, is preferable to the first approach because it is more attuned to the difficulty, and in some cases, the impossibility, of viewing FET through the sole optic of legitimate expectations.

Second, investment contracts may contain undertakings assumed by the State towards the investor, and which the investor relied upon when making the investment. This does not make every representation-backed expectation arising from an investment contract a legitimate expectation that some FET clauses protect. Legitimate expectations may be a helpful litmus test for when a breach of contract amounts to a violation of FET if it operates, as Schreuer suggests, within narrow confines. If a breach of contract has to affect the security and stability of a legal framework before it can amount to a violation of FET, not many contractual breaches are likely to meet the test. If, in contrast, legitimate expectations in a contractual setting are defined more generally as representations given by the host State and relied on by the investor when making an investment, it is arguable

---

[99] Dumberry, 'The Protection of Investors' Legitimate Expectations', pp. 51–62. One exception is *International Thunderbird Gaming Corporation v. Mexico*, UNCITRAL-NAFTA, Arbitral Award, 26 January 2006 (van den Berg, Ariosa, Wälde), para. 147; especially Separate Opinion of T. Wälde in the same award, para. 44: '[T]he breach of legitimate expectations created by specific assurances now constitutes a self-standing subcategory of the "fair and equitable treatment" standard under Art. 1105 of the NAFTA.'

[100] Signed 18 September 1998, entered into force 1 April 2000.

[101] ICSID Case No. ARB/05/17, Award, 6 February 2008 (Tercier, Paulsson, El-Kosheri), para. 191.

[102] Award, ibid., pp. 193–5.

that a contractual undertaking by the host State to guarantee payment for the provision of services or works which induced the investor to sign the contract qualifies as a legitimate expectation. When taken to the extreme, a broad definition of legitimate expectations has the potential to turn every breach of contract into a violation of FET. More tribunals that refer to legitimate expectations in a contract-based FET claim appear partial to a broad definition of legitimate expectations.[103] However, because they consider legitimate expectations as merely one of several components of FET, and not the only component, contractual breaches are also analysed with respect to the other components like non-arbitrariness and due process. By avoiding exclusive reliance on legitimate expectations, tribunals have also managed to avoid a doubtful situation where 'any violation of a contractual obligation by a host State or one of its entities automatically amounts to a violation of the FET standard'.[104]

Third, the second approach where legitimate expectations are at best one of several components of FET, applies to a broader range of contractual breaches. A State that abruptly cancels an investment contract between an investor and a State entity may not have given any specific undertaking to induce the investor. Here, even if the investor cannot show that the breach of contract was a breach of legitimate expectations, it may, depending on the facts, have an arguable case for arbitrariness, or lack of due process, in their various manifestations. Moreover, the content of FET can evolve over time. For example, although earlier arbitral awards do not include freedom from coercion and harassment in the formulation of FET, recent arbitral awards and academic commentary expressly acknowledge it as a feature of FET.[105] As Section 3.4 will show, contractual breaches that have formed the basis of an FET claim take many different forms. In this regard, the second approach, which recognises that the content of FET may vary over time and from case to case is preferable for contract-based FET claims. Not all forms of contractual breaches can be assimilated to breaches of legitimate expectations.

One result of tribunals hearing contract-based FET claims favouring the second approach where FET comprises different components, is

---

[103] See for instance *Duke Energy Electroquil Partners and Anor* v. *Ecuador*, ICSID Case No. ARB/04/19, Award, 18 August 2008 (Kaufmann-Kohler, Pinzón, van den Berg), para. 340: '[S]uch expectations must arise from the conditions that the State offered the investor and the latter must have relied upon them when deciding to invest.'

[104] Schreuer, 'Fair and Equitable Treatment (FET)', p. 90.

[105] See for instance *Ioan Micula* v. *Romania*, Award, para. 519; Dolzer and Schreuer, *Principles of International Investment Law*, pp. 159–60.

the broad alignment of the FET standard for contractual protection and the core standard for contractual protection. Another result is the possibility of developing the content of FET, given the contemporary ring of certain aggravating circumstances, such as orchestrated campaigns of coercion and harassment by the host State, that can accompany a breach of contract.[106]

3.3.2   *The Return to the Minimum Standard of Treatment*

Concerns that some arbitral tribunals use their interpretive license to give an overly expansive meaning to FET that captured even minor infringements of investor protection, prompted some States to reconsider the wisdom of concluding investment treaties with open-textured FET clauses. Arbitral tribunals that saw fit to reduce FET to the single component of legitimate expectations, were usually interpreting open-textured FET clauses which presented FET as an autonomous standard of international law whose content had neither precedent nor peer.[107] Be that as it may, the prevailing interpretive approach, as discussed earlier, assigns several components to FET, one of which may be respect for legitimate expectations. The more settled components though, are non-arbitrariness and due process, which are also the anchor components of the core standard for contractual protection. Therefore, even before more States began clarifying the content of FET in newer generation investment treaties, a considerable

---

[106]   In McLachlan's words, '[t]he result is a convergence, on these issues, between treaty practice and custom, in which the modern understanding of the content of the customary right is being elaborated primarily through the treaty jurisprudence', 'Investment Treaties and General International Law', p. 394.

[107]   See for instance Art. 3(1) of the Agreement on Encouragement and Reciprocal Protection of Investments between the Kingdom of the Netherlands and the Czech and Slovak Federal Republic (signed 29 April 1991, entered into force 1 October 1992) which directs Contracting States to 'ensure fair and equitable treatment to the investments of investors of the other Contracting Party'. The *Saluka* tribunal held that FET is 'closely tied to the notion of legitimate expectations which is the dominant element of that standard', para. 302, see also discussion Section 2.1.1. Arbitral tribunals that have adopted the *Saluka* formulation of FET include *Suez, Sociedad General de Aguas de Barcelona, S.A. and Anor.* v. *Argentine Republic*, ICSID Case No. ARB/03/17, Decision on Liability, 30 July 2010 (Salacuse, Kaufmann-Kohler, Nikken), para. 223, also 224–6; *El Paso Energy International Company* v. *Argentina*, ICSID Case No. ARB/03/15, Award, 31 October 2011 (Caflisch, Bernadini, Stern), para. 348; and *Ioan Micula and Ors* v. *Romania*, ICSID Case No. ARB/05/20, Award, 11 December 2013 (Lévy, Alexandrov, Abi-Saab), para. 667 (fn. 133). The notable exception is *International Thunderbird Gaming Corporation* v. *Mexico*, para. 147, where the tribunal reduced the explicitly MST-aligned FET in NAFTA Art. 1105 to the single component of legitimate expectations.

number of arbitral awards imparting content to FET already favoured a return to MST.

The World Investment Reports of 2015, 2016 and 2017 surveyed fifty-seven investment protection agreements concluded between 2014 and 2016, and noted a treaty-making trend where '[f]air and equitable treatment [was] equated to the minimum standard of treatment of aliens under customary international law'.[108] The 2015 Report identified two policy objectives driving this trend. The first is the '[p]reserv[ation] [of] the right to regulate in the public interest'.[109] The second is the '[a]void[ance] [of] overexposure to litigation'.[110] The 2017 Report observed that some of the newest investment protection agreements contained 'unique, innovative features', which include 'specifying that the mere act of taking, or the failure to take, an action that may be inconsistent with an investor's expectations does not constitute a breach of FET, even if it results in loss or damage to the investment'.[111] By expressly linking FET to the minimum standard for alien protection, and by expressly excluding the preservation of investor expectations as a component of FET, the new generation of investment protection agreements reinforce the equation between FET on contractual protection and the core standard on contractual protection. Two of the most notable among them are mega-regional agreements, so called because they represent regional groupings of three or more States who collectively account for more than 25 per cent of world trade.[112]

The only mega-regional agreement currently in force is the Comprehensive Economic and Trade Agreement between Canada and the European Union.[113] Articles 8.10(1), 8.10(2) and 8.10(3) of the CETA provide:

(1) Each Party shall accord in its territory to covered investments of the other Party and to investors with respect to their covered investments

---

[108] UNCTAD, 'World Investment Report 2015', online: unctad.org/en/PublicationsLibrary/wir2015_en.pdf (accessed 31 December 2017), p. 113; 'World Investment Report 2016', online: unctad.org/en/PublicationsLibrary/wir2016_en.pdf (accessed 31 December 2017), p. 113; and 'World Investment Report 2017', online: unctad.org/en/PublicationsLibrary/wir2017_en.pdf (accessed 31 December 2017), p. 121.

[109] 'World Investment Report 2015', p. 113.

[110] Ibid., p. 113.

[111] Ibid., p. 120. The 2016 Report did not comment specifically on new generation FET clauses.

[112] P. Draper, S. Lacey and Y. Ramkolowan, 'Mega-Regional Trade Agreements: Implications for the African, Caribbean, and Pacific Countries', ECIPE Occasional Paper No 2/2014, online: www.ecipe.org (accessed 31 December 2017), p. 8.

[113] Signed 30 October 2016, provisionally entered into force 21 September 2017.

fair and equitable treatment and full protection and security in accordance with paragraphs 2 through 7.

(2) A Party breaches the obligation of fair and equitable treatment referenced in paragraph 1 if a measure or series of measures constitutes:

    (a) denial of justice in criminal, civil or administrative proceedings;

    (b) fundamental breach of due process, including a fundamental breach of transparency, in judicial and administrative proceedings;

    (c) manifest arbitrariness;

    (d) targeted discrimination on manifestly wrongful grounds, such as gender, race or religious belief;

    (e) abusive treatment of investors, such as coercion, duress and harassment; or

    (f) a breach of any further elements of the fair and equitable treatment obligation adopted by the Parties in accordance with paragraph 3 of this Article.

(3) The Parties shall regularly, or upon request of a Party, review the content of the obligation to provide fair and equitable treatment. The Committee on Services and Investment, established under Article 26.2.1(b) (Specialised committees), may develop recommendations in this regard and submit them to the CETA Joint Committee for decision.

The mega-regional whose projected entry into force by 2018 was derailed by US withdrawal from the pact concluded with eleven other countries,[114] is the Trans-Pacific Partnership (TPP).[115] Articles 9.6(1), 9.6(2)(a), 9.6(4) and 9.6(5) of the TPP provide:

(1) Each Party shall accord to covered investments treatment in accordance with applicable customary international law principles, including fair and equitable treatment and full protection and security.

(2) For greater certainty, paragraph 1 prescribes the customary international law MST of aliens as the standard of treatment to be afforded to covered investments. The concepts of 'fair and equitable treatment' and 'full protection and security' do not require treatment in addition to or beyond that which is required by that standard, and do not

---

[114] These countries are Australia, Brunei Darussalam, Canada, Chile, Japan, Malaysia, Mexico, New Zealand, Peru, Singapore and Vietnam.

[115] Signed 4 February 2016, not yet in force. The eleven remaining TPP signatories have agreed to conclude the Comprehensive Agreement for Trans-Pacific Partnership (CPTPP). This development is current as of 31 January 2018.

create additional substantive rights. The obligations in paragraph 1 to provide:

(a) 'fair and equitable treatment' includes the obligation not to deny justice in criminal, civil or administrative adjudicatory proceedings in accordance with the principle of due process embodied in the principal legal systems of the world ...

(4) For greater certainty, the mere fact that a Party takes or fails to take an action that may be inconsistent with an investor's expectations does not constitute a breach of this Article, even if there is loss or damage to the covered investment as a result.

(5) For greater certainty, the mere fact that a subsidy or grant has not been issued, renewed or maintained, or has been modified or reduced, by a Party, does not constitute a breach of this Article, even if there is loss or damage to the covered investment as a result.

CETA Article 8.10 and TPP Article 9.6 align FET and MST in different ways. CETA Article 8.10 enshrines FET as a multi-component treatment standard, thereby precluding any attempt to reduce the content of FET to a single component, like the protection of legitimate expectations. It identifies 'fundamental breach of due process' (Article 8.10(2)(b)) and 'manifest arbitrariness' (Article 8.10(2)(c)), the two anchor components of the core standard for contractual protection, as discrete components of FET. It also identifies denial of justice in judicial and administrative proceedings (Article 8.10(2)(a)) and discrimination on wrongful grounds (Article 8.10(2)(d)), which can be subsumed under the broader rubric of denial of justice to aliens,[116] as components of FET. Finally, CETA Article 8.10 caters for content development, notwithstanding the alignment of FET to MST. It identifies the abusive treatment of investors (Article 8.10(2)(e)), which was not considered in older arbitral awards that contributed to the formulation of the core standard for contractual protection, as an aggravating circumstance that will establish the violation of FET. It also empowers the Contracting Parties to supplement or revise the current list of components that define FET (Articles 8.10(2)(f) and 8.10(3)), allowing the content of FET as MST to evolve over time. In contrast, TPP Article 9.6 expressly links FET to 'the customary international law minimum standard of treatment of aliens' (Article 9.6(2)), without articulating a complete list of

---

[116] M. S. McDougal, L-C. Chen and H. D. Laswell, 'The Protection of Aliens from Discrimination and World Public Order: Responsibility of States Conjoined with Human Rights' (1976) 70 AJIL 432 at 433–7 and 443.

different components. Included in the list, though, is 'the obligation not to deny justice in criminal, civil or administrative adjudicatory proceedings in accordance with the principle of due process' (Article 9.6(2)(a)), which, like CETA Article 8.10(2)(a), is a subset of the broader category of denial of justice to aliens encompassing State acts other than those associated with adjudicatory functions. And given the reference to MST, the Article 9.6 list should also include non-arbitrariness and respect for due process in the carrying out of non-adjudicatory acts by States.[117] Finally, Article 9.6 expressly excludes frustrated investor expectations (Article 9.6(4)), and the non-issuance, non-maintenance and non-renewal of grants and subsidies (Article 9.6(5)), as possible grounds for FET violation, forestalling dilution of FET as MST through expansive interpretations of FET.

Even with the general alignment of FET to MST, defining the core standard of treatment for contracts through a list of components whose content and level of detail may vary from one tribunal to the next, may render unpredictable whether a breach of contract amounts to a violation of the core standard of treatment. Arbitral tribunals can nonetheless obtain some guidance from earlier arbitral awards. It is possible to glean from existing arbitral *jurisprudence* different categories of contractual breaches that tribunals may be inclined to regard as a violation of the core standard of treatment. How each of these categories may implicate aggravating circumstances that entail a finding of State responsibility for a breach of contract, is where the discussion now turns.

3.4   Contractual Breaches That Violate the Core Standard of Treatment

As with all findings of State responsibility when host State conduct is measured against international standards, the devil lurks in the details. It is not

---

[117] One example of a non-adjudicatory act by a State that can be tested for propriety against due process is the unilateral cancellation of an investment contract, see Section 3.4.5. On the rare occasion when an FET clause limits claims to those arising from a denial of justice in adjudicatory proceedings, it appears that non-adjudicatory acts, even if arbitrary or lacking in due process, cannot amount to a violation of FET, see Association of South East Asian Nations (ASEAN) Comprehensive Investment Agreement (signed 26 February 2009, entered into force 24 February 2012) ('ACIA'), Art. 11(2)(a): 'For greater certainty: fair and equitable treatment requires each Member State not to deny justice in any legal or administrative proceedings in accordance with the principle of due process'. Unlike TPP Art. 9.6(2)(a), which conveys that denial of justice in adjudicatory proceedings is *one of several possible components* of FET, ACIA Art. 11(2)(a) identifies denial of justice in adjudicatory proceedings as *the only component* of FET.

always easy to tell when State conduct crosses the line and becomes internationally wrongful. To understand why a breach of contract may be considered a violation of the core standard of treatment in one case but not in another, it is necessary to situate the breach in its proper factual context. Yet, one may disagree with the significance attached to certain factual occurrences by the arbitral tribunal, and consequently, with the outcome of the claim. Based on earlier arbitral awards, most of which address contract-based FET claims, contractual breaches underlying claims alleging the violation of the core standard of treatment tend to fall into one of five categories: non-payment (Section 3.4.1); cumulative acts and omissions (Section 3.4.2); breaches committed in a sovereign capacity (Section 3.4.3); forced renegotiation (Section 3.4.4); and cancellation (Section 3.4.5). When discussing the different categories of contractual breaches that may give rise to a violation of the core standard of treatment, a closer examination of the facts of each case is unavoidable. What these categories convey is the variety of ways that contract-based international claims can come about; they do not suggest that a breach of contract must fall within a particular category to violate the core standard of treatment. So long as a breach of contract implicates one of the established components of the core standard of treatment, such as non-arbitrariness or respect for due process, discussed in the preceding sections, the investor has an arguable claim.

3.4.1   Non-payment

Before investors had the opportunity to bring FET claims against host States for contractual breaches, arbitral tribunals rarely determined the legality of contractual non-payment by host States in accordance with the core standard of treatment. Prior to the proliferation of investment treaties, contract claims were typically presented by home States to host States either through diplomatic channels,[118] or before Mixed Claims Commissions.[119] Home States rarely invoked international law in diplomatic correspondence when attempting to secure payment on behalf of their nationals from defaulting host States,[120] while Mixed Claims Commissions rarely applied

---

[118] See discussion at Chapter 1, Section 1.2.

[119] See discussion at Chapter 1, Section 1.3.

[120] See for instance *Réclamation Pemarchan, Lettre du Consulat Général de France au Vénézuéla à Monsieur le Ministre des Affaires Etrangères* (4 December 1869), Archives Diplomatiques La Courneuve, 752SUP/476; *Réclamation Buisson, Lettre du Ministre de France au Brésil à Son Excellence Monsieur le Ministre des Affaires Etrangères* (22 December 1913), Archives Diplomatiques La Courneuve, 144CPCOM/104; *Réclamation Taximètre*

international law to decide claims brought by home States on behalf of their nationals against host States for defaulting on payment due under a contract.[121] The dearth of earlier discussions on the engagement of State responsibility for contractual non-payment, deferred the issue of whether and when contractual non-payment violates the core standard of treatment to arbitral tribunals hearing contract-based FET claims.

Arbitral tribunals appear to agree that contractual non-payment, in and of itself, cannot amount to a violation of FET.[122] But arbitral *jurisprudence* is less instructive on whether aggravating circumstances need to be present for non-payment to be internationally wrongful, and what they might be. The arbitral tribunals in *Bureau Veritas, Inspection, Valuation, Assessment and Control, BIVAC B.V.* v. *The Republic of Paraguay*,[123] and *SGS Société Générale de Surveillance S.A.* v. *Republic of the Philippines* did not rule out the possibility that contractual non-payment can violate FET, but did not clearly link internationally wrongful non-payment to one or more established component/s of FET.[124] In contrast, the arbitral tribunal in *SGS Société Générale de Surveillance S.A.* v. *The Republic of Paraguay*

(Argentine), *Note Interne du Ministère des Affaires Etrangères* (17 November 1917), Archives Diplomatiques La Courneuve, 137CPCOM/42; *Réclamation La Maison Bos, Lettre du Consulat des Pays-Bas de Messine provisoirement à Palerme à Son Excellence Ministre Plenipotentiaire des Pays-Bas à Rome* (27 January 1912), Nationaal Archief Den Haag, 2.05.26/781; cf. *Réclamation Sabatier, Lettre du Consul Général de Hollande à Singapour au Consul de France à Singapour* (28 March 1911), Archives Diplomatiques La Courneuve, 138CPCOM/6; *Réclamation Derbès, Note Interne du Ministère des Affaires Etrangères* (26 April 1911), Archives Diplomatiques La Courneuve, 144CPCOM/103.

[121] See for instance *Illinois Central Railroad Company, George W. Cook, Singer Sewing Machine Co. (USA v. United Mexican States)* (1928) 4 RIAA 411; *American Bottle Company (USA v. United Mexican States)* (1929) 4 RIAA 435; cf. *Chattin Claim*, p. 287. As pointed out in Section 3.2, the presiding commissioner in the *Chattin Claim* was wrong to rely on *Illinois Central Railroad Company* as authority for the proposition that 'the non-performance of government contracts', which naturally encompasses non-payment, automatically engages a host State's international responsibility. The Commission in *Illinois Central Railroad Company* clarified that the contract claim presented by the United States, which concerned Mexico's liability to make payment due under a sale and purchase contract, did not involve the 'international responsibility of governments', p. 23.

[122] *Biwater Gauff (Tanzania) Ltd.* v. *United Republic of Tanzania*, ICSID Case No. ARB/05/22, Award, 24 July 2008 (Hanotiau, Born, Landau), para. 602. This formulation was adopted in *Walter Bau* v. *Thailand*, UNCITRAL, Award, 1 July 2009 (Barker, Lalonde, Bunnag), paras. 635–6.

[123] ICSID Case No. ARB/07/9, Decision of the Tribunal on Objections to Jurisdiction, 29 May 2009 (Knieper, Fortier, Sands), paras. 125–6.

[124] ICSID Case No. ARB/02/6, Decision of the Tribunal on Objections to Jurisdiction, 29 January 2004 (El-Kosheri, Crawford, Crivellaro (partially dissenting)), para. 162.

implicitly accepted that contractual non-payment violates FET if there is proof of bad faith and arbitrariness.[125]

The tribunal in *BIVAC* v. *Paraguay* left open the question of whether 'a persistent failure to make payment on an outstanding debt, no matter how unreasonable or unwarranted, could of itself ever amount to a violation of the obligation to provide fair and equitable treatment in circumstances in which a contractually agreed remedy remains available'.[126] This case involved a claim for unpaid invoices issued pursuant to customs inspections services rendered. Proceedings have been stayed after the tribunal recommended that BIVAC submit its claim against Paraguay to the courts in Asunción.[127] The tribunal in *SGS* v. *Philippines* also found that a failure to pay might be a breach of FET. This was another case on unpaid invoices for customs inspection services rendered. According to this tribunal, 'an unjustified refusal to pay sums admittedly payable under an award or a contract at least raises arguable issues under [an FET clause]'.[128] That said, the tribunal did not proceed to hear the merits of this claim. The claimant, bound by an exclusive jurisdiction clause in the contract, subsequently submitted its claim to the Filipino courts for adjudication. The tribunal then awarded the claimant the exact amount that a Filipino court found was owed by the Philippines under the contract. Neither the *BIVAC* nor the *SGS* v. *Philippines* tribunal referred to the various components of FET, as identified in earlier arbitral awards, when signalling the potential for contractual non-payment to violate FET. Instead, both tribunals took the view that when contractual non-payment is demonstrably 'unreasonable or unwarranted' or 'unjustified', there is a tenable, as opposed to a winning, FET claim. Neither tribunal identified aggravating circumstances that can accompany contractual non-payment, and which can turn a tenable FET claim into a winning one.

In *SGS* v. *Paraguay*, the arbitral tribunal held that an FET claim should be heard on the merits when 'Claimant's allegations with respect to unfair or inequitable treatment by Paraguay extend beyond mere non-payment in breach of the Contract'.[129] By reciting SGS's allegations that Paraguay

---

[125] ICSID Case No. ARB/07/29, Award (Alexandrov, Donovan, Mexia), 10 February 2012, incorporating the Decision on Jurisdiction (Alexandrov, Donovan, Mexiá), 12 February 2010, para. 150.

[126] Decision of the Tribunal on Objections to Jurisdiction, paras. 125–6.

[127] ICSID Case No. ARB/07/9, Further Decision on Objections to Jurisdiction, 9 October 2012 (Knieper, Fortier, Sands), para. 294(c).

[128] Decision of the Tribunal on Objections to Jurisdiction, para. 162.

[129] Decision on Jurisdiction, para. 150.

'acted in bad faith, capriciously, arbitrarily and in a non-transparent manner towards SGS' by refusing to compensate SGS for services rendered
under a customs inspection contract,[130] and by reserving judgment on
the success of the FET claim until SGS proves its allegations, the arbitral
tribunal implicitly accepted that SGS's catalogue of allegations is a list of
discrete aggravating circumstances that should accompany contractual
non-payment for an FET claim to prevail. Arbitrariness, which is synonymous with caprice and non-transparent conduct, is an anchor component
of FET, while bad faith conduct, although hard to prove, undeniably violates FET. The arbitral award rendered in SGS v. Paraguay has been called
'[t]he high-water mark for interpreting the fair and equitable standard of
treatment in respect of an investment-as-contract', for its supposed elevation of simple contractual non-payment to a violation of FET.[131] This
characterisation is not borne out by the analysis in the award. Although
the arbitral tribunal did not explore how Paraguay's non-payment was a
demonstration of bad faith or arbitrariness at the merits stage, this was due
to SGS's withdrawal of its FET claim, and not the result of any noticeable
inclination on the part of the tribunal to regard contractual non-payment,
in the absence of aggravating circumstances, as an FET violation.[132]

Construing non-payment as a violation of FET can be challenging
because it is not entirely clear which FET component non-payment readily implicates. An 'unjustified refusal to pay', in the words of the SGS v.
Philippines tribunal, may denote arbitrariness or bad faith. Yet, the inability to demonstrate that a host State defaulting on payment due under a
contract is arbitrary, or an act of bad faith, may be the reason why the
claimant in SGS v. Paraguay withdrew its FET claim. It is not unusual for
a host State facing genuine financial difficulties to default on its contractual payments. In this regard, the Waste Management (No. 2) tribunal dis-
couraged 'resort to conspiracy theories, unsupported by solid evidence',
to accuse a host State of setting out to 'destroy or frustrate the investment
by improper means'.[133] When non-payment is neither arbitrary nor an act
of bad faith, an aggrieved investor committed to bringing an FET claim
may be compelled to argue that non-payment frustrates legitimate expectations for payment due under a contract. That said, even if legitimate

---

[130] Decision on Jurisdiction, para. 149; see also para. 147.
[131] Douglas, The International Law on Investment Claims, p. 390. This comment was made in
        light of Douglas' prediction that contract-based FET claims are, on the whole, unlikely to
        succeed. The finding of SGS v. Paraguay tribunal, in Douglas' view, probably went too far.
[132] See also Award, para. 146.
[133] Award, paras. 138–9.

expectations are a stand-alone component of FET, which a sizeable number of tribunals do not accept, it is questionable if an expectation to be paid for services or works rendered qualifies as a legitimate expectation. According to Schreuer's definition of FET-protected legitimate expectations, an expectation regarding payment due under a contract is probably not a protected expectation. As non-payment is a common and recurrent feature of economic life, its impact on the security and stability of a legal framework is likely to be minimal. The arbitral tribunal in *Biwater* v. *Tanzania* was also sceptical that payment-related expectations are protected by an FET clause. According to the tribunal, an investor can entertain no greater expectation to be paid promptly by a State or State entities than by an individual because 'Government institutions were to be treated as any other customer'.[134] On the facts of *Biwater* v. *Tanzania*, payment from some Government institutions was forthcoming once the claimant, who contracted to provide water distribution services, cut off their water supply. Due to the remedy of self-help on which the claimant relied, 'arrears in their payments is not sufficient to establish a breach by [Tanzania] of the fair and equitable treatment principle'.[135]

The ensemble of arbitral awards on non-payment contract-based FET claims permits two deductions. First, if claimants are swift to allege but often struggle to prove that contractual non-payment was accompanied by aggravating circumstances, a breach of contract for non-payment is unlikely to violate the core standard of treatment. Second, even if respect for legitimate expectations is a discrete component of FET, payment-related expectations are unlikely to be regarded as legitimate expectations that benefit from FET protection, and whose frustration is a violation of FET.

3.4.2   Cumulative Acts and Omissions

Like non-payment, cumulative acts and omissions took shape as a distinct category of contractual breach that potentially violates the core standard of treatment with the appearance of contract-based FET claims. Modern investment projects can be extremely complex endeavours. From sophisticated investment and financing structures, to mandatory performance and periodic reporting requirements under updated host State legislation or extremely detailed investment contracts, to protracted, multiple or recurrent administrative procedures associated with the issuance or renewal of

---

[134] Award, para. 635.
[135] Award, para. 635.

permits, licenses and authorisations, an investment is the sum of many moving parts. A one-off delay on the part of the host State in the issuance of one of several licenses an investor requires to operate the investment, for instance, may not arouse suspicion. But repeated episodes of delay at different junctures during the life cycle of the investment may seriously hamper the investor from performing its end of the contractual bargain and reaping the benefit of its investment. Therefore, in finding an FET violation through the totality of a host State's actions and omissions towards a protected investment, tribunals try to discern conscious and concerted effort by the host State over an extended period of time to put the foreign investor out of business.[136] The situation here is different from an outright cancellation, the subject of Section 3.4.5, because the investment contract is usually kept alive in form, but gradually stripped of value in substance.

Arbitral tribunals have found that the giving of false assurances by government officials, or the persistent failure by the host State to respect the terms of a renegotiated investment contract violate FET. The investor in *Metalclad Corporation* v. *The United Mexican States* was repeatedly assured by the federal government that a construction permit from the municipal government where a hazardous landfill project was supposed to take place will be awarded, and that construction works could proceed in the meantime. Contrary to the assurances the investor received, the permit was denied, and the construction works brought to a standstill. The tribunal found that Mexico's failure to 'ensure a transparent and predictable framework for Metalclad's business planning and investment … demonstrates a lack of orderly process and timely disposition in relation to an investor of a Party acting in the expectation that it would be treated fairly

---

[136] The cumulative acts and omission referred to in this section can be likened to 'creeping violations of the FET standard', enunciated in *El Paso* v. *Argentina*, Award, para. 518, as 'a succession or an accumulation of measures which, taken separately, would not breach that standard but, when taken together, do lead to such a result'. On Argentina's application for annulment, the ad hoc Committee held that '[p]aragraph 518 is not the basis for the conclusion that the Tribunal reached in paragraph 519 of the Award, in which it found that there had been a violation of fair and equitable treatment by the cumulative effects of the measures adopted by Argentina. Thus, there was no creation of a new standard nor was another law applied to the case', ICSID Case No. ARB/03/15, Decision of the ad hoc Committee on the Application for Annulment of The Argentine Republic, 22 September 2014 (Oreamuno, Cheng, Knieper), para. 182. The novelty of 'creeping' FET violations, drawn from 'creeping' expropriations, awaits further exploration. For a brief critique, see S. Vesel, 'A "Creeping" Violation of the Fair and Equitable Treatment Standard?' (2014) 30(3) *Arbitration International* 553.

and justly'.[137] Therefore, the FET component that Mexico's cumulative acts and omissions towards Metalclad implicate is arbitrariness. In *Walter Bau v. Thailand*, a highway construction contract was modified with the agreement of the parties and Thailand undertook to raise toll fees for the use of the highway.[138] Despite repeated requests by the concessionaire, in which the claimant was a minority shareholder, to increase tolls, Thailand refused to do so. In addition, Thailand made important changes to the roading network, such as increasing the capacity and service levels of adjacent toll-free roads, that diverted traffic as well as profits away from the newly constructed highway. The temporary closure of a nearby airport also reduced traffic flow on the highway. The prolonged refusal to raise highway tolls was arguably explicable in light of the government's hesitation to incur public discontent,[139] but having negotiated a toll increase with the concessionaire, it was arbitrary for the government to then reduce tolls in contravention of its contractual commitment.[140] The claimant's expectations for a 'reasonable rate of return' on its investment were, in the tribunal's view, 'legitimate expectations [which] are definitely part of FET'.[141] The tribunal found that the toll decrease, traffic re-routing and airport closure amounted to 'a series of cumulative acts and omissions [where] [o]ne of these may not on its own be enough, but taken together, they can constitute a breach of FET obligations'.[142]

Acts and omissions that involve the use of regulatory power may tilt the balance in favour of the investor bringing the FET claim, as the *Impregilo S.p.A.* v. *Argentine Republic* and *SAUR International SA* v. *Republic of Argentina* awards illustrate. Both awards addressed the question of whether the emergency economic measures taken by Argentina, which greatly impaired the investment of water concessionaires, violated FET. The *Impregilo* v. *Argentina* tribunal applied the 'fair and equitable treatment standard based on a theory of legitimate expectations', adding that 'conduct in the exercise of sovereign powers' was required for a violation of FET.[143] It held that the various acts and omissions committed in the provincial government's capacity as a contracting party may have breached

---

[137] ICSID Case No. ARB(AF)/97/1, Award, 30 August 2000 (Lauterpacht, Civiletti, Siqueiros), para. 99.
[138] Award, para. 12.14.
[139] Award, para. 6.7.
[140] Award, para. 12.26.
[141] Award, para. 12.1.
[142] Award, para. 12.4.
[143] ICSID Case No. ARB/07/17, Award, 21 June 2011 (Danelius, Brower, Stern), para. 294.

the concession, but did not violate FET because there was no misuse of public power. Argentina's refusal to renegotiate the terms of the concession after its adjustment of the currency exchange rate, when renegotiation was clearly an option that could have kept the claimant financially afloat, was a misuse of regulatory power, a breach of the claimant's legitimate expectations for a reasonable rate of return on its investment, and a violation of FET.[144] The *SAUR* v. *Argentina* tribunal found that inordinate delays on the part of the provincial government in implementing the changes in a renegotiated water concession led to the claimant's 'financial asphyxiation' and the eventual termination of the water concession.[145] By doing so, the provincial government had exercised its regulatory power in a manner that violates FET. The *SAUR* v. *Argentina* tribunal did not refer to any particular component or components of FET when evaluating the claim. But by stressing that the delays were 'excessive', 'without justification' and 'deliberate', the tribunal came very close to saying that Argentina's treatment of SAUR was arbitrary. Even though the proper use of regulatory power is not widely recognised as a stand-alone component of FET, it may be possible, after *Impregilo* v. *Argentina* and *SAUR* v. *Argentina*, to subsume the misuse of regulatory power under the more established component of non-arbitrariness, or the more controversial component of legitimate expectations.

Cumulative acts and omissions can also take a more sinister turn. In *Anatolie Stati and Ors* v. *Kazakhstan*, the tribunal characterised the actions taken by Kazakhstan pursuant to a presidential order to investigate the claimants' accounts and activities in relation to the performance of a hydrocarbon concession as 'a string of measures of coordinated harassment by various institutions of the Respondent and has to be considered as a breach of the obligation to treaty investors fairly and equitably'.[146] The concession was granted in 2002 and the campaign of harassment began at the end of 2008 when, according to the claimants, Kazakhstan wanted to acquire the concession for the State-owned oil company at a fire-sale price.[147] These measures included the financial police compelling various Kazakh authorities to agree with its seemingly arbitrary assessment that

---

[144] Award, paras. 298–309.
[145] Affaire CIRDI No. ARB/04/4, Décision sur La Compétence et sur la Responsabilité, 6 June 2012 (Fernández-Armesto, Hanotiau, Tomuschat), para. 506. Author's translation from the original French.
[146] SCC Arbitration V (116/2010), Award, 19 December 2013 (Böckstiegel, Haigh, Lebedev), para. 1086.
[147] Award, ibid., para. 2.

the claimants were using an unauthorised pipeline system to transport gas, incessant and duplicate inspections carried out by seven different Kazakh agencies which forced the claimants to halt normal operations without the possibility of seeking remedies, trumped-up criminal charges against the claimants' employees for engaging in 'illegal entrepreneurial activity', and deliberate foiling by the president's influential son-in-law of the claimants' attempts to secure gas sales, export rights and crucial financing.[148] Kazakhstan's 'coordinated harassment' of the investor was a clear violation of FET, because it flouted both the anchor components of non-arbitrariness and respect for due process.

3.4.3 Acta Iure Imperii

As discussed in Section 3.2, contractual breaches *iure imperii* unaccompanied by compensation for injury suffered or prospect of redress violate the core standard for contractual protection. The unilateral cancellation of a concession by legislative decree without compensation, as seen in the *Shufeldt Claim*, and the revocation of a public tender by executive decree and subsequent denial of judicial redress by the combined efforts of the executive and legislature, as seen in the *Brown Claim*, are examples of internationally wrongful contractual breaches *iure imperii*.[149] While older arbitral awards blend *acta iure imperii* with the absence of compensation and genuine prospect of redress into a suite of aggravating circumstances that turn a breach of contract into a violation of the core standard of treatment, more recent arbitral awards showcase the uncertainty that the application of this tried-and-tested formula to contract-based FET claims may engender.

A number of arbitral tribunals hearing contract-based FET claims readily accept that contractual breaches *iure imperii* potentially violate FET.[150] This calls for a determination on whether the contractual breach in question was committed in the State's sovereign capacity (*iure imperii*) or

---

[148] Award, ibid., paras. 1089–95.

[149] See also *Delagoa Bay Railway Arbitration*, *Cheek Claim*, and *Claim of the George D. Emery Co.*, at note 46.

[150] *Duke Energy Electroquil Partners and Anor* v. *Ecuador*, ICSID Case No. ARB/04/19, Award, 18 August 2008 (Kaufmann-Kohler, Pinzón, van den Berg), para. 345; also *Consortium RFCC c. Royaume du Maroc*, Affaire CIRDI No. ARB/00/6, Sentence Arbitrale, 22 December 2003 (Briner, Cremades, Fadlallah), para. 51; *Impregilo SpA* v. *Pakistan*, ICSID Case No. ARB/03/3, Decision on Jurisdiction, 22 April 2005 (Guillaume, Cremades, Landau), para. 260; *Siemens AG* v. *Argentina*, ICSID Case No. ARB/02/8, Award, 6 February 2007 (Sureda, Brower, Janeiro), para. 308.

non-sovereign capacity (*iure gestionis*). In some cases, the use of sovereign prerogatives like legislative and executive decrees to interfere with a contract is apparent.[151] In other cases, whether State conduct should be classified as sovereign or non-sovereign is less clear-cut. Yet, arbitral tribunals hearing contract-based FET claims offer little explanation for their chosen classification. Two arbitral awards which illustrate the difficulty of telling contractual breaches *iure imperii* apart from contractual breaches *iure gestionis* are *Toto Costruzioni Generali S.p.A.* v. *The Republic of Lebanon*, and *Bayindir Insaat Turizm Ticaret Ve Sanayi A.S.* v. *Islamic Republic of Pakistan*.

In *Toto* v. *Lebanon*, the host State undertook to carry out expropriations of various parcels of land in preparation for the execution of a highway construction contract which it concluded with the claimant. The expropriations were delayed and the claimant argued that the delay amounted to a violation of FET. The tribunal rejected this argument as it 'fail[ed] to see how Toto could have legitimately expected that the parcels would be expropriated earlier than they actually were'.[152] Although the tribunal agreed that 'only when the State acted as sovereign authority – and not merely as a contracting partner – was there treaty protection of fair and equitable treatment',[153] it is not entirely clear if delayed expropriations are a breach of contract *iure gestionis*. While a delay in contractual performance may be committed by any contracting party, both sovereign and non-sovereign, it is at least arguable that when contractual performance involves the exercise of sovereign power to expropriate property, a delay in contractual performance in this particular situation can be construed as a breach of contract *iure imperii*. It is hardly self-evident, as the tribunal's brief discussion seems to suggest, that a delay in the performance of a sovereign function which adversely affects the claimant's performance of its own contractual obligations, and results in uncompensated financial injury, is nonetheless FET-compliant.

In *Bayindir* v. *Pakistan*, one of the grounds raised by Bayindir in its FET claim was the forcible expulsion of its personnel from their offices and the site of the construction works. The tribunal held that 'Pakistan can reasonably justify the expulsion by Bayindir's poor performance ... with the consequence that the expulsion must be seen in the framework of the

---

[151] *Inmaris Perestroika Sailing Maritime Services GmbH and Others* v. *Ukraine*, ICSID Case No. ARB/08/8, Excerpts of Award, 1 March 2012 (Alexandrov, Rubins, Cremades), paras. 273–5.

[152] ICSID Case No. ARB/07/12, Award, 7 June 2012 (van Houtte, Schwebel, Moghaizel), para. 162.

[153] Award, ibid., para. 162.

contractual relationship, not as an exercise of sovereign power'.[154] Bayindir's expulsion was secured by the presence of the Pakistani army, which was mobilised to evict Bayindir's personnel from the work site. It is not easy to see why army mobilisation is not an exercise of sovereign power and the tribunal did not elaborate on this point when discussing Bayindir's FET claim. The tenor of its analysis implied that as Bayindir chose to continue performing the contract despite the major political changes occurring in Pakistan which put the longevity of its project in jeopardy, it bore the risk of having its contract terminated by whatever means, including forcible expulsion by government troops, and could not benefit from the protection conferred by an FET clause.[155] This in turn suggests that whether a breach of contract was committed in a sovereign or non-sovereign capacity was not pivotal to the success or failure of Bayindir's FET claim.

Given the propensity for disagreement over the sovereign or non-sovereign character of contractual breaches, applying the *acta iure imperii–acta iure gestionis* distinction to contract-based FET claims adds considerable uncertainty to the scope of contractual protection under a given FET clause. As the FET standard covers the entire spectrum of host State conduct, and not just sovereign acts, it may not be necessary to distinguish between contractual breaches carried out in a sovereign capacity and those that are not when assessing host State compliance with FET. A breach of contract violates FET because it flouts one or more of the components of FET, like non-arbitrariness or due process, whether or not it constitutes a sovereign act. No arbitral tribunal or commentator has acknowledged sovereign acts as a component of FET because the exercise of sovereign prerogatives is not inherently incompatible with FET. Therefore, when referring to contractual breaches *iure imperii* in connection with the core standard of treatment, it is the absence of compensation and redress for injury caused that aggravate the injury inflicted by *acta iure imperii*, and that elevate the contractual breach to a violation of international law. Some tribunals nonetheless insist on viewing the *acta iure imperii-acta iure gestionis* distinction as a preliminary filter for contract-based FET claims, possibly to limit the number of successful claims. For these tribunals, the *acta iure imperii–acta iure gestionis* distinction may be a precaution against the casual engagement of State responsibility for contractual breaches.

---

[154] ICSID Case No. ARB/03/29, Award, 27 August 2009 (Kaufmann-Kohler, Berman, Böckstiegel), para. 461.
[155] Award, ibid., paras. 184–90.

To add to the uncertainty, there is a possibility that contractual interference *iure imperii* that is unaccompanied by compensation for injury caused to the investor will not be considered a violation of FET. In *AES Summit Generation Limited and Anor.* v. *The Republic of Hungary*, the claimants argued that the reintroduction of administrative pricing by Hungary, designed to lower the profit margins of energy operators, was a breach of the more generous pricing terms in two purchase and sale agreements which it concluded with Hungarian State-owned entities.[156] The claimants based their FET claim on the sovereign character of the breach, and the arbitrariness and lack of due process that coloured Hungary's decision to reintroduce administrative pricing.[157] The arbitral tribunal agreed that the change in law was a sovereign act that interfered with the original contracts and caused financial injury to the claimants.[158] However, it disagreed with the claimants that Hungary acted arbitrarily and without respect for due process. The tribunal held that Hungary's decision to reintroduce administrative pricing, which was reasonably motivated by the desire to reduce the financial burden on energy consumers, was not arbitrary.[159] It then held that Hungary's irregularity-laden process for reintroducing the administrative pricing decrees, 'while sub-optimal [*sic*], did not fall outside the acceptable range of legislative and regulatory behaviour'.[160] According to the *AES* tribunal, procedural irregularities or failings must be 'manifestly unfair or unreasonable (such as would shock, or at least surprise a sense of juridical propriety)' to violate FET.[161] Whether non-respect for due process is mild or serious is very much a matter of perception, which can vary from one tribunal to the next. Incorporating a sliding scale of severity into the analysis on due process violations, just like applying the *acta iure imperii–acta iure gestionis* distinction to exclude non-sovereign contractual breaches from FET protection, is likely to reduce the likelihood of the engagement of State responsibility for FET violations.

3.4.4   Coerced Renegotiation

The few instances where investors were forced to renegotiate their contracts with the host State came to light in arbitral awards analysing the

---

[156]   ICSID Case No. ARB/07/22, Award, 23 September 2010 (von Wobeser, Stern, Rowley), paras. 4.3–4.25.
[157]   Award, ibid., para. 9.3.36.
[158]   Award, ibid., paras. 9.3.27–9.3.35.
[159]   Award, ibid., paras. 10.3.15–10.3.34, also 9.3.37.
[160]   Award, ibid., para. 9.3.73, also 9.3.41–9.3.72.
[161]   Award, ibid., para. 9.3.40.

investors' FET claims. These awards highlight how a genuine attempt at renegotiation cannot be about the host State imposing its will on the foreign investor. A host State that initiates a renegotiation of an investment contract, only to ride roughshod over the investor during the negotiation process, will most likely violate FET.

In *Desert Line Projects* v. *Yemen*, the Omani claimant signed a total of eight road construction contracts with Yemen. Yemen defaulted on various progress payments and the matter was referred to arbitration in Yemen. The arbitrators held that the Yemeni government owed a substantial debt to the claimant, but despite the binding validity of this arbitral award on Yemen, no payment was forthcoming. Yemen subsequently concluded a settlement agreement with the reluctant claimant, where the amount judged owing in the earlier arbitral award was reduced by half. When the matter was submitted to investment treaty arbitration, the tribunal found that the methods employed by Yemen to persuade the claimant to settle for an amount far less than what it was entitled to amounted to a violation of FET:[162]

> The settlement agreement according to which the prevailing party in an arbitral proceeding renounces half of its rights without due consideration can only be valid if it is the result of an authentic, fair and equitable negotiation. In the case at hand, the rejection of the outcome of a mechanism for the resolution of the claims rendered in a local arbitration by two arbitrators selected by the Parties, and assisted in their deliberations by a local Yemeni magistrate; coupled with the subjection of the Claimant's employees, family members, and equipment to arrest and armed interference, as well as the subsequent peremptory 'advice' that it was 'in [his] interest' (Exh. CM-113) to accept that the amount awarded be amputated by half, falls well short of minimum standards of international law and cannot be the result of an authentic, fair and equitable negotiation.

The tribunal noted that Yemen relied on a potent mix of financial duress – refusal to pay which brought the claimant to the brink of bankruptcy just prior to the signing of the settlement, and physical duress – harassment of the claimant's work sites by armed men, arrests and threats to the personal safety of the claimant's employees, to coerce the claimant into signing the settlement agreement.[163] As the settlement agreement was the product of Yemen's violation of its treaty obligation to accord FET to protected investments, the tribunal declared that 'the Settlement Agreement is not entitled to international effect'.[164] As mentioned in Section 3.3.1.3.,

---

[162] Award, para. 179.
[163] Award, paras. 181–6.
[164] Award, para. 194.

the tribunal in *Desert Line Projects* v. *Yemen* did not extrapolate generally applicable components of FET from the closely worded Article 3 of the Oman-Yemen investment treaty. Overt coercion and harassment of a foreign investor by the host State arguably indicates a complete disregard for due process that upholds the rule of law. This is fundamentally incompatible with the core standard of treatment, whether the claim is framed as a denial of justice as MST, or a denial of FET.

The facts of *Desert Line Projects* v. *Yemen* are extreme. A claimant need not be physically intimidated in order for a tribunal to find that its consent to a renegotiated investment contract was vitiated by coercion. In *Suez* v. *Argentina*, AASA, an Argentinian company formed by a consortium which included the claimants, was awarded a thirty-year concession to operate water distribution and waste water services in the city of Buenos Aires. One of the most important changes Argentina made to its regulatory framework in response to the economic crisis of the early 2000s was the abolition of automatic tariff adjustments in the public utilities sector in accordance with international indices. This gravely affected the profitability of the Suez concession. It is against this backdrop of economic instability and depressed profits that Argentina broached the renegotiation of the concession with AASA. The tribunal noticed a marked difference in the way the concession was renegotiated and revised pre- and post-crisis. The post-crisis renegotiation process challenged by the claimants as a breach of FET 'had an extremely forceful character quite different from what the legal framework provided and from the way previous negotiations had taken place'.[165] The numerous changes demanded by Argentina of the concession, which were already secured by newly enacted legislation, led the tribunal to question if 'Argentina sought to structure the "renegotiation" process in such a way as to severely limit or indeed curtail the contractual freedom of AASA in order to arrive at a predetermined result desired by Argentina'.[166] The *Suez* tribunal held that the legal framework of the concession gave AASA legitimate expectations that its views and input will matter in any contractual renegotiation process. Therefore the high-handed manner in which Argentina conducted the renegotiation was a violation of FET because it frustrated AASA's legitimate expectations. Alternatively, inviting AASA to renegotiate on the one hand while unilaterally fixing the new contractual terms on the other is duplicitous conduct that is arguably indicative of bad faith. Therefore, another component of FET that coerced

---

[165] Decision on Liability, para. 241.
[166] Decision on Liability, para. 242.

or false renegotiations may implicate, one that is less controversial than legitimate expectations, is bad faith.

3.4.5   Cancellation

Cancellations *per se* do not violate the core standard of treatment. Only cancellations that are arbitrary or evince a lack of due process, and sometimes both, violate the core standard of treatment. Arbitral tribunals hearing contract-based denial of justice claims and contract-based FET claims are likely to rule that a cancellation is arbitrary if the host State is unable to offer a cogent justification for the cancellation, or if the cancellation is a disproportionate response to the investor's shortcomings as a contracting party. Whether a cancellation violates the core standard of treatment by denying the investor due process depends on the availability of compensation, and, more often, the investor's prospects for obtaining effective redress for the injury suffered. A due process determination may be less straightforward than an arbitrariness determination, because the prevailing political climate and popular sentiment in a host State towards the cancelled contract can be invisible barriers to the pursuit of local remedies.

A cancellation is arbitrary if the host State offers no explanation whatsoever to the investor or to the arbitral tribunal for the cancellation. In the *Claim of the Salvador Commercial Company* first discussed in Section 3.2, a majority of the US-El Salvador Mixed Claim Commission found the timing of an edict issued by the El Salvador government to close the port from which the US investors had an exclusive concession to trade highly suspect. The concession was rendered worthless by the edict just as the concessionaires were starting to see sustainable returns on their investment. The El Salvador government subsequently issued trading concessions bearing the same terms as those originally granted on an exclusive basis to the US investors. Notably, El Salvador did not attempt to justify its decision to close the port to the arbitral tribunal. Instead, it argued that the US investors had no basis for complaint since, having decided to invest in El Salvador, they were bound by the laws of El Salvador.[167] El Salvador also asserted that an international claim was premature as the US investors did not exhaust local remedies.[168] Neither argument was persuasive. The first argument runs contrary to the established principle that a State cannot take shelter from its international obligations by invoking

---

[167] *USA v. El Salvador* (1902), p. 476.
[168] Ibid.

its national laws.[169] The second argument is superseded by the agreement of El Salvador to submit the dispute between itself and the US investors to arbitration.[170] The majority of the arbitral tribunal held that the cancellation was arbitrary. Unlike El Salvador, respondent States hoping to avoid a finding of international responsibility will probably attempt to justify the cancellation of the contract to the arbitral tribunal. Arbitral tribunals will then scrutinise the proffered justification, and have been known to reject those that appear dubious. In *Gemplus S.A. and Ors* v. *The United Mexican States*, the arbitral tribunal hearing a contract-based FET claim was sceptical that having a foreign concessionaire run a national vehicle registry in Mexico, with the aim of lowering the frequency of car thefts and criminal activity, posed 'imminent peril to national security', thereby warranting a takeover by the Mexican government.[171] According to the arbitral tribunal, Mexico's invocation of national security manifested 'a clear intention ... to terminate the Concession and Concession Agreement without due regard to the Claimants' legal rights'.[172] In light of this overt intent, the list of deficiencies supplied by Mexico with respect to the claimants' performance of the concession prior to its termination came across as afterthoughts, cobbled together to give the impression that there were many good reasons for termination. The way in which Mexico orchestrated the termination of the concession in *Gemplus* v. *Mexico* was criticised by the tribunal as 'irrational, perverse and tainted with bad faith towards the Concessionaire', and amounted to a violation of FET.[173]

A cancellation by the host State is arguably arbitrary if it is an overreaction to the investor's missteps as a contracting party. In *Occidental Petroleum Corporation and Anor* v. *The Republic of Ecuador*, the claimants argued that the cancellation of an oil concession by Ecuador, in response to the second claimant's unauthorised sub-contracting of its concessionary rights, was simultaneously 'unfair, arbitrary, discriminatory and disproportionate'.[174] The cancellation was motivated by political opposition to and public strikes against the second claimant's actions. It appears

---

[169] *Certain Norwegian Loans Case* (*France* v. *Norway*) (Preliminary Objections) [1957] ICJ Rep 9, Separate Opinion of Judge Lauterpacht, p. 37.

[170] *USA* v. *El Salvador* (1902), p. 468.

[171] See the conjoined arbitrations *Gemplus SA et al* v. *United a Mexican States* (ICSID Case No. ARB(AF)/04/3) and *Talsud SA* v. *United Mexican States* (ICSID Case No. ARB(AF)/04/4), Award, 16 June 2010 (Fortier, Gómez, Veeder), para. 7-25.

[172] Award, ibid., para. 7-70.

[173] Award, ibid., paras. 4-183, 4-187.

[174] ICSID Case No. ARB/06/11, Award, 5 October 2012 (Fortier, Williams, Stern), paras. 203, 206, 237, 238 and 239.

from the award that the parties and the arbitral tribunal devoted most of their attention to the contested proportionality of the cancellation. In a first for contract-based FET claims, the arbitral tribunal held that proportionality is the key component of FET.[175] And on the facts, the tribunal found that cancellation was a disproportionate response to the second claimant's conduct, and a violation of FET, because any 'deterrence message' that Ecuador hoped to send to the wider oil and gas community with the cancellation was overshadowed by the 'total loss of an investment worth many hundreds of millions of dollars'.[176] Moreover, Ecuador admitted in its counterclaim that alternative responses to the second claimant's conduct, such as the negotiation of a new concession, were available.[177] Apart from being disproportionate, Ecuador's cancellation of the concession may also be arbitrary. Textbook arbitrary conduct is the failure to offer any or a sufficiently convincing reason for the measure taken. El Salvador's cancellation of the trading concession in *Claim of the Salvador Commercial Company* was arbitrary because there was no attempt to justify the cancellation. Mexico's cancellation of a concession to operate a national vehicle registry on the ground of national security in *Gemplus S.A.* v. *Mexico* was arbitrary because it was unable to show how exactly a foreign concessionaire posed a threat to national security. Similarly, it may be said that Ecuador's cancellation of the oil concession to quell civil unrest was arbitrary because it could not explain why it eschewed less drastic options that would achieve the same end.

A cancellation can evince a lack of due process when a host State is contractually obliged to give the investor an opportunity to cure the defects in its performance of the contract, but chooses to terminate while thwarting the investor from exercising its contractual right to cure.[178] The arbitral award in point is *Rumeli Telekom* v. *Kazakhstan*. Here, an investment

---

[175] Award, ibid., paras. 402–9. Although several arbitral tribunals have adopted a proportionality analysis for FET claims (see B. Kingsbury and S. Schill, 'Investor-State Arbitration as Governance: Fair and Equitable Treatment, Proportionality and the Emerging Global Administrative Law' in A. J. van den Berg (ed.), *50 Years of the New York Convention – ICCA International Arbitration Conference* (The Hague: Kluwer Law International, 2009) 5, p. 18–24; and A. Kulick, *Global Public Interest in International Investment Law* (Cambridge: Cambridge University Press, 2012), p. 184.), it is uncertain if this approach will gain more adherents in the future.

[176] Award, ibid., para. 450.

[177] Award, ibid., paras. 429–35.

[178] Conversely, when a host State exercises a contractual right to cancel the contract in response to breaches committed by the investor, there is no violation of FET; see *Vannessa Ventures Ltd* v. *Venezuela*, ICSID Case No. ARB(AF)/04/6, Award, 16 January 2013 (Lowe, Brower, Stern), paras. 221–2.

contract was concluded between the claimants and Kazakhstan whereby in return for their efforts in developing the telecommunications industry which were to be documented in periodic reports submitted to a governmental Investment Committee, they would receive various tax breaks and incentives from Kazakhstan to boost their investment. According to the investment contract, should the claimants fail to discharge their contractual obligations, Kazakhstan was entitled to suspend the contract, notify the claimants of the suspension and ask the claimants to address their failings. On the basis that the claimants had made limited progress since acquiring their telecommunications license and had fallen behind in their reporting duties, Kazakhstan notified the claimants of its intent to terminate the investment contract and gave the claimants one month to file the missing reports. The claimants missed the deadline by a few days and the contract was terminated. After the claimants wrote to various ministries to complain about the abrupt termination, a Working Group was set up to consider the validity of the termination. The claimants had no genuine prospect of defending themselves as they were invited to the meeting of the Working Group just two days before the meeting was scheduled to take place. Moreover, this invitation was extended on the same day that the claimants were informed of criminal proceedings being brought against their executives in Kazakh courts. The Working Group issued a three-and-a-half-page report recording that the contract was validly terminated on grounds which were entirely different to those previously communicated to the claimants. The tribunal found that the manner in which the investment contract was terminated was 'arbitrary, unfair, unjust, lacked in due process and did not respect the investor's reasonable and legitimate expectations',[179] while the way in which the Working Group reached its decision 'lacked transparency and due process and was unfair, in contradiction with the requirements of the fair and equitable treatment principle'.[180] Therefore, it was not the cancellation of the investment contract *per se* that violated FET, but the lip service that Kazakhstan paid to due process.[181]

---

[179] Award, para. 615.
[180] Award, para. 618.
[181] Kazakhstan arguably created a hostile environment for the claimants, and an investment contract cancelled by the host State amidst demonstrable hostility by local authorities is likely to be construed as a violation of FET, see *Metalclad* v. *Mexico*, Award, op. cit., para. 99; *Wena Hotels Ltd* v. *Egypt*, ICSID Case No. ARB/98/4, Award, 8 December 2000 (Leigh, Fadlallah, Wallace), para. 84; and *Compañia de Aguas del Aconquija SA & Vivendi Universal* v. *Argentina*, ICSID Case No. ARB/97/3, Award, 20 August 2007 (Kaufmann-Kohler, Verea, Rowley), para. 7.4.19.

Another way which the cancellation of an investment contract implicates the due process component of FET is if the host State, after promising not to do so, makes a public announcement to terminate an investment contract before the expiry of the contractual notice period for termination. This *volte-face* took place in *Biwater Gauff* v. *Tanzania*. Here, three contracts for the provision or water and sewerage services were concluded between a local company, City Water, incorporated by Biwater Gauff, and Tanzania. Despite the unsatisfactory performance of the contracts by the local company which led to both public and political opposition to the local company, Tanzania insisted that the contractual relationship will not be brought to an end before the expiry of the contractual notice period. Shortly after, Tanzania announced that it was terminating one of the contracts. In the arbitral tribunal's opinion, this sudden public announcement 'inflamed the situation, and polarised public opinion still further, thereby ensuring that from May 2005 onwards, the process by which the Lease Contract was terminated and City Water was removed did not – and could not – follow a normal contractual course'.[182] The arbitral tribunal did not explain why contractual termination, even if it was a surprise termination, denied the investor due process since the investor always has the option of seeking local remedies for premature termination. However, due to the unpopularity of City Water, and the high-profile manner which Tanzania chose to dissociate itself from City Water, hopes for obtaining redress for premature termination from Tanzanian courts appeared slim. Biwater Gauff was left with little choice but to accept the termination and bow out of the venture. An investor who is placed by the host State in a position of grave disadvantage in its pursuit of contractual remedies is arguably denied due process.[183]

3.5   Conclusion

When the breach of an investment contract by a host State is arbitrary or lacking in due process, it falls short of the core standard for contractual protection and becomes a violation of international law. The core standard for contractual protection, which derives from the minimum standard for alien protection, is the denial of justice. Denial of justice in the context of

---

[182] Award, para. 627.
[183] See J. E. Alvarez, 'The Public International Law Regime Governing International Investment' (2009) 344 *Recueil des Cours* 193 at 344: 'A State's mere failure to act, particularly to provide a remedy for a breach of the State own representations to an investor, seems capable of grounding a violation of general international law or FET today.'

alien protection is particularised in the *Neer Claim* as conduct amounting to 'an outrage, to bad faith, to wilful neglect of duty, or to an insufficiency of governmental action so far short of international standards that every reasonable and impartial man would readily recognize its insufficiency'. Denial of justice in the context of contractual protection is adapted in the *Chattin Claim*, the *Claim of the Salvador Commercial Company*, the *International Fisheries Company Case*, the *Mexican Union Railway Case*, the *Shufeldt Claim* and the *Brown Claim* to mean arbitrary contractual breaches, or contractual breaches carried out in a sovereign capacity that are unaccompanied by compensation for the injured investor or avenues for redress. The *Neer*-plus formula for denial of justice as MST for investment contracts is largely preserved, and occasionally supplemented, by the interpretation given to open-textured FET clauses in investment treaties by arbitral tribunals hearing contract-based FET claims. There is general agreement in arbitral *jurisprudence* that non-arbitrariness and respect for due process are the key components of FET. Additionally, bad faith conduct undoubtedly violates FET. But due to the scarcity of instances where a host State is shown to have acted in bad faith, bad faith is not routinely identified as a discrete component of bad faith. Furthermore, some tribunals identify the safeguarding of investor expectations and freedom from host State coercion and harassment as additional components of FET. Of the more common categories of contractual breaches, cumulative acts and omissions, *acta iure imperii*, coerced renegotiations and cancellations are more likely to implicate recognised components of FET, thereby engaging State responsibility, than non-payment. This is because non-payment is typically a response to the investor's unsatisfactory contractual performance, or the result of host State impecuniosity, offering claimants little fodder for arguing that non-payment is either arbitrary or a snub at due process.

4

State Responsibility and Expropriation

4.1 Introduction

General international law recognises the right of States to expropriate alien property. However, expropriations that do not meet settled, cumulative conditions for a lawful expropriation, will give rise to the international responsibility of the expropriating State.[1] These conditions are the payment of compensation, the pursuit of public purpose and compliance with due process. To the extent that alien contracts are a species of or can be assimilated to alien property, the general international law on expropriation protects both in the same way. Investment treaties also recognise the right of States to expropriate, subject to stipulated conditions of lawfulness. The object of expropriation here is an investment, as defined by the treaty. To the extent that investment contracts fall within the definition of protected investments, contractual rights are protected from unlawful expropriation by investment treaties. The framing of a breach of contract claim as an unlawful expropriation claim, whether under general international law or under investment treaty law, is not new. The sizeable body of arbitral *jurisprudence* on contract-based unlawful expropriations suggests that, apart from the different ways that contractual rights are characterised under general international law and investment treaty law (contract as property

---

[1] I. Brownlie, 'Causes of Action in the Law of Nations' (1979) 50(1) BYIL 13 at 33; also J. F. Williams, 'International Law and the Property of Aliens' (1928) 9 BYIL 1 at 13; A. Fachiri, 'International Law and the Property of Aliens' (1929) 10 BYIL 32 at 51; A. K. Kuhn, 'Nationalization of Foreign-Owned Property in Its Impact on International Law' (1951) 45 AJIL 709 at 711; R. L. Bindschedler, 'La Protection de la Propriété Privée en Droit International Public' (1959) 90 *Recueil des Cours* 174 at 187; F. Münch, 'Les Effets d'Une Nationalisation à l'Etranger' (1959) 89 *Recueil des Cours* 411 at 463 and 467; B. Weston, '"Constructive Takings" Under International Law: A Modest Foray into the Problem of "Creeping Expropriation"' (1975–6) 16 *Vanderbilt Journal of International Law* 103 at 129; T. Wälde and A. Kolo, 'Environmental Regulation, Investment Protection and "Regulatory Taking" in International Law' (2001) 50 ICLQ 811 at 824–5.

under the former, and contract as investment under the latter), the same considerations apply to the existence and legality of an expropriation.

This chapter analyses the three considerations that inform every finding of State responsibility for the unlawful expropriation of an investment contract. One, whether the investment contract qualifies as an object of expropriation; two, whether the breach of contract amounts to an expropriation; and three, whether the expropriation is unlawful.

4.2   The Object of Expropriation

An expropriation is the taking of property or of an investment by the State.[2] If contracts are a species of property or investment, it follows that existing contractual rights may also be taken away by the State.[3] Tribunals rarely elaborate on the propriety of assimilating contractual rights to property rights, or to a protected investment under an investment treaty.[4] This has led to criticism that applying an expropriation analysis to contractual rights begets 'form triumphing over substance in international

---

[2] Expropriation is broadly defined in international law. State interference with or dispossession of alien property, even if that property is not subsequently put to use by the State, can be regarded as an expropriation. See M. Sornarajah, *The International Law on Foreign Investment*, 4th edn (Cambridge: Cambridge University Press, 2017), p. 453 (footnote omitted), also 432–3:

> Interference with the exercise of property or ownership rights by the host [S]tate could amount to takings which require compensation. Once the jurisprudential fact that ownership itself involves a bundle of tangible rights in relation to property is acknowledged, then it follows that it is not only the outright taking of the whole bundle of rights but also the restriction of the use of any part of the bundle that amounts to a taking under the law.

[3] Unlawful expropriation claims involving illusory contractual rights are infrequently brought and tend to be summarily dismissed. See *Wintershall* v. *Qatar*, 28 ILM 795, Partial and Final Awards, 5 February 1988 and 31 May 1988 (Stevenson, Brownlie, Cremades), 814–6; *Robert Azinian and Ors* v. *Mexico*, ICSID Case No. ARB(AF)/97/2, Award, 1 November 1999 (Paulsson, Civiletti, Wobeser), para. 100; *Emmis International Holding BV and Ors* v. *Hungary*, ICSID Case No. ARB/12/2, Award, 16 April 2014 (McLachlan, Lalonde, Thomas), paras. 193–255. This chapter focuses on unlawful expropriation claims involving existing contractual rights.

[4] Recent exceptions are *Emmis* v. *Hungary*, Award, paras. 164–6 and 168–9; *Vigotop Limited* v. *Hungary*, ICSID Case No. ARB/11/22, Award, 1 October 2014 (Sachs, Bishop, Heiskanen), paras. 312–632; and *Accession Mezzanine Capital and Ors* v. *Hungary*, ICSID Case No. ARB/12/3, Award, 17 April 2015 (Rovine, Lalonde, Douglas), paras. 147–57; also in *Koch Minerals SARL and Anor.* v. *Bolivarian Republic of Venezuela*, ICSID Case No. ARB/11/19, Partial Dissenting Opinion of Arbitrator Zachary Douglas, 30 October 2017, paras. 3–12.

law'.[5] This section examines the propriety of viewing of contractual rights as property under general international law (4.2.1), and of contractual rights as protected investments under investment treaty law (4.2.2).

4.2.1 Contract as Property in General International Law

The assimilation of contract to property was neither sporadic nor accidental. Kriebaum and Schreuer observe that international tribunals are 'unanimous in extending the concept of the protected property to rights arising from contracts'.[6] When the law of State responsibility developed at the turn of the twentieth century, Lauterpacht urged recourse to domestic law for guidance.[7] Over time, the practice of supplementing lacunae in international law with reference to domestic law grew. Contemporary writers accept that 'the domestic law analogy is perhaps inevitable', and ponder instead 'the proper analogy with domestic private law or domestic public law'.[8] To this end, disputes between private investors and host States have been analogised to domestic public law disputes between private individuals and home States.[9] Writing in the specific context of expropriation claims, Lowe credits the 'municipal public-law tradition ... as a rich and powerful source of analytical tools'.[10] Notably, the principal terrain on which the definitional limits of property have been tested are domestic public law decisions on the constitutional protection of property. The accumulation of centuries worth of judicial experimentation on assimilating contractual rights to property creates a valuable repository

---

[5] Z. Douglas, 'Property, Investment and the Scope of Investment Protection Obligations' in Z. Douglas, J. Pauwelyn, and J. E. Viñuales (eds.), *The Foundations of International Investment Law: Bringing Theory into Practice* (Oxford: Oxford University Press, 2014), pp. 363, 391; same author, *The International Law on Investment Claims*, pp. 213–24.

[6] U. Kriebaum and C. Schreuer, 'The Concept of Property in Human Rights Law and International Investment Law' in S. Breitenmoser, B. Ehrenzeller, and M. Sassoli (eds.), *Human Rights, Democracy and the Rule of Law: Liber Amicorum Luzius Wildhaber* (Baden-Baden: Nomos, 2007), pp. 1, 6 and 8–10; also *Biloune and Anor v. Ghana and Anor*, 95 ILR 184, Award, 30 June 1990 (Schwebel, Wallace, Leigh), paras. 204–5.

[7] H. Lauterpacht, *Private Law Sources and Analogies of International Law* (London: Longmans, 1927), pp. 134–43.

[8] M. Koskenniemi, 'Doctrines of State Responsibility' in J. Crawford, A. Pellet, and S. Olleson (eds.), *The Law of International Responsibility* (Oxford: Oxford University Press, 2010), pp. 45, 47.

[9] G. Van Harten, *Investment Treaty Arbitration and Public Law* (Oxford: Oxford University Press, 2007), pp. 45–7 and 59; S. Schill, 'International Investment Law and Comparative Public Law – An Introduction' in S. Schill (ed.), *International Investment Law and Comparative Public Law* (Oxford: Oxford University Press, 2010), pp. 3–38.

[10] V. Lowe, 'Regulation or Expropriation?' (2002) 55 *Current Legal Problems* 447 at 465.

of information and insight on the aggregate practice of States which general international law is founded upon. Careful reference to domestic law (4.2.1.1), is necessary to understand why the equation of contract to property has gained traction in international law (4.2.1.2).

4.2.1.1 Precedent on Contract as Property in Domestic Law

The gradual assimilation of contractual rights to property in domestic law is observable from the evolving meaning of property (4.2.1.1.1), the changing limits of constitutional protection for property rights (4.2.1.1.2) and judicial endorsement of contract as property in cases on constitutional interpretation (4.2.1.1.3).

4.2.1.1.1 The Meaning of Property   More than 300 years ago when property was synonymous with chattel or land ownership, a claimant could assert no proprietary right over fees due from an unlicensed wine seller, because a 'licence properly passeth no interest, nor alters or transfers property in any thing'.[11] The advent of modern technology and trading practices saw the creation, use, exchange and circulation of both corporeal and incorporeal goods and things. The traditional definitional boundary of property was being redrawn by claims that asserted a right to property in intangible forms, such as copyright[12] and contract.[13] The notion of property is not static. Rights that would not have been considered property in the 1600s, like those accruing from a contractual license, gradually gained acceptance as a species of property.[14] It became increasingly harder to maintain a strict dichotomy between contract and property. As Gray remarked,[15]

> '[P]roperty' is not all it is cracked up to be. By now it should be becoming obvious that the notion of 'property' readily collapses back into contract or,

---

[11] *Thomas* v. *Sorrell* [1973] Vaugh 330, p. 351.

[12] *Victoria Park Racing and Recreation Grounds Co. Ltd.* v. *Taylor* [1937] 58 CLR 479. Although the claim that the defendants had acted in breach of copyright by broadcasting the numbers of the winning horses after a race was dismissed, this was because the plaintiffs had failed to take measures to prevent anyone but themselves to transmit the information obtained.

[13] *Tulk* v. *Moxhay* [1848] 41 ER 1143.

[14] A. W. B. Simpson, *A History of the Land Law*, 2nd edn (Oxford: Oxford University Press, 1986), pp. 74–7. Property now includes rights as diverse as the right to confidential information, see *Smith-Kline and French Laboratories (Australia) Ltd. and Ors* v. *Secretary, Department of Community Services and Health* [1990] 95 ALR 87, pp. 134–6 (per Gummow J), and the right to pension benefits, see C. A. Reich, 'The New Property' (1964) 73 *Yale Law Journal* 733 at 742 and 768–74; M. J. Radin, *Reinterpreting Property* (Chicago, IL: University of Chicago Press, 1993), pp. 14–6.

[15] K. Gray, 'Property in Thin Air' (1991) 50(2) *Cambridge Law Journal* 252 at 303.

more broadly, into a number of arrangements based on assent. No quantum step differentiates contract from 'property', for 'property' has no clear threshold.

Gray's epiphany is shared by other influential contributors to the modern concept of property[16] and even resonates to some extent with Penner, who argues that contract and property should ideally be studied as distinct branches of law.[17] While Penner would disagree with the generalisation that "'property" readily collapses back into contract', he accepts that contracts are a 'legally effective mode by which the enjoyment of property can be shared or transferred'.[18] After all, Penner admits, no theory of property can deny 'the manifest truth that some property owes its very existence to the institution of contract'.[19] The possibility that contracts are a species of property cannot be ruled out even if the classical Roman law–inspired distinction between rights *in rem* and rights *in personam* is adopted. Rights *in rem* refer to rights enforceable against the world at large, while rights *in personam* usually refer to rights which are personal to and can only be enforced by and against contracting parties. Traditionally, only rights *in rem* which belong to a closed list qualify as property.[20] Additionally, English law recognises certain rights *in personam*, such as receipt of a money debt or transfer, as property.[21] Therefore, when a contract creates rights *in rem*, or, arguably, certain rights *in personam*, that contract may be a form of property.

Investment contracts and the rights accruing thereunder are always property if one subscribes to Gray's wholesale assimilation of contract to property. Investment contracts that create, transfer or relinquish title to

---

[16] B. Ackerman, *Private Property and the Constitution* (New Haven, CT: Yale University Press, 1977), pp. 26–9; D. Kennedy and F. Michelman, 'Are Property and Contract Efficient?' (1980) 8 *Hofstra Law Review* 711 at 714 and 739; R. Cotterrell, 'The Law of Property and Legal Theory' in W. Twining (ed.), *Legal Theory and Common Law* (Oxford: Basil Blackwell, 1986), pp. 81, 90 and 92; C. Sunstein, 'On Property and Constitutionalism' (1993) 14 *Cardozo Law Review* 907 at 908, 911–12, and 933; cf. R. Posner who maintains the distinction between contract and property in *Economic Analysis of Law*, 9th edn (The Hague: Wolters Kluwer, 2014), Chapters 3–4.

[17] J. Penner, *The Idea of Property in Law* (Oxford: Oxford University Press, 2000), pp. 34–8 and 52.

[18] J. Penner, 'Basic Obligations' in P. Birks (ed.), *The Classification of Obligations* (Oxford: Clarendon, 1997), pp. 91, 107; also *The Idea of Property in Law*, p. 52.

[19] Penner, *The Idea of Property in Law*, p. 165, also 182.

[20] T. W. Merrill and H. E. Smith, 'Optimal Standardization in the Law of Property: The *Numerus Clausus* Principle' (2000) 110 *Yale Law Journal* 1 at 68–9.

[21] F. H. Lawson and B. Rudden, *The Law of Property*, 3rd edn (Oxford: Clarendon, 2002), pp. 44–5; Penner, *The Idea of Property in Law*, p. 165; also Douglas, *The International Law on Investment Claims*, p. 383.

property rights also satisfy Penner's narrower understanding of property.[22] Investment contracts that generate rights *in rem*, as well as certain rights *in personam*, may also be property. An example of a right *in rem* is the grant of an exclusive right to mine for bauxite in a stipulated area of the host State's territory, and to share in the proceeds of the sale of bauxite together with the host State.[23] The foreign investor can enforce this property right against anyone who tries to mine and market bauxite in contravention of the grant. An example of a right *in personam* is payment for the provision of services,[24] or remuneration for construction works done.[25] Tribunals hearing claims arising from breaches of investment contracts have equated a contractual right to payment, a traditional *in personam* right, to a property right that can be expropriated.[26] Regardless of whether the total or partial assimilation of contract to property eventually takes hold, the widening notion of property sustains the argument that contractual rights can, as a matter of principle, be expropriated.

4.2.1.1.2   Constitutional Protection for Property Rights   Constitutions protect private individuals against the State. Having a right to own property rings hollow if the State can take property away at will.[27] Provisions in

---

[22] Like Penner, Douglas favours a narrower understanding of property, see Z. Douglas, 'The Hybrid Foundations of Investment Treaty Arbitration' (2003) 74(1) BYIL 151 at 191 (fn. 291) where he argues that even if contractual rights expressly qualify for protection under investment treaties, they 'should be interpreted narrowly as those contracts that regulate the investor's rights to property in the host State'.

[23] *Revere Copper and Brass Inc.* v. *Overseas Private Investment Corporation*, 56 ILR 258, Award, 24 August 1978 (Haight, Wetzel, Bergan (dissenting)), pp. 269–70.

[24] *SGS Société Générale de Surveillance S.A.* v. *Republic of Philippines*, ICSID Case No. ARB/02/6, Decision of the Tribunal on Objections to Jurisdiction, 29 January 2004 (El-Kosheri, Crawford, Crivellaro (partially dissenting)), paras. 19–20 (customs inspection services).

[25] *Autopista Concesionada de Venezuela CA (Aucoven)* v. *Venezuela*, ICSID Case No. ARB/00/5, Award, 23 September 2003 (Kaufmann-Kohler, Böckstiegel, Cremades), paras. 21–5 (highway construction).

[26] *Emmis* v. *Hungary* Award, para. 169; also *Bayindir Insaat Turzim Ticaret Ve Sanayi AS* v. *Pakistan*, ICSID Case No. ARB/03/29, Decision on Jurisdiction, 14 November 2005 (Kaufmann-Kohler, Berman, Böckstiegel), para. 255.

[27] The assimilation of contract to property translates into the objective of strengthening constitutional protection for the basic rights held by every individual. This objective is expressed in the Preamble to the European Convention on Human Rights as 'the maintenance and further realisation of human rights and fundamental freedoms' (signed 4 November 1950, entry into force 3 September 1953), 213 UNTS 221. To this end, the Grand Chamber of the European Court of Human Rights has found that 'the extent of the State's interference with freedom of contract and contractual relations' is relevant to a determination of a State's

different constitutions governing the right to property, notwithstanding some textual variation, all confirm that any interference with private property by the State must conform to constitutional safeguards. The US Constitution permits the government to deprive an individual of his property only if the taking is done in accordance with 'due process of law[,] ... for public use, and with just compensation'.[28] The German Constitution provides that the taking of private property by the State must be done 'for the public good ... [and] ordered by or pursuant to a law that determines the nature and extent of compensation ... [which] shall be determined by establishing an equitable balance between the public interest and the interests of those affected'.[29] The Australian Constitution obliges Parliament to ensure that laws affecting an individual's right to property reflect 'the acquisition of property on just terms'.[30] The South African Constitution prohibits the 'arbitrary deprivation of property' and provides that property may only be expropriated 'for a public purpose or in the public interest; and subject to compensation'.[31] The Malaysian Constitution guarantees that '[n]o law shall provide for the compulsory acquisition or use of property without adequate compensation'.[32]

A snapshot of constitutional provisions protecting the right to property shows that contracts are not expressly protected as a species of property. The assimilation of contract to property was hardly self-evident, especially in countries like Germany and South Africa where property in private law is limited to corporeal things. Property in the German Constitution and in the German Civil Code is denoted by the same term, 'Eigentum'.[33]

---

compliance with Art. 1 of the First Protocol, which protects a person's right to 'the peaceful enjoyment of his possessions' and 'the use of property', see *Case of Hutten-Czapska v. Poland* (Grand Chamber), App. No. 35014/97, 19 June 2006, para. 168. Kriebaum and Schreuer appear to regard 'possessions' and 'property' in Art. 1 of the First Additional Protocol as interchangeable terms, noting that while the ECHR 'has refrained from offering a general definition ... it has generally adopted a broad concept of property in its case law on this provision', 'The Concept of Property in Human Rights Law and International Investment Law', p. 2.

[28] US Bill of Rights, Amendment V.
[29] Basic Law for the Federal Republic of Germany, Art. 14(3). Official English translation provided by the German Federal Ministry of Justice, 'Gesetze im Internet', online: www .gesetze-im-internet.de (accessed 31 December 2017).
[30] Commonwealth of Australia Constitution Act, 9 July 1900, Cap. 12, Art. 51(xxxi).
[31] Constitution of the Republic of South Africa, 18 December 1996, No. 108/1996, Sections 25(1), 25(2)(a) and 25(2)(b).
[32] Constitution of Malaysia, 27 August 1957, Art. 13(2).
[33] Basic Law for the Federal Republic of Germany in the revised version published in the Federal Law Gazette Part III, classification number 100-1, as last amended by the Act of

In South Africa, courts are accustomed to viewing property as the physical manifestation of ownership in private law. Which interpretation of constitutionally protected property best achieves the objective of constitutional protection may be a question of perspective, but how well an individual is protected against arbitrary interference with his rights by the State is directly proportional to how comprehensive the definition of constitutionally protected property is. Van der Walt argues that the assimilation of contracts to constitutionally protected property in South Africa and beyond is necessary because an individual should not be left with no cause of action when State action deprives him of his contractual rights:

> There are a number of private law and commercial rights that are protected quite adequately by the common law or legislation, albeit not as property, but that could only be protected as property for the sake of constitutional conflicts. The best examples are commercial rights like licenses and quotas that are protected by legislation and money debts that are protected by the common law ... However, for constitutional purposes, for example in a dispute with the [S]tate about legislation that allegedly deprives their holders of these rights, section 25 [the constitutional property guarantee] may well be the only constitutional provision under which these rights can be protected, and then there is a case for the argument that these rights should be regarded as property for constitutional purposes.[34]

In the United States, contractual rights and property rights are addressed separately in the Constitution. The Contract Clause in Article 1 prohibits state governments from passing any 'law impairing the obligation of contracts', whereas the Takings Clause in the Fifth Amendment prohibits the federal government from taking private property unless the taking is done for public use and upon the payment of just compensation.[35] The application of the Contract Clause and the Takings Clause to different levels of government was deliberate. The depressed post-independence economy prompted many states to pass legislation compelling creditors to either write off private debts or to accept repayment in kind.[36] The Contract Clause was adopted specifically to 'prevent the states from enacting laws

---

21 July 2010 (Federal Law Gazette I 944), Art. 14(3); Civil Code BGB in the version promulgated on 2 January 2002 (Federal Law Gazette I 42, 2909; 2003 I 738), last amended by Art. 1 of the Statute of 27 July 2011 (Federal Law Gazette I 1600), s. 90.

[34] A. J. Van der Walt, *Property and Constitution* (Pretoria: Pretoria University Law Press, 2012), p. 124.

[35] US Bill of Rights, Amendment V, Art. I(10). The reference to due process in Amendment V is known separately as the Due Process Clause.

[36] D. W. Kmiec and J. O. McGinnis, 'The Contract Clause: A Return to the Original Understanding' (1986–7) 14 *Hastings Constitutional Law Quarterly* 525 at 533.

retroactively relieving debtors from the payment of their private debts'.[37] Since legislation impairing contractual obligations would affect interstate commerce, Congress should oversee such important legislative activity without being bound by the Contract Clause. In contrast, property was often taken for military use by the federal government during the American Revolution without payment of compensation.[38] The Takings Clause applied only to the federal government because the framers of the US Constitution believed that property was far more vulnerable to confiscation by the federal government than by state governments. On the face of it therefore, the Contract Clause does not bind the federal government. Nonetheless, the US Supreme Court mended the loophole of the federal government being able to breach contracts with impunity by treating contractual rights as property which would be protected by the Takings Clause.[39] Even Merrill who maintains a 'pervasive distinction between contract rights and property rights' under US private law,[40] accepts that contracts qualify as property under the US Constitution:[41]

> Most choses in action originate as contract rights, as do bonds, common stock, and even money issued by the government. These interests are commonly regarded as property and are assumed to be protected by the Takings Clause.

The possibility of property encompassing contractual rights whenever constitutional protection is invoked has also been acknowledged by the German Federal Constitutional Court. In a series of decisions over the course of two decades, the Federal Constitutional Court held that non-corporeal things, including contractual rights, qualify as 'Eigentum' for constitutional protection.[42]

When the right to property was recognised as a stand-alone right in the Indian Constitution, Indian courts were very generous with the definition

---

[37] M. W. McConnell, 'Contract Rights and Property Rights: A Case Study in the Relationship between Individual Liberties and Constitutional Structure' (1988) 76(2) *California Law Review* 267 at 280. For further discussion on constitutional constraints on the liberty of contract, see D. Bernstein, *Rehabilitating Lochner: Defending Individual Rights against Progressive Reform* (Chicago, IL: University of Chicago Press, 2011), pp. 90–107.

[38] McConnell, 'Contract Rights and Property Rights', p. 292.

[39] *Bowen v. Public Agencies Opposed to Social Security Entrapment*, 477 US 41 (1986), p. 56.

[40] Merrill and Smith, 'Optimal Standardization in the Law of Property', p. 68.

[41] T. W. Merrill, 'The Landscape of Constitutional Property' (2000) 86 *Virginia Law Review* 885 at 991.

[42] For a concise summary of the German position, see A. J. Van der Walt, *Constitutional Property Clauses – A Comparative Analysis* (South Africa: Juta & Co., 1999), pp. 151–3.

of constitutionally protected property.[43] The courts held that even executory contractual rights, such as rights arising from a permit, are deserving of constitutional protection.[44] Perhaps the former Chief Justice of India, Hiyadatullah, was right to observe that the trend of enlarging the scope of constitutionally protected property stems from how '[a]ll property is now exposed to the vagaries of political thinking'.[45]

4.2.1.1.3 Judicial Elaboration on Contract as Property

US courts assimilated contractual rights to property progressively. During the time when the Takings Clause was binding only on the federal government, the Supreme Court held that the taking of property rights by state governments could be regulated by the Contract Clause.[46] After the Fourteenth Amendment containing the Equal Protection Clause was adopted, the Supreme Court invoked the 'equal protection of the laws' to apply the Takings Clause to the impairment of contractual obligations by state governments.[47] The willingness of the Supreme Court to regard contracts as property eligible for constitutional protection has generated a substantial body of case law. Among the many different types of contracts that now qualify as constitutionally protected property in the United States are employment contracts,[48] contracts for the purchase of government bonds[49] and contracts containing assurances of governmental deregulation for a given sector.[50]

---

[43] Before 1979, the right to property was secured in Art. 31 of the 1950 Constitution of India. Since the repeal of Art. 31, the right to property has to be implied from other constitutional provisions on the acquisition of property by the State.

[44] *Rabindra Kumar* v. *Forest Officer* (1955) AIR (Manipur) 49, pp. 53–4; also *Dwarkadas Shrinivas* v. *The Sholapur Spinning and Weaving Co. Ltd. and Others* (1954) AIR (Supreme Court) 119, p. 139 (per Ghulam Hassan J).

[45] M. Hidayatullah, *Right to Property and the Indian Constitution* (Calcutta: Calcutta University Press, 1983), p. 203.

[46] *Fletcher* v. *Peck*, 10 US (6 Cranch) 87 (1810), pp. 136–7.

[47] See for instance *City of El Paso* v. *Simmons*, 379 US 497 (1965), p. 535.

[48] *Perry* v. *Sindermann*, 408 US 593 (1972), p. 601 (per Stewart J for the Court); *Vail* v. *Board of Education*, 705 F 2d 1435 (7th Cir. 1983), pp. 1437–8 (per Wood J), affirmed *Board of Education* v. *Vail*, 466 US 377 (1984).

[49] *Eastern Enterprises* v. *Apfel*, 524 US 498 (1998), p. 555 (per Stevens J, Souter J, Ginsburg J, and Breyer J), dissenting from the majority on the applicability of the Due Process Clause or the Takings Clause to determine the constitutionality of a challenged statute. The majority did not comment on whether contracts for the purchase of government bonds were constitutionally protected property.

[50] J. G. Sidak and D. F. Spulber, *Deregulatory Takings and the Regulatory Contract* (Cambridge: Cambridge University Press, 1997), pp. 213–55.

In South Africa, many were evicted from their houses during the apartheid and forced to relocate to racially segregated areas. The end of the apartheid saw a wave of claims for the restoration or reparation of appropriated housing rights. The Constitutional Court of South Africa had to consider what the relationship between the right to property which was protected under Section 25 of the Constitution, and the right to housing which was protected under Section 26, was. In a series of rulings, it found that the right to housing was an extension of the right to property.[51] When the right to housing conferred by a tenancy or lease, both of which are contractual in origin, receives equal protection under the Constitution from the right to housing consequent upon property ownership, contractual rights are constitutionally protected property. The broadening scope of constitutionally protected property can also be seen in constitutional discourse outside the housing context. In *National Credit Regulator* v. *Opperman*, the legislature passed a law cancelling credit lending agreements. Affected creditors argued that the new statutory provision was unconstitutional because it deprived them of their contractual right of restitution, thus arbitrarily depriving them of property in contravention of Section 25(1). By a majority,[52] the Constitutional Court prefaced its finding of unconstitutionality with the observation that 'Section 25 deals with property and not with ownership',[53] and noted the gradual acceptance as property by the Court of rights which are not grounded in the ownership of corporeal things.[54] The Constitutional Court added that since other jurisdictions like Germany already recognise contracts as constitutionally protected property, treating a contractual right to restitution as property eligible for constitutional protection in South Africa was both 'logical and realistic'.[55]

---

[51] See for instance *Port Elizabeth Municipality* v. *Various Occupiers* (2005) 1 SA 217, para. 19 (per Sachs J); *Residents of the Joe Slovo Community, Western Cape* v. *Thubelisha Homes and Ors* (2010) 3 SA 454, para. 343 (per Sachs J).

[52] *National Credit Regulator* v. *Opperman* (2013) 2 BCLR 170. The dissent of Cameron J, which was joined by Froneman and Jafta JJ, disagreed with the majority's interpretation of the contested statutory provision which deprived it of legal effect, but did not dispute the majority's treatment of contractual rights as constitutionally protected property in Section 25(1).

[53] Ibid., para. 61.

[54] *Laugh It Off Promotions CC* v. *SAB International (Finance) BV t/a Sabmark International (Freedom of Expression Institute as amicus curiae)* (2005) 8 BCLR 743 (trademark); *Phumelela Gaming and Leisure Ltd* v. *Grndlingh and Ors* (2006) 8 BCLR 883 (trademark); *Law Society of South Africa* v. *Minister for Transport* (2011) 2 BCLR 150 (loss of earning capacity).

[55] *National Credit Regulator*, para. 63.

English law also embraces a broad meaning of property whereby a contractual right is cognisable as property so long as it is 'definable, identifiable
by third parties, capable in its nature of assumption by third parties, and
ha[s] some degree of permanence or stability'.[56] In 1998, the UK Parliament
enacted the Human Rights Act which gives the ECHR the force of law
in England, Wales, Scotland and Northern Ireland. Article 1 of the First
Protocol prohibits Member States from depriving their nationals of their
possessions or property 'except in the public interest and subject to the conditions provided for by law and by the general principles of international
law'. English courts have held that a contractual right to payment,[57] and to
pension benefits qualify as property under Article 1 of the First Protocol.[58]
In *Wilson* v. *First County Trust Ltd. (No. 2)*, the then House of Lords held that
a contractual right to the repayment of a loan was a property right which
could not be restricted by a statutory provision requiring the creditor to
obtain the debtor's consent before a court can enforce the loan agreement:[59]

> Here, the transaction between the parties provided for repayment of the
> loan and for the car to be held as security. What is in issue is the 'lawful-
> ness' of overriding legislation. The proposition advanced by the Secretary
> of State would mean that however arbitrary or discriminatory such leg-
> islation might be, if it was in existence when the transaction took place
> a court enforcing human rights values would be impotent. A Convention
> right guaranteeing a right of property would have nothing to say. That is not
> an attractive conclusion.

The liberal English notion of property has influenced the approach of
courts in jurisdictions where English judicial decisions are routinely consulted. The High Court of Australia has consistently held that contracts
are property which can only be acquired by the State on 'just terms' under
Section 51(xxxi) of the Constitution.[60]

---

[56] *National Provincial Bank Ltd.* v. *Ainsworth* [1965] AC 1175 (House of Lords), pp. 1247–8
(per Lord Wilberforce).

[57] *The Commissioners for Her Majesty's Revenue and Customs* v. *John Richard Smith* [2007]
EWHC 488, para. 26 (per Warren J).

[58] *In re Malcolm* [2004] EWCA Civ 1748, para. 28 (per Chadwick LJ); also *R* v. *Croydon
London Borough Council and Anor Appeal* [2009] UKSC 8, para. 38 (per Baroness Hale of
Richmond JSC).

[59] *Wilson* v. *First County Trust Ltd. (No. 2)* [2003] UKHL 40, para. 41 (per Lord Nicholls of
Birkenhead).

[60] *Mutual Pools and Staff Pte Ltd.* v. *Commonwealth of Australia* [1994] 179 CLR 155, p. 174
(per Mason CJ) and p. 186 (per Deane and Goudron JJ); *Smith* v. *ANL Ltd.* [2000] 204
CLR 493, p. 505 (per Gleeson CJ) and pp. 522–3 (per Kirby J); also *Attorney-General for
the Northern Territory* v. *Chaffey and Anor* [2007] 231 CLR 651, p. 668 (per Gleeson CJ,
Gummow, Hayne and Crennan JJ).

In Malaysia, the leading case on the definition of constitutionally pro-
tected property is *Selangor Pilot Association* v. *Malaysia*.[61] The Federal
Court, Malaysia's highest court, held that that goodwill arising from the
grant of a license by the government to provide pilotage services is property worthy of constitutional protection under Article 13(1).[62] The Privy
Council heard the appeal against this decision.[63] Allen suggested that the
Privy Council ascribed a narrower meaning to property in the Malaysian
Constitution by holding that a license is not property.[64] On the contrary,
the outcome of the appeal from the Federal Court did not turn on the
definition of property in Article 13(1), but whether the deprivation complained of amounted to a 'compulsory acquisition' within the meaning of
Article 13(2).[65] Therefore, recent decisions of the Malaysian High Courts
continue to cite the Federal Court decision in *Selangor Pilot Association* v.
Malaysia and older Indian cases as authorities for a wide definition of property, and not the Privy Council decision.[66] Reliance on Indian authorities
which regarded contract as property deserving of constitutional protection implied that Malaysian courts were inclined towards the same view.

The one occasion in Malaysia when a contractual right was not treated as
property stemmed from a misreading of the Indian case that was cited. In
Station Hotels v. *Malayan Railway Administration*, the Kuala Lumpur High
Court held that a contractual right to benefit from a lease of premises did
not qualify as property under Article 13(1) of the Federal Constitution.[67]
The High Court claimed that it was guided in its definition of property by
the written opinion of Hiyadatullah CJ in the Indian Supreme Court decision of *Achutan* v. *Kerala*. Remarkably, the passage that it quoted did not
disclose the position of the Indian Supreme Court on the definition of property under the Indian Constitution, and addressed instead the entirely separate issue of whether a right to property can be considered a fundamental

---

[61] *Selangor Pilot Association* v. *Malaysia* (1975) 2 MLJ 66.
[62] Ibid., pp. 71–2.
[63] *Government of Malaysia and Anor* v. *Selangor Pilot Association* (1977) 1 MLJ 133.
[64] T. Allen, 'Commonwealth Constitutions and the Right Not to Be Deprived of Property'
     (1993) 42 ICLQ 523 at 533; also A. Harding, *Law, Government and the Constitution in
     Malaysia* (The Hague: Kluwer Law International, 1996), p. 227.
[65] *Selangor Pilot Association* v. *Malaysia*, pp. 135–6 (per Viscount Dilhorne).
[66] *Adong bin Kuwau and Ors* v. *Kerajaan Negeri Johor and Anor* (1997) 1 MLJ 418 (High Court
     Johor Bahru), pp. 432–3; *Amit bin Salleh and Ors* v. *The Superintendent, Land and Survey
     Department Bintulu and Ors* (2005) MLJ 258 (High Court Bintulu) (unreported judgment);
     Mohamad Rambli bin Kawi v. *Superintendent of Lands Kuching and Anor* (2010) 8 MLJ 441
     (High Court Kuching), pp. 466–7.
[67] *Station Hotels* v. *Malayan Railway Administration* (1977) 1 MLJ 112, pp. 114–5. This finding
     of the High Court was not challenged on appeal to the Federal Court.

right. All that Hiyadatullah CJ had to say was that the petitioner '[had not] shown how ... the Constitution may be invoked to prevent cancellation of a contract in exercise of powers conferred by one of the terms of the contract itself'.[68] The Kuala Lumpur High Court may have opposed the assimilation of contractual rights to constitutionally protected property in 1977, but it was remiss to base its decision on an Indian case that did not support its findings. Therefore, even if *Station Hotels* v. *Malayan Railway Administration* renders Malaysian law on the assimilation of contractual rights to property unsettled since it has never been expressly overruled, Malaysian constitutional discourse, like that of the other jurisdictions surveyed, favours the assimilation of contract to property.

4.2.1.2   Precedent on Contract as Property in International Law

The push for a more generous definition of property in domestic public law was mirrored in international law. This can be seen from the meaning given by commentators to property (4.2.1.2.1), and the findings of international courts and tribunals (4.2.1.2.2).

4.2.1.2.1   The Meaning of Property   Some commentators allude to the assimilation of contract to property by including contractual breaches in a discussion on State interference with property rights. Schwarzenberger argued that the termination of an investment contract by a State was, like an unlawful expropriation of property, 'an elementary breach of good faith' which 'violates the minimum standards of international law and ... the general principles of law recognized by civilised nations'.[69] Seidl-Hohenveldern considered the engagement State responsibility for a breach of contract while addressing the 'property rights of aliens'.[70]

Higgins adopted a more nuanced view on the assimilation of contract to property. While she accepted a liberal concept of property, and acknowledged the possibility of assimilation, she did not advocate the wholesale assimilation of contract to property:[71]

---

[68] *Achutan* v. *Kerala* (1959) AIR (Supreme Court) 490, p. 492.
[69] G. Schwarzenberger, 'The Protection of British Property Abroad' (1952) 5 *Current Legal Problems* 295 at 296.
[70] I. Seidl-Hohenveldern, 'International Economic Law – General Course on Public International Law' (1986) 198 *Recueil des Cours* 9 at 171.
[71] R. Higgins, 'The Taking of Property by the State' (1982) 176 *Recueil des Cours* 263 at 270–1 (original emphasis).

[T]here is virtual consensus on the *meaning* of property ... the notion of 'property' is not restricted to chattels. Sometimes rights that might seem more naturally to fall under the category of contract rights are treated as property.

Other commentators who explicitly endorse contract as property do not share Higgins' reserve. Lipstein, in his study on the conflict of laws rules applied by international tribunals, argued that knowing when the existence of a right is a question of domestic or international law is:[72]

[A]n essential factor in deciding claims for State responsibility ... whenever property rights are involved, whether they be contractual or concerned with tangible property, real or personal.

Sampliner, in his review of expropriation claims brought under US investment treaties, did not attempt to distinguish the types of contracts or contractual rights that could be assimilated to property from those that could not:[73]

Although international law has not developed a singular definition of 'property', the term has been acknowledged to encompass all forms of tangible property as well as intangible property, such as intellectual property and contract rights, that entail the right of exclusive use and the right of disposal.

From the foregoing, there appears to be broad agreement that the meaning of property is sufficiently wide to encompass contractual rights. Moreover, many international tribunals have upheld the proposition that contractual breaches can found expropriation claims.

4.2.1.2.2 International Decisions on Contract as Property A key arbitral award on contract as property in international law is the *Norwegian Shipowners' Claim*.[74] As part of its war mobilisation efforts in 1916, the US

---

[72] K. Lipstein, 'Conflict of Laws before International Tribunals (ii)' (1943) 29 *Transactions of the Grotius Society* 51 at 55.

[73] G. H. Sampliner, 'Arbitration of Expropriation Cases under US Investment Treaties – A Threat to Democracy or the Dog That Didn't Bark?' (2003) 18(1) *ICSID Review – Foreign Investment Law Journal* 1 at 14. Schwebel offered indirect support to the assimilation of contract to property by arguing that a breach of contract may entitle a claimant to the same international law remedies as an unlawful expropriation of property, see S. M. Schwebel, 'International Protection of Contractual Arrangements' (1959) 53 *American Society of International Law Proceedings* 266 at 272–3. It is arguable that if interference with contractual rights is remedied in the same way as interference with property rights, then contractual rights are, for all intents and purposes, a species of property.

[74] *Norwegian Shipowners' Claim* (*Norway v. United States*), (1922) 1 RIAA 307, Award, 13 October 1922 (Anderson, Vogt, Valloton). The Permanent Court of Arbitration tribunal

government requisitioned all ships being constructed in local shipyards that were contracted to foreign owners. The US government admitted that compensation was due to the Norwegian shipowners for their cancelled contracts, but as the quantum of compensation could not be agreed on, the dispute was referred to arbitration. The US government argued that as contractual rights are intangible, cancelled contracts are not equivalent to takings of property. The PCA tribunal disagreed, holding that '[t]hese *contracts were the property*, or created it ... [and] "physical property" is only one of the elements or aspects of the "property" under the municipal law of the United States, as well as under the law of Norway and other States'.[75]

Another notable arbitral award is the *Shufeldt Claim*, where the sole arbitrator regarded the rights of a US investor in a chicle extraction contract concluded with the Guatemalan government as property. Remarkably, even the Guatemalan government which was contesting the claim confirmed this:[76]

> There can not be any doubt that property rights are created under and by virtue of a contract, and the Guatemala Government admit this in section 103 of their Answer as follows: 'The Republic of Guatemala does not deny that the grantee or assignee of a legal and binding contract acquires property rights subject to the terms and conditions of the contract.' There is therefore no need to discuss this question further. Shufeldt did, in view of my findings, possess the rights of property given to him under the contract.

The American-Turkey Claims Commission in the *Hoachoozo Palestine Land and Development Co. Case* also took the view that contracts embody property rights, making it possible to regard a contract as a species of property in international law:[77]

> In a case in which complaint is made that governmental authorities have confiscated contractual property rights, the preliminary question is one of domestic law as to the rights of the claimant under a contract in the light of the domestic proper law governing the legal effect of the contract. The next question for determination is whether in the light of principles or rules of international law rights under the contract have been infringed.

---

was not the first tribunal to endorse contract as property. For an even earlier arbitral award, see *Réclamation Chemins de Fer de Lourenço Marques* (*Etats-Unis d'Amerique, Grande-Bretagne, Portugal*), Award, 13 June 1891 in Fontaine (ed.), *Pasicrisie Internationale*, pp. 397, 402.

[75] Ibid., p. 334 (original emphasis).

[76] *Shufeldt Claim* (*Guatemala* v. *United States*) (1930) 2 RIAA 1079, Award, 24 July 1930 (Sisnett), p. 1097.

[77] Excerpted in Lipstein, 'Conflict of Laws', p. 54.

Even the Permanent Court of International Justice accepted that contractual rights can be assimilated to property rights. In the *Case Concerning Certain German Interests in Polish Upper Silesia*, Germany claimed that the assumption of control by the Polish government over a German-owned nitrate factory at Chorzów, including its tangible and intangible assets, was an unauthorised 'measure of liquidation' pursuant to Article 6 of the Convention Relating to Upper Silesia (the Geneva Convention).[78] Article 6 referred specifically to the conditional expropriation of property but was silent on whether contractual rights were covered.[79] The Court pointed out that since Article 6 was one of several provisions grouped under the heading of 'Expropriation' in the Geneva Convention, the German claim was in substance a claim for unlawful expropriation.[80] The Court did not find it necessary to explain the equivalence of contractual rights to property rights and appeared to assume that contract and property were interchangeable under Article 6. It held that so long as the Polish measure challenged by Germany did not conform to the provisions on expropriation in the Geneva Convention, 'Poland has unlawfully expropriated the contractual rights [of] the lawful owner of the Chorzów factory'.[81]

The Iran-US Claims Tribunal treats contract as a species of property. The expropriation provision in the US-Iran Treaty of Amity is Article IV(2):[82]

> Property of nationals and companies of either High Contracting Party, including interests in property, shall receive the most constant protection and security within the territories of the other High Contracting Party, in no case less than that required by international law. Such property shall not be taken except for a public purpose, nor shall it be taken without the prompt payment of just compensation.

Article IV(2) defines expropriation solely with reference to property and interests in property, and no specific mention is made of contracts or

---

[78] *Case Concerning Certain German Interests in Polish Upper Silesia* (*Germany* v. *Poland*) (Merits) (1926) PCIJ, Series A, No. 7, p. 12.

[79] Convention between Germany and Poland Relating to Upper Silesia. Signed 15 May 1922, entered into force 3 June 1922. Article 6 provides:

> Poland may expropriate in Polish Upper Silesia, in conformity with the provisions of Articles 7 to 23, undertakings belonging to the category of major industries including mineral deposits and rural estates. Except as provided in these clauses, the property, rights and interests of German nationals or of companies controlled by German nationals may not be liquidated in Polish Upper Silesia.

[80] *Case Concerning Certain German Interests in Polish Upper Silesia*, p. 21.

[81] Ibid., p. 44.

[82] Treaty of Amity, Economic Relations, and Consular Rights between the United States of America and Iran. Signed 15 August 1955, entered into force 16 June 1957. 284 UNTS 93.

of contractual rights. Yet, investment contracts are frequently assimilated to property. In *Phillips Petroleum* v. *Iran*, the claimant argued that its contractual right to explore and exploit petroleum resources in the Persian Gulf was expropriated when the new Iranian government that came into power after the 1979 revolutions cancelled the contract. The tribunal agreed with the claimant that its claim was one for expropriation, and held that 'contract rights, such as those taken by the Respondents in the present Case, are "interests in property" protected by the Treaty of Amity'.[83] In *Amoco International Finance* v. *Iran*, the tribunal held that contractual rights are property under Article IV(2), because '[e]xpropriation, which can be defined as a compulsory transfer of property rights, may extend to any right which can be the object of a commercial transaction, i.e., freely sold and bought, and thus has a monetary value'.[84] In *Mobil Oil* v. *Iran*, the tribunal held that 'the lawfulness of an expropriation must be judged by reference to international law ... even when the expropriation is of contractual rights', but found it unnecessary to pronounce on whether contract is property because the claim was settled.[85] By repeatedly acknowledging that a claim for the breach of an investment contract can be framed as a claim for expropriation, the IUSCT clearly accepted that the only way in which Article IV(2) of the Treaty of Amity applies to contractual disputes, is if contract is property or generates interests in property.

Finally, contract is also viewed as property in the US Investment Guaranty Program. This Program commits the US government to the indemnification of qualifying US investors for losses suffered in overseas ventures. In return, the investor must assign all remaining rights in the investment to the US government. Once the indemnity is paid, the Program subrogates any outstanding claim or cause of action against the foreign government to the United States. Expropriation is defined in part in the Contract of Guaranty concluded between US investors and the Agency for International Development (AID) as the taking of measures by a foreign government that prevents the US investor 'from exercising substantial control over the use

---

[83] *Phillips Petroleum* v. *Iran* (1989) 21 IUSCTR 79, Award, 29 June 1989 (Briner, Khalilian, Aldrich), para. 105; see also *Oil Field of Texas* v. *Iran and Anor*, 69 ILR 565, Award, 7–8 December 1982 (Lagergren, Bellet, Mangård, Kashani (dissenting), Holtzmann, Shafeiei (dissenting), Aldrich, Mosk (concurring), Sani (dissenting)), p. 584 (Concurring Opinion of Richard Mosk); *McHarg* v. *Iran* (1986) 13 IUSCTR 286, Award, 17 December 1986 (Böckstiegel, Mostafavi, Holtzmann (dissenting and concurring in part)), pp. 291–2 and 302; *Starrett Housing Corporation and Anor* v. *Iran and Ors*, 85 ILR 350, Award, 14 August 1987 (Lagergren, Ameli, Holtzmann (concurring)), p. 392.

[84] 27 ILM 1320, Partial Award, 14 July 1987 (Virally, Brower (concurring), Moin), pp. 1342-52.

[85] *Mobil Oil* v. *Iran*, 86 ILR 231, Award, 14 July 1987 (Virally, Brower, Ansari), p. 255.

and disposition of its property'. Although there is no specific mention of contractual rights in the extensive provision on expropriation, the notion of property is considered sufficiently broad to cover contractual rights. In *Valentine Petroleum and Chemical Corporation* v. *AID*, the US investors sought indemnification from the AID for the unilateral termination of an oil concession contract by the Haitian government.[86] The tribunal held that expropriatory action 'certainly is not limited to the taking of physical property ... [and] the definition in the Contract of Guaranty is broad enough to include ... [the] abrogation of concessionary rights'.[87]

4.2.2 Contract as Investment in Investment Treaty Law

Although the critical equation in a claim for the unlawful expropriation of contractual rights under general international law is between contract and property, the equation changes when the claim is brought under an investment treaty. This is because investment treaties confer protection on qualifying investments, and not on qualifying property.[88] As Kriebaum and Schreuer point out, '[i]nternational investment law does not normally speak of property but of "investments"'.[89] The difference is not purely semantic because qualifying investments are not limited to property rights. What may not qualify as property may, depending on how investment is defined in an applicable treaty, nonetheless qualify as a protected investment. Under investment treaty law therefore, the assimilation is not between contract and property, but between contract and investment.[90]

---

[86] *Valentine Petroleum & Chemical Corp.* v. *AID*, 44 ILR 79, Award, 15 September 1967 (De Vries, Rogers, Sebes).

[87] Ibid., p. 87.

[88] The ASEAN Comprehensive Investment Agreement (signed 26 February 2009, entered into force 24 February 2012), retains the contract-as-property equation. Annex 2(1) provides: 'An action or a series of related actions by a Member State cannot constitute an expropriation unless it interferes with a tangible or intangible property right or property interest in a covered investment.' The contract-as-property equation is also retained in newer treaties such as the Comprehensive Economic and Trade Agreement (signed 30 October 2016, provisional entry into force 21 September 2017), Annex 8-A(1)(b); the Comprehensive and Progressive Agreement for Trans-Pacific Partnership (TPP-11) (signed 23 January 2018, not yet in force), Annex 9-B(1); the European Union-Singapore Investment Protection Agreement (pending signature and ratification, text as of April 2018), Annex 1(1); and the European Union-Mexico Global Agreement (pending signature and ratification, text as of April 2018), Annex on Expropriation (1) and (3).

[89] 'The Concept of Property in Human Rights Law and International Investment Law', p. 2.

[90] *Caratube International Oil Company LLP & Anor* v. *Republic of Kazakhstan*, ICSID Case No. ARB/13/13, Award, 27 September 2017 (Lévy, Aynès, Salès (partially concurring and partially dissenting)), paras. 822–6; cf. *Accession Mezzanine Capital* v. *Hungary*, Award, para. 154;

When investment treaties expressly list contractual rights as a protected investment (4.2.1), it follows that contractual rights are susceptible to expropriation (4.2.2).

4.2.2.1   The Meaning of Investment

The protection accorded by an investment treaty covers investments enumerated in the treaty.[91] Many bilateral and multilateral investment treaties identify contractual rights as a species of investment. The US-Argentina investment treaty provides that 'investment' includes:[92]

> [A]ny right conferred by law or contract.

The Hungary-Switzerland investment treaty provides that 'investment' includes:[93]

> [C]oncessions, including concessions of exploration, extraction or exploitation of natural resources, as well as any right conferred by law, by contract, or by a decision rendered by an authority applying the law.

'Investment' according to the Energy Charter Treaty includes:[94]

> [A]ny right conferred by law or contract.

And 'investment' in the ASEAN Comprehensive Investment Agreement (ACIA) includes:[95]

> [R]ights under contracts, including turnkey, construction, management, production or revenue-sharing contracts.

From a plain reading of the text, some investment treaties, like the US-Argentina investment treaty, the Hungary-Switzerland investment treaty

---

and *Ampal-American Israel Corporation and Ors* v. *Arab Republic of Egypt*, ICSID Case No. ARB/12/11, Decision on Jurisdiction, 1 February 2016 (Fortier, McLachlan, Orrego Vicuña), para. 255 and Decision on Liability and Heads of Loss, 21 February 2017 (Fortier, McLachlan, Orrego Vicuña), paras. 337 and 347.

[91] It is unusual when an investment treaty does not contain a definition of investment, but see Convention between the Government of the French Republic and the Government of the Federal Socialist Republic of Yugoslavia on the Protection of Investments. Signed 28 March 1974, entered into force 3 March 1975.

[92] Treaty between United States of America and the Argentine Republic Concerning the Reciprocal Encouragement and Protection of Investment. Signed 14 November 1991, entered into force 20 October 1994. Article I(1)(a)(v).

[93] Accord entre la Confédération Suisse et la République Populaire Hongroise concernant la promotion et la protection réciproques des investissements. Signed 5 October 1988, entered into force 16 May 1989. Article 1(2)(e), author's translation from the original French.

[94] Signed 17 December 1994, entered into force 16 April 1998. 2080 UNTS 95 ('ECT'), Art. 1(6)(f).

[95] Signed 26 February 2009, entered into force 24 February 2012, ('ACIA'). Article 4(c)(v).

and the ECT, appear to recognise any contractual right as a protected investment. Apart from claims concerning rights arising from ordinary sale and purchase contracts, it is doubtful if tribunals should try to shrink the scope of treaty protection for contractual rights, in disregard of express treaty language.[96] The situation is different when treaties, such as the ACIA, are more specific about which contractual rights qualify as protected investments. Here, there is always the possibility that a claim founded on the host State's interference with the foreign investor's contractual rights does not come within the jurisdiction of an investment treaty tribunal due to the absence of an underlying protected investment.

Some investment treaties do not refer to contracts or contractual rights in the definition of a protected investment. This does not mean that contractual rights can never benefit from treaty protection. A claimant can still try to show that a contract qualifies as a protected investment by arguing that the contractual rights in question are akin to rights expressly recognised by the treaty as investments.

The claimants in *Emmis* v. *Hungary* brought unlawful expropriation claims under the Hungary-Switzerland and Hungary-Netherlands investment treaties for the non-renewal of a broadcasting license. The Hungary-Switzerland investment treaty expressly includes contractual rights in its definition of protected investments, but the Hungary-Netherlands investment treaty does not. Instead, the latter contains an asset-based definition of investment where

> [i] movable and immovable property as well as any other rights *in rem* in respect of every kind of asset; [ii] rights derived from shares, bonds and other kinds of interests in companies and joint ventures; [iii] title to money, goodwill and other assets and to any performance having an economic value; [iv] rights in the field of intellectual property, technical processes and know-how; and [v] rights granted under public law, including rights to prospect, explore, extract and win natural resources,[97]

qualify for treaty protection. After setting out the authorities which advise that, under general international law, contractual rights are a species of property that can be expropriated, the tribunal in *Emmis* v. *Hungary* held that contractual rights which come within an asset-based treaty definition of protected investments can also be expropriated:[98]

---

[96] Cf. Douglas, 'The Hybrid Foundations of Investment Treaty Arbitration', p. 191 (fn. 291).

[97] Agreement between the Swiss Confederation and the Hungarian People's Republic on the Reciprocal Promotion and Protection of Investments. Signed 5 October 1988, entered into force 16 May 1989. Article 1(a).

[98] Award, *op. cit.*, para. 169.

> [T]he loss of a right conferred by contract may be capable of giving rise to a claim of expropriation but only if it gives rise to an asset owned by the claimant to which a monetary value may be ascribed.

When a treaty is silent on whether contracts and contractual rights are protected investments, it may be tempting to deduce that all contractual rights are thus ineligible for treaty protection. The approach of the tribunal in *Emmis* v. *Hungary* is nonetheless preferable because it endeavours to further the goal of investment protection without overextending the scope of treaty protection to rights which are not expressly recognised as investments.

4.2.2.2   Investments Are Subject to the Right of Host States to Expropriate

Whether or not a particular investment treaty lists contractual rights as protected investments or the types of contractual rights that benefit from treaty protection, all investment treaties contain provisions regulating the expropriation of protected investments. Although the scope of protection for contractual rights may differ considerably from one investment treaty to the next, the way that investment treaties address the expropriation of protected investments is largely similar.

According to Article 13(1) of the ECT:

> Investments of Investors of a Contracting Party in the Area of any other Contracting Party shall not be nationalized, expropriated or subjected to a measure or measures having effect equivalent to nationalization or expropriation (hereinafter referred to as 'Expropriation') except where such Expropriation is: (a) for a purpose which is in the public interest; (b) not discriminatory; (c) carried out under due process of law; and (d) accompanied by the payment of prompt, adequate and effective compensation.

And Article 14(1) of the ACIA provides:

> A Member State shall not expropriate or nationalise a covered investment either directly or through measures equivalent to expropriation or nationalisation ('expropriation'), except: (a) for a public purpose; (b) in a non-discriminatory manner; (c) on payment of prompt, adequate and effective compensation; and (d) in accordance with due process of law.

Investment treaties permit host States to expropriate protected investments, so long as the expropriation is accompanied by prompt, adequate and effective compensation, public purpose and due process.[99] Some investment treaties

---

[99] It has been observed that the 'requirement of due process is not systematically included in investment protection treaties ... [resulting in] not much case law on the issue', U. Kriebaum and A. Reinisch, 'Property, Right to, International Protection' in R. Wolfrum (ed.), *The Max Planck Encyclopedia of Public International Law* (Oxford: Oxford University Press, 2008), online: www.mpepil.com/home (accessed 31 December 2017), para. 22.

may also require the expropriation to be non-discriminatory. Treaty conditions for a lawful expropriation thus mirror the conditions under general international law.

Based on the foregoing, there is strong support for characterising investment contracts as objects of expropriation. The inquiry does not stop here. Even if investment contracts can be expropriated, State responsibility is only engaged when an expropriation has taken place and does not comply with customary or treaty law. The next two sections discuss when a breach of an investment contract amounts to an expropriation, and when that expropriation becomes unlawful.

4.3   The Existence of Expropriation

Not every breach of contract amounts to an expropriation. According to some early writers, a contractual breach is expropriatory only if justice is denied to the foreign investor seeking redress in the courts of the host State.[100] Some modern-day tribunals adhere to this narrower understanding of expropriation. In *Waste Management Inc.* v. *United Mexican States (No. 2)*, the tribunal held that before interference by the host State with a contractual right can amount to an expropriation, 'it is necessary to show an effective repudiation of the right, unredressed by any remedies available to the Claimant, which has the effect of preventing its exercise entirely or to a substantial extent'.[101] Other tribunals are more generous with the characterisation of conduct as expropriatory. According to the tribunal in *Metalclad Corporation* v. *The United Mexican States*, an expropriation includes any 'covert or incidental interference with the use of property which has the effect of depriving the owner, in whole or in significant part, of the use or reasonably-to-be-expected economic benefit of property even if not necessarily to the obvious benefit of the host State'.[102] Drawing on existing arbitral awards, this section attempts to identify contractual

---

[100] Borchard, *The Diplomatic Protection of Citizens Abroad*, p. 284; J. J. Herz, 'Expropriation of Foreign Property' (1941) 35 AJIL 243 at 245.
[101] *Waste Management Inc.* v. *United Mexican States (No. 2)*, ICSID Case No. ARB(AF)/00/3, Award, 30 April 2004 (Crawford, Civiletti, Gómez), para. 175; see also *Caratube International Oil Company* v. *Kazakhstan*, Award, para. 908; *Koch Minerals SARL and Anor.* v. *Bolivarian Republic of Venezuela*, ICSID Case No. ARB/11/19, Award, 30 October 2017 (Veeder, Lalonde, Douglas (partially dissenting)), para. 7.50.
[102] *Metalclad Corp.* v. *The United Mexican States*, ICSID Case No. ARB(AF)/97/1, Award, 30 August 2000 (Lauterpacht, Civiletti, Siqueiros), para. 103.

breaches that amount to expropriations (4.3.1), and contractual breaches that do not (4.3.2).

4.3.1   Expropriatory Contractual Breaches

As contractual breaches can be committed by a private individual as well as a State, while expropriations can only be carried out by a State, expropriatory contractual breaches must first and foremost constitute *acta iure imperii* (4.3.1.1). Moreover, breaches committed in a State's sovereign capacity usually have to bring about the cancellation of the investment contract to be expropriatory (4.3.1.2).

4.3.1.1   Acta Iure Imperii

According to the tribunal in *Waste Management (No. 2)* v. *Mexico*, 'nationalization and expropriation are inherently governmental acts'.[103] The identification of a 'governmental act' requires a distinction to be drawn between acts done by a State *iure imperii* (in a sovereign capacity) and *iure gestionis* (in a non-sovereign capacity). For a breach of contract to be construed as an expropriation under international law, it has to qualify as a 'governmental act'. This qualification stands notwithstanding the absence of the *iure imperii-iure gestionis* distinction from the Articles on State Responsibility.[104] This is because Article 12 provides that State responsibility is engaged upon the non-conformity by a State with its international obligation, 'regardless of its origin or character'.[105] Therefore, when a State is under a primary obligation to expropriate within the confines of customary or treaty law, with expropriation being a manifestation of *acta iure imperii*, the secondary rules on State responsibility as enshrined in the ILC Articles do not alter the conditions for a violation of the primary obligation.[106] And unless a breach of contract is simultaneously *acta iure imperii*, the existence of an expropriation is not proved.

---

[103] *Waste Management (No. 2)* v. *Mexico*, Award, para. 174.

[104] Crawford, 'Revising the Draft Articles on State Responsibility', p. 435 at 440.

[105] See also ILC, 'Draft Articles on Responsibility of States for Internationally Wrongful Acts, with Commentaries', vol. II, Part Two, pp. 54–7.

[106] Where the primary obligation is violated by a State-owned or State-linked entity possessing separate legal personality from the host State, the normal rules of attribution found in ASR Chapter II, in particular Article 5, determine if that entity's *acta iure imperii* can be imputed to the host State.

One category of 'governmental acts' that has the potential to bring about the expropriatory breach of an investment contract is legislation. As the power to legislate is an essential attribute of sovereignty, the passing of legislation which affects investment contracts can, in some situations, amount to an expropriation.[107]

Legislative measures purporting to suspend the performance of an investment contract, or to modify key contractual terms which make continued performance by the foreign investor extremely onerous, are arguably expropriatory. The arbitral tribunals in *Himpurna* v. *PT (Persero)*,[108] *Patua* v. *PT (Persoro)*,[109] and *Karaha Bodas* v. *Pertamina*[110] all concluded that Indonesia's suspension of sales energy contracts by legislative decree in the aftermath of the 1997 Asian financial crisis expropriated the claimants' contractual rights. The legislative decree provided that the suspended contracts would be reviewed and possibly reinstated in due course. Yet, the State entities with whom the claimants contracted did nothing to jumpstart a review process, nor did they exhibit any inclination to work with the claimants to persuade the government to lift the suspension. The tribunals in the *Himpurna* and *Patua* awards pointed out that with no end to the suspension in sight, 'the claimant would soon go bankrupt'.[111] Expropriatory legislative measures were also the focal point in *Revere Copper* v. *OPIC*, where a newly elected Jamaican government decided to tighten regulations over the bauxite mining industry. The government enacted a series of legislative provisions to shorten the duration of mining licenses, revoke certain guarantees previously given to foreign investors and impose a bauxite levy that promised to lower the profit margins of mining companies. In the view of the tribunal, the claimant 'still has all the rights property that it had before the events of 1974; it is in possession of the plant and other facilities; it has its Mining Lease; it can operate as it did

---

[107] Mann, 'State Contracts and State Responsibility', p. 572 at 577–8; Amerasinghe, 'State Breaches of Contracts with Aliens and International Law', p. 881 at 885–6; Pazarci, 'La Responsabilité Internationale des Etats à l'Occasion des Contrats Conclus Entre Etats et Personnes Privées Etrangères', p. 354 at 371–2; F. Rigaux, 'Les Situations Juridiques Individuelles Dans un Système de Relativité Générale de Droit International Privé' (1989) 213 *Recueil des Cours* 154 at 209–14.

[108] Award, 4 May 1999 (Paulsson, de Fina, Setiawan) in A. J. van den Berg (ed.), Yearbook Commercial Arbitration (The Hague: Kluwer Law International, 2000), vol. 15, p. 11.

[109] Award, 4 May 1999 (Paulsson, de Fina, Setiawan) in (1999) 14 *Mealey's International Arbitration Report* B1.

[110] Final Award, 18 December 2000 (Derains, Bernadini, El Kosheri) in (2001) 16 *Mealey's International Arbitration Report* C1.

[111] *Himpurna v. PT (Persoro)* Award, para. 191; *Patua v. PT (Persoro)* Award, para. 309.

before'.[112] However, the modifications which the claimant had no choice but to accept amounted to a *de facto* expropriation since they represented 'the destruction by Government actions of its contract rights'.[113]

Ascertaining if a breach of contract is *acta iure imperii*, and in turn expropriatory, in the absence of legislative activity is less straightforward. The *iure imperii-iure gestionis* distinction, which developed in the context of granting States jurisdictional immunity before foreign courts, is notoriously difficult to apply in practice.[114] In disputes over breaches of investment contracts, where the State argues that it was acting in a purely contractual capacity, 'it might be difficult to draw this distinction, as not every kind of conduct can be clearly ascribed to one or the other type'.[115]

Still, difficulty in application is not a reason for jettisoning the *iure imperii-iure gestionis* distinction when the existence of an expropriation hinges on the act complained of being a 'governmental act'. The arbitral tribunal in *Vigotop* v. *Hungary* refashioned the *iure imperii-iure gestionis* distinction into a three-part test to determine if the termination of an investment contract by Hungary was expropriatory. The dispute in *Vigotop* v. *Hungary* arose from the cancellation of a concession for the development of tourist sites and attractions in Hungary. Vigotop argued that the cancellation was equivalent to an unlawful expropriation under the Cyprus-Hungary investment treaty, while Hungary countered that it was merely exercising its contractual right to terminate. The tribunal decided the expropriation claim by examining: (i) whether Hungary had public policy reasons for termination; (ii) whether Hungary had contractual grounds for termination; and (iii) whether Hungary abused its contractual right to terminate in order to avoid paying compensation.[116] If, on the facts, the answer to limb (i) is negative, there is no expropriation at all since the State is not acting in its sovereign capacity.[117] The expropriation claim

---

[112] Award, p. 291.

[113] Award, p. 292.

[114] H. Lauterpacht, 'The Problem of Jurisdictional Immunities of Foreign States' (1951) 28 BYIL 220 at 222 and 224; J. Crawford, 'International Law and Foreign Sovereigns: Distinguishing Immune Transactions' (1983) 54 BYIL 74 at 98–102; Chinkin, 'A Critique of the Public/Private Dimension', p. 387; M. Koskenniemi, *From Apology to Utopia* (Cambridge: Cambridge University Press, 2005), pp. 488–9; also the Dissenting Opinions of Judges Yusuf, p. 25 and Trindade, p. 171, para. 177 in *Jurisdictional Immunities of the State (Germany v. Italy: Greece intervening)* (Judgment) [2012] ICJ Rep 99.

[115] *Sempra Energy International* v. *Argentina*, ICSID Case No. ARB/02/16), Award, 28 September 2007 (Orrego Vicuña, Lalonde, Rico), para. 311.

[116] Ibid., paras. 312–632.

[117] Ibid., para. 328.

can be dismissed at this stage. If the answer to limb (i) is positive, then limb (ii) would have to be considered. This is because if the State has valid contractual grounds for termination, the presence of public policy reasons does not necessarily render the termination expropriatory. Conversely, the absence of valid contractual grounds for termination would place the contractual breach squarely within the province of an expropriation.[118] When there are both public policy and contractual reasons for termination, the tie-breaker for a finding of expropriation is limb (iii). If the termination is not effected to avoid payment of compensation, it is not expropriatory.[119]

The *Vigotop* test has the benefit of flexibility because the relevance of limbs (ii) and (iii) to the existence of expropriation depends on the facts of each case. On the facts of *Vigotop* v. *Hungary*, the tribunal found that there was no expropriation as Hungary had both public policy as well as valid contractual grounds for termination, and was not trying to avoid paying compensation. The problem with the *Vigotop* test is the compulsory limb (i). The pursuit of public purpose or policy is one of several indicia for the legality of an expropriation (see Section 4.4.2). By listing it as a criterion for the *existence* of an expropriation, the tribunal in *Vigotop* v. *Hungary* risked conflating a finding of expropriation with a finding of unlawfulness. The tribunal did not have to deal with the conflation because it found that as there was no expropriation on the facts, there was no need to pronounce on legality.

One way of maintaining distinctive criteria for the existence and legality of an expropriatory breach of contract, is for limb (i) of the *Vigotop* test to direct a tribunal to assess the mode rather than the objective of a contractual breach. A State would have 'stepped out of the contractual shoes' if it breaches an investment contract in a way that cannot be replicated by a private contracting party.[120] Examples include denying permits or licenses without which the investor cannot perform the contract,[121] deporting the investor[122] or dispatching military personnel to secure the investor's

---

[118] Ibid., para. 329.

[119] Ibid., para. 330.

[120] *Vigotop* v. *Hungary* Award, para. 328, where the tribunal adopted the words of Vigotop's expert, N. Schrijver, as the 'key question' in its expropriation analysis.

[121] *Metalclad* v. *Mexico* Award, cited previously; *Southern Pacific Properties (Middle East) Limited* v. *Arab Republic of Egypt*, ICSID Case No. ARB/84/3, Award on the Merits, 20 May 1992 (Jiménez de Aréchaga, Pietrowski, El Mahdi (dissenting)); *Biloune and Anor* v. *Ghana and Anor*, 95 ILR 184, Award, 30 June 1990 (Schwebel, Wallace, Leigh).

[122] *Case of Ahmadou Sadio Diallo* (*Guinea* v. *Democratic Republic of the Congo*) (Preliminary Objections, Judgment) [2007] ICJ Rep 582.

eviction from a work site.[123] Whatever its weaknesses, the *Vigotop* test must be lauded for trying to capture the dominant traits of an expropriatory breach of contract. It is a rare and genuine attempt to overcome the difficulties associated with applying the *iure imperii-iure gestionis* distinction to contract-based expropriation claims.

4.3.1.2   Cancellation

It is generally accepted that the cancellation of an investment contract *iure imperii* is expropriatory.[124] Cancellation can be direct or indirect.

A direct cancellation is likely to involve the promulgation of legislation terminating the particular contract, or nationalising the particular industry for which the contract was concluded.[125]

An indirect cancellation usually comprises a series of measures which, when taken in isolation, do not put an end to the investment contract, but in totality render it impossible or impracticable for the investor to perform its end of the original contractual bargain.[126] These measures can include but are not limited to unilateral profit-sharing adjustments,[127] the refusal or revocation of previously promised or granted licenses and permits necessary for the performance of the contract,[128] the eviction of the investor from the place of performance[129] and, in some extreme cases, the harassment and intimidation of the investor's employees.[130]

Occasionally, one measure in a series of measures taken by the host State that brings about the cancellation of the investment contract may qualify on its own as an expropriation. In *Metalclad* v. *Mexico*, the claimant procured a permit from the federal government to construct and operate a hazardous waste landfill in Guadalcazar, which is located within

---

[123] See *Bayindir* v. *Pakistan* Decision on Jurisdiction, cited previously.

[124] G. White, 'Wealth Deprivation: Creditor and Contract Claims' in R. B. Lillich (ed.), *International Law of State Responsibility for Injuries to Aliens* (Virginia: University Press of Virginia, 1983), pp. 149, 151; I. Brownlie, 'International Law at the Fiftieth Anniversary of the United Nations: General Course on Public International Law' (1995) 25 *Recueil des Cours* 9 at 152–3; C. F. Dugan et al., *Investor-State Arbitration* (Oxford: Oxford University Press, 2008), p. 460.

[125] *AHS Niger and Ors* v. *Republic of Niger*, ICSID Case No. ARB/11/11, Award, 15 July 2013 (Mantilla-Serrano, Hubert, Kenfack-Douajni), paras. 119–26.

[126] *Koch Minerals* v. *Venezuela* Award, para. 7.51.

[127] *Revere Copper* v. *OPIC* Award.

[128] *SPP* v. *Egypt* Award on the Merits; *Biloune* v. *Ghana* Award.

[129] *GMR Malé International Airport Pte Ltd.* v. *The Republic of Maldives and Anor* [2013] SGCA 16.

[130] *Wena Hotels Limited* v. *Arab Republic of Egypt*, ICSID Case No. ARB/98/4, Award, 8 December 2000 (Leigh, Fadlallah, Wallace).

the Mexican state of San Luis Potosí. The state government subsequently issued a land use permit for the construction of the landfill. Barely a year after constructions began, the municipality of Guadalcazar ordered the cessation of all work on the landfill since no municipal construction permit was issued. The claimant protested that it had acted on the advice of federal officials who did not think that a permit from the municipality was necessary for works to proceed. Nevertheless, the claimant submitted an application for a municipal construction permit and resumed work on the landfill. After construction works were completed, the claimant was informed by the municipal government that its application for the construction permit was denied. The municipality then obtained an injunction from the Mexican courts to stop the claimant from operating the landfill. After trying and failing to resolve the dispute over the landfill in Guadalcazar with the state government, the claimant brought arbitration proceedings against Mexico under Chapter 11 of NAFTA. Several months later, the governor of San Luis Potosí issued an Ecological Decree declaring the area where the landfill stood as a natural area for the protection of a rare breed of cactus. Operation of the landfill ceased for good.

The tribunal in *Metalclad* v. *Mexico* found that the representations of the federal government, the denial of a municipal construction permit, as well as the resort to an injunction to hinder the claimant from operating the landfill were 'measures ... amount[ing] to an indirect expropriation'.[131] The federal permit was as good as cancelled even if the Ecological Decree had not been passed. The tribunal added that since the 'Decree had the effect of barring forever the operation of the landfill ... the implementation of the Ecological Decree would, in and of itself, constitute an act tantamount to expropriation'.[132] This finding reinforces the need for an investment contract to be cancelled *iure imperii* for there to be an expropriation. The sovereign act here was the promulgation of the Ecological Decree by the governor of San Luis Potosí.

Tribunals may not elevate the cancellation of an investment contract to an expropriation if the cancellation is a response to the claimant's defective or non-performance of the contract. In *Carl Sax* v. *St Petersburg*, the claimant contracted with the city of St Petersburg to develop and construct an airport terminal.[133] The claimant was responsible for submitting a financing proposal for the project by a given date and for establishing a joint

---

[131] Ibid., para. 107.
[132] Ibid., paras. 109 and 111.
[133] SCC-UNCITRAL, Final Award, 30 March 2012 (Blessing, Runeland, Bushev).

stock company, with Russians holding two-thirds of the shares, to over-see the project. The claimant failed to meet the deadline, and the financ-ing terms in the proposal that was eventually submitted were not what his Russian partners previously agreed to. Absent accord on how the pro-ject should be financed, the Russian respondents saw the project as still-born and cancelled the investment contract. The claimant argued that the cancellation was an expropriation of his contractual rights. The tribunal rejected this argument, holding that since 'the project did not proceed and became entirely stale ... the Russian Parties could no longer be considered bound to work towards an implementation of the Project'.[134] Moreover, as 'it is the case of the Foreign Parties' failure to provide what they had firmly undertaken to provide[,] ... the Tribunal sees no merits in ... an expropria-tion claim'.[135] Notably, there was nothing inherently governmental about the manner in which the City of St Petersburg cancelled the contract.

4.3.2   Non-expropriatory Contractual Breaches

As long as a breach of contract is not committed *iure imperii*, it cannot be an expropriation. This is why forced renegotiations, which any indi-vidual or State can initiate, are rarely expropriatory (4.3.2.1). That said, some contractual breaches committed *iure imperii*, such as those which only result in fractional interference with contractual rights, are also non-expropriatory (4.3.2.2).

4.3.2.1   Forced Renegotiations

Whether forcibly renegotiated contracts evince expropriation is controver-sial. Muchlinski argues that when a foreign investor renegotiates an invest-ment contract with the host State under duress, the coercive actions of the host State amount to an expropriation.[136] But he also accepts that apart from threats of physical injury to person or property which generally elude legal justification,[137] 'no absolute rules can be laid down' to guide a tribunal in determining if an investor's consent to renegotiate was involuntary.[138]

Tribunals are generally reluctant to consider the exertion of pressure on the investor by the host State to renegotiate as a measure tantamount to

---

[134] Ibid., para. 630.
[135] Ibid., paras. 631–2.
[136] P. Muchlinski, *Multinational Enterprises and the Law* (Oxford: Blackwell, 1995), pp. 500–1.
[137] D. Vagts, 'Coercion and Foreign Investment Rearrangements' (1978) 72 AJIL 17 at 30 where violence is called 'the antithesis of the ordinary market'.
[138] Muchlinski, *Multinational Enterprises and the Law*, p. 500.

expropriation. In *The Government of the State of Kuwait* v. *The American Independent Oil Company*, the majority rejected the claimant's argument that its consent to renegotiate an oil concession contract was, despite the presence of 'strong economic pressure', vitiated by duress:[139]

> [T]he Company made a choice; disagreeable as certain demands might be, it considered that it was better to accede to them because it was still possible to live with them. The whole conduct of the Company shows that the pressure it was under was not of a kind to inhibit its freedom of choice.

No other tribunal has come as close to considering the effect of a forcibly renegotiated investment contract in connection with a claim for expropriated contractual rights. In *Desert Line* v. *Yemen*, the Omani claimant persuaded the tribunal that the forced renegotiation of several contracts for the construction of asphalt roads was an act of duress by Yemen that violated the fair and equitable treatment standard in Article 3 of the Oman-Yemen investment treaty.[140] It has been suggested that 'had Desert Line framed its argument solely in terms of expropriation before the ICSID tribunal, it is unclear whether it would have been successful'.[141]

Unlike cancellations *iure imperii*, renegotiations are a way of preserving the contractual relationship even if the original contractual bargain can no longer be held. A renegotiation tends to be borne from commercial sense. Furthermore, a renegotiation aims to adapt contractual rights to changing circumstances, rather than abrogate them. Since renegotiations are 'an integral feature of the foreign investment process',[142] a demand by the host State to renegotiate should not be an immediate cause for alarm for the foreign investor. Salacuse, an experienced negotiator of investment contracts, urges investors to part with the notion that contracts can be carved in stone. If a contractual relationship is worth maintaining, then 'it may be

---

[139] *The Government of the State of Kuwait* v. *The American Independent Oil Company*, 21 ILM 976, Award, 24 March 1982 (Reuter, Sultan, Fitzmaurice (partially dissenting)), paras. 41 and 44.

[140] *Desert Line Projects LLC* v. *The Republic of Yemen*, ICSID Case No. ARB/05/17, Award, 6 February 2008 (Tercier, Paulsson, El-Kosheri), paras. 151–86 and 191–4.

[141] O. R. Jones and C. Dunn, 'Consent, Forced Renegotiation and Expropriation in International Law' (2010) 26(3) *Arbitration International* 391 at 407.

[142] S. B. Asante, 'Stability of Contractual Relations in the Transnational Investment Process' (1979) 28 ICLQ 401 at 413; more generally K. P. Berger, 'Renegotiation and Adaptation of International Investment Contracts: The Role of Contract Drafters and Arbitrators' (2003) 36 *Vanderbilt Journal of Transnational Law* 1347; and S. M. Kröll, 'The Renegotiation and Adaptation of Investment Contracts' in N. Horn and S. M. Kröll (eds.), *Arbitrating Foreign Investment Disputes: Procedural and Substantive Legal Aspects* (The Hague: Kluwer Law International, 2004), p. 425.

more realistic and wiser to think of an international deal as a *continuing negotiation* between the parties to the transactions as they seek to adjust their relationship to the rapidly changing international environment in which they must work together'.[143]

Immutable investment contracts belong to a bygone era when host States were not fully aware that turning back on sweeping assurances not to alter contractual undertakings raised the issue of their responsibility under international law. The wisdom of giving these assurances, whether through stabilisation clauses in investment contracts (Chapter 5, Section 5.2.2.2), or through umbrella clauses in investment treaties (Chapter 5, Section 5.3), has since been called into question. If States today are unlikely to abstain from contractual modifications, foreign investors should be prepared to renegotiate. Unless renegotiations are secured through the exercise of sovereign powers, and resorted to as a pretext for cancellation without compensation (recall the *Vigotop* test discussed earlier at Section 4.3.1.1), they are not illustrative of expropriations.

4.3.2.2   Fractional Interference with Contractual Rights

A breach of contract by the host State that does not wholly or substantially deprive the investor of his contractual rights, even if it is committed in a sovereign capacity, will not be regarded as an expropriation.

In *Nykomb* v. *Latvia*, Windau, a wholly owned subsidiary of the claimant entered into a contract with Latvenergo, a State-owned enterprise, for the generation and distribution of electricity. According to the terms of the contract, Latvenergo was to purchase electricity from Windau at a rate that was fixed by contract and confirmed by statute. The relevant statutory provisions were later repealed and Latvenergo stopped making payment to Windau. Windau argued that the State was complicit in the default in payment and had therefore committed an expropriatory breach of contract under Article 13 of the ECT. The tribunal agreed that Latvenergo's failure to pay was attributable to the State because Latvenergo 'was clearly an instrument of the State in a highly regulated electricity market'.[144] It disagreed that the failure to pay was expropriatory:[145]

---

[143] J. W. Salacuse, *The Three Laws of International Investment: National, Contractual, and International Frameworks for Foreign Capital* (Oxford: Oxford University Press, 2013), p. 297 (original emphasis).

[144] *Nykomb Synergetics Technology Holding AB* v. *Latvia*, SCC-ECT, Award, 16 December 2003 (Haug, Schütze, Gernandt), p. 31.

[145] Ibid., p. 32.

The decisive factor for drawing the border line towards expropriation must primarily be the degree of possession taking or control over the enterprise the disputed measures entail. In the present case, there is no possession taking of Windau or its assets, no interference with the shareholder's rights or with the management's control over and running of the enterprise apart from ordinary regulatory provisions laid down in the production licence, the off-take agreement, etc. The Tribunal therefore concludes that the withholding of payment at the double tariff does not qualify as an expropriation or the equivalent of an expropriation under the Treaty.

An investor who still exercises control over his contractual rights has clearly not been deprived of them. This is why taxation and devaluation measures that are *acta iure imperii*, and which may affect the performance or profitability of an investment contract but do not otherwise interfere with an investor's exercise of his contractual rights, are *prima facie* non-expropriatory.[146] Moreover, if the investor consents to alterations to the original contract, he cannot subsequently claim that those alterations amount to an expropriation.[147]

4.4   The Unlawfulness of Expropriation

An expropriatory breach of contract engages the international responsibility of the host State only if it is unlawful. The three settled indicia of an unlawful expropriation are the absence of compensation (4.4.1), the absence of public purpose (4.4.2) and the absence of due process (4.4.3). An expropriatory breach of contract is lawful if *all* three indicia are *absent*. But an expropriatory breach of contract will be unlawful so long as any *one* of the three indicia is *present*.

4.4.1   Absence of Compensation

Acceptable standards of compensation for expropriation range from 'full', to 'prompt, adequate and effective', to 'appropriate', to 'equitable'.[148] Without

---

[146] J. Crawford, *Brownlie's Principles of Public International Law* (Oxford: Oxford University Press, 2012), p. 621; also *Sergei Paushok and Ors* v. *Mongolia*, UNCITRAL, Award on Jurisdiction and Liability, 28 April 2011 (Lalonde, Grigera Naón, Stern), paras. 330–6; *El Paso Energy International Company* v. *Argentina*, ICSID Case No. ARB/03/15, Award, 31 October 2011 (Caflisch, Bernadini, Stern), paras. 294–9. For a persuasive account of why taxation is not equivalent to expropriation under domestic law, see J. Penner, 'Misled by Property' (2005) 18 *Canadian Journal of Law & Jurisprudence* 75 at 79–86.

[147] C. McLachlan, L. Shore, and M. Weiniger, *International Investment Arbitration: Substantive Principles* (Oxford: Oxford University Press, 2007), para. 8.74.

[148] C. Brown, *A Common Law of International Adjudication* (Oxford: Oxford University Press, 2007), pp. 205–6.

a common standard, the adequacy or inadequacy of any compensation received by the investor will depend on the standard of compensation the tribunal adopts. Claimants are more likely to press for 'full' compensation, whereas host States are more likely to argue that 'equitable' compensation suffices. Most investment treaties adopt the higher 'prompt, adequate and effective' standard of compensation for expropriations,[149] arguably easing the claimant's task of proving that the compensation awarded, if at all, was inadequate. Due to the lack of more specific guidelines to measure the adequacy of compensation, the ultimate finding usually rests on the battle between expert valuation reports.[150]

In *Guaracachi America* v. *Bolivia*, the claimants prevailed because the tribunal agreed with the claimants' valuation expert that the expropriated company 'had a positive value'.[151] Bolivia's failure to pay any compensation upon expropriation was therefore unlawful. In contrast, UK investors in Northern Rock, a bank that traded on the London Stock Exchange, were unsuccessful in challenging the zero compensation they received from the UK government when the bank was nationalised in 2008. The ECHR and the English courts agreed with the independent valuer that the value of Northern Rock's shares, immediately before the UK government announced its decision to nationalise, was nil.[152] Foreign investors in Northern Rock on the other hand have the option of bringing a treaty claim against the United Kingdom. The United Kingdom agreed to pay 'prompt, adequate, and effective' compensation to protected investors in its investment treaties.[153] It is at the very least arguable that nil compensation is inadequate compensation.

Apart from an unfavourable report on the value of the claimant's expropriated investment, the absence of compensation may not be indicative of unlawfulness if the host State pleads that the expropriation was a non-compensable regulatory taking.[154] Here, because the host State is alleging

---

[149] UNCTAD, *Bilateral Investment Treaties 1995–2006: Trends in Investment Rulemaking* (New York, NY and Geneva: United Nations, 2007), p. 52.

[150] B. Sabahi, *Compensation and Restitution in Investor-State Arbitration: Principles and Practice* (Oxford: Oxford University Press, 2011), pp. 183–5.

[151] *Guaracachi America, Inc. and Rurelec PLC* v. *The Plurinational State of Bolivia*, PCA Case No. 2011-17, Award, 31 January 2014 (Júdice, Conthe, Vineusa), para. 438.

[152] *Case of Grainger and Ors* v. *United Kingdom* (European Court of Human Rights Fourth Section), App. No. 34940/10, 10 July 2012, paras. 20–2 and 35–43.

[153] N. J. Calamita, 'The British Bank Nationalizations: An International Law Perspective' (2009) 58(1) ICLQ 119 at 124–8.

[154] *Ronald S. Lauder* v. *Czech Republic*, UNCITRAL, Final Award, 3 September 2001 (Briner, Cutler, Klein), para. 198; *Tecnicas Medioambientales Tecmed S.A.* v. *United Mexican States*, ICSID Case No. ARB(AF)/00/2, Award, 29 May 2003 (Grigera Naón, Rozas, Verea), para. 119.

that no compensation is due, it bears the burden of proving the proper exercise of its police powers. While the evidential threshold for a non-compensable regulatory taking awaits refinement,[155] it is generally accepted 'that governments have the right to protect, through non-discriminatory actions, *inter alia*, the environment, human health and safety, market integrity and social policies without providing compensation for any incidental deprivation of foreign owned property'.[156] Whether the stated purpose can be proved and persuade the tribunal that no compensation is due will depend on the facts of each case. There is to date little progress on what sets a regulatory taking apart from a compensable expropriation, or what measures other than general taxation affecting property represent a valid exercise of a State's police powers.[157] That said, bare assertions that a State has an unfettered right to regulate its domestic affairs are unlikely to impress a tribunal. Although most tribunals will probably be reluctant to second-guess a State's exact motivations, a State must still offer some proof that its refusal to compensate was justified.

In *ADC* v. *Hungary*, the claimants won a tender to build and operate two terminals of the Budapest-Ferihegy International Airport. After the terminals were completed and in service, Hungary adopted a new model of regulation for its aviation industry and passed a decree recognising the State as the majority owner in any provider of air travel facilities. The turn-key and management contracts concluded between the claimants and the Hungarian Air Traffic and Airport Administration (ATAA) were swiftly terminated with no offer of compensation. Hungary denied that the absence of compensation was unlawful because it was within its sovereign right to 'regulate its own economy, to enact and modify laws, to secure the proper application of law and to accede to international organizations'.[158] It added that if the claimants wanted compensation, they should have discussed the matter with the ATAA or approached the Hungarian courts.[159]

---

[155] One view posits that regulatory takings which frustrate the investor's 'legitimate expectations built on a reasonable reliance upon representations and undertakings by the Host State are compensable'. Z. Douglas and J. Paulsson, 'Indirect Expropriation in Investment Treaty Arbitrations' in H. Horn and S. M. Kröll (eds.), *Arbitrating Foreign Investment Disputes – Procedural and Substantive Legal Aspects* (The Hague: Kluwer Law International, 2004), pp. 145, 158.

[156] C. Yannaca-Small, '"Indirect Expropriation" and the "Right to Regulate" in International Investment Law (2004)', online: www.oecd-library.org (accessed 31 December 2017), p. 22.

[157] *Emanuel Too* v. *Greater Modesto Insurance Associates*, (1989) 23 IUSCTR 378, Award, 29 December 1989 (Briner, Aldrich, Khalilian), para. 26.

[158] *ADC Affiliate Limited and Anor* v. *Hungary*, ICSID Case No. ARB/03/16, Award of the Tribunal, 2 October 2006 (Kaplan, Brower, van den Berg), para. 384.

[159] Ibid., para. 398.

The claimants replied that Hungary could not simply assert a 'right to regulate' to avoid its treaty obligation to compensate.[160] The tribunal agreed with the claimants that the right to regulate did not grant Hungary *carte blanche* to expropriate contractual rights without compensation:[161]

> It is the Tribunal's understanding of the basic international law principles that while a sovereign State possesses the inherent right to regulate its domestic affairs, the exercise of such right is not unlimited and must have its boundaries ... In the present case, had the Claimants ever envisaged the risk of any possible depriving measures, the Tribunal believes that they took that risk with the legitimate and reasonable expectation that they would receive fair treatment and just compensation and not otherwise.

Characterising an uncompensated expropriation as a regulatory taking will not circumvent a finding of unlawfulness when there is plenty of evidence on record to suggest that the host State merely wanted to exit a current contract with a foreign investor and enter into a more profitable arrangement with a different investor. In *Kardassopoulos v. Georgia*, the claimant oil traders were dispossessed of their concession for the exclusive development and control of a pipeline transporting oil from the Azeri oil fields on the Caspian Sea to the Black Sea. It started with media reports that the government was planning to offer the claimants' concession to a consortium made up of large multinational oil companies. The rumours were subsequently confirmed by a legislative decree that terminated the claimants' concessionary rights without compensation. The ordeal ended with the conferral of the concession originally awarded to the claimants to the consortium.

Georgia is not precluded from reconsidering the award of the concession to a company set up by two individual oil traders. But a change of heart does not justify the absence of compensation. Nor does it prove that the expropriation is a regulatory taking. In the view of the tribunal in *Kardassopoulos v. Georgia*, 'this deprivation was not an exercise of the State's *bona fide* police powers'.[162] The tribunal also explained that although the expropriation did not qualify as a regulatory taking, it was plausibly undertaken for a public purpose since the development of the pipeline was significant to the Georgian economy.[163] This suggests that the notion of a public purpose is broad; broader than that of police powers.

---

[160] Ibid., para. 403.
[161] Ibid., paras. 423–4.
[162] *Ioannis Kardassopoulos and Ron Fuchs v. Georgia*, ICSID Case Nos. ARB/05/18 and ARB/07/15, Award, 3 March 2010 (Fortier, Orrego Vicuña, Lowe), para. 387.
[163] Ibid., para. 391.

4.4.2 Absence of Public Purpose

Given the expansiveness of public purpose, Dolzer and Schreuer note that 'this requirement has rarely been questioned by the foreign investor'.[164] Not only is evidence of the absence of public purpose hard to come by,[165] tribunals may be disinclined to play the role of shadow policy makers who scrutinise the purpose of State action with an overly critical eye.[166] There are of course some tribunals which are prepared to accord less deference to the host State. The tribunal in *ADC* v. *Hungary* was unreceptive to Hungary's explanation that its partial nationalisation of the aviation sector, which resulted in the expropriation of the claimants' contractual rights, was done for a public purpose:[167]

> Although the Respondent repeatedly attempted to persuade the Tribunal that the Amending Act, the Decree and the actions taken in reliance thereon were necessary and important for the harmonisation of the Hungarian Government's transport strategy, laws and regulations with the EU law, it failed to substantiate such a claim with convincing facts or legal reasoning.

The tribunal's reasoning above is difficult to follow. Hungary's accession to the European Union was a momentous event and a matter of national importance. The modification of existing laws and adoption of new laws on the aviation industry in preparation for accession pursued a public purpose. The expropriation was objectionable because it was uncompensated, not because it occurred. The rebuke that Hungary was short on 'convincing facts and legal reasoning' was probably undeserved. If accession to the EU does not count as public purpose, then, to borrow a phrase from the tribunal, one 'can imagine no situation where this requirement would have been met'.[168]

---

[164] Dolzer and Schreuer, *Principles of International Investment Law*, p. 99; also E. Nwogugu, 'Legal Problems of Foreign Investments' (1976) 153 *Recueil des Cours* 167 at 226: 'There is very little if any evidence of cases where the taking of private property has been held to be unlawful under international law merely because it was not for public purpose.'

[165] History shows that expropriations tend to take place for a multitude of reasons, making it impractical to reduce State actions to a core motive that either fulfils or flouts the requirement of public purpose. See G. Ingram, *Expropriation of US Property in South America* (Santa Barbara, CA: Praeger, 1974), pp. 2–13.

[166] J. Kurtz, 'Adjudging the Exceptional at International Investment Law: Security, Public Order and Financial Crisis' (2010) 59(2) ICLQ 325 at 365–70 convincingly calls for restraint.

[167] Award of the Tribunal, para. 430.

[168] Award of the Tribunal, para. 432.

4.4.3   Absence of Due Process

The absence of due process is a criticism of procedures for redress made available by the host State to the foreign investor. This particular indicia of unlawfulness is rarely discussed by tribunals in connection with a claim for expropriation.[169] The clearest, and thus far unchallenged, depiction of what due process signifies is found in *ADC* v. *Hungary*:[170]

> '[D]ue process of law', in the expropriation context, demands an actual and substantive legal procedure for a foreign investor to raise its claims against the depriving actions already taken or about to be taken against it. Some basic legal mechanisms, such as reasonable advance notice, a fair hearing and an unbiased and impartial adjudicator to assess the actions in dispute, are expected to be readily available and accessible to the investor to make such legal procedure meaningful. In general, the legal procedure must be of a nature to grant an affected investor a reasonable chance within a reasonable time to claim its legitimate rights and have its claims heard. If no legal procedure of such nature exists at all, the argument that 'the actions are taken under due process of law' rings hollow.

The tribunal in *ADC* v. *Hungary* found that there was an absence of due process because Hungary did not show, to the tribunal's satisfaction, that Hungarian law provided 'methods for the Claimants to review the expropriation' of their contractual rights.[171] Rejecting Hungary's argument that the expropriation was done in preparation for EU accession and therefore reflected a public purpose, the tribunal was highly sceptical that Hungarian law provided any meaningful recourse for foreign investors. It remains to be seen if future tribunals will emulate the *ADC* v. *Hungary* tribunal in subjecting host State assurances that due process was complied with to such rigorous analysis.

Another indicia of unlawfulness that may arise for consideration in conjunction with the absence of due process is discrimination. Discrimination is relative. As one commentator put it, '[i]n today's world of heterogeneous situations no absolute concept of non-discrimination can thus garner any warm support'.[172] Discrimination is not established by a difference in treatment – the difference must be unreasonable to warrant a finding of

---

[169] See for instance *Fireman's Fund Insurance Company* v. *United Mexican States*, ICSID Case No. ARB(AF)/20/01, Award, 17 July 2006 (van den Berg, Lowenfeld, Olavarrieta), p. 208.

[170] Award of the Tribunal, para. 435.

[171] Award of the Tribunal, para. 438.

[172] A. F. M. Maniruzzaman, 'Expropriation of Alien Property and the Principle of Non-Discrimination in International Law of Foreign Investment: An Overview' (1998–9) 8 *Journal of Transnational Law & Policy* 57 at 64.

unlawfulness.[173] Differential treatment is discriminatory when a foreign investor is consistently prejudiced by measures taken by the host State when other foreign investors holding identical or very similar contractual rights remain unaffected.[174] Showing that an expropriation is discriminatory becomes difficult, if not impossible, when there is a lack of comparable situations. This may happen when the claimant is the sole service provider selected through a tendering process.[175] If there is no basis for comparing the treatment received by the claimant to the treatment received by a direct competitor, there is no basis for alleging that the expropriation was discriminatory.

It is unusual for the expropriation of an investment contract to be discriminatory. The establishment of the New International Economic Order may not have secured in concrete terms the type of economic justice that former colonies in Asia, Africa and the Americas strove for in the 1960s and 1970s,[176] but it did raise awareness of the frequency of inequitable bargains struck in contracts for natural resource exploitation.[177] The nationalisation of the Dutch-run tin mining industry by Indonesia,[178] of British Petroleum by Nigeria,[179] and of the British and US-led copper industry in Chile,[180] are examples of vital industries targeted by host States for expropriation partly because they had a proven track record of profitability. If the expropriations are viewed solely in terms of the nationality of those

---

[173] M. N. Shaw, *International Law*, 6th edn (Cambridge: Cambridge University Press, 2008), p. 842; *Antoine Goetz et Consorts c Burundi*, Affaire CIRDI ARB/95/3, Sentence, 10 February 1999 (Weil, Bedjaoui, Bredin), para. 121.

[174] *CME Czech Republic BV* v. *Czech Republic*, UNCITRAL, Partial Award, 13 September 2001 (Kühn, Schwebel, Hándl), para. 612; *Nykomb* v. *Latvia*, Award, 16 December 2003 (Haug, Schütze, Gernandt), para. 4.3.2(a); *ADC* v. *Hungary*, Award of the Tribunal, 2 October 2006 (Kaplan, Brower, van den Berg), para. 442.

[175] *Dallah Real Estate and Tourism Holding Company* v. *The Ministry of Religious Affairs, Government of Pakistan*, ICC Case No. (unknown), Final Award, 23 June 2006, unpublished, excerpted in [2010] UKSC 46; *GMR* v. *Maldives*.

[176] M. Salomon, 'From NIEO to Now and the Unfinishable Story of Economic Justice' (2013) 62(1) ICLQ 31 at 43.

[177] Sornarajah, *The International Law on Foreign Investment*, pp. 48–52; also E. Penrose, G. Joffe, and P. Stevens, 'Nationalisation of Foreign-Owned Property for a Public Purpose: An Economic Perspective on Appropriate Compensation' (1992) 55 *Modern Law Review* 351 at 361–4.

[178] Lord A. McNair, 'The Seizure of Property and Enterprises in Indonesia' (1959) 6(3) *Netherlands International Law Review* 218.

[179] The official reason given by Nigeria for the takeover was displeasure over the pro-apartheid policy that the United Kingdom adopted towards South Africa, see S. J. Kobrin, 'Expropriation as an Attempt to Control Foreign Firms in LDCs: Trends from 1960 to 1979' (1984) 28(3) *International Studies Quarterly* 329 at 337–8.

[180] Ingram, *Expropriation of US Property in South America*, pp. 211–92.

whose property was taken, then it would appear that there is systematic discrimination against foreign investors which may also fall short of the national treatment standard.[181] If the 'entire history of the investment project' reveals that the foreign investor was conferred rights to exploit an exceptionally lucrative industry on terms which suggest that broader public interests were not taken into account when the contract was signed, then the expropriation of that particular investor's contractual rights is not discriminatory.[182] This is precisely why the termination or renegotiation of long-term petroleum contracts whose original terms promised a windfall for the investor at the expense of the host State, are not regarded as discriminatory expropriations.[183]

4.5   Conclusion

State responsibility will be engaged for an unlawfully expropriated investment contract. There are ample domestic and international precedents for the proposition that an investment contract can be the object of expropriation. The practice of foreign investors framing contractual breaches by the host State as expropriation claims under general international law lives on with protected investors invoking expropriation clauses in investment treaties when host States breach investment contracts. The crux of the analysis for expropriation claims founded on breaches of investment contracts is the existence of an expropriation. In this regard, arbitral *jurisprudence* is largely consistent on two essential features of expropriated contracts: one, that the breach was committed in the State's sovereign capacity; and two, that the breach resulted in the substantial deprivation of the investor's contractual rights. Until recently, the first of the two features has been the more elusive. The difficulty of sorting contractual breaches committed by States into *acta iure imperii* and *acta iure gestionis* is now alleviated to some extent by the *Vigotop* test. This is a helpful test because it proposes indicators which are applicable across a range of factual matrixes to filter expropriatory contractual breaches from non-expropriatory contractual

---

[181] According to this standard, host States are obliged to treat foreign investors as least as favourably as local investors in like circumstances. For a succinct overview on the interpretation of this treaty standard, see Dolzer and Schreuer, *Principles of International Investment Law*, pp. 198–206.

[182] Penrose, Joffe, and Stevens, 'Nationalisation of Foreign-Owned Property', p. 363.

[183] *The Government of the State of Kuwait* v. *The American Independent Oil Company* Award; Z. A. Al Qurashi, 'Renegotiation of International Petroleum Agreements' (2005) 22(4) *Journal of International Arbitration* 261 at 262–8.

breaches. It is hoped that the *Vigotop* test will be considered by future tribunals. The final step to a finding of State responsibility is the presence of unlawfulness in the expropriation of an investment contract. Given the evidential hurdles of proving an absence of public purpose, and the infrequency of expropriations carried out without due process, the presence of unlawfulness will most likely turn on the absence of compensation.

State Responsibility and Internationalisation

5.1 Introduction

State responsibility is engaged whenever a State breaches an international obligation by which it is bound.[1] International law governs the characterisation of the breach as internationally wrongful.[2] As investment contracts do not usually generate international obligations, a breach of contract usually does not, in and of itself, violate international law. Concerns over the vulnerability of investment contracts to unfavourable changes in host State laws motivated some scholars to theorise that these contracts may nonetheless be removed from the influence of national law and relocated within the protective ambit of international law.[3] The purported effect of identifying international law as the law applicable to the merits of a contractual dispute is the elevation of contractual obligations to international obligations. Treating every breach of a contractual obligation by a State like a breach of its international obligation, enables sanction of the State by international law and is a strong deterrent to contractual interference. The conversion of contractual obligations to international obligations is known as 'internationalisation'.[4]

Unlike the submission of contractual protection to a core standard of treatment as discussed in Chapter 3, or to the same regime governing alien property protection as discussed in Chapter 4, the very notion of contractual protection through internationalisation is highly controversial. This chapter

---

[1] ILC, 'Draft Articles on Responsibility of States for Internationally Wrongful Acts, with Commentaries' (2001), *Yearbook of the International Law Commission*, vol. II, Part Two ('Articles on State Responsibility'), Art. 2.

[2] Articles on State Responsibility, Art. 3.

[3] F. A. Mann, 'The Proper Law of Contracts Concluded by International Persons' (1959) 35 BYIL 34 at 46; W. Friedmann, 'Half a Century of International Law' (1964) 50(8) *Virginia Law Review* 1333 at 1340 and 1342–3.

[4] V. V. Veeder credits *Lena Goldfields v. USSR*, *The Times*, 3 September 1930, as the award that floated the idea of internationalisation, likening it to 'the caveman's discovery of fire', see 'The Lena Goldfields Arbitration', p. 747 at 772.

evaluates the impact of internationalisation on the development of the law of State responsibility for breaches of investment contracts by critiquing attempts and counter-attempts at internationalisation. These attempts and counter-attempts can be grouped into two main categories. The first category, which I will call panoptic internationalisation, concerns the internationalisation of investment contracts as a matter of principle (5.2). The second category, which I will call umbrella clause internationalisation, concerns the internationalisation of investment contracts by invoking an umbrella clause in an applicable investment treaty (5.3). The chapter then concludes by considering the compatibility of umbrella clause internationalisation with the existing framework of investment protection established by investment treaties (5.4).

5.2   Panoptic Internationalisation

The overarching rationale for internationalising investment contracts, so the proponents of internationalisation assert, is investor protection. According to Weil,

> [i]f the penetration of public international law in the domain of contracts concluded between States and foreign nationals has crept into ideas as it has into positive law, this is essentially because public international law better protects investors than any other legal order; it is the demand of practicality which, more than any other consideration, has traversed the traditional barrier separating investment contracts from the international legal order.[5]

As States have been known to legalise changes to investment contracts without compensation for any resulting loss,[6] the calculated denial of recourse to affected investors is a real risk.[7] Be that as it may, foreign

---

[5] P. Weil, 'Problèmes Relatifs aux Contrats Passés entre un Etat et un Particulier' (1969) 128(3) *Recueil des Cours* 95 at 122. Author's translation from the original French.

[6] In 1975, the United Kingdom passed the Petroleum and Submarine Pipe Lines Act, imposing new licensing and tax regulations on oil production in the North Sea. This resulted in substantial changes to existing licenses between the United Kingdom and both local and foreign contractors. The Act did not provide for compensation for any loss suffered as a result of the legislative changes. To criticisms that the Act gave the United Kingdom *carte blanche* to unilaterally rewrite its contractual obligations, the United Kingdom insisted that it was within the legitimate exercise of its sovereign powers to alter contractual obligations without prior consultation and without compensation. For an overview of the impact of the Petroleum and Submarine Pipe Lines Act on North Sea oil concessions concluded with the United Kingdom, see Bowett, 'State Contracts with Aliens', p. 49 at 58–9 (fn. 40).

[7] Uncompensated *iure imperii* interference with investment contracts that causes financial injury to affected investors is likely to violate the core standard for contractual protection, see discussion at Chapter 3, Section 3.2.2.

investment can never be risk-free. What many investors have done is to quantify the risk of adverse legislative changes, such as nationalisation, and factor it into their profit-sharing arrangements with the host State.[8] Other investors (or their legal advisers) try to devise a legal solution to what they perceive as a legal problem – the ability of States to change their laws. For those in search of a legal solution, internationalisation is at first glance attractive, because it disables States from legislating to the detriment of investors with impunity. Judging States in accordance with international law which they cannot change at will, is far more reassuring than judging States in accordance with national law which they can apparently alter to their greatest advantage.

On closer inspection, internationalisation appears to overstate the sovereign prerogative to legislate, as well as the extent to which international law protects contractual rights. The Separate Opinion of Judge Lauterpacht in the *Norwegian Loans Case* clarified that a State's actions may be legal under national law but illegal under international law if 'national legislation ... [is] contrary, in its intention or effects, to the international obligations of the State'.[9] A breach of contract, the normal consequences of which a State tries to erase via legislation, *may* violate international law *if and only if* the State is simultaneously in breach of an international obligation by which it is bound. One example is expropriation, which was discussed in the previous chapter. Passing a law to expropriate an investment contract without compensation is not the end of the matter for the host State. It could still be in breach of its international obligation to compensate for expropriation.[10] But internationalisation is not content with the existing

---

[8] E. Engel and R. Fischer, 'Optimal Resource Extraction Contracts under Threat of Expropriation' in W. Hogan and F. Sturzenegger (eds.), *The Natural Resources Trap – Private Investment without Public Commitment* (Cambridge, MA: MIT Press, 2010) 161, p. 162; also M. A. Adelman, 'Economics of Exploration for Petroleum and Other Minerals' (1970) 8 *Geoexploration* 131 at 144–6; E. H. Leland, 'Optimal Risk Sharing and the Leasing of Natural Resources with Application to Oil and Gas Leasing of the OCS' (1978) 92(3) *Quarterly Journal of Economics* 413 at 414–5; M. Schnitzer, 'Expropriation and Control Rights: A Dynamic Model of Foreign Direct Investment' (1999) 17 *International Journal of Industrial Organization* 1113 at 1132; D. Johnston, *International Exploration Economics, Risk and Contract Analysis* (Tulsa, OK: PennWell Corporation, 2003), p. 135; L. T. Wells and R. Ahmed, *Making Foreign Investment Safe: Property Rights and National Sovereignty* (Oxford: Oxford University Press, 2007), pp. 283–93.

[9] (*France v. Norway*) [1957] ICJ Rep 9, 37.

[10] The obligation to compensate for expropriation has alternatively been termed a non-delictual financial obligation owed by the State to the dispossessed investor under international law. See R. Silvestre and J. Martha, *The Financial Obligation in International Law* (Oxford: Oxford University Press, 2015), p. 69.

stable of international obligations, wherever their location, owed by States to investors. Internationalisation demands absolute protection for investment contracts by elevating contractual obligations to international obligations. A breach of an internationalised investment contract *per se* engages State responsibility. International law may offer enhanced protection to investment contracts as compared to national law, but it is questionable if enhanced protection can be stretched to mean absolute protection.

Panoptic internationalisation once enjoyed moderate acclaim. However, because international law does not recognise the absolute sanctity of contract, it has become a magnet for criticism (5.2.1). Moreover, whether contractual rights are secured by virtue of being acquired rights or through a stabilisation clause, neither acquired nor stabilised rights are rights which international law incontrovertibly regards as sacrosanct and resistant to any form of State interference (5.2.2). If internationalisation is the vehicle for the engagement of State responsibility for any breach of contract, its deficiencies caution that the intended effect of internationalising investment contracts may be purely aspirational.

5.2.1   Theoretical Foundations and Flaws

Of the various theories advanced in support of internationalisation, the writings of the Vienna School led by Kelsen (5.2.1.1), and those of McNair (5.2.1.2), a former president of the ICJ, stand out.[11]

5.2.1.1   The Vienna School

It was the primary contention of the Vienna School that since the conduct of States was in reality driven by individuals, the ultimate objects of regulation by international law were individuals.[12] *Pacta sunt servanda*, as a basic norm of international law,[13] thus sanctioned the performance of obligations assumed by States towards individuals, in the same way that it did the performance of obligations assumed by States towards other States.[14] As the effect of applying *pacta sunt servanda* to contractual obligations and

---

[11] For an analysis and critique of other theories of internationalisation, see I. Alvik, *Contracting with Sovereignty* (Oxford: Hart Publishing, 2011), pp. 47–58.

[12] J. von Bernstorff, *The Public International Law Theory of Hans Kelsen* (Cambridge: Cambridge University Press, 2010), p. 72.

[13] H. Kelsen, *Principles of International Law*, 2nd edn (New York, NY: Holt, Rinehart and Winston, 1967), pp. 569–72.

[14] J. Kunz, 'La Primauté du Droit des Gens' (1925) 6 *Revue de Droit International et de Législation Comparée* 556 at 595–6; A. Verdross, 'La Primauté du Droit des Gens et La Conception Unitaire du Droit' (1927) 16 *Recueil des Cours* 287 at 288.

treaty obligations was identical, contractual obligations were equivalent to treaty obligations. That said, not all *pacta* are instruments of international law. An individual who breaches a contractual obligation owed to another individual cannot possibly incur responsibility for the violation of international law since an individual is by definition not a State. The application of *pacta sunt servanda* to treaties (international *pacta*) requires treaty obligations to be fulfilled as a matter of international law, whereas the application of *pacta sunt servanda* to contracts (domestic *pacta*) requires contractual obligations to be fulfilled as a matter of domestic law.[15] Without specifying the nature of the *pactum*, invoking *pacta sunt servanda* does not clarify whether it is international law or domestic law that a breach of the *pactum* potentially violates.

The Vienna School and its followers appeared unperturbed that their entire thesis rested on the ambiguity of *pacta sunt servanda*. Academics, like Wehberg, regarded the ability of *pacta sunt servanda* to convert contractual obligations to international obligations as a truism:[16]

> We have described above the rule of [p]*acta sunt servanda* as a general principle of law that is found in all nations. It follows, therefore, that the principle is valid exactly in the same manner, whether it is in respect of contracts between [S]tates or in respect of contracts between [S]tates and private companies.

The persistent failure to address the logical leap from the invoking of *pacta sunt servanda* to the conversion of contractual obligations into international obligations would prove to be the undoing of the Vienna School in respect of internationalisation. Notably, it has not attracted new followers since the early 1980s.

5.2.1.2   McNair

McNair presented a different theory of internationalisation from the Vienna School. He argued that general principles of law were more appropriate than national law as the *lex causae* in contractual disputes between foreign investors and developing host States:[17]

---

[15] See generally M. P. Sharp, 'Pacta Sunt Servanda' (1941) 41 *Columbia Law Review* 783.

[16] H. Wehberg, 'Pacta Sunt Servanda' (1959) 53 AJIL 775 at 786; see also A. Verdross, 'Quasi-International Agreements and International Economic Transactions' (1964) 18 *Yearbook of World Affairs* 230 at 234; W. Wengler, 'Les accords entre Etats et entreprises ́etrang ́eres sont-ils des trait ́es de droit international?' (1972) 76 *Revue Géneérale de Droit International Public* 313 at 343–5; J. F. Lalive, 'Les Contrats d'Etat: D ́eveloppements R ́ecents et Perspectives d'Avenir' (1983) 181 *Recueil des Cours* 163 at 192.

[17] McNair, 'The General Principles of Law Recognized by Civilized Nations', p. 1 at 4.

It is hardly to be expected that the nationals of countries enjoying a well-established system of law, which is familiar with contracts of this type, are likely to be readily disposed to enter into contracts with a foreign Government that are to be regulated by systems of law which are vague and have not been developed in the direction, or to the extent, necessary for dealing with this type of transaction.

McNair saw a direct correlation between a country's status as a capital exporter and the sophistication of its legal system. This view was shared by some arbitral tribunals interpreting oil concession contracts awarded by Middle Eastern States to UK and US investors in the 1950s.[18] McNair was persuaded of a 'marked contrast ... between the law of England or of most of the States in the North American Continent and the law of many Asiatic countries'.[19] Internationalisation was therefore a response and a remedy to the presumably inadequate laws of developing States.[20] As a theory driven by value judgments on the superiority or inferiority of certain legal systems of the world, it represented 'a very partisan, capitalist approach to contractual disputes',[21] which developing States duly rejected.

Resistance was most visible when developing States used their numerical edge in the UN General Assembly to press for the identification of the applicable law of an investment contract with host State laws in a series of important resolutions.[22] Although unpopularity does not invalidate McNair's theory,[23] the imperialistic undertone of internationalisation rendered it incompatible with the equality of nations which developing States

---

[18] *Petroleum Development Ltd* v. *The Sheikh of Abu Dhabi*, 18 ILR 144, Award, September 1951 (Asquith), p. 149; *Ruler of Qatar* v. *International Marine Oil Co.*, 20 ILR 534, Award, June 1953 (Bucknill), pp. 544–5; *Saudi Arabia* v. *Arabian American Oil Co. (Aramco)*, 27 ILR 117, Award, 23 August 1958 (Sauser-Hall, Badawi/Hassan, Habachi (dissenting)), pp. 153–72.

[19] McNair, 'The General Principles of Law Recognized by Civilized Nations', p. 1.

[20] Fatouros, 'International Law and the Internationalized Contract', p. 134 at 136; Sornarajah, 'The Myth of International Contract Law', p. 187 at 201.

[21] D. W. Bowett, 'State Contracts with Aliens', p. 49 at 51.

[22] Permanent Sovereignty Over Natural Resources, UNGA Res. 1803 (XVIII) (14 December 1962), GAOR Supp. 17, p. 15; UN General Assembly Resolution on a Charter of Economic Rights and Duties of States UNGA Res. A/Res/3281 (XXIX) (12 December 1974), see especially UNCTAD, Report of the Working Party of the Trade and Development Board, TD/B/AC.12/4, partially reproduced in Kuusi, *The Host State and the Transnational Corporation*, pp. 131–5. The Charter was passed with 120 votes; the 16 States that voted against the Charter or abstained were developed States, see (1975) 16 ILM 263 for the roll-call vote.

[23] C. N. Brower, 'The Charter of Economic Rights and Duties of States' (24–6 April 1975) *American Society of International Law Proceedings* 225 at 234.

were intent on bringing about. As stirringly put by Mexican President Echeverría in his address to the 1972 UNCTAD Conference:[24]

> The resentment accumulated against political colonialism is now turned against economic colonialism ... We must reinforce the precarious legal foundation of the international economy. It is impossible to have a just order and a stable world until such a time as rights and duties are created to protect weak States.

5.2.1.3   Criticism of Internationalisation

A theory of internationalisation that hindered the goal of attaining political and economic parity was destined for a shrinking audience and eventual decline. The tide turned when many began to question the viability of *pacta sunt servanda* as a means for internationalisation, the persuasive value of internationalisation and the place of internationalisation amidst the economic and legal progress achieved by developing States.

The glaring defect in the Vienna School's theory of internationalisation was how simply invoking *pacta sunt servanda* could displace national law as the default *lex causae* in claims against States for a breach of contract, and replace it with international law. Critics seized upon this disconnect to deride the internationalisation of contractual obligations.[25] Mann found the theory of internationalisation fostered by the Vienna School untenable because:[26]

> [It] stems from a fundamental error which would not have arisen if public international lawyers had had due regard to the character and teachings of private international law: in the type of case where there is room for the problem at all under customary public international law, no breach of contract in fact occurs and, consequently, the principle of *pacta sunt servanda* is not infringed. Contracts are governed by the law determined by the private international law of the forum.

Moreover, commentators discount the persuasive value of the handful of arbitral awards that promote internationalisation. Sornarajah

---

[24] UNCTAD, 'Proceedings of the United Nations Conference on Trade and Development: Third Session, Santiago de Chile' (13 April to 21 May 1972), UN Doc. A/PV.2315, para. 67.

[25] Jennings, 'State Contracts in International Law', p. 156 at 165–8; Amerasinghe, 'State Breaches of Contracts with Aliens and International Law', p. 881 at 897; Pazarci, 'La Responsabilité Internationale des Etats à l'Occasion des Contrats Conclus Entre Etats et Personnes Privées Etrangères', p. 354 at 371–2; G. R. Delaume, 'State Contracts and Transnational Arbitration' (1981) 75 AJIL 784 at 806; Sacerdoti, 'State Contracts and International Law: A Reappraisal', p. 26 at 46; Schwebel, 'On Whether the Breach by a State of a Contract with an Alien Is a Breach of International Law', pp. 425, 434.

[26] Mann, 'State Contracts and State Responsibility', pp. 572 at 580–1.

considered the legal foundation of internationalisation precarious at best because '[t]he mere fact that in some uncontested arbitral awards ... the existence of an "international contract law" was asserted, cannot convert opinions into international law'.[27] Others were concerned at how easy it seemed for contracts to be internationalised. In response to the holding of the sole arbitrator in *Texaco* v. *Libya* that the presence of an arbitration clause in an investment contract sufficed to convert contractual obligations into international obligations,[28] Fatouros remarked that '[t]he presence of an arbitration clause can hardly be construed as necessarily a sign of internationalization – are all charter parties entered into by [S]tates internationalized?'[29]

Internationalisation also loses some of its practical value as an insulation against changes in host State laws when neither international law nor national law recognises the absolute sanctity of contract. Claiming that a host State can be permanently bound to its contractual obligations through internationalisation exaggerates the level of protection international law confers on contractual rights. Asante, the former Solicitor-General of Ghana, exposed the pretence in the following terms:[30]

> [Even if] such an agreement were subject to public international law, the doctrine of *pacta sunt servanda* would be effectively qualified by the equally well-established international legal principle, *clausula rebus sic stantibus*, which sanctions the revision of international agreements on the basis of a fundamental change of circumstances ... With particular reference to agreements concluded with governments and public authorities, the civil and common law systems all recognise the principle that such contracts may not only be renegotiated at the instance of the government, in appropriate cases, but may even be unilaterally modified by the government in certain circumstances by virtue of the government's sovereign rights.

---

[27] Sornarajah, 'The Myth of International Contract Law', pp. 205–6. Although controversial arbitral awards on contractual protection may never become leading content-generators of international law, they are still a part of the larger body of arbitral awards which constitute a principal source of international law on contractual protection, and whose persuasive value cannot be cavalierly brushed off. See discussion at Chapter 2, Sections 2.2 and 2.4.1.

[28] 53 ILR 389, Award on the Merits, 19 January 1977 (Dupuy), p. 455. In addition to an arbitration clause, the sole arbitrator found that the presence of a choice-of-law clause referring to international law (pp. 452–4), as well as a stabilisation clause prohibiting the host State from making changes to the contract without the investors' consent (p. 389), were features of an internationalised investment contract.

[29] International Law and the Internationalized Contract, p. 136.

[30] S. B. Asante, 'International Law and Foreign Investment: A Reappraisal' (1988) 37 ICLQ 588 at 612–3.

McNair's early impression that the laws of certain States were lacking was outpaced by the publication of studies which demonstrated that the laws of many developing States did provide adequate protection for foreign investors.[31] As neither *pacta sunt servanda* nor poor laws offered a convincing rationale for treating contractual obligations as international obligations, the reputation of internationalisation which was built on 'theoretically vague concepts lacking a substantial degree of practical support',[32] suffered.

Most damagingly perhaps, the few contemporary supporters of internationalisation have not been able to rebut the criticisms levelled at internationalisation.[33] One supporter asserts that the internationalisation of investment contracts has been 'admitted as part of the doctrine',[34] when the weight of academic opinion swings the opposite way. Another supporter, Leben, argues that 'agreements in which the [S]tate as an international person contracts with a private person ... cannot be part of the reserved domain, for that would be to deny their very reason for being'.[35] Leben's concern, that investment contracts are meaningless pieces of paper if they are governed by the laws of the host State which the host State is free to amend, is shared by others.[36] Internationalisation may not be the best response when there are other less extreme solutions. One possibility, as noted in the opening paragraph to Section 5.2, is the factoring of adverse legislative changes into the economic arrangement with the host State. Another possibility is recourse to domestic public law remedies. For example, English law permits the seeking of judicial review when administrative action or inaction alters the rights and obligations of a claimant otherwise enforceable under private law.[37] The doctrine of *fait du prince* in

---

[31] A. Akinsanya, 'Host Government's Responses to Foreign Economic Control: The Experience of Selected African Countries' (1981) 30(4) ICLQ 769 at 770–4; see generally K. M. Al-Jumah, 'Arab State Contract Disputes: Lessons from the Past' (2002) 17(3) *Arab Law Quarterly* 215.

[32] A. S. El-Kosheri and T. F. Riad, 'The Law Governing a New Generation of Petroleum Agreements: Changes in the Arbitral Process' (1986) 1 *ICSID Review – Foreign Investment Law Journal* 257 at 259.

[33] Recent qualified support for the 'internationalisation' of investment contracts can be found in H. E. Kjos, *Applicable Law in Investor-State Arbitration: The Interplay Between National and International Law* (Oxford: Oxford University Press, 2013), pp. 213 and 222.

[34] J. Cantergreil, 'The Audacity of the Texaco/Calasiatic Award: Ren´e-Jean Dupuy and the Internationalization of Foreign Investment Law' (2011) 22(2) EJIL 441 at 445.

[35] C. Leben, *The Advancement of International Law* (Oxford: Hart, 2010), p. 153.

[36] See for instance R. Kreindler, 'The Law Applicable to International Investment Disputes' in Horn and Kröll (eds.), *Arbitrating Foreign Investment Disputes*, pp. 401, 417.

[37] *Council of Civil Service Unions and Ors v. Minister for the Civil Service* [1965] AC 374, pp. 408–9 (per Lord Diplock).

French administrative law entitles a claimant to full indemnification when losses are occasioned by legislative activity.[38] Neither possibility requires State responsibility to be engaged for every breach of contract.

5.2.2 The Engineered Inviolability of Contractual Rights

The objective of internationalisation, and its undoing, is making contracts inviolable. Whether contractual rights are likened to acquired rights (5.2.2.1), or purportedly safeguarded from unilateral modification or termination by the State with the inclusion of a stabilisation clause in an investment contract (5.2.2.2), the begetting of inviolable contracts from internationalisation is debatable.

5.2.2.1 Contractual Rights as Acquired Rights

The majority of the tribunal in *Saudi Arabia* v. *Aramco* suggested that contractual rights are acquired rights, which are therefore inviolable under international law:[39]

> Nothing can prevent a State, in the exercise of its sovereignty, from binding itself irrevocably by the provisions of a concession and from granting to the concessionaire irretractable rights. Such rights have the character of acquired rights. Should a new concession contract incompatible with the first, or a subsequent statute, abolish totally or partially that which has been granted by a previous law or concession, this could constitute a clear infringement ... which the State cannot do in respect of concessions, without engaging its responsibility.

The majority's contention that acquired rights are absolute rights is extraordinary. It is puzzling how commentators have credited, without criticising, this award for the proposition that a State cannot interfere with contractual rights without violating international law.[40] Lalive, for one, saw

---

[38] *L'arrêt Tanty*, Conseil d'Etat, CE, 28 November 1924.

[39] Award, 23 August 1958, p. 168. An earlier arbitral decision which alluded to the absolute sanctity of rights acquired from a concession is *The Sopron-Köszeg Local Company* (1930) 24 AJIL 164, Award, 18 June 1929, p. 167. The majority in *Saudi Arabia* v. *Aramco* comprised G. Sauser-Hall, who acted as counsel for Switzerland in the *Losinger Case* before the PCIJ ((*Switzerland* v. *Yugoslavia*) (27 June 1936) PCIJ, Series A/B, No. 67), and M. Hassan, an Egyptian judge. The dissenting arbitrator, S. Hanachy, an Egyptian former Cabinet minister, did not comment on the majority's legal arguments in his very brief opinion.

[40] R. Y. Jennings, 'Rules Governing Contracts between States and Foreign Nationals' in Southwestern Legal Foundation. International and Comparative Law Center, *Rights and Duties of Private Investors Abroad* (Albany, NY: Matthew Bender, 1965) 123, pp. 133–4; P. Weil, 'Droit International Et Contrats d'Etat' in *Mélanges Offerts A Paul Reuter – Le Droit International:*

no inconsistency in the majority's findings with his own observation that '[t]he [S]tate keeps its competence to enact legislation affecting acquired rights'.[41] The majority's attempt to engineer inviolable contractual rights by assimilating contractual rights to acquired rights should be read as a failure if international law does not recognise acquired rights as absolute rights. The *Aramco* award certainly 'merits more contemporaneous attention than it appears to attract',[42] if only because it is time to test the majority's understanding of acquired rights in international law for accuracy.

The *locus classicus* on acquired rights in international law is the *Case Concerning Certain German Interests in Polish Upper Silesia*. The PCIJ held that 'the principle of respect for vested rights' is open to 'derogation', whereby the expropriation of 'property, rights and interests' belonging to German nationals in Polish Upper Silesia either in accordance with treaty or customary conditions, is an act that 'generally accepted international law does not sanction'.[43] The mutability of acquired rights is acknowledged by the European Court of Human Rights,[44] international arbitral tribunals,[45] and national courts.[46] Commentators also accept

---

Unité Et Diversité (Paris: Pedone, 1981), pp. 549, 550–1; Schwebel, 'On Whether the Breach by a State of a Contract with an Alien is a Breach of International Law', pp. 433–4.

[41] P. Lalive, 'The Doctrine of Acquired Rights' in Southwestern Legal Foundation. International and Comparative Law Center, *Rights and Duties of Private Investors Abroad*, pp. 145, 167, 177–80 and 183; see also Mann, 'The Proper Law of Contracts Concluded by International Persons', p. 48; McNair, 'The Seizure of Property and Enterprises in Indonesia', p. 218 at 233–4.

[42] S. M. Schwebel, 'The Kingdom of Saudi Arabia and Aramco Arbitrate the Onassis Agreement' (2010) 20(20) *Journal of World Energy Law and Business* 1 at 12.

[43] (*Germany v. Poland*) (Merits) (1926) PCIJ, Series A, No. 7, p. 22. See also the *Island of Palmas* award which involved the competing claims of sovereignty of the United States and the Netherlands over the island of Palmas located in the Philippine archipelago. The sole arbitrator, Huber, held that 'it cannot be sufficient to establish the title by which territorial sovereignty was validly acquired at a certain moment; it must also be shown that the territorial sovereignty has continued to exist and did exist at the moment which for the decision of the dispute must be considered as critical', (*United States v. The Netherlands*) (1928) 2 RIAA 829, Award of the Tribunal, 4 April 1928 (Huber), p. 839. In other words, acquired rights may be modified.

[44] *Case of Moskal v. Poland* (European Court of Human Rights Fourth Section), App. No. 10373/05, 15 September 2009, paras. 47–52; *Case of Grudić v. Serbia* (European Court of Human Rights Second Section), App. No. 31925/08, 17 April 2012, paras. 72–6.

[45] *Hudson's Bay Company's Claim* (*Great Britain v. United States*), Award, 1 July 1863, in Fontaine (ed.), *Pasicrisie Internationale*, pp. 44, 45; *Affaire Des Propriétés Religieuses* (*France, Royaume-Uni, Espagnole c Portugal*), (1920) RIAA 7, Sentence, Sentence, 4 September 1920 (Root, de Savornin Lohman, Lardy), p. 16; *Shufeldt Claim* (*Guatemala v. USA*) (1930) 2 RIAA 1079, Award, 24 July 1930 (Sisnett), p. 1100.

[46] *United States v. Juan Percheman*, 32 US 51 (1833) (US Supreme Court), pp. 87–8 (per Marshall CJ); *R v. International Trustee for the Protection of Bondholders A/G (2)* [1937]

that the creation of acquired rights is no bar to their lawful modification or extinction.[47]

The conviction of governments that they are not irrevocably bound by contractual rights obtained under previous governments upon State succession or regime change, further attests to the mutability of acquired rights.[48] This is evident from the report of the Transvaal Concessions Commission which was tasked to explain the status of existing concessionary rights in light of the British annexation of the South African Republic:[49]

> [T]he new Government is justified in cancelling or modifying a concession when ... [t]he maintenance of the concession is injurious to the public interest. In this last case however, the question of compensation arises, inasmuch as it would be inequitable that a concessionaire should lose without compensation a right duly acquired ...

Moreover, as respect for acquired rights is usually pleaded in a claim that the State has unlawfully expropriated property, acquired rights have been likened to property rights.[50] This subjects acquired rights to the rules governing the taking of alien property in international law.[51] Acquired rights

---

AC 500 (UK House of Lords), pp. 554–5 (per Lord Atkin), 559–60 (per Lord Russell of Killowen) and 575 (per Lord Roche); *Kahler* v. *Midland Bank Ltd* [1950] AC 24 (UK House of Lords), p. 56 (per Lord Radcliffe).

[47] S. S. Ko, 'The Concept of Acquired Rights in International Law: A Survey' (1977) 24(1–2) *Netherlands International Law Review* 120 at 131–2; also S. de Sza´szy, 'The Protection of Acquired Private Rights of Foreigners in International Law' (1930) 36 *International Law Association Reports of Conferences* 583 at 586; G. Karckenbeeck, 'La Protection Internationale Des Droits Acquis' (1937) 5 *Recueil des Cours* 317 at 337–8.

[48] A. Cavaglieri, 'La Notion Des Droits Acquis Et Son Application En Droit International Public' (translated by R. Genet) (1931) *Revue Générale de Droit International Public* 257 at 264; B. A. Wortley, *Expropriation in Public International Law* (Cambridge: Cambridge University Press, 1959), pp. 125–8; Lalive, 'The Doctrine of Acquired Rights', at p. 167.

[49] A. Lyttleton, A. M. Ashmore, and R. K. Loveday, *Report of the Transvaal Concessions Commission (19 April 1901)* (London: Wyman & Sons, 1901), p. 8.

[50] A. Fachiri, 'Expropriation and International Law' (1925) 6 BYIL 159 at 168–70; J. C. Witenberg, 'Protection of Private Property' (1930) 36 *International Law Association Reports of Conferences* 301 at 341; S. Friedmann, *Expropriation in International Law* (translated by I. C. Jackson) (London: Stevens & Sons, 1953), p. 126; A. Newcombe, 'The Boundaries of Regulatory Expropriation in International Law' (2005) 20(1) *ICSID Review – Foreign Investment Law Journal* 1 at 8.

[51] *United States* v. *Juan Percheman*, pp. 87–8; *Van Marle and Ors* v. *The Netherlands* in Report of the European Commission of Human Rights, App. Nos 8543/79, 8674/79, 8675/79 and 8685/79, 8 May 1984, pp. 26–7; note also the partially dissenting opinions in *Case of Andrejeva* v. *Latvia* (European Court of Human Rights Grand Chamber), App. No. 55707/00, 18 February 2009, para. 21 and *Case of Vistiņš and Perepjolkins* v. *Latvia* (European Court of Human Rights Grand Chamber), App. No. 71243/01, 25 October 2012,

cannot be absolute if they can be expropriated like property. Calling contractual rights acquired rights subjects the former to the same level of protection international law accords the latter; it does not entitle contractual rights to greater protection than acquired rights. As it stands, the majority award in *Aramco* which advocates that acquired rights are absolute rights is a fundamental departure from the international law on acquired rights as laid down in the *Case of German Interests In Polish Upper Silesia*. For these reasons, the *Aramco* vision of inviolable contractual rights should be rejected.

5.2.2.2   Contractual Rights as Stabilised Rights

The risk that a host State may unilaterally modify or terminate rights found in investment contracts, to the detriment of the private contracting party, is never far from the mind of foreign investors. The more savvy among them (or their legal team) have devised a clause that expressly forbids the host State from modifying any aspect of the investment contract without the consent of the foreign investor. Such a clause freezes contractual rights at the date of the making of the contract, stabilising them, and is therefore commonly referred to as a stabilisation clause. By purporting to insulate contractual rights from future change, a stabilisation clause tries to engineer inviolable contractual rights.[52] This is reflected in the argument that any interference with contractual rights by the host State is a breach of the stabilisation clause which in turn constitutes a violation of international law.[53] The equation of stabilised contractual rights to inviolable rights raises 'one of the most complex issues in international economic law'.[54] There are several reasons why reliance on stabilisation clauses to obtain inviolable contractual rights is controversial.

---

paras. 1–6, where the majority was chided for omitting to consider the doctrine of acquired rights which would have complemented the analysis on the lawfulness of expropriating property under the Convention.

[52] W. Peter, *Arbitration and Renegotiation of International Investment Agreements* (The Hague: Kluwer Law International, 1995), p. 215.

[53] *Anglo-Iranian Oil Co. (United Kingdom v. Iran)* (Preliminary Objection) [1952] ICJ Rep 93, Observations and Submissions Presented by the Government of the United Kingdom of Great Britain and Northern Ireland in Regard to the Preliminary Objection Lodged by the Imperial Government of Iran, para. 12; *Texaco v. Libya* Award on the Merits, pp. 455–7; *AGIP Spa v. The Government of the Popular Republic of the Congo*, ICSID Case No. ARB/77/1, Award, 30 November 1979 (Trolle, Dupuy, Rouhani) in 67 ILR 318, p. 338; P. Weil, 'Les Clauses de Stabilisation ou d'Intangibilité Insérée Dans Les Accords de Development Economique' in C. E. Rousseau (ed.), *Mélanges Offerts à Charles Rousseau* (Paris: Pedone, 1974), pp. 301, 318–19.

[54] T. Wälde and G. Ndi, 'Stabilizing International Investment Commitments: International Law versus Contract Interpretation' (1996) 31 *Texas International Law Journal* 215 at 238.

First, it is uncertain if States can, by contract, limit their sovereign prerogative to modify or terminate contracts via legislation. The United Kingdom argued before the ICJ in the *Anglo-Iranian Oil Company Case* that the stabilisation clause in an oil concession was 'inserted with the specific object of making it legally impossible for the Government of Iran to put an end to the concession by some such measure of nationalization'.[55] Yet, were the United Kingdom to switch places with Iran, it is doubtful if the United Kingdom would have accepted the argument that its sovereign powers can be curtailed by contract. Under English law, the Crown cannot proscribe the future exercise of its sovereignty in a contract.[56] During the Hague Codification Conference of 1930, the United Kingdom did not take a firm position on the ability of the Crown to contract away its sovereignty, merely noting that 'the sovereign authority of the State, its power to terminate by appropriate means any such concession or contract on grounds of public policy i.e., that the interests of the State require it, must be recognised'.[57] It is therefore unclear if, as far as the United Kingdom is concerned, international law requires a State to prioritise a contractual undertaking over a sovereign prerogative if the two should ever conflict. A stabilisation clause that forbids a State from exercising important sovereign powers, such as the power to legislate or the power to nationalise, may run afoul of domestic constitutional law which regulates the exercise of sovereign powers.[58] Similarly, a stabilisation clause that forbids a State from interfering with contractual rights in any manner whatsoever with

---

[55] Observations and Submissions Presented by the Government of the United Kingdom of Great Britain and Northern Ireland in Regard to the Preliminary Objection Lodged by the Imperial Government of Iran, para. 12.

[56] *Rederiaktiebolaget Amphitrite* v. *The King* [1921] KB 500, p. 503 (per Rowlatt J); *Cudgen Rutile (No. 2) Pty Ltd and Anor* v. *Gordon William Wesley Chalk* [1975] AC 520, p. 534 (per Lord Wilberforce); also *Williams & Humbert* v. *W & H Trade Marks (Jersey)* (1985) 75 ILR 268, pp. 314–5 (per Lord Templeman).

[57] Rosenne (ed.), *Conference for the Codification of International Law [1930]*, vol. II, p. 205.

[58] In 2007, the Federal High Court of Nigeria declared unconstitutional a legislative provision purporting to fetter Nigeria's sovereign prerogative to alter the existing fiscal regime on the oil and gas industry. For a commentary of the unpublished judgment in *Niger Delta Development Commission* v. *Nigeria Liquefied Natural Gas Company Ltd.*, see B. Adaralegbe, 'Stabilizing Fiscal Regimes in Long-Term Contracts: Recent Developments from Nigeria' (2008) 1(3) *Journal of World Energy Law & Business* 239 at 239–42. Note also Peter, *Arbitration and Renegotiation of International Investment Agreements*, p. 221 where it is argued that '[t]here is no reason why the host country could not validly enter into a contract with a stabilization clause, *so long as all constitutional and legislative requirements are respected*' (emphasis added).

the constant threat of sanction by international law wrests such a severe undertaking from the State that its enforceability is constantly in doubt.[59]

Second, since stabilisation clauses endeavour to block any interference with contractual rights by the host State, the only remedy that supports this intended effect is *restitutio in integrum*. This will comprise material restitution to fully restore the affected contractual rights, *and*, if contractual modification or termination was done pursuant to a legislative act, juridical restitution to annul the said act.[60] With the exception of the *Texaco* v. *Libya* award where the sole arbitrator tried to show that *restitutio in integrum* was 'the normal sanction for non-performance of contractual obligations' and actually ordered it,[61] tribunals usually refuse *restitutio in integrum* as an impracticable remedy.[62] If monetary compensation is the adequate remedy for interference with contractual rights, stabilised contractual rights are indistinguishable from regular contractual rights. It has been suggested that a stabilisation clause may entitle a foreign investor to higher compensation for the deprivation of his contractual rights.[63] Factoring stabilisation clauses into the quantification of damages for a

---

[59] G. White, *Nationalisation of Foreign Property* (London: Stevens & Sons, 1961), p. 178; E. J. de Ar´echaga, 'International Law in the Past Third of a Century' (1978) 159 *Recueil des Cour* 267 at 307–8; O. Schachter, 'International Law in Theory and Practice: General Course in Public International Law' (1982) 178 *Recueil des Cours* 1 at 314; P. Kahn, 'Contrats d'Etat et Nationalisation. Les Apports de la Sentence Arbitrale du 24 mars 1982' (1982) 109 *Journal de Droit International* 844 at 858; R. Brown, 'The Relationship between the State and the Multinational Corporation in the Exploitation of Resources' (1984) 33 ICLQ 218 at 222–4; Bowett, 'State Contracts with Aliens', pp. 58–9; Wälde and Ndi, 'Stabilizing International Investment Commitments', pp. 220–36 and 242; Sornarajah, *The International Law on Foreign Investment*, pp. 330–4; Dolzer and Schreuer, *Principles of International Investment Law*, pp. 75–7; see also R. Geiger, 'The Unilateral Change of Economic Development Agreements' (1974) 23 ICLQ 73 at 101–2.

[60] Commentary on Art. 35 of the Articles on State Responsibility in ILC, 'Draft Articles on Responsibility of States for Internationally Wrongful Acts, with Commentaries', vol. II, Part Two, p. 97.

[61] Award, on the Merits, 19 January 1977, pp. 507–9.

[62] *The Government of the State of Kuwait* v. *The American Independent Oil Company*, 21 ILM 976, Award, 24 March 1982 (Reuter, Sultan, Fitzmaurice (partially dissenting)). 1035; *LIAMCO* v. *Libya*, 62 ILR 140, Award, 12 April 1977 (Mahmassani), pp. 198–9; *BP* v. *Libya*, 53 ILM 297, Award, 10 October 1973 (Lagergren), pp. 347–8 and 353; *Mobil Oil* v. *Iran*, 86 ILR 231, Award, 14 July 1987 (Virally, Brower, Ansari), p. 273; and *INA Corporation* v. *Iran*, 75 ILR 595, Award, 13 August 1985 (Lagergren (separate opinion), Ameli, Holtzmann), p. 609.

[63] Aréchaga, 'International Law in the Past Third of a Century', pp. 307–8; Schachter, 'International Law in Theory and Practice', p. 314; also M. Sornarajah, 'Compensation for Expropriation: The Emergence of New Standards' (1979) 13 *Journal of World Trade Law* 108 at 114–15.

breach of contract seems a better way of acknowledging the foreign investor's risk minimisation strategy without attempting the dubious engineering
of inviolable contractual rights.

Third, a stabilisation clause is not a boilerplate feature of investment contracts and is only inserted when the foreign investor has sufficient bargaining
power to steer negotiations.[64] A stabilisation clause is thus most often found
in older investment contracts concluded between wealthy Anglo-American
or European investors and impoverished, less developed host States.[65] If stabilisation clauses do render contractual rights inviolable, then only those
investors with financial leverage can hope to be in possession of contractual
rights that resist all interference by the host State. Even so, the days of using
stabilisation clauses to venerate the contractual rights of wealthy investors
are probably over. A 2009 study of seventy-six modern investment contracts
found that a full stabilisation clause, namely one that purports to insulate all
contractual rights from all manner of interference by the host State, does not
appear in contracts concluded with the governments of 'South Asia, Eastern
Europe, Southern Europe, Central Asia or OECD countries'.[66] Developing
States that have achieved economic progress and are keen to preserve or
recover their regulatory autonomy will be extremely wary of stabilisation
clauses.[67] When States are no longer willing to trade sovereignty for foreign
capital injection, inviolable contractual rights will gradually become a thing
of the past. The verdict, in the words of one commentator, is that 'stabilization clauses are highly speculative in terms of contract stability'.[68]

The dwindling appeal of stabilisation clauses does not necessarily fore-
close fresh attempts to forge inviolable contractual rights by other means.

---

[64] Brown, 'The Relationship between the State and the Multinational Corporation', pp. 220–2.
[65] C. T. Curtis, 'The Legal Security of Economic Development Agreements' (1988) 29 *Harvard International Law Journal* 317 at 351–2.
[66] A. Shemberg, 'Stabilization Clauses and Human Rights', Research Project Conducted for International Finance Corporation and the United Nations Special Representative of the Secretary-General on Business and Human Rights (27 May 2009), online: www.ifc.org (accessed 31 December 2017), p. 21.
[67] *Case Concerning the Barcelona Traction, Light and Power Company, Limited (Belgium v. Spain)* (Second Phase) [1970] ICJ Rep 3, Separate Opinion of Judge Padilla Nervo, p. 250:

> Perhaps modern international business practice has a tendency to be soft and partial towards the powerful and the rich, but no rule of law could be built on such flimsy bases. Investors who go abroad in search of profits take a risk and go there for better or for worse, not only for better. They should respect the institutions and abide by the national laws of the country where they chose to go.

[68] Peter, *Arbitration and Renegotiation of International Investment Agreements,* p. 230; cf. generally P. Cameron, *International Energy Investment Law: The Pursuit of Stability* (Oxford: Oxford University Press, 2010), paras. 2.19–56.

It appears that the inspiration for umbrella clauses in modern investment treaties may have come from the stabilisation clause in the oil concession contract between Anglo-Iranian Oil Company and Iran.[69] A typical umbrella clause provides that host States 'shall observe any obligation it may have entered into with regard to investments'.[70] If umbrella clauses are meant to stabilise contractual rights in the same way as stabilisation clauses, then they continue the work of engineering inviolable contractual rights.[71] There is intense disagreement over whether umbrella clauses cast the sort of protective barrier over contractual rights that enables these rights to repel State interference, such that every breach of contract engages State responsibility. It is to umbrella clauses that the discussion now turns.

5.3   Umbrella Clause Internationalisation

If a host State breaches an umbrella clause in an investment treaty, its international responsibility will be engaged for violating a treaty obligation. What is less categorical, and the focus of this section, is whether the breach of a contractual obligation by a host State suffices to violate an umbrella clause. Umbrella clause claims are unusual because they sometimes evince an overlap between traditionally distinct contract claims (breach of contract) and treaty claims (breach of treaty). We begin by elaborating on the contract-treaty claim distinction and overlap (5.3.1). We then examine possible reasons for why recourse to canons of treaty interpretation, namely Articles 31 and 32 of the Vienna Convention on the Law of Treaties,[72] is equivocal on umbrella clause internationalisation (5.3.2), before discussing different degrees of umbrella clause internationalisation (5.3.3).

5.3.1   The Contract-Treaty Claim Distinction and Overlap

In a pure contract claim, the foreign investor argues that the host State is in breach of contract and should be held liable in accordance with the proper law of the contract. In a pure treaty claim, the foreign investor argues that

---

[69] Sinclair, 'The Origins of the Umbrella Clause in the International Law of Investment Protection', p. 411 at 412.

[70] Treaty between United States of America and the Argentine Republic Concerning the Reciprocal Encouragement and Protection of Investment (signed 14 November 1991, entered into force 20 October 1994), Art. II(2)(c).

[71] C. Titi, 'Les Clauses de Stabilisation dans les Contrats d'Investissement: Une Entrave au Pouvoir Normatif de l'Etat d'Accueil' (2014) 2 *Journal de Droit International* 541 at 551.

[72] Adopted 23 May 1969, entered into force 27 January 1980, 1155 UNTS 331.

the host State is in breach of a treaty obligation and should be held responsible under international law. In contract-based disputes submitted to investment treaty arbitration, the line separating a contract claim from a treaty claim may not always be clear. Investment treaties set out obligations owed directly by host States to protected investors. In the preponderance of investor-State disputes submitted to investment treaty arbitration therefore, the investor's grievance lies in the State's non-compliance with its treaty obligations. When the dispute is contractual in origin, the investor will argue that a breach of contract is entwined with a breach of treaty. It is nonetheless important to maintain a conceptual distinction between contract claims and treaty claims. According to the unchallenged pronouncement of the ad hoc committee in *Vivendi* v. *Argentina*, '[e]ach of these claims will be determined by reference to its own proper or applicable law – in the case of the BIT, by international law; in the case of the Concession Contract, by the proper law of the contract'.[73]

Not every breach of contract is concurrently a breach of treaty.[74] Umbrella clauses, because of their resemblance to stabilisation clauses, reintroduce internationalisation to investment protection. If one rejects umbrella clause internationalisation, contractual obligations are not promoted to treaty obligations, and there is minimal to no overlap between a contract claim and a treaty claim. On the contrary, if one accepts umbrella clause internationalisation, contractual obligations can be elevated to treaty obligations, and there will be some, if not a total, overlap between a contract claim and a treaty claim.

5.3.2   The Interpretation of Umbrella Clauses

How an umbrella clause protects the contractual rights of investors is a question of treaty interpretation. In this regard, Articles 31 and 32 of the VCLT encapsulate standard interpretive guidelines. It may be easy to underestimate the interpretive task at hand because an umbrella clause, due to its brevity, appears to issue a straightforward directive to the

---

[73] *Compañia de Aguas del Aconquija S.A. and Vivendi Universal* v. *Argentine Republic*, ICSID Case No. ARB/97/3, Decision on Annulment, 3 July 2002 (Fortier, Crawford, Fernández Rozas), para. 96.

[74] See discussion at Chapter 3, Section 3.4 for categories of contract claims that potentially violate the FET standard found in investment treaties, and at Chapter 4, Sections 4.3.1 and 4.4 for contractual breaches that may amount to unlawful expropriations under the applicable investment treaties.

arbitral tribunal.[75] Yet, perceptions on what the directive is can vary significantly from one person to the next. According to Mann, an umbrella clause merely reflects the duty of host States to 'act in accordance with the requirements of good faith'.[76] Weil, on the other hand, states categorically that 'the invocation of an umbrella [clause] transforms contractual obligations into international obligations, thereby assuring the immutability of the contract with the penalty of a treaty violation'.[77]

The confusion is borne out in the awards issued in the aftermath of *SGS* v. *Pakistan*, where an investment treaty tribunal considered for the first time the effect of an umbrella clause on contractual protection.[78] This section uses *SGS* v. *Pakistan* as a case study to illustrate the interpretive challenge that an umbrella clause poses. It suggests that neither the principal (5.3.2.1), nor the supplementary means of interpretation (5.3.2.2), offer conclusive answers on the character of protection that an umbrella clause confers on contractual rights.

5.3.2.1   Principal Means of Interpretation

The dispute in *SGS* v. *Pakistan* arose from outstanding payment owed by Pakistan to SGS under a customs inspection services contract, as well as the termination of the said contract by Pakistan. After unsuccessfully seeking redress from Swiss courts, SGS filed a request for arbitration with ICSID pursuant to the dispute settlement provision in the Switzerland-Pakistan investment treaty. One of the claims submitted to the ICSID tribunal by SGS was that Pakistan, in committing a breach of the contract,

---

[75] A. Sinclair, 'State Contracts in Investment Treaty Arbitration', PhD thesis, University of Cambridge (2013), p. 139: 'A typical umbrella clause is mandatory and apparently clear in its intended effect'.

[76] F. A. Mann, 'British Treaties for the Promotion and Protection of Foreign Investment' (1981) BYIL 241, 249.

[77] Weil, 'Problèmes Relatifs aux Contrats Passés entre un Etat et un Particulier', p. 130; see also I. F. Shihata, 'Applicable Law in International Arbitration: Specific Aspects in the Case of the Involvement of State Parties' in I. F. Shihata (ed.), *The World Bank in a Changing World* (Dordrecht: Martinus Nijhoff, 1995), vol. 2, p. 595; E. Gaillard, *La Jurisprudence du CIRDI* (Paris: Pedone, 2004), vol. I (*SGS* v. *Philippines*), pp. 833–4; S. Alexandrov, 'Breaches of Contract and Breaches of Treaty – The Jurisdiction of Treaty-based Arbitration Tribunals to Decide Breach of Contract Claims in *SGS* v. *Pakistan* and *SGS* v. *Philippines*' in T. Weiler (ed.), *International Investment Law and Arbitration: Leading Cases from the ICSID, NAFTA, Bilateral Treaties and Customary International Law* (London: Cameron May, 2005), pp. 555, 566.

[78] *SGS Société Générale de Surveillance SA* v. *Islamic Republic of Pakistan*, ICSID Case No. ARB/01/13, Decision of the Tribunal on Objections to Jurisdiction, 6 August 2003 (Feliciano, Faurès, Thomas).

violated Article 11, the umbrella clause in the Switzerland-Pakistan investment treaty:[79]

> Either Contracting Party shall constantly guarantee the observance of commitments it has entered into with respect to the investments of the investors of the other Contracting Party.

Counsel for SGS argued that the wording of Article 11 was sufficiently clear for the tribunal to find that:

> If I am the government and if I breach a contract, by the same token I will breach a treaty, so the useful effect of this is to create this mirror effect, to say that I will elevate in essence, and that's what it does, it may be far-reaching but that's what it does, to elevate breaches of contract as breaches of a treaty.[80]

Notably, Pakistan did not refute the argument that Article 11 protects contractual rights by transforming all contractual breaches into treaty violations. Instead, Pakistan reasoned that given the exclusive forum selection clause in the contract, the tribunal should only hear an Article 11 claim after a determination of whether Pakistan has breached the contract has been made in the contractually agreed forum. Pakistan appeared to accept that Article 11 did have the 'far-reaching' effects that counsel for SGS said it did.

According to Article 31(1) of the VCLT, the principal means of interpretation are the 'the terms of the treaty in their context' and the treaty's 'object and purpose'. Although the tribunal in *SGS v. Pakistan* did not refer specifically to the VCLT, its interpretive approach is reminiscent of Article 31(1):[81]

> A treaty interpreter must of course seek to give effect to the object and purpose projected by that Article and by the BIT as a whole. That object and purpose must be ascertained, in the first instance, from the text itself of Article 11 and the rest of the BIT.

Turning first to the text of Article 11, the tribunal found that SGS had greatly exaggerated the effect of this provision on contractual rights:[82]

> The text itself of Article 11 does not purport to state that breaches of contract alleged by an investor in relation to a contract it has concluded with a State (widely considered to be a matter of municipal rather than international law) are automatically 'elevated' to the level of breaches of

---

[79] Ibid., para. 97.
[80] Ibid., para. 99.
[81] Ibid., para. 165.
[82] Ibid., para. 166.

international treaty law. Thus, it appears to us that while the Claimant has sought to spell out the consequences or inferences it would draw from Article 11, the Article itself does not set forth those consequences.

Without commenting on Pakistan's apparent acquiescence in SGS's reading of Article 11, the tribunal opined that Article 11 could not be construed in the way suggested by SGS without '[c]lear and convincing evidence that such was indeed the shared intent of the Contracting Parties' to the investment treaty.[83] One may reasonably ask if the tribunal's unwillingness to accept SGS's interpretation, which Pakistan did not object to, was because the text of Article 11 illuminated the character of protection conferred on contractual rights, or because as the first tribunal to interpret an umbrella clause, it was understandably hesitant to conclude that Article 11 alters the default position where a breach of contract by a State does not in and of itself violate international law. The tribunal added that while States are free to conclude umbrella clauses that elevate all contractual obligations into international obligations, there has to be 'clear and persuasive evidence' that such an expansive interpretation was intended.[84] In the case of Article 11, this evidence was missing.

Having dismissed SGS's argument that Article 11 turns every breach of contract into a breach of treaty for lack of textual support, the tribunal proceeded to explain why an expansive reading of Article 11 is untenable in light of the object and purpose of the investment treaty. With respect to the character of protection conferred on contractual rights, the tribunal held that other treaty provisions on substantive protection (Articles 3 to 7) will be rendered 'superfluous ... if a simple breach of contract, or of municipal statute or regulation, by itself, would suffice to constitute a treaty violation on the part of a Contracting Party and engage the international responsibility of the Party'.[85] Moreover, given the 'structure and sequence' of the treaty, the placement of Article 11 towards the end of the treaty was taken by the tribunal as a reliable indication that Article 11 did not offer substantive protection to qualifying investments, unlike Articles 3 to 7. The tribunal deduced that

[t]he separation of Article 11 from those obligations by the subrogation article and the two dispute settlement provisions (Articles 9 and 10), indicates to our mind that Article 11 was not meant to project a substantive obligation like those set out in Articles 3 to 7, let alone one that could, when

---

[83] Ibid., para. 167.
[84] Ibid., para. 173.
[85] Ibid., para. 168.

read as SGS asks us to read it, supersede and render largely redundant the substantive obligations provided for in Articles 3 to 7.[86]

In rejecting SGS's reading of Article 11 without proposing an alternative interpretation, the award in *SGS* v. *Pakistan* appeared to strip Article 11 of all legal effect. Crawford criticises the tribunal's insistence on 'clear and convincing evidence' and 'clear and persuasive evidence' before the consequences of invoking an umbrella clause can be spelt out, as 'effectively depriv[ing] the umbrella clause of any content, contrary to the principle of *effet utile* and to the apparent intent of the drafters'.[87] But what could the drafters of the Switzerland-Pakistan investment treaty have intended for Article 11 if its meaning was still obscure after an examination of the text and the treaty's object and purpose? Swiss and Pakistani officials involved in the negotiation and drafting of the investment treaty would presumably be in the best position to offer clarification on the character of protection offered by Article 11. However, the tribunal in *SGS* v. *Pakistan* made no attempt to consult the relevant Swiss or Pakistani authorities who might have shed further light on Article 11. The next section considers if recourse to supplementary means of interpretation as provided in Article 32 of the VCLT, such as 'the preparatory work of the treaty and the circumstances of its conclusion', would have assisted the *SGS* v. *Pakistan* tribunal in its interpretation of Article 11.

5.3.2.2 Supplementary Means of Interpretation

Considering that disputes submitted to investment treaty arbitration always involve a respondent State that was party to the applicable investment treaty, States should reproduce and rely on records of the drafting history of umbrella clauses in their written submissions to the tribunal. And yet, despite some arbitral tribunals highlighting the pertinence of the '*travaux* of the BIT' to the interpretation of an umbrella clause,[88] publicly available written submissions of host States generally do not contain any discussion of the *travaux* on an umbrella clause. In *SGS* v. *Pakistan*, Pakistan did not supply the *travaux* of the Switzerland-Pakistan investment treaty, and the tribunal neither pressed Pakistan for it, nor requested its production by Switzerland. After the award in *SGS* v. *Pakistan* was

---

[86] Ibid., para. 170.
[87] Crawford, 'Treaty and Contract in Investment Arbitration', p. 351 at 368.
[88] *CMS Gas Transmission Company* v. *The Argentine Republic*, ICSID Case No. ARB/01/8, Decision of the ad hoc Committee on the Application for Annulment of the Argentine Republic, 25 September 2007 (Guillaume, Elaraby, Crawford), para. 95(f).

issued, Switzerland wrote a letter to the Deputy-Secretary General of ICSID, criticising the narrow interpretation the tribunal gave to Article 11.[89] Switzerland clarified that Article 11 does not elevate the breach of 'every imaginable commitment' to a breach of treaty, only:[90]

> [C]ommitments that a host State has entered into with regard to specific Investments of an investor, or investments of a specific investor, which played a significant role in the Investor's decision to invest or to substantially change an existing investment. i.e. commitments which were of such a nature that the investor could rely on them. Most typically but not exclusively, such commitments by the host State would be in the form of an Investment authorization by the competent authority of the host State or a written agreement between the host State or a competent authority of that State, on the one hand, and the investor, on the other.

Remarkably, Switzerland also asserted that its interpretation of Article 11, which rejects investment contract internationalisation, is the appropriate interpretation for umbrella clauses in general:[91]

> This interpretation is supported by the use of provisions such as Article 11 by countries like the United States, the United Kingdom, Germany, France and the Netherlands in the bilateral investment treaties. It also agrees with the meaning of a corresponding provision given by the negotiating parties of the Multilateral Agreement on Investment (MAI) in the framework of the OECD which Switzerland actively supported. In the light of the importance of establishing the intention of the Contracting Parties that concluded the BIT at issue it should be noted that negotiations for the MAI took place in the same time period as those between Switzerland and Pakistan.

The detailed explanation provided by Switzerland on the meaning that should have been ascribed to the umbrella clause in the Switzerland-Pakistan investment treaty demonstrates how States can influence the

---

[89] Letter from the Swiss Secretariat for Economic Affairs to the ICSID Secretary-General, 'Umbrella Clauses in Bilateral Investment Agreements', 1 October 2003, 19 *Mealey's International Arbitration Reports*, E1.

[90] Ibid., E2.

[91] Letter from the Swiss Secretariat for Economic Affairs to the ICSID Secretary-General, E2. No corresponding provision to Art. 11 was agreed upon during negotiations for the MAI. And in any event, negotiations for the MAI were abandoned in 1998. Furthermore, it is debatable if the Swiss view of including umbrella clauses in investment treaties to secure qualified contractual protection is representative of the views of other States that have concluded investment treaties containing umbrella clauses. The circumstances surrounding State and private codification projects on international law, which produced likely forerunners of umbrella clauses, also lend support to the view that umbrella clauses stand for absolute contractual protection, see discussion at Chapter 1, Section 1.4.

interpretation of treaty provisions *ex post*.[92] Yet, pre- or post-award elucidations by States on how an investment treaty provision should be interpreted are rare.[93] This may be because '*traxaux* of the BIT' do not exist. Relying on extensive interviews conducted with government officials intimately connected with the conclusion of BITs in their respective countries, political scientists Poulsen and Aisbett discovered that many countries have traditionally viewed the signing of investment treaties as 'photo opportunities' with visiting heads of State and pay significantly less attention to the terms of the treaty.[94] They have rarely bothered to keep records of the negotiations, if negotiations indeed took place. Some

---

[92] Roberts, 'Power and Persuasion in Investment Treaty Interpretation', p. 179 at 220.

[93] There are two other instances of post-award elucidations. The first is the series of meetings between representatives of the Netherlands and the Czech Republic in 2002 after the Partial Award in *CME Czech Republic BV* v. *Czech Republic*, UNCITRAL, Partial Award, 13 September 2001 (Kühn, Schwebel, Hándl) was rendered. In the Final Award, the tribunal was guided by the common position reached by Dutch and Czech officials on the interpretation of the Netherlands-Czech Republic investment treaty: see Final Award, 14 March 2003 (Kühn, Schwebel, Brownlie), paras. 87–93, 400, 437 and 504. The second and more recent is the exchange of letters between Laos and China in 2014 over the applicability of the China-Laos investment treaty to investments made in Macau. In *Sanum Investments Ltd.* v. *Laos*, the tribunal found that investments made in Macau, a Portuguese protectorate until 1999, after which it became a Special Administrative Region of China, were protected by the China-Laos investment treaty concluded in 1993: see PCA Case No. 2013-13, Award on Jurisdiction, 13 December 2013 (Sureda, Stern, Hanotiau), paras. 219–300. On 7 January 2014, the Laotian Ministry of Foreign Affairs wrote to the Chinese Embassy in Vientiane, expressing the view that the China-Laos investment treaty did not extend to Macau, and seeking Chinese views on the same matter. The Chinese Embassy agreed with Laos's interpretation of the scope of the treaty. This exchange of letters was pivotal to the decision of the High Court of Singapore to grant Laos' application to set aside the Award on Jurisdiction, see *Government of the Lao People's Democratic Republic* v. *Sanum Investments Ltd.* [2014] SGHC 15. The High Court's decision was reversed on appeal; see *Sanum Investments Ltd.* v. *Government of the Lao People's Democratic Republic* [2016] SGCA 57. For a critique of the decision of the Court of Appeal, Singapore's apex court, see J. Ho, 'Circumstantial Indicia in Treaty Interpretation' (2018) 33(1) *ICISD Review: Foreign Investment Law Journal* 67–73.

[94] L. Poulsen and E. Aisbett, 'When the Claim Hits: Bilateral Investment Treaties and Bounded Rational Learning' (2013) 65(2) *World Politics* 273 at 280 and 296 (Table 6). Officials from the following twenty-nine countries participated in the study: Cambodia, Canada, Chile, China, Costa Rica, Croatia, Czech Republic, Denmark, Dominican Republic, Democratic Republic of Congo, Ecuador, Finland, Germany, Ghana, Estonia, Jamaica, Japan, Lebanon, Malaysia, Mexico, Netherlands, Pakistan, South Africa, Sri Lanka, Sweden, Switzerland, Thailand, United Kingdom and United States. This groundbreaking research appears to defeat, or at least cast serious doubt on the view that there is solid

> evidence of the origins of the umbrella clause, including the intentions of the drafters involved in producing the first formulations of the umbrella clause ... [to] suggest[] that the umbrella clause had been intended effectively to ensure that [S]tate contracts (and other 'obligations' of the host State) are lifted out of

countries draw up a model investment treaty and adopt it as template.[95] A new investment treaty can be swiftly concluded if treaty negotiators are content to import provisions from the model treaty.

Pakistan was unable to point the tribunal in *SGS* v. *Pakistan* to any *travaux* on the umbrella clause for a good, yet unsettling, reason:[96]

> [T]he claim in 2001 took everyone within the Pakistani bureaucracy by complete surprise. When learning of the dispute, Pakistan's attorney general – one of the top experts on international public law in South Asia – actually had to look up 'BITs' and 'ICSID' on Google. And when inquiring with the relevant ministries, there were almost no records of Pakistan's past BIT negotiations with Switzerland. There were no files or documentation in any of the responsible ministries and no indication that the treaty had ever been discussed in Parliament. In fact, the treaty itself was nowhere to be found, and the government had to request a copy from Switzerland through formal channels.

Pakistan's experience may have been the most unforgettable of all the countries surveyed by Poulsen and Aisbett. Investment treaties are not always the products of significant negotiation and meticulous drafting. As a result, the wording of an umbrella clause does not necessarily contain clear directives on contractual protection.[97] In light of Pakistan's unfamiliarity with the circumstances under which the Switzerland-Pakistan investment treaty was concluded, Switzerland's elaboration of the objective of Article 11 more likely reflected Swiss views, rather than views jointly held by Switzerland and Pakistan. Therefore, even after applying the canons of interpretation found in Articles 31 and 32 of the VCLT, it is still not entirely clear whether an umbrella clause protects contractual rights by elevating some or all contractual obligations into international obligations, or by some other method. This ambiguity has fostered different degrees of umbrella clause internationalisation.

---

the domain of the host State's legal system so that, at least, the obligation to perform such obligations is not governed exclusively by the proper law,

Sinclair, 'State Contracts in Investment Treaty Arbitration', p. 163.

[95] See chapter contributions in C. Brown (ed.), *Oxford Commentaries on International Law – Commentaries on Selected Model Investment Treaties* (Oxford: Oxford University Press, 2013).

[96] Poulsen and Aisbett, 'When the Claim Hits', p. 280.

[97] Cf. *Noble Ventures* v. *Romania*, ICSID Case No. ARB/01/11, Award, 12 October 2005 (Böckstiegel, Lever, Dupuy), p. 56; *Bureau Veritas, Inspection, Valuation, Assessment and Control, BIVAC B.V.* v. *The Republic of Paraguay*, ICSID Case No. ARB/07/9, Decision of the Tribunal on Objections to Jurisdiction, 29 May 2009 (Knieper, Fortier, Sands), para. 141.

5.3.3   Degrees of Umbrella Clause Internationalisation

In the wake of the less than compelling interpretation given to the umbrella clause in the Switzerland-Pakistan investment treaty by the *SGS* v. *Pakistan* tribunal,[98] whether umbrella clauses internationalise investment contracts invited further reflection. The looming question is whether an umbrella clause protects contractual rights by transforming all contractual obligations into international obligations. In response, three degrees of umbrella clause internationalisation emerged. The first, which rejects umbrella clause internationalisation, posits that while an umbrella clause sets forth an international obligation on the part of a host State to respect commitments undertaken, an umbrella clause does not convert contractual obligations which are governed by the proper law of the contract, most likely national law, into international obligations governed by international law (5.3.3.1). The second, which advocates partial umbrella clause internationalisation, accepts that a breach of contract can rise to the level of a treaty violation only if the host State was acting in a sovereign capacity. International law is not violated simply because a contractual obligation is breached but because it is breached pursuant to the exercise of sovereign power (5.3.3.2). The third is in favour of umbrella clause internationalisation. In other words, every breach of a contractual obligation is a breach of an international obligation (5.3.3.3).

5.3.3.1   No Internationalisation: *SGS* v. *Philippines*

When a breach of contract is the basis for an umbrella clause claim but will be judged by the tribunal in accordance with the proper law of the contract and not international law, there is scant allowance for internationalisation. Although every contractual obligation attracts the protection of an umbrella clause, no contractual obligation is assimilated to an international obligation. By this approach, a breach of contract is far more likely to engage a host State's liability under national law, and not its international responsibility even when an umbrella clause is invoked.

As explained by the tribunal in *SGS* v. *Philippines*, the first tribunal to reject umbrella clause internationalisation:[99]

---

[98] For a succinct critique, see C. Schreuer, 'Travelling the BIT Route: Of Waiting Periods, Umbrella Clauses and Forks in the Road' (2004) 5 *Journal of World Investment and Trade* 231 at 253–4.

[99] ICSID Case No. ARB/02/6, Decision of the Tribunal on Objections to Jurisdiction, 29 January 2004 (El-Kosheri, Crawford, Crivellaro (partially dissenting)) (original emphasis). Art. X(2) provides: 'Each of the Contracting Parties shall observe all obligations entered into

[The umbrella clause] makes it a breach of the BIT for the host State to fail to observe binding commitments, including contractual commitments, which it has assumed with regard to specific investments. But it does not convert the issue of the extent or content of such obligations into an issue of international law ... It is a conceivable function of a provision such as Article X(2) of the Swiss-Philippines BIT to provide assurances to foreign investors with regard to the performance of obligations assumed by the host State under its own law with regard to specific investments – in effect, to help secure the rule of law in relation to investment protection.

Stressing that the logic applied by the *SGS* v. *Philippines* tribunal to umbrella clauses was straightforward, one member of the tribunal subsequently added the clarification that:[100]

The purpose of the umbrella clause is to allow enforcement without internationalisation and without transforming the character and content of the underlying obligation.

According to the *SGS* v. *Philippines* award therefore, the protection conferred by umbrella clauses on contractual rights is the enforcement of contractual obligations against host States by investment treaty tribunals. This reading of an umbrella clause respects the difference between a contract claim and a treaty claim as set out by the ad hoc committee in *Vivendi* v. *Argentina*, the leading decision on the contract-treaty claim distinction. The endgame of arguing that a breach of contract simultaneously violates an umbrella clause is therefore to bring a contract claim within the purview of investment treaty arbitration. Umbrella clauses thus authorise investment treaty tribunals to decide contract claims by applying the proper law of the contract.[101]

Although one commentator claims that the interpretive approach of the tribunal in *SGS* v. *Philippines* is the approach that other tribunals interpreting umbrella clauses are converging towards,[102] the rationale adopted by the *SGS* v. *Philippines* tribunal has, perhaps because of its subtlety, eluded many who have referred to its findings. Some tribunals endorse the *SGS* v. *Philippines* award and yet fail to appreciate what the tribunal was saying. The mischaracterisation, misunderstanding and worst of all, misquoting

---

with respect to an investment in its territory made by an investor of the other Contracting Party.' Author's translation from the original French.

[100] Crawford, 'Treaty and Contract in Investment Arbitration', p. 370.

[101] For a critique of the interpretation given to Art. X(2) of the Swiss-Philippines BIT by the arbitral tribunal in *SGS* v. *Philippines*, see Gaillard, *La Jurisprudence du CIRDI* (*SGS* v. *Philippines*), pp. 903–5.

[102] J. Antony, 'Umbrella Clauses since *SGS* v. *Pakistan* and *SGS* v. *Philippines* – A Developing Consensus' (2013) 29(4) *Arbitration International* 607 at 618 and 638.

of the *SGS* v. *Philippines* tribunal on umbrella clauses is commonplace. The dubious honour for the most severe mischaracterisation probably goes to the *Noble Ventures* v. *Romania* tribunal:[103]

> [I]n *SGS* v. *Philippines, supra*, the treaty clause was formulated so as to assimilate the host State's contractual obligations to its treaty obligations under the bilateral investment treaty.

The *SGS* v. *Philippines* award has also been misunderstood and wrongly criticised. According to the tribunals in *El Paso Energy International Company* v. *The Argentine Republic* and *Pan American Energy LLC and Anor* v. *The Argentine Republic*, the tribunal in *SGS* v. *Philippines* had drawn 'contradictory conclusions':[104]

> [T]he Tribunal stated that, although the umbrella clause transforms the contract claims into treaty claims, first 'it does not convert the issue of the *extent or content* of such obligations into an issue of international law' (Decision, [para.] 128, original emphasis), which means that the 'contract claims/treaty claims' should be assessed according to the national law of the contract and not the treaty standards ... In other words, the Tribunal asserts that a treaty claim should not be analysed according to treaty standards, which seems quite strange.

The two tribunals appear to have missed the point that the tribunal in *SGS* v. *Philippines* was making. First, the *SGS* v. *Philippines* tribunal did not state that 'the umbrella clause transforms the contract claims into treaty claims'. On the contrary, it found that an umbrella clause '*does not* convert questions of contract law into questions of treaty law'.[105] Second, the purpose of maintaining a distinction between contract claims and treaty claims is to ensure that contractual claims are subjected to the proper law of the contract. According to the *SGS* v. *Philippines* tribunal, the function of an umbrella clause is to 'provide assurances to foreign investors with regard to the performance of obligations *assumed by the host State under its own law*'.[106] Nowhere is it suggested that 'treaty claims should be assessed according to the national law of the contract'. Finally, after pointing out that an umbrella clause 'does not change the proper law of the [investment

---

[103] Award, 12 October 2005, p. 59.
[104] *El Paso Energy International Company* v. *Argentina*, ICSID Case No. ARB/03/15, Decision on Jurisdiction, 27 April 2006 (Caflisch, Stern, Bernadini), p. 76; *Pan American Energy and BP Argentina Exploration Company* v. *Argentina*, ICSID Case Nos ARB/03/13 and ARB/04/8, Decision on Preliminary Objections, 27 July 2006 (Caflisch, Stern, Bernadini), para. 105.
[105] Decision on Jurisdiction, para. 126 (emphasis added).
[106] Decision on Jurisdiction, para. 128 (emphasis added).

contract] from the law of the Philippines to international law', it is hardly strange that a contractual claim 'should not be analysed according to treaty standards'.

The *SGS* v. *Philippines* award is often misquoted as a complementary award to the *Noble Ventures* v. *Romania* award.[107] The latter tribunal is in favour of umbrella clause internationalisation.[108] The *SGS* v. *Philippines* award, which expressly rejects umbrella clause internationalisation, cannot be reconciled with the *Noble Ventures* v. *Romania* award. One begins to doubt the care which certain tribunals read the *SGS* v. *Philippines* and *Noble Ventures* v. *Romania* awards before citing them both as authority for umbrella clause internationalisation.[109]

Recent attempts by commentators to fuse anti-internationalisation and pro-internationalisation arbitral awards leave readers to unravel a series of contradictory propositions. According to one commentator, umbrella clauses impose on the one hand 'an international treaty obligation on host countries that requires them to respect obligations they have entered into regarding investments protected by the treaty ... [by] plac[ing] such obligations under the protective umbrella of international law', but do not on the other 'transform a contractual or other obligation governed by domestic law into an international obligation governed by international law'.[110] Other commentators have readily endorsed the diametrically opposed readings of umbrella clauses advanced in the *SGS* v. *Philippines* and *Noble Ventures* v. *Romania* awards, seemingly oblivious to their incompatibility.[111]

At present, only the majority of the tribunal in *Eureko B.V.* v. *Republic of Poland*,[112] the ad hoc committee in *CMS Gas Transmission Company* v. *The Republic of Argentina*,[113] the tribunal in *Toto Costruzioni Generali*

---

[107] The complementary authority for *Noble Ventures* v. *Romania* is in fact *BIVAC* v. *Paraguay*, para. 141.

[108] Award, 12 October 2005, p. 54.

[109] *SGS Société Générale de Surveillance SA* v. *The Republic of Paraguay*, ICSID Case No. ARB/07/29, Award, 10 February 2012 (Alexandrov, Donovan, Mexiá), incorporating the Decision on Jurisdiction, 12 February 2010 (Alexandrov, Donovan, Mexia), para. 170 (fn. 98).

[110] Salacuse, *The Three Laws of International Investment*, pp. 390–1.

[111] Kjos, *Applicable Law in Investor-State Arbitration,* pp. 251–3.

[112] Partial Award (ad hoc), 19 August 2005 (Fortier, Schwebel, Rajski (dissenting)), paras. 256–7.

[113] ICSID Case No. ARB/01/8, Decision of the ad hoc Committee on the Application for Annulment of the Argentine Republic, 25 September 2007 (Guillaume, Elaraby, Crawford), paras. 95–7.

S.p.A. v. *The Republic of Lebanon*,[114] and four commentators have fully grasped the *SGS* v. *Philippines* tribunal's refusal to endorse umbrella clause internationalisation.[115]

5.3.3.2   Partial Internationalisation: *Joy Mining* v. *Egypt*

The first investment treaty award to endorse the distinction between breaches of contract committed by a host State *iure gestionis* and *iure imperii*, the former falling outside the jurisdiction of the arbitral tribunal constituted pursuant to an investment treaty containing an umbrella clause, was *Joy Mining Machinery Limited* v. *Arab Republic of Egypt*. Here, the tribunal cited no earlier arbitral awards to support the integration of this distinction into the umbrella clause in the UK-Egypt investment treaty, and simply assumed that contractual breaches *iure gestionis* do not qualify for treaty protection:[116]

> Disputes about the release of bank guarantees are a common occurrence in many jurisdictions and the fact that a State agency might be a party to the Contract involving a commercial transaction of this kind does not change its nature. It is still a commercial and contractual dispute to be settled as agreed to in the Contract, including the resort to arbitration if and when available. It is not transformed into an investment or an investment dispute.

In contrast, contractual breaches *iure imperii* will qualify for treaty protection because such contractual breaches amount to treaty violations that come within the jurisdiction of the tribunal. Umbrella clause internationalisation is only partial because unless it is established that the host State has breached a contract in its sovereign capacity, the presence of an umbrella clause in an investment treaty has no bearing on either a State's liability under national law, or its responsibility under international law for a breach of contract.

Other investment treaty tribunals have elaborated on the significance of applying the *iure gestionis–iure imperii* distinction when interpreting

---

[114] *Toto Costruzioni Generali S.p.A.* v. *The Republic of Lebanon*, ICSID Case No. ARB/07/12, Decision on Jurisdiction, 11 September 2009 (van Houtte, Feliciani, Moghaizel), para. 202.

[115] Gaillard, *La Jurisprudence du CIRDI*, pp. 90–5; Schreuer, 'Travelling the BIT Route', p. 255; M. Sasson, *Substantive Law in Investment Treaty Arbitration – The Unsettled Relationship between International and Municipal Law* (The Hague: Kluwer, 2010), pp. 184–5 and 192; Sinclair, 'State Contracts in Investment Treaty Arbitration', pp. 145–7. It may be helpful, as Schreuer suggests, to think of the *SGS* v. *Philippines* approach as extending '[t]he range of remedies … from redress for violations of international law to relief for breach of domestic law'.

[116] *Joy Mining Machinery Limited* v. *Egypt*, ICSID Case No. ARB/03/11, Award on Jurisdiction, 6 August 2004 (Orrego Vicun̄a, Craig, Weeramantry), para. 79, also 72, 75 and 81.

umbrella clauses.[117] The relevance of this distinction to a finding of State responsibility for contractual breaches is apparently confirmed by earlier arbitral awards. The tribunal in *Impregilo S.p.A.* v. *Islamic Republic of Pakistan* concluded on a 'review of jurisprudence' that:[118]

> In order that the alleged breach of contract may constitute a violation of the BIT, it must be the result of behaviour going beyond that which an ordinary contracting party could adopt. Only the State in the exercise of its sovereign authority ('*puissance publique*'), and not as a contracting party, may breach the obligations assumed under the BIT. In other words, the investment protection treaty only provides a remedy to the investor where the investor proves that the alleged damages were a consequence of the behaviour of the Host State acting in breach of the obligations it had assumed under the treaty.

This 'review of jurisprudence' consists of twelve arbitral awards that Schwebel credits for the proposition that 'the use of the sovereign authority of a State, contrary to the expectations of the parties, to abrogate or violate a contract with an alien, is a violation of international law'.[119] Reliance on these decisions, which are a mix of awards rendered by Mixed Claims Commissions and *ad hoc* arbitral tribunals, is problematic. With the exception of the *Shufeldt Claim*, which concerned a claimant's entitlement to compensation by Guatemala after its contract had been terminated by legislative decree,[120] the pertinence of the *Texaco, Revere Copper, AGIP* and

---

[117] *CMS Gas Transmission Company* v. *The Argentine Republic*, ICSID Case No. ARB/01/8, Awa Award, 12 May 2005 (Orrego Vicuña, Lalonde, Rezek), para. 299; *El Paso Energy International Company* v. *Argentina*, Decision on Jurisdiction, paras. 66–82; *Pan American Energy* v. *Argentina*, Decision on Preliminary Objections, paras. 97–110; *Sempra Energy International* v. *Argentine Republic*, ICSID Case No. ARB/02/16, Award, 28 September 2007 (Orrego Vicuña, Lalonde, Morelli Rico), paras. 310–11.

[118] ICSID Case No. ARB/03/3, Decision on Jurisdiction, 22 April 2005 (Guillaume, Cremades, Landau), para. 260. This case, like *Abaclat and Others* v. *Argentina*, ICSID Case No. ARB/07/5, Decision on Jurisdiction and Admissibility, 4 August 2011 (Tercier, van den Berg, Abi-Saab (dissenting)), is unusual because the applicable investment treaty did not contain an umbrella clause. The claimants relied on the most-favoured-nation (MFN) clause in the Italy-Pakistan investment treaty (Agreement between the Government of the Islamic Republic of Pakistan and the Government of the Italian Republic on the Promotion and Protection of Investments (signed 19 July 1997, entered into force 22 June 2001)) and the Italy-Argentina investment treaty (Fra la Repubblica Italiana e la Repubblica Argentina Sulla Promozione e Protezione Degli Investimenti (signed 22 May 1990, entered into force 14 October 1993)) respectively to import the umbrella clause from other investment treaties concluded by Argentina.

[119] Schwebel, 'On Whether the Breach by a State of a Contract with an Alien is a Breach of International Law', pp. 425, 431–3.

[120] (*Guatemala* v. *USA*) (1930) 2 RIAA 1079, p. 1095. See also discussion at Chapter 1, Section 1.3.3.3 and Chapter 3, Section 3.2.2.

Elf Aquitaine arbitral awards to Schwebel's proposition is not easily discernible. The distinction between sovereign and commercial acts was only mentioned in passing in the *Texaco* award and is of remote consequence to the sole arbitrator's findings.[121] It was not even alluded to in the *Revere Copper*, *AGIP* and *Elf Aquitaine* awards.[122]

Nonetheless, the 'review of jurisprudence' by the tribunal in *Impregilo* v. *Pakistan* has been deemed accurate. According to the tribunal in *Sempra Energy International* v. *The Argentine Republic*:[123]

> The decisions dealing with the issue of the umbrella clause and the role of contracts in a Treaty context have *all* distinguished breaches of contract from Treaty breaches on the basis of whether the breach has arisen from the conduct of an ordinary contract party, or rather involves a kind of conduct that only a sovereign State function or power could effect.

Although the *iure gestionis–iure imperii* distinction is critical to a finding of expropriation,[124] it does not mean that the distinction must apply in all other contexts. Notably, the law of State responsibility 'do[es] not, generally speaking, rest on a distinction between conduct *iure imperii* and conduct *iure gestionis*'.[125] It is debatable if the tribunal in *Joy Mining* v. *Egypt* was correct to hold that only contract claims that overlap with treaty claims fall within the jurisdiction of the tribunal. The jurisdiction *ratione materiae* of a tribunal in investment treaty arbitration is established on the existence of a protected investment and a qualifying dispute as defined by the relevant treaty. When these conditions are satisfied, the tribunal has jurisdiction over the claims submitted, regardless of whether they originated in a contract and regardless of whether the treaty contains an umbrella clause. The international responsibility of a host State for the violation of treaty obligations is determined at the merits phase of the

---

[121] *Texaco Overseas Petroleum Company/California Asiatic Oil Company* v. *The Government of the Libyan Arab Republic*, 53 ILR 389, Award on the Merits, 19 January 1977 (Dupuy), p. 467.

[122] *Revere Copper and Brass Inc.* v. *Overseas Private Investment Corp.*, *AGIP* v. *Congo* Award; *Elf Aquitaine Iran* v. *National Iranian Oil Company*, (1984) *Revue de l'Arbitrage* 401, Preliminary Award, 14 January 1982 (Gomard).

[123] Award, 28 September 2007, p. 310 (fn. 112) (emphasis added); cf. *Duke Energy Electroquil Partners and Anor* v. *Ecuador*, ICSID Case No. ARB/04/19, Award, 18 August 2008 (Kaufmann-Kohler, Pinzón, van den Berg), para. 320: 'Another open question is whether sovereign interference is needed to constitute a breach of an umbrella clause. While, as indicated by Respondent, language to that effect appears in some cases ... a majority of decisions do not formulate such distinction.'

[124] See discussion at Chapter 4, Section 4.3.1.1.

[125] Crawford, 'Revising the Draft Articles on State Responsibility', p. 435 at 440.

arbitration. Relying on an umbrella clause subject to the *iure gestionis–iure imperii* distinction as a bar to jurisdiction is impractical due to the order in which submissions on jurisdiction and submissions on the merits are made to the tribunal. The *Impregilo* v. *Pakistan*, *El Paso* v. *Argentina* and *PanAm* v. *Argentina* tribunals were unable to ascertain after the hearing on jurisdiction if the contractual breaches complained of were sovereign acts that violated the umbrella clause because the parties had yet to present their arguments on the merits.[126] There is thus little to commend the *iure gestionis–iure imperii* distinction as a jurisdictional criterion.[127] As Crawford points out, the distinction 'imposes a characterisation test at the level of breach for which there is no textual warrant and which is capable of producing arbitrary results'.[128]

5.3.3.3   Full Internationalisation: *Noble Ventures* v. *Romania*

If the effect of an umbrella clause is to transform all contractual obligations into international obligations, then there is umbrella clause internationalisation whereby State responsibility is engaged for every breach of contract. This is an extremely expansive, and possibly unwarranted, reading of umbrella clauses. Unlike the *SGS* v. *Philippines* line of awards, the tribunal need not decide a contract claim in accordance with the proper law of the contract, since a contract claim is automatically transformed into a treaty claim. And unlike the *Joy Mining* v. *Romania* line of awards, jurisdiction is established and State responsibility is engaged even if the host State breaches the contract in a commercial capacity.

According to the tribunal in *Noble Ventures* v. *Romania*, the first tribunal to endorse umbrella clause internationalisation:[129]

> An umbrella clause is usually seen as transforming municipal law obligations into obligations directly cognizable in international law ... [whereby] the host State may incur international responsibility by reason of a breach of its contractual obligations towards the private investor of the other Party, the breach of contract being thus 'internationalized', i.e. assimilated to a breach of the treaty.

---

[126] *Impregilo* v. *Pakistan*, Decision on Jurisdiction, para. 316c; *El Paso* v. *Argentina*, Decision on Jurisdiction, para. 86; *Pan American Energy* v. *Argentina*, Decision on the Preliminary Objections, para. 115.

[127] This finds support in *SGS* v. *Paraguay*, Decision on Jurisdiction, para. 136.

[128] 'Treaty and Contract in Investment Arbitration', p. 368.

[129] Award, 12 October 2005, paras. 53–4.

The tribunals in *BIVAC* v. *Paraguay*,[130] *Duke Energy* v. *Ecuador*,[131] and most recently in *SGS* v. *Paraguay*[132] also recognised umbrella clause internationalisation. The tribunal in *BIVAC* v. *Paraguay* was explicit that an umbrella clause does more than confer jurisdiction on an investment treaty tribunal to decide a contract claim in accordance with the proper law of the contract; it transforms every contractual obligation into a treaty obligation:[133]

> Article 3(4) of the BIT does have the effect for which BIVAC argues, namely that it gives the Tribunal jurisdiction over a claim that arises from or is produced directly in relation to the Contract. This is not, however, the end of the matter. Assuming that Article 3(4) does import the obligations under the Contract into the BIT, giving this Tribunal jurisdiction to interpret and apply the Contract as such, *then it must have imported into the BIT all of the obligations owed by Paraguay to BIVAC under the Contract.*

The criticism levelled by Switzerland at the *SGS* v. *Pakistan* tribunal cautions that the effect of an umbrella clause on contractual rights may not be evident just by looking at the wording of an umbrella clause. Nonetheless, tribunals in favour of umbrella clause internationalisation all appear to rely exclusively on textual interpretation.[134] For instance, the *BIVAC* v. *Paraguay* tribunal found that 'the broadly worded text of Article 3(4) of the [Netherlands-Paraguay] BIT has been significant' to its endorsement of umbrella clause internationalisation.[135] Yet, it is doubtful if the text of Article 3(4) compels the internationalisation of contractual obligations.[136] Article 3(4) of the Netherlands-Paraguay investment treaty provides:[137]

> Each Contracting Party shall observe any obligation it may have entered into with regard to investments of the other Contracting Party.

---

[130] Decision of the Tribunal on Objections to Jurisdiction, paras. 141–2.

[131] Award, para. 325.

[132] Decision on Jurisdiction, pp. 168–9; see also *David Minotte and Robert Lewis* v. *Poland*, ICSID Case No. ARB/AF/10/1, Award, 16 May 2014 (Lowe, Mendelson, Romero), p. 203, where the tribunal implied that the breach of an existing 'legal obligation', such as a contractual obligation, may suffice to violate an umbrella clause.

[133] Decision of the Tribunal on Objections to Jurisdiction, para. 142 (emphasis added).

[134] *SGS* v. *Paraguay*, Decision on Jurisdiction, para. 170; also *LG & E Energy Corp.* v. *Argentina*, Decision on Liability (de Maekelt, Rezek, van den Berg), 3 October 2006 (ARB/02/1), paras. 170–1; *Enron Corporation Ponderosa Assets* v. *Argentina*, Award (Orrego Vicuña, van den Berg, Tschanz) 22 May 2007 (ARB/01/3), paras. 269, 274.

[135] Decision of the Tribunal on Objections to Jurisdiction, para. 141.

[136] Cf. E. Gaillard, *La Jurisprudence du CIRDI*, vol. II (*Noble Ventures c. Romania*), pp. 195, 209–15.

[137] Decision of the Tribunal on Objections to Jurisdiction, para. 19.

Article 3(4) is not materially different from Article X(2) of the Switzerland-Philippines investment treaty,[138] or Article 2(2) of the UK-Egypt investment treaty,[139] which the *SGS* v. *Philippines* and *Joy Mining* v. *Egypt* tribunals respectively found did not give rise to umbrella clause internationalisation. Article 3(4) also bears close resemblance to what appears to be the earliest version of an umbrella clause, namely Article II of the 1959 Abs-Shawcross Draft Convention on Investments Abroad:[140]

> Each Party shall at all times ensure the observance of any undertakings, which it may have given in relation to investments made by nationals of any other Party.

Although the drafters of the Abs-Shawcross Draft Convention maintained that Article II represented one of the 'fundamental principles of international law regarding the treatment of the property, rights, and interests of aliens' which draws no distinction 'between the rule [of *pacta sunt servanda*] applicable to treaties and that applicable to contracts with aliens',[141] the ability of Article II to internationalise contracts was not widely accepted.[142] While the meaning of Article II may appear plain to some from its wording, the scepticism expressed by others over the integration of the controversial notion of internationalisation into an investment treaty cannot be ignored. To borrow a phrase from Schwarzenberger, the *Noble Ventures* v. *Romania* line of awards which promote umbrella clause internationalisation, represents '[a] far-reaching departure from the law as it stands and may tilt the balance too far in favour of the investor'.[143]

---

[138] For text of Art. X(2), see *SGS* v. *Philippines*, Decision of the Tribunal on Objections to Jurisdiction.

[139] Art. 2(2) provides: 'Each Contracting Party shall observe any obligation it may have entered into with regard to investments of nationals or companies of the other Contracting Party.'

[140] UNCTAD, 'International Investment Instruments: A Compendium, Volume III (Regional Integration, Bilateral and Non-governmental Instruments)', online: http://unctad.org/en/Docs/dtci30vol3_en.pdf (accessed 31 December 2017). A nearly identical version of Art. II later appeared as Art. 2 in the 1967 OECD Draft Convention on the Protection of Foreign Property (signed 12 October 1967, not yet in force), C(67)102, p. 14.

[141] Abs and Shawcross, 'The Proposed Convention to Protect Private Foreign Investment', p. 115 at 119–20; also Lord H. Shawcross, 'The Problems Foreign Investment in International Law' (1961) 102 *Recueil des Cours* 335 at 351–5.

[142] For possible reasons underlying the resistance to absolute contractual protection that Abs-Shawcross Draft Convention Art. II attempted to secure, see discussion at Chapter 1, Section 1.4.2.

[143] G. Schwarzenberger, 'The Abs-Shawcross Draft Convention on Investments Abroad: A Critical Commentary' (1960) 9 *Journal of Public Law* 147 at 154–5; cf. Gaillard, *La Jurisprudence du CIRDI*, vol. II (*Noble Ventures c. Romania*), pp. 209–15.

5.4 Investment Contract Internationalisation within Investment Treaty Protection

Whichever degree of umbrella clause internationalisation one finds agreeable, the presence of an umbrella clause in an applicable investment treaty 'add[s] extra protection to the investor'.[144] The no-internationalisation approach of the *SGS* v. *Philippines* tribunal nonetheless lends an investor the authority of an investment treaty tribunal to enforce contractual obligations against a State according to the proper law of the contract. The partial-internationalisation approach of the *Joy Mining* v. *Egypt* tribunal sanctions the use and abuse by a State of its sovereign powers to repudiate contractual obligations owed to an investor. And the full-internationalisation approach of the *Noble Ventures* v. *Romania* tribunal offers the highest possible level of protection to contractual rights, by assimilating every breach of contract to a breach of treaty.

As the purpose of concluding investment treaties is to further the goal of investment protection, it is only natural that the protection of contractual rights, so long as they qualify as investments under the applicable investment treaty, is correspondingly enhanced. To interpret umbrella clauses in a way that strengthens contractual rights is therefore, in the most general sense, compatible with the existing framework of investment protection generated by investment treaties. However, enhanced protection for investment contracts under investment treaties does not necessarily lie in the engagement of State responsibility for contractual breaches. The availability of enhanced protection for contractual rights raises two related issues that this section will address. The first is the possibility of enhanced protection becoming excessive (5.4.1), and the second is the viability of multilateralising the enhanced protection of contractual rights using MFN clauses (5.4.2).

5.4.1 *The Improbability of Absolute Contractual Protection*

Neither international law in general nor investment treaties in particular prohibit all manner of host State interference with foreign investment. For example, treaty provisions on expropriation do not stipulate that a host State commits a treaty violation by the mere fact of expropriation.

---

[144] C. Schreuer, 'Investment Treaty Arbitration and Jurisdiction over Contract Claims – The *Vivendi I* Case Considered' in T. Weiler (ed.), *International Investment Law and Arbitration: Leading Cases from the ICSID, NAFTA, Bilateral Treaties and Customary International Law* (London: Cameron May, 2005), pp. 281, 301.

The same goes for treaty standards of protection such as fair and equitable treatment. An act of the host State that compromises the rights of a foreign investor does not in and of itself lead to a finding that there has been a violation of the treaty obligation to accord an investor fair and equitable treatment. Treaty protection for rights that qualify as investments is therefore not absolute. A host State can interfere with a foreign investor's rights, including contractual rights, without incurring international responsibility so long as its conduct does not infringe treaty provisions or standards.

Of the three views on umbrella clause internationalisation discussed in Section 5.3.3, the more popular *SGS* v. *Philippines* and *Joy Mining* v. *Egypt* approaches, while enhancing contractual protection, do not treat investment contracts as inviolable. The *SGS* v. *Philippines* approach urges the application of national law to the breach of contractual obligations by a State, while the *Joy Mining* v. *Egypt* approach views the engagement of international responsibility as a likelihood only when a contract is breached by a State in its sovereign capacity. In contrast, the *Noble Ventures* v. *Romania* approach, which stands for umbrella clause internationalisation, clearly regards investment contracts as inviolable. Accordingly, an umbrella clause does not allow a State to breach a contract without violating international law. It is arguable that the *Noble Ventures* v. *Romania* brand of contractual protection is excessive because contracts are turned into super-investments that that command a much higher level of protection than other types of protected investments.

When the performance of a contractual obligation is delayed or denied, there is a *prima facie* breach of contract. Should the investor choose to seek redress under an applicable investment treaty containing an umbrella clause, it must show how the contractual breach rises to the level of a treaty violation that engages the international responsibility of the host State. If umbrella clauses truly establish a treaty obligation *not to breach* investment contracts, then State responsibility will be engaged for all manner of contractual breaches attributable to the host State. Compare this with the situation where an investment is made in the host State without a contract and which is subsequently taken pursuant to a nationalisation decree providing for nominal compensation. The investor seeking redress under the same investment treaty not only needs to show that an expropriation has occurred before the host State can be held responsible for a treaty violation but is also expected to demonstrate that one of the investment treaty's substantive protections has been breached. An umbrella clause that enables the owner of a contract claim to prevail without having to prove the breach of any of the investment treaty's substantive protections therefore creates two regimes of investment protection within the same treaty: a preferential regime for contract-based investments since State responsibility is far more easily engaged and a less-preferential regime for all other investments.

Even if many investments are contracted for by host States,[145] this does not recast the goal of *investment* protection which produced the BIT generation as the goal of *investment contract* protection. Wälde wrote that investment contracts occupied at best a position of auxiliary importance in pioneering efforts to draft multilateral rules on investment protection because 'the solutions emerging were all about expropriation (including expropriation of contracts and contractually organised investments) in its direct and indirect forms'.[146] Umbrella clause internationalisation, by exalting contractual rights above all other rights, arguably ignores the broader historical context which led to the conclusion of investment treaties.

5.4.2 *The Multilateralisation of Enhanced Contractual Protection*

If umbrella clauses offer enhanced protection to contractual rights, some claimants may consider themselves disadvantaged if the applicable investment treaty does not contain an umbrella clause. A few have argued that a treaty obligation to accord MFN treatment to qualifying investments imports an umbrella clause to the applicable investment treaty, so long as umbrella clauses are present in other investment treaties concluded by the respondent State.[147] Although one tribunal summarily dismissed this argument,[148] another has been more receptive. In *Abaclat and Others* v. *Argentine Republic*, a mass claim for unpaid sovereign bonds was brought pursuant to the Argentina-Italy investment treaty which does not contain an umbrella clause.[149] The arbitral tribunal agreed with the claimants that '[b]y not respecting its obligations under the bonds, Argentina would have violated [the umbrella clause in the] Argentina-Chile BIT, which in turn, constitutes a violation of [the MFN clause] in the Argentina-Italy

---

[145] Salacuse, *The Three Laws of International Investment* pp. 164–6.
[146] T. Wälde, 'The "Umbrella" Clause in Investment Arbitration – A Comment on Original Intentions and Recent Cases' (2005) 6 *Journal of World Investment & Trade* 183 at 193.
[147] *Impregilo* v. *Pakistan*, Decision on Jurisdiction, paras. 220–1; *EDF International S.A. and Ors* v. *Argentina*, ICSID Case No. ARB/03/23, Award, 11 June 2012 (Park, Kaufmann-Kohler, Remón), para. 922.
[148] *Impregilo* v. *Pakistan*, Decision on Jurisdiction, para. 223.
[149] Signed 22 May 1990, entered into force 14 October 1993.

BIT'.[150] There is therefore some potential in relying on MFN clauses to multilateralise the enhanced protection of contractual rights under investment treaties.

MFN clauses stipulate the base level of protection that qualifying investors under an investment treaty are entitled to, namely, treatment that is 'no less favourable' than that accorded to investors from non-party States to the investment treaty.[151] Although MFN clauses pertain to the treatment of investors by the host State for the duration of the investment, they tend to be invoked by claimants seeking recourse to a particular dispute settlement procedure that is not provided for in the applicable investment treaty.[152] In analysing the misuse of MFN clauses, Paparinskis argues that the incomparability of different dispute settlement procedures does not support the conclusion that a claimant who does not have the option of seeking ICSID arbitration for instance, is being treated less favourably than a claimant who does.[153] For Paparinskis, an MFN clause secures more favourable *substantive* treatment and not *procedural* entitlement for an investor because '[i]f a particular issue is addressed by techniques and approaches that are too distinct to be more or less favourable, the MFN clause would have no application'.[154]

---

[150] Decision on Jurisdiction and Admissibility, paras. 312(v) and 314. The dissenting arbitrator did not comment on this aspect of the majority's holding. See also *EDF* v. *Argentina*, Award, para. 937.

[151] UNCTAD, 'Most-Favoured-Nation Treatment – Series on Issues in International Investment Agreements II (2010)', online: http://unctad.org/en/Docs/diaeia20101_en.pdf (accessed 31 December 2017), pp. 23–4 and 41–57.

[152] For an overview of this growing phenomenon, see Y. Radi, 'The Application of the Most-Favoured-Nation Clause to the Dispute Settlement Provisions of Bilateral Investment Treaties: Domesticating the "Trojan Horse"' (2007) 18(4) EJIL 757. Two recent awards where the MFN clause in the applicable investment treaty was invoked by investors claiming ICSID arbitration are *Kılıç İnşaat İthalat İhracat Sanayi Ve Ticaret Anonim Şirketi* v. *Turkmenistan*, ICSID Case No. ARB/10/1, Award, 2 July 2013 (Rowley, Park, Sands), paras. 4.2.1 and 4.2.2 and *Garanti Koza LLP* v. *Turkmenistan*, ICSID Case No. ARB/11/2, Decision on the Objections to Jurisdiction for Lack of Consent, 3 July 2013 (Townsend, Lambrou, de Chazournes), paras. 65–6. See also *Sanum Investments Ltd.* v. *Laos*, PCA Case No. 2013-13, Award on Jurisdiction, 13 December 2013 (Sureda, Hanotiau, Stern), para. 179–85.

[153] M. Paparinskis, 'MFN Clauses and International Dispute Settlement: Moving Beyond *Maffezini* and *Plama*?' (2011) 26(2) *ICSID Review: Foreign Investment Law Journal* 14 at 37 and 49–50; see also Z. Douglas, 'The MFN Clause in Investment Arbitration: Treaty Interpretation Off the Rails' (2011) 2(1) *Journal of International Dispute Settlement* 97 at 105 and 107.

[154] Ibid., p. 51; see also C. Schreuer, 'Coherence and Consistency in International Investment Law' in R. Echandi and P. Sauvé (eds.), *Prospects in International Investment Law and Policy* (Cambridge: Cambridge University Press, 2013), pp. 391, 394. The tribunal in

This particular view of MFN clauses renders uncertain if umbrella clauses can or should be multilateralised via MFN clauses. This is because the character of enhanced protection conferred on contractual rights by umbrella clauses can be either procedural or substantive. According to the *SGS* v. *Philippines* approach where an umbrella clause guarantees the enforcement of contractual rights under the proper law of the contract by an investment treaty tribunal, but not a finding of State responsibility for a breach of contract, the form of protection conferred is procedural. According to the *Joy Mining* v. *Egypt* and *Noble Ventures* v. *Romania* approaches where an umbrella clause has a direct bearing on the engagement of State responsibility for interference with contractual rights, the form of protection envisaged is substantive. If the procedural-substantive distinction is introduced to MFN clauses and then transposed to umbrella clause claims, the protection conferred by an umbrella clause on contractual rights can be multilateralised only if one adopts the *Joy Mining* v. *Egypt* or *Nobel Ventures* v. *Romania* approaches to umbrella clause internationalisation. This is not necessarily desirable. Unless there is a more objective way of classifying State actions as sovereign or non-sovereign, the multilateralisation of the *Joy Mining* v. *Egypt* approach to umbrella clauses will only serve to multiply real or perceived inconsistencies in classification. The multilateralisation of the *Nobel Ventures* v. *Romania* approach which upholds absolute protection for contractual rights is arguably even less appealing. Umbrella clause internationalisation renders host States extremely vulnerable to sanction by international law for contractual breaches. The vast majority of States already rejected internationalisation in the 1970s because it encroached on their newly acquired economic autonomy. Internationalisation is unlikely to experience a renaissance today when States strive to preserve their regulatory autonomy while welcoming foreign investment and investors.[155]

Sanum v. Laos supplied a different rationale for rejecting the argument that MFN clauses can be invoked to import dispute settlement procedures from other investment treaties:

> [T]o read into that clause a dispute settlement provision to cover all protections under the Treaty when the Treaty itself provides for very limited access to international arbitration would result in a substantial rewrite of the Treaty and an extension of the States Parties' consent to arbitration beyond what may be assumed to have been their intention, given the limited reach of the Treaty protection and dispute settlement clauses,

Award on Jurisdiction, 13 December 2013, para. 358.

[155] Umbrella clauses will probably be excluded from the future treaty practice of the United States, see 2012 US Model Bilateral Investment Treaty which does not contain an umbrella

Moreover, excluding enhanced procedural protection for contractual rights from the ambit of an MFN clause is ironic when the rejection of umbrella clause internationalisation merits greater recognition and acceptance. The *SGS* v. *Philippines* approach clarifies that the submission of a contract claim to investment treaty arbitration does not oblige the tribunal to apply international law to vindicate contractual rights. It serves as a reminder that contractual breaches *per se* rarely violate international law. And most importantly, it reflects the correct understanding of the law of State responsibility on contractual breaches, which has enabled it to steer clear of the controversies surrounding the partial internationalisation (*Joy Mining* v. *Egypt*), or internationalisation (*Nobel Ventures* v. *Romania*), of investment contracts. Therefore, while the procedural-substantive distinction may curb claimants from treaty shopping for preferred dispute settlement procedures, it is not an illuminating distinction in the context of umbrella clause claims. It inadvertently encourages the spread of umbrella clause internationalisation, which promises absolute protection for contractual rights. For this reason, it is advisable to avoid the procedural–substantive distinction when contemplating the possibility of multilateralising the enhanced protection offered by umbrella clauses on contractual rights via MFN clauses.

5.5   Conclusion

While the presence of an umbrella clause in an investment treaty promises enhanced protection for investment contracts, the case for absolute protection via umbrella clause internationalisation remains controversial. In their eagerness to check the legislative power of States, the proponents of panoptic and umbrella clause internationalisation have not paused to consider if international law has ever recognised the absolute sanctity of contract. Nor do they appear to have considered if States intend to achieve the absolute sanctity of contract by concluding investment treaties containing umbrella clauses. Internationalisation faces a wall of resistance because it enlists international law for an objective that international law cannot and States may not fulfil. In the same way that international law does not recognise the absolute protection of aliens, nor the absolute protection of alien property, both branches having been adapted for contractual protection, it is short on support for a case on absolute contractual

---

clause: US Department of State, '2012 U.S. Model Bilateral Investment Treaty', online: www.state.gov/documents/organization/188371.pdf (accessed 31 December 2017).

protection. And while States are undoubtedly free to bind themselves to standards of investment protection that are more generous than those under general international law in their investment treaties,[156] the spectrum of views on *how* umbrella clauses enhance protection for investment contracts dilute the possibility that umbrella clauses necessarily facilitate the engaging of State responsibility for contractual breaches.

This chapter has shown, using *SGS v. Pakistan* as an illustration, that deducing the meaning of an umbrella clause through textual, contextual and circumstantial interpretation can, due to various and unseen motivations behind the conclusion of investment treaties, be a challenge. When even the negotiating States to an investment treaty are unsure of why an umbrella clause was included and what its drafters intended its effect to be, tribunals hearing contract-based umbrella clause claims are left to decide if umbrella clauses actually internationalise investment contracts. As the weight of arbitral *jurisprudence* leans away from full umbrella clause internationalisation, the tentative conclusion at this juncture is that umbrella clauses can enhance protection for investment contracts without requiring the assimilation of contractual obligations to treaty obligations.

Gravitation towards a uniform reading of umbrella clauses may come from the use of MFN clauses to secure and multilateralise-enhanced protection for contractual rights. If every investment treaty tribunal hearing a contract claim can only do so in conjunction with an umbrella clause claim, constant reflection on the different degrees of umbrella clause internationalisation over time may produce a preferred approach. In this regard, the *SGS v. Philippines* approach which enhances protection for investment contracts while firmly rejecting internationalisation is a strong contender. According to this approach, State responsibility is never engaged for a breach of contract *per se*. State responsibility will only be engaged when the State thwarts the enforcement of the investor's contractual rights by the investment treaty tribunal. A breach of the umbrella clause, and the engagement of State responsibility, will occur if, for instance, the State refuses to pay damages awarded by the tribunal to the investor for a breach of contract. Just like how only contractual breaches that fall short of the core standard of treatment, or that amount to an unlawful expropriation, trigger a finding of State responsibility, an internationalisation-free interpretation of umbrella clauses for contract-based claims heeds the accumulated and authoritative wisdom that contractual protection under international law is qualified, not absolute.

---

[156] R. R. Baxter, 'Treaties and Custom' (1970) 129 *Recueil des Cours* 25 at 96.

6

The Emerging International Law on Investment Contract Protection

6.1 Introduction

Investment contract protection through the application of the core standard of treatment, or the regime on expropriation, is markedly less controversial than protection through investment contract internationalisation. Although there are different approaches to the number and nature of components that define the minimum standard of treatment for investment contracts, and those that define the fair and equitable standard of treatment, the anchor MST components of non-arbitrariness and respect for due process are also the most widely accepted FET components.[1] Shared content attests to the existence of a core standard of treatment. Additionally, the conditions for an unlawful expropriation, namely, conduct *iure imperii* that substantially deprives a foreign investor of property or a protected investment, and that is uncompensated, or lacking in public purpose or due process, apply whether the investor seeks to engage State responsibility under general international law or under investment treaty law.[2] In contrast, internationalisation, which transforms contractual obligations into international obligations to secure absolute contractual protection, encounters fierce resistance whether the investor invokes general international law or an umbrella clause in an investment treaty.[3] Acceptance of the core standard of treatment and the rules on expropriation as markers of State responsibility for breaches of investment contracts, and antipathy towards internationalisation, characterise the emerging international law on investment contract protection.

The different receptions to different legal routes for the pursuit of investment contract protection is an important, yet unexplained, phenomenon. It raises the question of the respective roles that pre-existing general international law and investment treaty law play in the development of an

---

[1] See discussion at Chapter 3, Sections 3.2 and 3.3.
[2] See discussion at Chapter 4, Sections 4.2.1 and 4.4.
[3] See discussion at Chapter 5, Sections 5.2 and 5.3.

international law on investment contract protection.[4] The extent to which general international law informs the interpretation and content of treaty provisions and vice versa is a topic of recurring interest and relevance in the study and practice of international law.[5] It is especially pertinent

---

[4] The use of the term 'general international law' instead of 'customary international law' as a contrast to investment treaty law in this chapter is deliberate. General international law is the more encompassing category that, in addition to customary rules of international law, comprises treaty law. See Baxter, 'Treaties and Custom', p. 25 at 99–104; G. Tunkin, 'Is General International Law Customary Law Only?' (1993) 4 EJIL 534 at 541, as well as other sources of international law such as arbitral awards; see J. Crawford, 'Multilateral Rights and Obligations in International Law' (2006) 319 *Recueil des Cours* 325 at 392–7; also d'Aspremont, *Formalism and the Sources of International Law*, pp. 205–6. As the international law on contractual protection developed principally through arbitral awards before investment treaties entered the scene, see discussion at Chapters 2; 3, Section 3.2; 4, Section 4.2.1.2.2; and 5, Section 5.2, the pre-existing law is non-customary and, at first glance, non-specific to *investment contract* protection. Therefore, 'general international law' is an appropriate term because it conveys the presupposed generality of pre-existing law, while compelling an inquiry into the presupposed specificity of investment treaty law on *investment contract* protection. As Crawford pointed out in his Hague Academy lecture, pp. 396–7: 'The relations between different "sources" of law are not matters of hierarchy but of coverage. Where a particular issue is covered by more than one, the question is not which is the more cogent but which is the more specific – the more telling rather than the more compelling, one might say.'

[5] For studies, see Baxter, 'Treaties and Custom', pp. 36–98; G. Tunkin, 'International Law in the International System' (1975) 147 *Recueil des Cours* 1 at 132–41; W. M. Reisman, 'The Cult of Custom in the Late 20th Century' (1987) 17 *Canadian Western International Law Journal* 133 at 135; M. E. Villiger, *Customary International Law and Treaties: A Manual on the Theory and Practice of the Interrelation of Sources*, 2nd edn (The Hague: Kluwer Law International, 1997), pp. 149–224; A. D'Amato, 'Treaty-Based Rules of Custom' in A. D'Amato (ed.), *International Law Anthology* (Cincinnati, OH: Anderson Publishing, 1994), pp. 94–101; Y. Dinstein, 'The Interaction between Customary International Law and Treaties' (2007) 322 *Recueil des Cours* 243 at 383–96; H. Thirlway, *The Sources of International Law* (Oxford: Oxford University Press, 2014), pp. 71–2 and 129–41.

For practice, see *Case of the SS Wimbledon* (*United Kingdom* v. *Japan*) (17 August 1923) PCIJ, Series A, No. 1, paras. 30–48; *North Sea Continental Shelf Cases* (*Federal Republic of Germany* v. *Denmark; Federal Republic of Germany* v. *Netherlands*) (Judgment) [1969] ICJ Rep 3, pp. 38–41; *Case Concerning Military and Paramilitary Activities in and against Nicaragua* (*Nicaragua* v. *United States of America*) (Judgment) [1986] ICJ Rep 14, pp. 82–97; *Case Concerning Oil Platforms* (*Islamic Republic of Iran* v. *United States of America*) (Judgment) [2003] ICJ Rep 161, p. 182; *LG & E Energy Corp.* v. *Argentina*, ICSID Case No. ARB/02/1, Decision on Liability, 3 October 2006 (de Maekelt, Rezek, van den Berg), para. 245; *Enron Creditors Recovery Corp. and Anor* v. *Argentina*, ICSID Case No. ARB/01/3, Award, 22 May 2007 (Orrego Vicuña, van den Berg, Tschanz), para. 333; *Case Concerning Ahmadou Sadio Diallo* (*Republic of Guinea* v. *Democratic Republic of The Congo*) (Preliminary Objections) [2007] ICJ Rep 582, pp. 614–7; *CMS Gas Transmission Company* v. *The Argentine Republic*, ICSID Case No. ARB/01/8, Decision of the ad hoc Committee on the Application for Annulment of the Argentine Republic, 25 September 2007 (Guillaume, Elaraby, Crawford), para. 129; *Sempra Energy International* v. *Argentina Republic*, Decision on the Argentine Republic's Application for Annulment of

in the context of investment protection where the typical laconicism of investment treaty provisions invites recourse to general international law to supply the content of investment protection,[6] and the multiplication of identically or similarly worded investment treaty provisions potentially generates custom.[7] Within the narrower confines of investment contract protection, the prevalence of contract-based treaty claims offers ample opportunity to examine how general international law on contractual protection interacts with key investment treaty provisions on contractual protection. This interaction produced the divergent receptions to investment contract protection through claims for violation of the core standard of treatment and unlawful expropriation and through claims for internationalisation. It is therefore also indicative of how the emerging international law on investment contract protection is likely to develop.

This chapter argues that the general international law applicable to investment contract protection, namely the core standard of treatment derived from the MST of aliens and the law on expropriation of alien property, is a stabilising force in the emerging international law on investment contract protection. Subjecting investment contract protection to the FET

---

the Award, 29 June 2010 (Söderlund, Edward, Jacovides), para. 200; *Continental Casualty* v. *Argentina*, ICSID Case No. ARB/03/9, Award, 5 September 2008 (Sacerdoti, Veeder, Nader), paras. 167 (fn. 242) and 168; *El Paso Energy International Company* v. *Argentina*, ICSID Case No. ARB/03/15, Award, 31 October 2011 (Caflisch, Bernadini, Stern), para. 613.

[6] Douglas, *The International Law on Investment Claims*, p. 81; also O. Schachter, 'Private Foreign Investment and International Organization' (1959–60) 45 *Cornell Law Quarterly* 415 at 424; V. Pechota, 'The Limits of International Responsibility in the Protection of Foreign Investments' in M. Ragazzi (ed.), *International Responsibility Today: Essays in Honour of Oscar Schachter* (Leiden: Martinus Nijhoff, 2005), pp. 171, 175.

[7] McLachlan, 'Investment Treaties and General International Law', p. 361 at 392 and 400–1; more cautiously Crawford, *Brownlie's Principles of Public International Law*, p. 31; see also International Law Association Committee on Formation of Customary (General) International Law, 'Statement of Principles Applicable to the Formation of General Customary International Law', Final Report of the Committee (2000), which leaves the door open for the transformation of select investment treaty provisions into custom, p. 48:

> Some have argued that provisions of bilateral investment protection treaties (especially the arrangements about compensation or damages for expropriation) are declaratory of, or have come to constitute, customary law. But ... there seems to be no special reason to assume that this is the case, unless it can be shown that these provisions demonstrate a widespread acceptance of the rules set out in these treaties outside the treaty framework. In short, there is no presumption that a series of treaties gives rise to a new rule of customary law, though this does not preclude such a metamorphosis occurring in particular cases.

standard or the expropriation clause in investment treaties is uncontroversial because either treaty claim finds purchase in pre-existing general international law. Seeking investment contract protection through umbrella clause internationalisation is, in contrast, highly contested because pre-existing general international law does not recognise absolute contractual protection (Section 6.2). Aligning the content of investment treaty provisions with corresponding content in general international law is advisable, since significant deviations from pre-existing general international law that exponentially enhance contractual protection are susceptible to rejection or revision by States and therefore unlikely to leave a lasting imprint on legal development. Moreover, interpreting investment treaty protection for investment contracts with reference to the position under general international law is necessary by virtue of Article 31(3)(c) of the Vienna Convention on the Law of Treaties and desirable for attaining a measure of juridical stability (Section 6.3).[8] This chapter concludes with a few remarks on the growing implausibility of interpreting investment treaty protection for investment contracts in isolation from its broader normative legal environment, with contemporary wisdom contemplating the impact of internationally wrongful investor misconduct on findings of State responsibility (Section 6.4).

6.2 The Relationships between General International Law and Investment Treaty Law

Just as there are different ways for custom and treaty to co-exist,[9] there is probably more than one way for general international law to interact with investment treaty law. A decade ago, McLachlan argued that the

---

[8] Signed 23 May 1969, entered into force 27 January 1980, 1155 UNTS 331.
[9] Dinstein, 'The Interaction between Customary International Law and Treaties', pp. 383–96 identifies seven 'modes of coexistence of treaty and custom'. They are (i) complementarity; (ii) parallelism; (iii) renvoi; (iv) subordination; (v) extension of range; (vi) filling in loopholes and providing definitions; and (vii) overlap. Which 'mode of coexistence' best captures the interplay between a body of customary rules and the corresponding treaty or treaties, to the extent that such rules or treaties exist, depends on the explicitness of customary and treaty content and language. These 'modes of coexistence' may also be employed for non-customary rules of international law and treaty rules. For example, if existing rules of international law are more abundant and explicit in content than corresponding or comparable rules in applicable treaties, and if there is no treaty prohibition from recourse to external rules, then external rules are likely to overlap with treaty rules (mode (vii)) while simultaneously filling in the gaps for treaty rules (mode (vi)).

relationship between general international law and investment treaties is 'symbiotic':[10]

> The obligations owed by States as a matter of custom are not necessarily identical to the related obligation undertaken by treaty, but nor is the treaty to be regarded as inhabiting its own watertight compartment. Rather the content of the treaty obligation may be informed by general international law. In turn, the promulgation of the treaty obligation, and its application by arbitral tribunals, may inform the progressive development of general international law.

McLachlan identified FET clauses as the flag-bearers of the 'symbiotic' relationship, 'in view of the substantial body of evidence for the prior existence of a minimum standard if treatment as a matter of custom; the almost universal inclusion of the standard in modern times in very similar terms; and its inclusion in many model treaties published by states'.[11] While there is considerable support for observing that the content of FET is informed by the content of MST,[12] McLachlan's prediction, that the content of FET will in turn shape general international law, has been seriously undermined by three significant developments which took place in the decade since it was made. The first is the rise of frustrated investor expectations as a stand-alone ground for the violation of FET.[13] This led to disagreement among arbitral tribunals over the propriety of lowering the threshold for State conduct violating FET, which generated conflicting interpretations of FET.[14] The absence of broad consensus on the most up-to-date, comprehensive content of FET greatly diminishes the likelihood that general international law will be conditioned by arbitral *jurisprudence* on FET. The second is the increasing precision in treaty definitions of FET, when States choose to include FET clauses in newer investment treaties.[15] Greater precision spells greater variation in treaty language, which in turn demands treaty-specific interpretations of FET ill-suited for general applicability. The third is the growing reservations of States towards FET clauses, which further quells aspirations that the content of FET will infiltrate general

---

[10] McLachlan, 'Investment Treaties and General International Law', p. 364.

[11] McLachlan, 'Investment Treaties and General International Law', pp. 400–1.

[12] See discussion at Chapter 3, Sections 3.2 and 3.3.

[13] *Saluka Investments B. V. v. The Czech Republic*, UNCITRAL, Partial Award, 17 March 2006 (Watts, Fortier, Behrens), paras. 301–2.

[14] See discussion at Chapter 3, Section 3.3.1.

[15] See for instance Association of South East Asian Nations (ASEAN) Comprehensive Investment Agreement, signed 26 February 2009, entered into force 24 February 2012, Art. 11(2)(a); and EU-Canada Comprehensive Economic and Trade Agreement, signed 30 October 2016, provisionally entered into force 21 September 2017, Arts. 8.10(1), 8.10(2) and 8.10(3).

international law. India, for instance, included an FET clause in its 2003 Model Bilateral Investment Treaty,[16] but not in its 2016 Model Bilateral Investment Treaty.[17] The omission is significant as India has terminated all its existing bilateral investment treaties and plans to negotiate new treaties using its 2016 Model BIT as a template.[18] Other countries have already concluded investment protection agreements without FET clauses. One example is the investment chapter in the 2015 China-Australia Free Trade Agreement.[19] Whatever the relationship between general international law and investment treaties may be, time has shown that it is not 'symbiotic'.[20]

The margin of differentiation in the content of investment treaty law generated by arbitral awards, and the changing policies of States towards the content of investment treaties, turn investment treaty law into a moving target. The difficulty of pinning down a moving target to a fixed relationship status with general international law is compounded by the arguably mixed character of investment treaties. While some ubiquitous treaty provisions like expropriation clauses mirror the position on the taking of property under both domestic law and general international law, it is not self-evident whether equally ubiquitous archetypal FET clauses, or less ubiquitous umbrella clauses, are meant to be construed as reflections or rejections of pre-existing general international law on investment protection.[21] Despite uncertainty and inevitable disagreement over the content of certain laconic treaty provisions, Contracting States to investment treaties rarely offer clarifications aimed at streamlining legal

[16] ITALaw, 'Indian Model Text of Bilateral Investment Protection and Promotion Agreement (BIPA) (2003)' online: www.italaw.com/sites/default/files/archive/ita1026.pdf (accessed 31 December 2017), Art. 3(2).

[17] Investment Policy Hub, 'Model Text for the Indian Bilateral Investment Treaty (2016)', online: investmentpolicyhub.unctad.org/Download/TreatyFile/3560 (accessed 31 December 2017).

[18] Financial Times, 'India Overhauls Its Investment Treaty Regime (16 July 2016)', online: www.ft.com/content/53bd355c-8203-34af-9c27-7bf990a447dc (accessed 31 December 2017).

[19] Signed 17 June 2015, entered into force 20 December 2015.

[20] The potential for investment treaty provisions to coalesce into custom, once a topic of academic interest, has been rendered moot for the foreseeable future by political and other developments. Therefore, this chapter focuses on the import of general international law to investment treaty law, leaving the vice versa for another occasion.

[21] Investment treaties, by virtue of their arguably mixed character, limit the explanatory and predictive value of the Baxter paradox, which posits that the more States are parties to treaties which are not declaratory of general international law, the less likely those treaties generate custom, see Baxter, 'Treaties and Custom', pp. 75–91. The operation of the paradox requires treaties that are solely declaratory or constitutive of international law. As investment treaties may well be a bit of both, the Baxter paradox neither confirms nor denies their ability to generate custom.

content generated by future arbitral awards.[22] States wholly entrusted arbitral tribunals with the task of treaty interpretation, acquiescing in arbitral tribunals obtaining guidance from MST when defining FET, and experimenting with umbrella clauses as tools of internationalisation. The result is some investment treaty provisions retaining a connection with general international law, while others seem to break away by purporting to set a standard of protection over and above what is provided for under general international law.

Building on the analysis on the content of FET, expropriation and umbrella clause protection presented in the three preceding chapters, this section demonstrates two possible relationships between general international law and investment treaty law. The first is a relationship of stabilisation, so called because general international law supplies the anchor content of FET and expropriation, restraining without necessarily precluding the development of investment treaty law on contractual protection (6.2.1). The second is a relationship of separation, so called because qualified contractual protection under general international law does not inform absolute contractual protection through umbrella clause internationalisation, leaving investment treaty law free to develop unfettered by any pre-existing law (6.2.2).

6.2.1   A Relationship of Stabilisation: Core
Standard of Treatment and Expropriation

Stabilisation denotes the absence or minimisation of change between the content of investment contract protection under pre-existing general international law and under later-in-time investment treaty law. General international law completely stabilises investment treaty law if the content of the latter is wholly imitative of and therefore wholly identical to the content of the former. Alternatively, general international law has a fractional stabilising effect on investment treaty law if the content of the latter is partly derivative of the content of the former, and partly novel. In this alternative scenario, the extent to which general international law stabilises investment treaty law is a matter of degree. Stabilisation occurs when novel content is deemed an unwarranted departure from the level of

---

[22] The notable exceptions are the Interpretive Note of the NAFTA Free Trade Commission on Art. 1105 (NAFTA Law, 'Interpretive Note of the NAFTA Free Trade Commission on Article 1105'), and the Letter from the Swiss Secretariat for Economic Affairs to the ICSID Secretary-General, 'Umbrella Clauses in Bilateral Investment Agreements'.

contractual protection conferred under general international law, prompting attempts to reject novel content in favour of, or refashion novel content in accordance with, the pre-existing position. As novel content usually broadens the scope of State responsibility for breaches of investment contracts, stabilisation seeks to reduce that scope and limit host State exposure to claims for violations of international law.

As discussed in Chapters 3 and 4 respectively, FET shares common components with, but is not identical to denial of justice as MST on investment contract protection. Likewise, the conditions for an unlawful expropriation under investment treaty law are very similar but not identical to those under general international law. Therefore, the current relationship between general international law on the one hand, and FET and investment treaty-based expropriation on the other, is one of fractional stabilisation. FET stabilisation is observable from enduring resistance to the inclusion of frustrated investor expectations as a discrete component of FET, in addition to the anchor components of arbitrariness and disregard for due process drawn from MST (6.2.1.1). Investment treaty-based expropriation stabilisation is observable from attempts by arbitral tribunals to base the viability of an expropriation claim on the presence of property attributes in the allegedly expropriated object, even when the applicable treaty expressly caters for the expropriation of a list of qualifying investments, where property is only one entry on that list (6.2.1.2).

6.2.1.1   MST-Linked FET and Rationalising the Limited Appeal of Preserving Investor Expectations

Chapter 3 located support for the alignment of FET with MST in, amongst other circumstances, the mixed reception of arbitral tribunals to the investor expectations as a discrete component of FET,[23] and the decision of States to entirely exclude or shrink the scope of investor expectations from FET protection in newer investment treaties.[24] Continuing from where Chapter 3 left off, this section locates the limited appeal of construing the frustration of investor expectations, in and of itself, as a violation of FET, in general international law. While arbitral *jurisprudence* defining FET maintains the MST on investment contract protection, thereby establishing a core standard of treatment, it also supplements the anchor components of arbitrariness and disregard for due process. The violation

---

[23] See discussion at Chapter 3, Sections 3.3.1.1 and 3.3.1.2.
[24] See discussion at Chapter 3, Section 3.3.2.

of FET through host State conduct in bad faith,[25] that coerces, harasses or is otherwise abusive of the foreign investor,[26] and that frustrates investor expectations,[27] are creatures of arbitral *jurisprudence*. Yet, only frustrated investor expectations attracts opposition or qualification when characterised as an independent component of FET.[28]

Bad faith conduct by the host State was expressly listed by the Commission in the *Neer Claim*, a key arbitral award from which the core standard of treatment for contractual protection was derived, as a trigger for 'international delinquency'.[29] That said, State conduct falling short of bad faith is usually already capable of amounting to an 'international delinquency'. A common example is a State's failure to comply with its treaty obligations. So long as it can be established that the said obligation is binding on the State and has been breached by conduct attributable to the State under international law,[30] there is no need to show that the State acted in bad faith. Therefore, a finding of 'international delinquency' may, but rarely turns on bad faith. As bad faith represents a metaphorical ceiling for host State misconduct, it is unobjectionable to identify bad faith as a discrete component of FET. If the investor is able to amass evidence proving that the host State acted in bad faith, then its FET claim should succeed. Similarly, abusive treatment of an investor by a host State, especially actual or threatened physical violence,[31] or the employment of pressure tactics to completely inhibit the investor's freedom of choice,[32] are sanctionable under general international law. The perpetration of physical violence by a State against persons is a violation of international human rights law.[33] Duress, although more often invoked as a defence for the commission

---

[25] See discussion at Chapter 3, Section 3.3.1.2.
[26] See discussion at Chapter 3, Section 3.4.4.
[27] See discussion at Chapter 3, Section 3.3.1.1.
[28] See discussion at Chapter 3, Section 3.3.1.
[29] *Neer Claim* (*USA* v. *United Mexican States*) (1926) 4 RIAA 60, p. 61.
[30] ILC, 'Draft Articles on Responsibility of States for Internationally Wrongful Acts, with Commentaries', vol. II, Part Two, Art. 2: 'There is an internationally wrongful act of a State when conduct consisting of an action or omission: (a) is attributable to the State under international law; and (b) constitutes a breach of an international obligation of the State.'
[31] Vagts, 'Coercion and Foreign Investment Rearrangements', p. 17 at 30.
[32] *The Government of the State of Kuwait* v. *The American Independent Oil Company*, 21 ILM 976, Award, 24 March 1982 (Reuter, Sultan, Fitzmaurice (partially dissenting)), paras. 41 and 44.
[33] Every person's right to life, freedom from inhuman or degrading treatment or punishment, and freedom from arbitrary arrest, detention or exile, are enshrined in the 1948 Universal Declaration of Human Rights, signed 10 December 1948, Arts. 3, 5, 9 and 30.

of internationally wrongful acts,[34] can also constitute an internationally wrongful act when it involves the use of force.[35] Economic duress on the other hand, while not necessarily internationally wrongful, may justify the rescission of the act or transaction that duress was employed to bring about.[36] In the context of investment contract protection, duress by the host State contravenes the letter and the spirit of investment treaties to promote and protect foreign investment. An investor facing extreme economic duress imposed by a host State to agree to revised contractual terms, is not in an entirely dissimilar situation from an investor who is coerced into agreement by threats of harm to his well-being.

Unlike bad faith conduct or abusive conduct towards a foreigner, there is little to no trace of frustrated investor expectations being capable of triggering a host State's responsibility under general international law. The prospect of frustrated investor expectations amounting to a violation of international law was unknown before the appearance of FET claims. It was not identified as part of the general international law on the protection of aliens or alien property, as part of FET in archetypal FET clauses in older generation investment treaties, or in the earliest attempts to impart content and meaning to FET. As a discrete component of FET, the preservation of investor expectations is of recent vintage, originating in the arbitral award in *Saluka Investments B.V.* v. *The Czech Republic* in 2006.[37] The sudden elevation of investor expectations to prominence when defining FET enabled the engagement of State responsibility for an infinite variety of unmet expectations, including self-induced, and vastly lowered the threshold for

---

[34] See for instance Art. 31(1)(d) of the Rome Statute of the International Criminal Court, signed 17 July 1998, entered into force 1 July 2002, 2187 UNTS 90: 'In addition to other grounds for excluding criminal responsibility provided for in this Statute, a person shall not be criminally responsible if, at the time of that person's conduct:

The conduct which is alleged to constitute a crime within the jurisdiction of the Court has been caused by duress resulting from a threat of imminent death or of continuing or imminent serious bodily harm against that person or another person, and the person acts necessarily and reasonably to avoid this threat, provided that the person does not intend to cause a greater harm than the one sought to be avoided. Such a threat may either be:
(i) Made by other persons; or
(ii) Constituted by other circumstances beyond that person's control.'

[35] The procurement of consent to a treaty by threat or use of force is a form of duress that violates international law. VCLT Art. 52 provides: 'A treaty is void if its conclusion has been procured by the threat or use of force in violation of the principles of international law embodied in the Charter of the United Nations.'

[36] See for instance VCLT Art. 51 which provides: 'The expression of a State's consent to be bound by a treaty which has been procured by the coercion of its representative through acts or threats directed against him shall be without any legal effect.'

[37] UNCITRAL, Partial Award, 17 March 2006 (Watts, Fortier, Behrens), paras. 301–2.

internationally wrongful State conduct. The response to the heightened vulnerability of host States to FET violations, which other components like bad faith and abuse did not engender, was swift and sustained. Attempts to remove investor expectations from FET purview,[38] or to restrict protected investor expectations to those pertaining to specific undertakings given by the host State to the claimant investor,[39] or the transparency and stability of the legal framework of the host State governing the investment contract,[40] emerged in arbitral awards rendered in the wake of *Saluka Investments v. Czech Republic*. These attempts are repeated in more recent arbitral awards.[41] Developments in arbitral *jurisprudence* are reflected in newer generation investment treaties that populate the content of FET with customary international law which does protect investor expectations,[42] omit or explicitly reject investor expectations as a discrete component of FET,[43] or carefully qualify investor expectations entitled to FET protection.[44] Notably, newer generation investment treaties that define FET in granular detail with a list of components usually include, without qualification or annotation, bad faith or abusive treatment of the investor as discrete components of FET.[45] The concerted efforts of arbitral tribunals and States to expunge or contain investor expectations as a potential trigger for FET violations, while simultaneously embracing bad faith and abuse as discrete components of FET, indicate that the greater the deviation of a proposed component from the baseline protection offered to aliens under general international law, the more susceptible that component is to stabilisation through eradication or moderation.

---

[38] See for instance *MTD Equity Sdn. Bhd. and Anor* v. *Republic of Chile*, ICSID Case No. ARB/01/7, Decision on Annulment, 21 March 2007 (Guillaume, Crawford, Ordóñez Noriega), para. 67.

[39] See for instance *Deutsche Bank AG* v. *Democratic Socialist Republic of Sri Lanka*, ICSID Case No. ARB/09/02, Award, 31 October 2012 (Hanotiau, Williams, Khan (dissenting)), para. 420.

[40] See for instance *AES Summit Generation Limited and Anor.* v. *The Republic of Hungary*, ICSID Case No. ARB/07/22, Award, 23 September 2010 (von Wobeser, Stern, Rowley), para. 9.3.30.

[41] See for instance *Urbaser S.A. and Anor.* v. *The Argentine Republic*, ICSID Case No. ARB/07/26, Award, 8 December 2016 (Bucher, Martínez-Fraga, McLachlan), paras. 626–32.

[42] See for instance Agreement between Japan and the State of Israel for the Liberalization, Promotion and Protection of Investment, signed 1 February 2017, not yet in force, Art. 4.

[43] See for instance the Comprehensive Economic and Trade Agreement (CETA) (signed 30 October 2016, provisional entry into force 21 September 2017), Art. 8.10(3); the Comprehensive and Progressive Agreement for Trans-Pacific Partnership (TPP-11) (signed 23 January 2018, not yet in force), Art. 9.6(4); and the European Union-Singapore Investment Protection Agreement (pending signature and ratification, text as of April 2018), Art. 2.4(3) and accompanying fn 11.

[44] CETA Art. 8.10(2)(e); EU-Singapore IPA Art. 2.4(2)(d).

[45] CETA Art. 8.10(2)(e); EU-Singapore IPA Art. 9.4(2)(d).

6.2.1.2   Only Property-like Investments Can Be Expropriated

Chapter 4 pointed out that '[a]lthough the critical equation in a claim for the unlawful expropriation of contractual rights under general international law is between contract and property', the equation in a claim for the unlawful expropriation of contractual rights under investment treaty law is between contract and investment.[46] Investment treaties guard against the unlawful expropriation of protected investments, of which property is one of several stipulated categories of protected investments. On a plain reading of treaty terms, rights arising from an investment contract can form the object of an unlawful expropriation claim so long as they qualify as a species of protected investment, even if they are not akin to property.

Although most arbitral tribunals hearing contract-based unlawful expropriation claims brought under an investment treaty have adapted to the contract-as-investment equation, some tribunals have seen fit to return to the contract-as-property equation. The rationale for adopting the older equation must have been self-evident to the arbitral tribunal in *Ampal-American Israel Corp. and Ors* v. *Arab Republic of Egypt*, which did not explain its endorsement. Here, the claimants framed the uncompensated termination of a Gas Supply and Purchase Agreement by the Egyptian authorities as an unlawful expropriation under Article III(1) of the Treaty between the United States of America and the Arab Republic of Egypt Concerning the Reciprocal Encouragement and Protection of Investments.[47] Article III(1) of the US-Egypt investment treaty refers to the expropriation of protected 'investment', not property:[48]

> No *investment* or any part of an *investment* of a national or company of either Party shall be expropriated or nationalized by the other Party or by –
> a subdivision thereof – or subjected to any other measure, direct or indirect, if the effect of such other measure, or a series of such other measures, would be tantamount to expropriation or nationalization (all expropriations, all nationalizations and all such other measures hereinafter referred to as expropriation') – unless the expropriation
>
> (a) is done for a public purpose;
> (b) is accomplished under due process of law;
> (c) is not discriminatory;
> (d) is accompanied by prompt and adequate compensation, freely realizable; and
> (e) does not violate any specific contractual engagement ...

---

[46] See discussion at Chapter 4, Section 4.2, especially Section 4.2.2.
[47] Signed 11 March 1986, entered into force 27 June 1992
[48] (emphasis added).

Moreover, Article I(c) of the US-Egypt investment treaty defines a protected investment as:

> [E]very kind of asset owned or controlled and includes but is not limited to:
>   (i) tangible and intangible property, including rights, such as mortgages, liens and pledges;
>   ...
>   (vi) any right conferred by law or contract, but not limited rights to within the confines of law to search for or utilize natural resources, and rights to manufacture, use and sell products;
>   ...

Without explaining why Article I(c)(vi) did not suffice to establish that rights arising from a terminated contract were capable of being expropriated in accordance with Article III(1), the tribunal in *Ampal-American* v. *Egypt* asserted in its Decision on Jurisdiction that 'the key issue under the Treaty in respect of a claim for unlawful expropriation ... is whether there has been a loss of property right constituted by the contract'.[49] After analysing the merits of the unlawful expropriation claim, the tribunal concluded in its Decision on Liability and Heads of Loss that there was an unlawful expropriation of 'the Claimants' property interest in the GSPA'.[50] It is not apparent why the tribunal in *Ampal-American* v. *Egypt* saw the need to apply the contract-as-property equation when Articles I(c)(vi) and III(1) of the US-Egypt investment treaty unambiguously called for the application of the contract-as-investment equation. Furthermore, it is superfluous for Article I(c) to list 'tangible and intangible property' separately from 'any right conferred by law or contract', if contractual rights have to be assimilated to property in order to qualify as an object of expropriation.

The arbitral tribunal in *Accession Mezzanine Capital and Ors* v. *Hungary* also replaced the contract-as-investment equation with the contract-as-property equation. But unlike the tribunal in *Ampal-American* v. *Egypt*, this tribunal proffered an explanation for doing so:[51]

> Pure contractual rights cannot be expropriated or taken because they are incapable of being alienated to a third party. For that reason they cannot be equated with property rights. Contracts can, however, be the source of

---

[49] *Ampal-American Israel Corp. and Ors* v. *Arab Republic of Egypt*, ICSID Case No. ARB/12/11, Decision on Jurisdiction, 1 February 2016 (Fortier, McLachlan, Orrego Vicuña), para. 255.

[50] *Ampal-American Israel Corp. and Ors* v. *Arab Republic of Egypt*, ICSID Case No. ARB/12/11, Decision on Liability and Heads of Loss, 21 February 2017 (Fortier, McLachlan, Orrego Vicuña), para. 347, also 337.

[51] *Accession Mezzanine Capital and Ors* v. *Hungary*, ICSID Case No. ARB/12/3, Award, 17 April 2015 (Rovine, Lalonde, Douglas), paras. 154 and 157.

intangible property such as debts and other choses-in-action. There is no doubt that debts and other choses-in-action are capable of being expropriated. But the object of the expropriation in such a case is the debt or chose-in-action and not the contract itself ... The distinction between a contract as a source of bilateral personal obligations and the contract as a source of property rights is critical because international law distinguishes between a state's mere non-performance of its contractual obligations to a foreign party, which cannot constitute an expropriation, and a state's taking of intangible property, which can.

Although arguably more illuminating than the *Ampal-American v. Egypt* awards which merely record the asserted propriety of adopting the contract-as-property equation, the explanation in the *Accession Mezzanine Capital* v. *Hungary* award is unsatisfying. It does not complement the definition of a protected investment in the applicable Agreement between the Government of the United Kingdom of Great Britain and Northern Ireland and the Government of the Hungarian People's Republic for the Promotion and Reciprocal Protection of Investments. According to Article 1(a):[52]

> [T]he term 'investment' means every kind of asset connected with economic activities which has been acquired since 31 December 1972 and in particular, though not exclusively, includes:
>
> (i) movable and immovable property and any other property rights such as mortgages, liens or pledges;
>
> ...
>
> (iii) claims to money and other assets or to any performance under contract having a financial value;
>
> ...
>
> (v) business concessions conferred by law or under contract, including concessions to search for, cultivate, extract or exploit natural resources[.]

The claimants in *Accession Mezzanine Capital* v. *Hungary* argued that the non-renewal of two expiring broadcasting licenses amounted to an unlawful expropriation of a protected investment under the UK-Hungary investment treaty.[53] The issue before the tribunal in relation to this

---

[52] Signed 9 March 1987, entered into force 28 August 1987 ('UK-Hungary investment treaty').
[53] UK-Hungary investment treaty, Art. 6(1) provides in relevant part:

> Neither Contracting Party shall nationalise, expropriate or subject to measures having effect equivalent to nationalisation or expropriation (hereinafter referred to as 'expropriation') the investments of investors of the other Contracting Party in its territory unless the following conditions are complied with: (a) the expropriation is for a public purpose related to the internal needs of that Party and is subject to due process of law; (b) the expropriation is non-discriminatory; and

contract-based unlawful expropriation claim was whether Hungarian law recognised an existing right of the license-holders to have their licenses renewed. The tribunal found that the claimants had no such rights under Hungarian law, but even if they did, 'the claim for expropriation would only have been cognisable in respect of rights that had the characteristics of property rights under Hungarian law'.[54] As the claimants based part of their case for renewal on the terms of the broadcasting licenses, the investment they sought to protect was arguably a claim 'to any performance under contract having a financial value' (Article 1(a)(iii)), or 'business concessions' in the form of potential broadcasting licences to exploit radio frequencies 'conferred by law' (Article 1(a)(v)). On the facts, the claimants were unable to show that they possessed a contractual right to renewal, or a right to renewal conferred by law.[55] The inability to satisfy either Article 1(a)(iii) or Article 1(a)(v) meant that the claimants were not in possession of a protected investment and justifies the tribunal's lack of jurisdiction over the dispute. Given the specific ability of Articles 1(a)(iii) and 1(a)(v) to weed out illusory contract-based unlawful expropriation claims, it is unclear why the arbitral tribunal in *Accession Mezzanine Capital* v. *Hungary*, by introducing the contract-as-property equation, insisted on viewing the claim through the optic of Article 1(a)(i). If all contractual rights for which protection under the UK-Hungary investment treaty is invoked must be tested for proprietary features, there will be no need for Articles 1(a)(iii) and 1(a)(v).

As investment treaty definitions of protected investments invariably encompass more than property, expanding the range of objects of expropriation, host States are potentially more vulnerable to unlawful expropriation claims brought under investment treaty law than under general international law. Concerns that host State responsibility may be too casually engaged for unlawful expropriation under investment treaties for contractual breaches, may have prompted certain arbitral tribunals to impose the requirement that contracts must resemble property before they can be expropriated.[56] At present, general international law on expropriation and

---

(c) the expropriation is followed by the payment of prompt, adequate and effective compensation.

[54] *Accession Mezzanine* v. *Hungry* Award, para. 158.

[55] Ibid., paras. 77–145.

[56] These concerns may have prompted a number of States to expressly limit expropriation claims to protected investments bearing proprietary features in newer treaties, see the ASEAN Comprehensive Investment Agreement (signed 26 February 2009, entered into

investment treaty law on expropriation differ on the character of an object of expropriation. Under general international law, an object of expropriation must be property or akin to property; under investment treaties, an object of expropriation can be any protected investment as defined by the applicable treaty. General international law fractionally stabilises investment treaty law on expropriation to the extent that guidance on the existence of an expropriation and the satisfaction of conditions for unlawfulness, but not on the character of an object of expropriation, continue to be sought by arbitral tribunals interpreting investment treaties from arbitral awards and other international decisions applying general international law. General international law fully stabilises investment treaty law on expropriation if all their conditions for an unlawful expropriation, including the condition for a property-like object of expropriation, are identical. Those in favour of suppressing any deviation in investment treaty law from the general international law on the protection of alien property, despite express treaty language to the contrary, are essentially rewriting the treaty that they have been tasked to interpret. The defensibility of stabilisation through deliberate disregard of express treaty language is doubtful. Unlike the possibility of variable content for open-textured provisions like FET, there is less interpretive leeway to disagree on whether Contracting States meant to limit expropriation claims to property-like investments. When the expropriation clause in an investment treaty is read in conjunction with the definitional clause, the two clearly anticipate the expropriation of both property-like and non-property-like investments.

6.2.2   A Relationship of Separation: Internationalisation

Separation denotes the absence of connection between qualified investment contract protection under pre-existing general international law and full umbrella clause internationalisation under later-in-time investment treaty law. Although the internationalisation of investment contracts was attempted well before umbrella clauses came to be regarded as tools of internationalisation,[57] those earlier attempts at making all

---

force 24 February 2012), Annex 2(1); CETA Annex 8-A(1)(b); TPP-11 Annex 9-B(1); and EU-Singapore IPA Annex 1(1).

[57] The idea of internationalisation likely surfaced in the 1930 arbitral award in *Lena Goldfields v. USSR*, The Times, 3 September 1930. It gained more defined contours in the 1950s to the 1970s in the innovative proposal to prevent Iran from interfering with the concessionary rights of the Anglo-Iranian Oil Company, as well as in a string of arbitral awards

contractual rights inviolable attracted too much scepticism and opposition over the years to merit recognition as part of general international law.[58] Full umbrella clause internationalisation therefore stood and fell on the interpretation of the applicable umbrella clause, with negligible guidance from general international law.

Given the varying interpretations ascribed by arbitral tribunals to identically or similarly worded umbrella clauses outlined in Chapter 5,[59] the more popular of which reject full umbrella clause internationalisation, instances of full umbrella clause internationalisation are infrequent and isolated. The difficulty of claiming textual support for full umbrella clause internationalisation is illustrated by the contrast between what an arbitral tribunal infers for contractual protection when interpreting an archetypal umbrella clause and what a State intends for contractual protection when concluding an investment containing such a clause. In *Noble Ventures v. Romania*, the arbitral tribunal has to interpret Article II(2)(c) of the treaty between the government of the United States of America and the government of Romania Concerning the Reciprocal Encouragement and Protection of Investment:[60]

> Each Party shall observe any obligation it may have entered into with regard to investments.

---

on terminated oil concessions in the Middle East. The proposal called for the inclusion of a non-interference clause in the concession, and its incorporation by reference into a treaty concluded between Iran and the United Kingdom, thereby elevating every breach of contract into a breach of treaty, see Lauterpacht, 'Anglo-Iranian Oil Company Ltd Persian Settlement', p. 4, quoted in Sinclair, 'The Origins of the Umbrella Clause in the International Law of Investment Protection', p. 411 at 415, also 414–7. The arbitral awards on internationalisation, in chronological order, are *Petroleum Development Limited v. The Sheikh of Abu Dhabi*, 18 ILR 144, Award, September 1951 (Asquith); *Ruler of Qatar v. International Marine Oil Co.*, 20 ILR 534, Award, June 1953 (Bucknill); *Saudi Arabia v. Arabian American Oil Co. (Aramco)*, 27 ILR 117, Award, 23 August 1958 (Sauser-Hall, Badawi/Hassan, Habachi (dissenting)); *Sapphire International Petroleum Ltd v. National Iranian Oil Company*, 35 ILR 136, Award, 15 March 1963 (Cavin); and possibly the most commented and controversial of them all, *Texaco Overseas Petroleum Company/California Asiatic Oil Company v. The Government of the Libyan Arab Republic*, 53 ILR 389, Award on the Merits, 19 January 1977 (Dupuy). The first known attempt at invoking an umbrella clause in an investment treaty to internationalise a contract was made in 2002–3, more than 70 years after *Lena Goldfields v. USSR*, see *SGS Société Générale de Surveillance S.A. v. Islamic Republic of Pakistan*, ICSID Case No. ARB/01/13, Decision of the Tribunal on Objections to Jurisdiction, 6 August 2003 (Feliciano, Faurès, Thomas).

58 See discussion at Chapter 5, Section 5.2.
59 See discussion at Chapter 5, Section 5.3.
60 Signed 28 May 1992, entered into force 15 January 1994.

Article II(2)(c) of the US-Romania investment treaty is nearly identical to the tabled 'respect clause' in the abandoned Multilateral Agreement on Investment:[61]

> Each Contracting Party shall observe any obligation it has entered into with regard to a specific investment of an investor of another Contracting Party.

Official commentary on the forerunners of the MAI 'respect clause', namely Article II of the 1959 Abs-Shawcross Draft Convention on Investments Abroad, and Article 2 of the 1967 OECD Draft Convention on the Protection of Private Foreign Investment, endorses absolute contractual protection through internationalisation.[62] The arbitral tribunal in *Noble Ventures* v. *Romania* inferred from the wording of Article II(2)(c) that the Contracting States to the US-Romania investment treaty were in favour of absolute contractual protection:[63]

> [T]wo States may include in a bilateral investment treaty a provision to the effect that, in the interest of achieving the objects and goals of the treaty, the host State may incur international responsibility by reason of a breach of its contractual obligations towards the private investor of the other Party, the breach of contract being thus 'internationalized', i.e. assimilated to a breach of the treaty. In such a case, an international tribunal will be bound to seek to give useful effect to the provision that the parties have adopted.
>
> ...
>
> In the present case, the formulation adopted at Art. II(2)(c) ... clearly falls into the category of the most general and direct formulations tending to an assimilation of contractual obligations to treaty ones; not only does it use the term 'shall observe' but it refers in the most general terms to 'any' obligations that either Party may have entered into 'with regard to investments'.

Neither the views of the United States, nor the respondent State Romania were sought to verify if Article II(2)(c) stood for full umbrella clause internationalisation. That said, neither the United States nor Romania has challenged the *Noble Ventures* v. *Romania* tribunal's interpretation of Article II(2)(c). Yet, a rare example of one State's articulated understanding of the MAI 'respect clause' suggests that the wording of an umbrella clause is

---

[61] OECD, 'The Multilateral Agreement on Investment Draft Consolidated Text, 22 April 1998, DAFFE/MAI(98)7/REV1', p. 116.

[62] Abs and Shawcross, 'The Proposed Convention to Protect Private Foreign Investment', p. 115 at 119–20; signed 12 October 1967, not yet in force, C(67)102, p. 14; see also Seidl-Hohenveldern, 'The Abs-Shawcross Draft Convention to Protect Private Foreign Investment', p. 100 at 104.

[63] *Noble Ventures, Inc.* v. *Romania*, ICSID Case No. ARB/01/11, Award, 12 October 2005 (Böckstiegel, Lever, Dupuy), pp. 51 and 53.

not necessarily indicative of the intent of Contracting States to fully, partially, or not internationalise investment contracts. In explaining how the
umbrella clause in Agreement between the Swiss Confederation and the
Islamic Republic of Pakistan on the Promotion and Reciprocal Protection
of Investments protects investment contracts,[64] Switzerland declared that
umbrella clauses, as well as the MAI 'respect clause', do not transform all
contractual obligations into international obligations:[65]

> [Umbrella clauses] are intended to cover commitments that a host State has
> entered into with regard to specific investments of an investor, or invest-
> ments of a specific investor, which played a significant role in the inves-
> tor's decision to invest or to substantially change an existing investment i.e.
> commitments which were of such a nature that the investor could reply on
> them ... This interpretation ... agrees with the meaning of a corresponding
> provision given by the negotiating parties of the Multilateral Agreement
> on Investment (MAI) in the framework of the OECD which Switzerland
> actively supported. In the light of the importance of establishing the inten-
> tion of the Contracting Parties that concluded the BIT at issue it should be
> noted that negotiations for the MAI took place in the same time period as
> those between Switzerland and Pakistan.

Absent anchor content in general international law, what umbrella
clauses mean for investment contract protection lies in the eyes of the
beholder. Full umbrella clause internationalisation seems a precarious
proposition because neither treaty text, nor the authors of treaty text, nor
the arbitral tribunals interpreting treaty text, lend it firm support. A relationship of separation between general international law and full umbrella
clause internationalisation leaves the latter to its very few devices for sur-
vival. Further marginalisation of full umbrella clause internationalisation is underway with States omitting umbrella clauses from,[66] or ruling
out umbrella clause internationalisation in recent investment treaties.
Finally and perhaps most importantly, if the Swiss view that umbrella
clauses protect only specific contractual undertakings given by the host
State is representative, breached undertakings can be construed as frustrated legitimate expectations that violate FET, or as an unlawful expropriation under investment treaty law. Umbrella clauses, whose content is

---

[64] Signed 11 July 1995, entered into force 6 May 1996. Article 11 provides: 'Either Party shall
constantly guarantee the observance of the commitments it has entered into with respect to
the investments of the investors of the other Contracting Party.'
[65] Letter from the Swiss Secretariat for Economic Affairs to the ICSID Secretary-General,
'Umbrella Clauses in Bilateral Investment Agreements', at E2.
[66] UNCTAD, 'World Investment Report 2015', p. 112–13; 'World Investment Report 2016',
pp. 111–13; and 'World Investment Report 2017', pp. 120–1.

ambiguous, and which serve no distinct contractual protection function from FET or expropriation clauses, seem destined for demise as tools of internationalisation.

6.3   The Case for Integrationist Investment Treaty Interpretation

Whether the relationship between general international law and investment treaty law is one of stabilisation or separation, arbitral *jurisprudence* strongly suggests that the content on contractual protection under the former is a point of reference for content creation on contractual protection under the latter. Observable recourse to general international law to moderate, staunch or reverse developments in investment treaty law that greatly enhance host State vulnerability to international law sanction for contractual breaches has become a key feature of the emerging international law on investment contract protection. Critics of this feature may contend that recourse to pre-existing general international law in investment treaty interpretation is justified only when the treaty contains an explicit directive to this effect and not as a general rule of interpretation.[67] This section argues that habitual recourse to general international law to supply or supplement the content of investment treaty law is defensible on both legal and policy grounds. Integrationist investment treaty interpretation is supported by Article 31(3)(c) of the VCLT (6.3.1). It also reinforces the foundational content of investment contract protection, offering some certainty at a time when States are either reconsidering the merits of concluding investment treaties, or experimenting with different modes and substantive details of investment protection when concluding investment treaties (6.3.2).

6.3.1   *The Relevance of VCLT Article 31(3)(c)*

The VCLT codifies the international law on treaties. Article 31, which sets out a three-pronged general rule of interpretation applicable to investment

---

[67] Support for interpreting investment treaties in isolation from general international law can be found in *Metalclad Corp. v. The United Mexican States*, ICSID Case No. ARB(AF)/97/1, Award, 30 August 2000 (Lauterpacht, Civiletti, Siqueiros), paras. 74–6 and 102–3; and in *Eureko B.V. v. Republic of Poland*, Partial Award (ad hoc), 19 August 2005 (Fortier, Schwebel, Rajski (dissenting)), paras. 231, 234–5, 238, 241 and 244–60. Notably, neither arbitral tribunal referred to VCLT Art. 31(3)(c). The arbitral tribunal in *Metalclad Corp. v. Mexico* did not refer to the VCLT at all. For an illuminating discussion on how arbitral tribunals either overlook or misapply VCLT Art. 31, see H. Y. Trinh, *The Interpretation of Investment Treaties* (The Hague: Brill, 2014), pp. 32–64.

treaties, is one of the most well-known and most commonly invoked VCLT provision by arbitral tribunals. In addition to the text and context of the treaty as elaborated in Articles 31(1) and 31(2), interpreters are obliged under Article 31(3) to consider what I call 'circumstantial indicia' of treaty content.[68] And according to Article 31(3)(c):

> There shall be taken into account, together with the context:
>
> ...
>
>   (c) any relevant rules of international law applicable in the relations between the parties.

Circumstantial indicia may not always be present to assist in treaty interpretation, but if they are, Article 31(3) is the 'gateway' for their incorporation.[69] When determining the content of investment treaty law on investment contract protection, pre-existing content of general international law must be taken into account if it is (1) 'relevant' and (2) 'applicable in the relations between the parties'. The second condition is easily met when the relevant rules are part of general international law, since general international law is applicable in the relations between all States. It will however serve as a filter when the external rule is found in a treaty to which only one or none of the Contracting States are party and which has not yet commanded acceptance by or compliance from non-parties.[70]

The key condition for interpreting investment treaty law in light of general international law, therefore, is relevancy. The existence of general international law on investment contract protection, in the form of a core standard of treatment and a regime on expropriation as evidenced in Chapters 3 and 4 respectively, creates the 'international normative environment' from which laconic investment treaty provisions invoked in the name of investment contract protection can draw meaning.[71] There is a continuum of investment contract protection, as opposed to the appearance of investment treaty law to fill the void in general international law. Disregarding general international law on the basis that Contracting States have not expressly authorised arbitral tribunals to take general international law into account when interpreting investment treaty provisions, also disregards the third prong of the canonical rule of treaty interpretation. VCLT Article 31(3)(c) saves Contracting States from repetition.

---

[68] Ho, 'Circumstantial Indicia in Treaty Interpretation' (2018) 33(1) *ICSID Review - Foreign Investment Law Journal* 67.

[69] Ibid., p. 72.

[70] Ibid., pp. 72–3.

[71] J.-M. Sorel, 'Article 31' in O. Corten and P. Klein (eds.), *The Vienna Convention on the Law of Treaties: A Commentary* (Oxford: Oxford University Press, 2011), vol. I, pp. 804, 828–9.

By supplying markers of State responsibility for contractual breaches, the general international law on investment contract protection is relevant to investment treaty law on investment contract protection. Therefore, it must be taken into account when interpreting how investment treaties protect investment contracts.

6.3.2   The Desirability of Certainty amid Change

Investment treaties were never all about investment protection. They are also symbols of the Contracting States' prevailing foreign policy, which can change over time. The archetypal laconic investment treaties of the 1990s, often drafted with little or no negotiation, were official symbols of economic and political friendship for many States. Concluding an investment treaty seemed to matter more than the content of investment protection. Pakistan for instance, promptly forgot about (as well as misplaced) the investment treaty it signed with Switzerland in 1995 and was only reminded of the treaty's existence after it was hit by a contract-based treaty claim brought by a Swiss investor in 2001.[72] Thereafter, the perception that archetypal laconic investment treaties were enabling arbitral tribunals to curtail the sovereign right to regulate for the benefit of foreign investors motivated States like South Africa, India, Indonesia and Ecuador to terminate all their investment treaties. These States turned to existing domestic legislation to protect foreign investment[73] or proposed different rules on investment protection for inclusion in future investment treaties.[74] Treaty termination sends a powerful political message on a terminating State's desire and determination either to reject investment treaty law for investment protection or to change that law. States that remain committed to investment protection through investment treaties are nonetheless wary of laconic treaty provisions and the considerable interpretive license they confer on arbitral tribunals, which may operate to routinely favour foreign investors. They address the concern of investment over-protection in newer investment treaties with detailed and heavily qualified substantive protection provisions[75] and occasionally the replacement of ad hoc

---

[72] Poulsen and Aisbett, 'When the Claim Hits', p. 273 at 280.
[73] This is South Africa's approach; see Financial Times, 'South Africa: BITs in Pieces (19 October 2012)', online: www.ft.com/content/b0eec497-5123-3939-92f7-a5fbcb73dd33 (accessed 31 December 2017).
[74] This is India's approach; see 'India Overhauls Its Investment Treaty Regime'.
[75] See for instance EU-Singapore IPA, Arts. 9.3, 9.4, 9.6.

arbitration as the designated mode of dispute resolution with a standing investment court or appellate tribunal.[76]

Despite the slew of changes targeting the deficiencies in the investment treaty regime, investment treaty law and investment dispute settlement remain highly politicised and polarising. One of President Donald J. Trump's loudest campaign promises, which he carried out shortly upon assuming office in 2016, was to withdraw the United States from the Trans-Pacific Partnership (TPP). Absent US participation, the fate of the TPP, and its investment chapter containing all the painstakingly negotiated safeguards against investment over-protection, hangs in the balance.[77] President Trump's cryptic assertion that multilateral free trade deals stand in the way of 'making America great again',[78] has also led to the renegotiation of NAFTA, which was concluded between the United States, Canada and Mexico in 1992.[79] Elsewhere, brewing hostility towards investment treaties and investment dispute settlement, often depicted in the media as giving profit-oriented private investors and arbitrators an unfair advantage over States acting in the public interest,[80] underscore ongoing multilateral efforts to debate and discuss how the investment treaty regime can be improved.[81] In a similar vein to how treaty conclusion in the past seemed to matter more than treaty content, taking action against investment treaties in the present appears to matter more than treaty content. Once political tools, investment treaties have become political targets. Their content, and even long-term existence, is likely to fluctuate in response to the winds of political change. As Jenks remarked, the content

---

[76] See for instance CETA, Arts. 8.27, 8.28, 8.29.

[77] The eleven remaining TPP signatories have agreed to conclude the Comprehensive Agreement for Trans-Pacific Partnership (CPTPP). This development is current as of 31 January 2018.

[78] Financial Times, 'US Trade Problems Begin at Home Not Abroad (20 November 2017)', online: www.ft.com/content/14b4ef1e-cbab-11e7-ab18-7a9fb7d6163e (accessed 31 December 2017).

[79] Signed 17 December 1992, entered into force 1 January 1994, (1993) 32 ILM 289 ('NAFTA').

[80] The New York Times, 'NAFTA's Powerful Little Secret; Obscure Tribunals Settle Disputes, but Go too Far, Critics Say (11 March 2001)', online: www.nytimes.com/2001/03/11/business/nafta-s-powerful-little-secret-obscure-tribunals-settle-disputes-but-go-too-far.html (accessed 31 December 2017); ABC, 'ISDS: The Devil in the Trade Deal (26 July 2015)', online: www.abc.net.au/radionational/programs/backgroundbriefing/isds-the-devil-in-the-trade-deal/6634538 (accessed 31 December 2017).

[81] UNCTAD, 'Improving Investment Dispute Settlement: UNCTAD Policy Tools (IIA Issues Note – International Investment Agreements, November 2017)', online: investmentpolicyhub.unctad.org/Upload/Documents/IMPROVING%20INVESTMENT%20DISPUTE%20SETTLEMENT-%20UNCTAD%20POLICY%20TOOLS.pdf (accessed 31 December 2017), pp. 2–3 and 12–14.

of a rapidly constructed body of international law on a matter 'previously regarded as within the exclusive jurisdiction of each State' is always subject to change.[82] Investment treaty law, which was constructed in less than three decades, is a law where:[83]

> Virtually all of the progress made remains highly precarious, liable to be destroyed by unilateral action contemptuous of wider interests which these developments in the law have attempted to express.

Investment contract protection under international law is derivative of the international minimum standard for alien protection and the international regime for alien property protection. It predates investment treaties and therefore its content and existence is not wholly dependent on the content and existence of investment treaties. Investment treaties may embellish on the foundational content of investment contract protection under general international law, but investment treaty law cannot supplant that foundational content. Interpreting investment treaty provisions in light of general international law weathers upheavals in treaty practice. It ensures a degree of predictability in the emerging international law on contractual protection, without compromising the duty of treaty interpreters to give effect to text that is specific to a given provision. Moreover, with integrationist investment treaty interpretation, investment contract protection will not be thrown into flux even if a world without investment treaties comes to pass. Integrationist investment treaty interpretation cultivates familiarity with general international law. In the absence of textual guidance from investment treaties, those tasked with the adjudication of international claims seeking the engagement of State responsibility for breaches of investment contracts can readily apply general international law. Given the uncertain future of investment treaties, general international law not only supplies the foundational, but also the fall-back content for the emerging international law on investment contract protection. The fall-back function of general international law is recognised in VCLT Article 43:

> The invalidity, termination or denunciation of a treaty, the withdrawal of a party from it, or the suspension of its operation, as a result of the application of the present Convention or of the provisions of the treaty, shall not in any way impair the duty of any State to fulfil any obligation embodied in the treaty to which it would be subject under international law independently of the treaty.

---

[82] W. Jenks, 'Economic and Social Change and the Law of Nations' (1973) 138 *Recueil des Cours* 455 at 490 and 501.

[83] Ibid., p. 501.

6.4   The Retreat of Isolationist Investment Treaty Interpretation

In addition to the justifiable interpretation of investment treaty law on investment contract protection in light of general international law on investment contract protection, States' investment treaty obligations can no longer be viewed in isolation from the broader suite of rules applicable to State and non-State actors involved in transnational investment. Recent contract-based investment treaty arbitrations indicate that host States are more prepared to draw the arbitral tribunal's attention to severe investor misconduct, often implicating human rights violations or environmental damage.[84] This is done with the objective of showing that an investor with 'unclean hands' is ineligible for treaty protection,[85] or that host State responsibility should be precluded, reduced or off-set for non-compliance with investment treaty obligations triggered by the investor's wrong-doing.[86] As investor wrongdoing is not addressed in investment treaties

---

[84] Cf. *Methanex Corp.* v. *USA*, NAFTA-UNCITRAL, Final Award of the Tribunal on Jurisdiction and Merits, 3 August 2005 (Veeder, Rowley, Reisman). The dispute arose from a ban imposed by the State of California on a gasoline additive known as methy tertiary-butyl ether (MTBE). MTBE is a non-biodegradable toxic chemical that is a potential human carcinogen. It is also highly soluble in water, causing substantial groundwater contamination once it is released into the environment. As the majority of Californian residents obtain their drinking water supplies from groundwater, the State of California decided to ban MTBE on the basis that it poses significant risk to the environment and human health. Methanex is a Canadian company that produces and sells methanol, a component chemical in MTBE. It also markets methanol in the United States through two local subsidiaries. Methanex brought a claim against the United States under Chapter 11 of NAFTA, alleging that the ban violated several treaty obligations owed to Methanex's investment in the US gasoline industry and seeking USD 970 million in damages (Final Award, Part II, paras. 26–8). The tribunal agreed with the United States that the MTEB ban did not relate to methanol-producing investors like Methanex, and as a result, it had no jurisdiction over Methanex's claim. Although the tribunal awarded legal costs against Methanex, no aspersions were cast on Methanex for bringing a Chapter 11 claim against the United States. The award conveyed the perception that investment treaties are solely concerned with the legality of State conduct under international law. Claims invoking investment treaty protection challenge that legality, while the task of tribunals specially constituted to hear these claims is to pronounce on that legality. Whether the corporate investor bringing the claim has violated international law is not in issue and need not be decided.

[85] *Copper Mesa Mining Corp.* v. *The Republic of Ecuador*, UNCITRAL-PCA Case No. 2012-2, Award (redacted), 15 March 2016 (Veeder, Cremades, Simma), paras. 5.39–5.4. According to the 'clean hands' principle, a claimant seeking relief from an international tribunal for a respondent's wrongful conduct may lack standing to bring its claim if the conduct complained of was undertaken in response to the claimant's own illegality, G. Fitzmaurice, 'The General Principles of International Law Considered from the Standpoint of the Rule of Law' (1957) 92 *Recueil des Cours* 1 at 199.

[86] *Perenco Ecuador Ltd.* v. *The Republic of Ecuador and Empresa Estatal Petróleos del Ecuador (Petroecuador)*, ICSID Case No. ARB/08/6, Interim Decision on the Environmental Counterclaim, 11 August 2015 (Tomka, Kaplan, Thomas), paras. 34–5.

which establish only Contracting State obligations, arbitral tribunals are obliged to look beyond investment treaty law to determine if and how investor wrongdoing impinges upon a finding of State responsibility for breaches of investment contracts. The impossibility of asking host States that have concluded investment treaties to undertake investment contract protection at all costs, corresponding retreat of isolationist investment treaty interpretation, and the complex issues of international responsibility raised, are captured in *Copper Mesa Mining* v. *Ecuador*.[87]

The story begins with Ecuador awarding three copper mining concessions for the cantons of Junín, Chaucha and Telimbela. Canadian mining firm Copper Mesa Mining Corporation (previously Ascendent Copper Corporation) acquired the Junín and Chaucha concessions and retained the option to acquire the Telimbela concession. The acquisition of the Junín concession turned out to be so unpopular with the local community, worried about the ecological and environmental impact of mining activities, that the clashes between the villagers and the foreign investor were depicted in two documentaries. The first is *The Curse of Copper*, a short film which was released in 2007.[88] The second is multiple award-winning *Under Rich Earth*, a full-length feature film that was released in 2008 to critical acclaim at numerous film festivals worldwide.[89] One scene composed of actual footage of the clashes in *Under Rich Earth* shows an armed representative of Copper Mesa spraying unarmed villagers in the eyes with a canister of what appears to be tear gas. Other frequent episodes of violence included the making of death threats, intimidation with weapons, physical assault, abduction and false imprisonment. While most of the violence was inflicted on the protesting villagers by Copper Mesa employees, the villagers occasionally retaliated in like manner. Given the extended catalogue of confrontations, the tribunal constituted to hear Copper Mesa's claim against Ecuador remarked that '[i]t was miraculous that no-one had been killed during one or more of these violent incidents'.[90]

Hoping to quell the escalating violence, Ecuador terminated the three concessions. Copper Mesa then brought a claim under the Agreement between the Government of Canada and the Government of the Republic

---

[87] See also *Urbaser* v. *Argentina*.
[88] Life on TERRA, 'Life on TERRA: The Curse of Copper – Part 1', online: lifeonterra.com/terra-318-the-curse-of-copper-part-one/ (accessed 31 December 2017).
[89] A synopsis of the film is available at *Under Rich Earth*, online: underrichearth.ryecinema.com/ (accessed 31 December 2017). DVD of the film on file with author.
[90] *Copper Mesa Mining* v. *Ecuador*, Award (redacted), para. 4.265.

of Ecuador for the Promotion and Reciprocal Protection of Investments,[91] alleging that the termination violated Ecuador's treaty obligations and seeking compensation for losses suffered. Notably, Copper Mesa admitted its role in the violence over the Junín concession and did not challenge Ecuador's submission that it had 'committed flagrant breaches of Ecuadorian and international human rights law'.[92] The tribunal factored investor wrongdoing into its assessment of the merits of Copper Mesa's claim. Unbidden by either party, the tribunal declared that it preferred to analyse Copper Mesa's conduct 'under analogous doctrines of causation and contributory negligence applying to the merits of the Claimant's claims arising from events subsequent to the acquisition of its investment'.[93] The tribunal located its approach in Article 39 of the ILC's Articles on State Responsibility:

> *Article 39*
> *Contribution to the injury*
>   In the determination of reparation, account shall be taken of the contribution to the injury by wilful or negligent action or omission of the injured State or any person or entity in relation to whom reparation is sought.

Articles on State Responsibility, Article 39, directs the tribunal to determine 'to what extent, the Claimant's worsening situation as the concessionaire in the Junín area was caused (in whole or in part) by its own acts or omission'.[94] The tribunal found that Copper Mesa, albeit provoked by local resistance, was responsible for 'recruiting and using armed men, firing guns and spraying mace at civilians ... as part of a premeditated,

---

[91] Signed 29 April 1996, entered into force 6 June 1997. On 3 May 2017, Ecuador's National Assembly voted to terminate a dozen of Ecuador's bilateral investment treaties, including the Canada-Ecuador investment treaty. One of the reasons for termination was the immense cost of defending and compensating investor claims, see Transnational Institute, 'Ecuador Terminates 16 Investment Treaties (18 May 2017)', online: www.tni.org/en/article/ecuador-terminates-16-investment-treaties (accessed 31 December 2017). However, termination does not mean immediate withdrawal of treaty protection from otherwise qualifying investments and investors. As provided for by Art. XVIII(2) of the Canada-Ecuador investment treaty:

> ... The termination of this Agreement shall become effective one year after notice of termination has been received by the other Contracting Party. In respect of investments or commitments to invest made prior to the date when the termination of this Agreement becomes effective, the provisions of Articles I to XVII inclusive of this Agreement shall remain in force for a period of fifteen years.

[92] *Copper Mesa Mining* v. *Ecuador*, Award (redacted), para. 5.42.

[93] Ibid., para. 5.65.

[94] Ibid., para. 6.98.

disguised and well-funded plan to take the law into its own hands'.[95] The sum of the investor's actions amounted, in the eyes of the tribunal, to 'a sustained act of folly'. In view of Copper Mesa's contribution to its own injury, the tribunal reduced the compensation payable by Ecuador for expropriating the Junín concession by 30 per cent.[96]

To be fair to the tribunal, Ecuador raised the issue of Copper Mesa's internationally wrongful conduct, without requesting a ruling on it. Moreover, invoking Articles on State Responsibility, Article 39, allowed the tribunal to put a price on investor wrongdoing without losing sight of the predetermined focus on host State responsibility in investment treaty arbitrations. However, the tribunal's acknowledgement that Ecuador was making 'grave allegations against the Claimant of violations of international law',[97] does not sit comfortably with the lesser given label of 'act[s] of folly'. Nor does it explain the invocation of Articles on State Responsibility, Article 39. Article 39 envisages a reduction in reparation payable by the injuring State when the victim has contributed to its own injury by conducting itself in a manner that was 'wilful or negligent'. Article 39 does not cover situations where the injured party's conduct was also internationally wrongful.[98] The ILC Commentary on Article 39 confirms that there is no assimilation of internationally wrongful conduct to 'wilful or negligent' conduct. Article 39 is only concerned with actions and omissions 'which manifest a lack of due care on the part of the victim of the breach for his or

---

[95] Ibid., para. 6.99.

[96] Ibid., paras. 6.102 and 7.30.

[97] Ibid., para. 5.42.

[98] None of the five investment treaty awards which the tribunal cited as precedent for the application of Articles on State Responsibility, Art. 39, to quantify an investor's contributory negligence, recorded allegations of investors violating international law, see Award (redacted), paras. 6.93–6.96. The allegation against the corporate investor in *MTD Equity Sdn Bhd and Anor* v. *The Republic of Chile* was poor business judgment in purchasing land absent adequate legal protection, see ICSID Case No. ARB/01/7, Award, 25 May 2004 (Sureda, Lalonde, Blanco), paras. 242–3, and Decision on Annulment, 21 March 2007 (Guillaume, Crawford, Ordóñez Noriega), paras. 99–101. The allegation against the investor in *Occidental Petroleum Corp. and Anor* v. *The Republic of Ecuador* was failure to comply with a contractual obligation to obtain ministerial authorization prior to the transfer of contractual rights, see Award, 5 October 2012 (Fortier, Williams, Stern), paras. 665, 671–3 and 679. Finally, the allegations against the investors in *Hulley Enterprises Limited* v. *Russia*, *Yukos Universal Limited* v. *Russia* and *Veteran Petroleum Limited* v. *Russia*, which shared a factual core, concerned tax avoidance and untimely bankruptcy proceedings; see Final Award (Fortier, Poncet, Schwebel), 18 July 2014 (PCA Case Nos. AA 226, AA 227 and AA 228), paras. 1608–1637.

her own property or rights'.[99] Any mention of international wrongfulness in the ILC Commentary is only ever associated with the conduct of the injuring State.

Notwithstanding the questionable downgrading of potentially internationally wrongful investor conduct to garden-variety negligence with the invocation of Articles on State Responsibility, Article 39, the arbitral award in *Copper Mesa Mining* v. *Ecuador* heralds a new era for investment contract protection under investment treaty law. The extent and quantification of State responsibility, once assessed with extensive or even exclusive reference to the applicable investment treaty provisions,[100] are now determined in conjunction with the investor's compliance with international law in the making and operation of its investment. Whether a host State's investment treaty obligations can be suspended vis-à-vis an investor committing human rights violations[101] or its international responsibility precluded or diminished on the basis that it acted in response to the investor's internationally wrongful conduct[102] are emerging questions that invite careful reflection. Much of the difficulty lies in the fact that

---

[99] ILC, 'Draft Articles on Responsibility of States for Internationally Wrongful Acts, with Commentaries', vol. II, Part Two, p. 110.

[100] Arbitral tribunals interpreting investment treaty provisions may also need to refer to domestic law in order to determine if the right for which the investor seeks treaty protection exists. For example, whether an investor holds title to property in a host State is a question for host State law, not international law. For a discussion on how domestic law assists arbitral tribunals in determining whether an investor possesses property rights in an investment contract that are capable of being enforced against a host State, see Sasson, *Substantive Law in Investment Treaty Arbitration*, pp. 83–7.

[101] A host State may invoke VCLT Art. 62, which permits a State to suspend the operation of a treaty on the basis that there has been '[a] fundamental change of circumstances which has occurred with regard to those existing at the time of the conclusion of a treaty, and which was not foreseen by the parties', and if '(a) the existence of those circumstances constituted an essential basis of the consent of the parties to be bound by the treaty; and (b) the effect of the change is radically to transform the extent of obligations still to be performed under the treaty.' A host State may argue that an investor's human rights violations, which post-date the making of the investment, amounts to a fundamental change in circumstances justifying the suspension of treaty protection since it would never have consented to extend, and should not be expected to extend, treaty protection to human rights violators. This argument is strengthened if the applicable investment treaty requires investors to uphold human rights in the host State. Such treaties are rare, but exist; see the Investment Agreement for COMESA (Common Market for Eastern and Southern Africa) Common Investment Area, signed 23 May 2007, not yet in force, Art. 16; and the Reciprocal Investment Promotion and Protection Agreement between the Government of the Kingdom of Morocco and the Government of the Federal Republic of Nigeria, signed 3 December 2016, not yet in force, Arts. 14(1) and 18(2).

[102] A host State may argue that its actions towards the investor were countermeasures to the investor's internationally wrongful conduct; see Articles on State Responsibility, Arts. 22

international law at present rarely identifies non-State actors as bearers of international obligations.[103] This may change if ongoing negotiations 'to elaborate an international legally binding instrument to regulate, in international human rights law, the activities of transnational corporations and other business enterprises', culminate in a multilateral treaty creating international obligations for corporate investors.[104] The clash between State obligations under investment treaties and investor obligations under various international soft law instruments,[105] the latter which may one day harden into international obligations, have already started to influence findings on State responsibility for investment contract protection. It will, in all likelihood, continue to do so.

6.5   Conclusion

The emerging international law on investment contract protection comprises general international law on which evolving investment treaty law perches. This chapter arrived at the characterisation through two observations.

First, Chapters 3–5 demonstrate that the emerging law recognises claims for the violation of the core standard of treatment, for unlawful expropriation and, to a much lesser degree, for internationalisation. I argued in this chapter that the different receptions to different genres of claims

---

and 49–54. State actions that meet the stringent Articles on State Responsibility criteria for countermeasures are not wrongful under investment treaty law.

[103]   The exception is the Rome Statute of the International Criminal Court, signed 17 July 1998, entered into force 1 July 2002, 2187 UNTS 90, Arts. 13, 15, 25 and 28, which allow the prosecution of individuals for international crimes.

[104]   UNHRC, Resolution 26/9 – Elaboration of an International Legally Binding Instrument on Transnational Corporations and other Business Enterprises with Respect to Human Rights, UN Doc. A/HRC/RES/26/9 (26 June 2014); see also UNHRC, 'First Intergovernmental Working Group Session Report' (5 February 2016), UN Doc. A/HRC/31/50, pp. 3-4; UNHRC, 'Second Intergovernmental Working Group Session Report' (4 January 2017), UN Doc. A/HRC/34/47, p. 3.

[105]   Two of the most well-known instruments are the UN Global Compact, 'The Ten Principles of the UN Global Compact', online: www.unglobalcompact.org/what-is-gc/mission/ principles (accessed 31 December 2017); and the Office of the UN High Commissioner for Human Rights, 'Guiding Principles on Business and Human Rights', online: www. ohchr.org/Documents/Publications/GuidingPrinciplesBusinessHR_EN.pdf (accessed 31 December 2017) ('UN Guiding Principles'). See also the OECD, 'Guidelines for Multinational Enterprises', online: www.oecd.org/corporate/mne/1922428.pdf (accessed 31 December 2017) ('OECD Guidelines'). Other relevant instruments are listed and discussed in I. Bantekas, 'Corporate Social Responsibility in International Law' (2004) 22 *Boston University International Law Journal* 309 at 317–25.

are conditioned by the general international law on investment contract protection. Since general international law readily sanctions contractual breaches that violate the core standard of treatment and that amount to an unlawful expropriation, but not internationalisation, investment treaty law appears to be more stable when it preserves the position in general international law, and less predictable when it deviates significantly, in the absence of unambiguous treaty language authorising the deviation, from the baseline position. This can be seen in how arbitral awards identifying bad faith or abuse on the part of the host State as discrete components of FET, both categories of host State misconduct already sanctionable under general international law, do not invite objection. The same goes for arbitral rulings that a host State has unlawfully expropriated rights arising from a contract, without considering if such rights also bear proprietary features, whenever the applicable investment treaty expressly recognises contractual rights as a protected investment. In contrast, attempts at identifying investor expectations as a discrete component of FET, and at umbrella clause internationalisation, render host States far more vulnerable to sanction under investment treaty law than under general international law for contractual breaches and are magnets for controversy. General international law therefore supplies the foundational content of investment contract protection, shaping the interpretation of investment treaty provisions applicable to investment contract protection by virtue of VCLT Article 31(3)(c) and enabling the approximation of investment treaty law to general international law.

Second, the content of investment treaty law is prone to change. I attribute this partly to the promise of differentiation described in Chapter 2, when the principal source of international law is arbitral awards which articulate investment treaty law absent a system of binding precedent.[106] I argued in this chapter that there are two additional factors contributing to change. The first is the fact that investment treaties are not only instruments of foreign investment protection but also instruments of foreign policy. Their content, as well as their conclusion and existence, is closely tied to political change. Due to concerns that older-generation archetype investment treaties may be conferring too much protection on foreign investors, some State have chosen to terminate all their existing investment treaties, while other States have concluded newer treaties that dictate new content, or alter or clarify existing content on investment treaty law. None of these changes are permanent or irreversible, rendering

---

[106] See discussion at Chapter 2, Section 2.3.

investment treaty law 'highly precarious'. The second is the rising prominence of investor misconduct in investment disputes. While investment treaty law is oriented towards establishing a State's responsibility for violations of investment treaty obligations, the severity of investor misconduct may nonetheless diminish the extent and quantification of State responsibility. If a host State expropriates an investment contract without compensation because the investor is believed to have violated international human rights law, it is at least arguable that investment treaty protection should be denied to that particular investor,[107] or that the wrongfulness of host State conduct is precluded because it was a legitimate response to the investor's misdeeds[108] or that host State responsibility is offset by investor responsibility for committing an internationally wrongful act.[109]

Together, the stabilising effect of general international law on investment treaty law, and the current direction of change in investment treaty law, albeit changeable at short notice, fosters an international law on investment contract protection where State responsibility will not be causally engaged for contractual breaches. With internationalisation likely to fade from view, contractual breaches by States will have to violate the core standard of treatment or constitute an unlawful expropriation in order to amount to an international wrong. Moving forwards, this will have an important bearing on the prospect of international investment contract claims, the topic of the next and final chapter.

---

[107] *Copper Mesa Mining* v. *Ecuador*, Award (redacted), at paras. 5.4 and 5.39. This leaves the investor with the option of pursuing local remedies.
[108] See above footnotes notes 101 and 102.
[109] *Urbaser* v. *The Argentine Republic*, Award, paras. 36 and 1138.

The Future of International Investment Contract Claims

7.1 Introduction

The preponderance of publicly known international investment contract claims seek treaty protection offered by fair and equitable treatment, expropriation and umbrella clauses. A contract-based FET claim entails the investor arguing that a breach of contract by the host State amounts to a denial of FET; a contract-based expropriation claim attempts the assimilation of a breach of contract to an unlawful expropriation by the host State; while a contract-based umbrella clause claim equates a breach of contract to a violation of a host State's treaty obligation to observe all undertakings given to protected investors. Regardless of whether the investor seeks treaty protection by invoking an FET, expropriation or umbrella clause in a contract-based dispute with the host State, the investor's objective is the same: the compensable engagement of the host State's international responsibility. To maximise the likelihood (or minimise the failure) of attaining this objective, investors usually formulate several treaty claims from the same set of facts. Where, for instance, the source of grievance for the investor is a breach of contract by the host State, and where the applicable investment treaty contains FET, expropriation and umbrella clauses, the investor may simultaneously bring FET, expropriation and umbrella clause claims.

Investor litigation strategy has kindled interest in the correlation between the different treaty claims, as well as in the relative success rates of the different treaty claims. In this regard, two observations have been made. One, that the distinctions between FET and expropriation claims, and FET and umbrella clause claims, are becoming porous. And two, that FET claims will become catch-all claims, more likely to succeed when other treaty claims fail. The content of FET applicable to investment contracts has already been explored in Chapter 3, Section 3.3.1, while the emergence of a stabilised, core standard of treatment was addressed in Chapter 3, Sections 3.2 and 3.3.2, as well as in Chapter 6, Section 6.2.1.1. Building on these findings, this chapter analyses the foregoing predictions of FET claims in the specific context of contract-based FET claims. It compares the character of substantive protection conferred by FET, expropriation and umbrella clauses to evaluate if distinctions between otherwise discrete contract-based treaty claims are readily collapsible (Section 7.2). It then considers the prospects of contract-based FET claims vis-à-vis contract-based expropriation and umbrella clause claims (Section 7.3). Drawing on Sections 7.2 and 7.3, the chapter concludes by considering if contract-based FET claims are indeed catch-all claims (Section 7.4).

7.2 The Uniqueness of Contract-based FET Claims

Observations that a denial of FET by the host State is akin to an unlawful expropriation, or a violation of an umbrella clause, have largely gone unchallenged. The merging of treaty protection under FET and expropriation clauses was first attempted by the tribunal in *Metalclad Corp. v. The United Mexican States*,[1] while the identity in character of treaty protection under FET and umbrella clauses was alluded to by the tribunals in *Metalpar S.A. and Buen Aire S.A. v. The Argentine Republic*,[2] and *Glamis Gold, Ltd. v. The United States of America*.[3] If FET, expropriation and umbrella clause claims are truly interchangeable, there will be no need for different provisions on substantive protection in investment treaties. FET claims can simply take the place of expropriation and umbrella clause claims, making expropriation and umbrella clauses redundant. The effect of erasing the boundaries between FET, expropriation and umbrella clause claims is so sweeping that the purported interchangeability of the different treaty claims invites further reflection. To this end, this section examines how protection under FET and expropriation clauses (7.2.1), and how protection under FET and umbrella clauses (7.2.2), correlate in contract-based treaty claims.

7.2.1 *Substantive Protection under FET and Expropriation Clauses Compared*

A breach of contract by a host State amounts to a denial of FET when it is carried out in a manner that violates a recognised limb of FET, such

---

[1] *Metalclad Corp. v. The United Mexican States*, ICSID Case No. ARB(AF)/97/1, Award, 30 August 2000 (Lauterpacht, Civiletti, Siqueiros), paras. 103–4.

[2] *Metalpar S.A. and Buen Aire S.A. v. The Argentine Republic*, ICSID Case No. ARB/03/5, Award on the Merits, 6 June 2008 (Blanco, Cameron, Chabaneix), paras. 185–6.

[3] *Glamis Gold Ltd. v. The United States of America*, NAFTA-UNCITRAL, Award, 8 June 2009 (Young, Caron, Hubbard), paras. 766–7.

as non-arbitrariness or due process.[4] In contrast, a breach of contract by a host State amounts to an expropriation when it results in a substantial deprivation of the investor's protected rights.[5] Additionally, in order for the expropriation to found a treaty claim, the investor has to challenge the legality of the expropriatory breach of contract.[6] Only expropriations that are not matched by adequate compensation, or the pursuit of public purpose, or respect for due process, are unlawful. While both FET and expropriation clauses regulate the manner of the contractual breach, the required showing of a substantial deprivation of protected rights in an expropriation claim but not in an FET claim is the critical and indelible point of distinction. Therefore, a successful FET claim does not necessarily beget a successful expropriation claim, and vice versa, because each claim follows a different line of inquiry.

In *Metalclad* v. *Mexico*, the arbitral tribunal appeared to conflate the different lines of inquiry. It took the view that facts which substantiated the denial of FET in the revocation of a construction permit also sufficed to prove an unlawful expropriatory breach of contract:[7]

> Thus, expropriation under NAFTA includes not only open, deliberate and acknowledged takings of property, such as outright seizure or formal or obligatory transfer of title in favour of the host State, but also covert or incidental interference with the use of property which has the effect of depriving the owner, in whole or in significant part, of the use or reasonably-to-be-expected economic benefit of property even if not necessarily to the obvious benefit of the host State. By permitting or tolerating the conduct of Guadalcazar in relation to Metalclad which the Tribunal has already held amounts to unfair and inequitable treatment breaching Article 1105 and by thus participating or acquiescing in the denial to Metalclad of the right to operate the landfill, notwithstanding the fact that the project was fully approved and endorsed by the federal government, Mexico must be held to have taken a measure tantamount to expropriation in violation of NAFTA Article 1110(1).

In all fairness, the arbitral tribunal did preface its holding on the interplay between NAFTA Articles 1105 (the FET clause) and 1110 (the

---

[4] Other generally accepted limbs include absence of bad faith and abusive conduct, see Chapter 3, Sections 3.3.1.2 and 3.4.4; and Chapter 6, Section 6.2.1.1. Less established limbs include proportionality and the preservation of investor expectations. See Chapter 3, Sections 3.3.1.2 and 3.3.1.3 and Chapter 6, Section 6.2.1.1.

[5] See Chapter 4, Sections 4.2.2, and 4.3.

[6] See Chapter 4, Section 4.4.

[7] *Metalclad* v. *Mexico*, Award, paras. 103–4.

expropriation clause),[8] with the reminder that an expropriation requires a deprivation of the 'economic benefit of property'. It was therefore implicit that the arbitral tribunal found that there was an expropriation because Mexico's conduct deprived Metalclad of the 'economic benefit of property'. Nonetheless, the arbitral tribunal's use of a successful FET claim to buttress an expropriation claim suggests the interchangeability of FET and expropriation claims. Regrettably, the arbitral tribunal in *Metalclad* v. *Mexico* did not elaborate on how the different lines of inquiry for FET and expropriation claims can be fused, thereby justifying the interchangeability of discrete treaty claims.

Tribunals hearing FET claims alongside expropriation claims in contract-based disputes after *Metalclad* v. *Mexico* rarely comment on the interchangeability of FET and expropriation claims. Although investors tend to prevail or fail on both their contract-based FET and expropriation claims,[9] occasions where investors prevail on the FET claim but not the expropriation claim caution that FET and expropriation claims are

---

[8] North American Free Trade Agreement, signed 17 December 1992, entered into force 1 January 1994, (1993) 32 ILM 289.

[9] *Wena Hotels Ltd* v. *Egypt*, ICSID Case No. ARB/98/4, Award, 8 December 2000 (Leigh, Fadlallah, Wallace), paras. 84 and 98; *Waste Management Inc.* v. *United Mexican States (No. 2)*, ICSID Case No. ARB(AF)/00/3, Award, 30 April 2004 (Crawford, Civiletti, Gómez), paras. 115 and 175; *Compañia de Aguas del Aconquija S.A. and Vivendi Universal* v. *Argentine Republic*, ICSID Case No. ARB/97/3, Award, 20 August 2007 (Kaufmann-Kohler, Verea, Rowley), paras. 7.4.19 and 7.5.8; *Parkerings-Compagniet AS* v. *Republic of Lithuania*, ICSID Case No. ARB/05/8, Award, 11 September 2007 (Lévy, Lew, Lalonde), paras. 337–8 and 445–7; *Rumeli Telekom A.S. and Anor* v. *Republic of Kazakhstan*, ICSID Case No. ARB/05/16, Award, 29 July 2008 (Hanotiau, Boyd, Lalonde), paras. 15–18 and 705–8; *Biwater Gauff (Tanzania) Ltd.* v. *United Republic of Tanzania*, ICSID Case No. ARB/05/22, Award, 24 July 2008 (Hanotiau, Born, Landau), paras. 519 and 622–8; *Continental Casualty* v. *Argentina*, ICSID Case No. ARB/03/9, Award, 5 September 2008 (Sacerdoti, Veeder, Nader), paras. 259 and 284; *Bayindir Insaat Turizm Ticaret Ve Sanayi A.S.* v. *Islamic Republic of Pakistan*, ICSID Case No. ARB/03/29, Award, 27 August 2009 (Kaufmann-Kohler, Berman, Böckstiegel), paras. 193–9 and 461; *Gemplus S.A. et al.* v. *United a Mexican States*, ICSID Case No. ARB(AF)/04/3, Award, 16 June 2010 (Fortier, Gómez, Veeder), paras. 7–76 and 8–25; *Inmaris Perestroika Sailing Maritime Services GmbH and Others* v. *Ukraine*, ICSID Case No. ARB/08/8, Excerpts of Award, 1 March 2012 (Alexandrov, Rubins, Cremades), paras. 273–5 and 304–5; *Occidental Petroleum Corporation and Anor* v. *The Republic of Ecuador*, ICSID Case No. ARB/06/11, Award, 5 October 2012 (Fortier, Williams, Stern), paras. 450 and 455; *Deutsche Bank AG* v. *Democratic Socialist Republic of Sri Lanka*, ICSID Case No. ARB/09/02, d, 31 October 2012 (Hanotiau, Williams, Khan (dissenting)), paras. 491 and 520–4; *SAUR* v. *Argentina*, Affaire CIRDI No. ARB/04/4, Décision sur La Compétence et sur la Responsabilité, 6 June 2012 (Fernández-Armesto, Hanotiau, Tomuschat), paras. 381–2 and 506–7.

not interchangeable.[10] The arbitral tribunal in *Sempra Energy* v. *Argentina*, which found for the investor's FET claim but not its expropriation claim, nearly refuted the possibility of identifying FET with expropriation claims:[11]

> It is quite true, as argued by the Claimant, that interference with contractual rights can in certain circumstances amount to an expropriation. Yet, in the instant case the Tribunal is not persuaded that such has been the result of the measures taken. In spite of all the difficulties which the Licensees and the investors have experienced, and which have doubtlessly affected rational management, they are still the rightful owners of the companies and their business. No one else has or could lawfully claim any such right. While the noted adverse effects can give rise to compensation, they cannot do so in connection with direct expropriation. The same is true with respect to the breach of stability clauses under the contract which, while potentially resulting in damage, is to be protected against and eventually compensated under a separate Treaty guarantee rather than under the heading of expropriation.

It was not until the *Accession Mezzanine Capital LP and Anor* v. *Hungary* award that the mooted identity of FET claims to expropriation claims in *Metalclad* v. *Mexico* was firmly rejected.[12]

> The [*Metalclad* v. *Mexico*] tribunal then upheld Metalclad's claim for expropriation under Article 1110 of NAFTA on precisely the same basis: By permitting or tolerating the conduct of [the municipality] in relation to Metalclad which the Tribunal has already held amounts to unfair and inequitable treatment breaching Article 1105 and by thus participating or acquiescing in the denial to Metalclad of the right to operate the landfill, notwithstanding the fact that the project was fully approved and endorsed by the federal government, Mexico must be held to have taken a measure tantamount to expropriation in violation of NAFTA Article 1110(1). There is little force in this statement as persuasive authority because it amounts to a conclusion that what is a breach of the fair and equitable standard must also be an expropriation. The Tribunal cannot accept this to be a correct

---

[10] *Sempra Energy International* v. *Argentine Republic*, ICSID Case No. ARB/02/16, Award, 28 September 2007 (Orrego Vicuña, Lalonde, Morelli Rico), paras. 280–1 and 303–4; *EDF International S.A. and Ors* v. *Argentina*, ICSID Case No. ARB/03/23, Award, 11 June 2012 (Park, Kaufmann-Kohler, Remón), paras. 1113 and 1004–5.

[11] Award, ibid., para. 281 (footnote omitted). The Award was subsequently annulled in its entirety for the tribunal's manifest excess of powers in failing to apply Art. XI of the US-Argentina investment treaty, Decision on the Argentine Republic's Application for Annulment of the Award, 29 June 2010 (Söderlund, Edward, Jacovides), para. 229. The annulment arguably diminishes the Award's persuasive value.

[12] *Accession Mezzanine Capital and Anor* v. *Hungary*, ICSID Case No. ARB/12/3, Award, 17 April 2015 (Rovine, Lalonde, Douglas), paras. 175–6 (footnote omitted).

statement of the law. There is no further analysis in the award as to whether the particular requirements of an expropriation have been satisfied; instead the *Metalclad* tribunal's principal findings in respect of the Article 1105 claim are simply repeated for the Article 1110 claim.

In noting that a successful expropriation claim called for the 'particular requirements of an expropriation [to be] satisfied', the arbitral tribunal in *Accession Mezzanine* v. *Hungary* drew attention to the different elements that make up an FET claim and an expropriation claim. A breach of contract by the host State can simultaneously be a denial of FET as well as an unlawful expropriation. But an unlawful expropriatory breach of contract is not proven simply because the breach of contract is shown to be a denial of FET. The 'particular requirements of an expropriation' claim are the existence of an expropriation (on which a showing of denial of FET is neutral), as well as the existence of a criterion of unlawfulness (on which a showing of denial of FET, unless the denial stems from due process violations, is also neutral).

7.2.2   Substantive Protection under FET and Umbrella Clauses Compared

As umbrella clauses oblige host States to observe all undertakings given to protected investors, such clauses potentially trigger the engagement of State responsibility for any breach of contract. The viability of elevating a host State's contractual obligations to international obligations via an umbrella clause, what I call umbrella clause internationalisation, is discussed in Chapter 5, Section 5.3.3.3. Given the known resistance of States to internationalisation, umbrella clauses are being viewed with increasing suspicion. In the World Investment Reports of 2015, 2016 and 2017, a survey of fifty-seven investment treaties and investment chapters in free trade agreements concluded between 2014 and 2016 revealed that forty-two of these agreements recorded 'an omission of the so-called umbrella clause'.[13] The reason for this trend in treaty-making, according to the 2015 Report, was to 'avoid overexposure to litigation'.[14]

The deliberate exclusion of umbrella clauses from the newer investment treaties undercuts the belief that FET clauses will become 'de facto'

---

[13] UNCTAD, 'World Investment Report 2015', p. 113; 'World Investment Report 2016', p. 113; and 'World Investment Report 2017', p. 121.

[14] Ibid., p. 113.

umbrella clauses.[15] Weaving an umbrella clause into an FET clause will, sooner or later, attract opposition. The entrenched disagreements over the character of protection umbrella clauses confer on investment contracts amplify the risk of misinterpretation when tribunals adjudicate contract-based umbrella clause claims. Some States hope to guide interpretation by drafting very detailed umbrella clauses,[16] while others hope to eradicate the risk altogether by dropping umbrella clauses from their investment treaties. Whether or not States choose to retain umbrella clauses in their treaty practice, the decision is probably contingent on the envisaged effects of umbrella clauses. Likening FET clauses to umbrella clauses defeats the purpose of negotiating and drafting FET clauses separately from umbrella clauses. It also defeats the purpose of excluding umbrella clauses from treaties if they can be reintegrated through FET clauses.

Aside from the impracticality of treating FET clauses like umbrella clauses, there are three important distinctions between the two types of clauses which obstructs their interchangeability.

First, the adequacy of investment contract protection under an FET clause requires an examination of the *manner* in which the contract was breached. A breach of contract in and of itself does not amount to a denial of FET. That breach must also offend at least one of the limbs of FET, such as non-arbitrariness or due process, to be considered a violation of the host State's treaty obligation to provide FET.[17] In contrast, an umbrella clause is unconcerned with the manner in which an investment contract is breached. Instead, a breach of contract in and of itself is sufficient to activate protection under an umbrella clause. According to the approach in *SGS Société Générale de Surveillance S.A.* v. *Republic of the Philippines* where umbrella clauses empower investment treaty tribunals to assess a breach of contract by applying the contractual proper law, protection for the 'rule of law' kicks in once the contract is breached, regardless of the manner of breach.[18] According to the approach in *Joy Mining Machinery Limited* v. *Arab Republic of Egypt*, a breach of contract carried out in a host

---

[15] L. Johnson and L. Sachs, 'International Investment Agreements, 2011–2012: A Review of Trends and New Approaches' in A. Bjorklund (ed.), *Yearbook on International Investment Law and Policy 2012–2013* (Oxford: Oxford University Press, 2013), pp. 219, 229.

[16] See for instance European Union-Singapore Investment Protection Agreement (pending signature and ratification, text as of April 2018), Art. 2.6 and accompanying fns 12 and 13.

[17] See Chapter 3, Sections 3.3.1, and 3.4.

[18] Decision of the Tribunal on Objections to Jurisdiction, 29 January 2004 (El-Kosheri, Crawford, Crivellaro (partially dissenting)), para. 128. See discussion at Chapter 5, Section 5.3.3.1.

State's sovereign capacity is a violation of the umbrella clause.[19] A breach of contract committed by a State in a particular capacity is not indicative of the manner of breach. What is being sanctioned here is the use by a State of its sovereign powers to breach a contract, and not the misuse of those powers.[20] Finally, according to the approach in *Noble Ventures, Inc. v. Romania,* where every breach of contract can be construed as a violation of the umbrella clause, the manner of breach is once again irrelevant. So long as a breach of contract has occurred, an umbrella clause dictates the engagement of State responsibility.[21]

Second, FET and umbrella clauses will be interchangeable if investment contracts indisputably create protected expectations for the investor, and if these expectations are indisputably an independent ground for the denial of FET. In this way, a breach of contract by the host State simultaneously activates protection under an umbrella clause, and violates an FET clause by frustrating investor expectations. The view that frustrated investor expectations alone give rise to a denial of FET is contested.[22] Moreover, the view that all contractual commitments by a State qualify as expectations eligible for FET protection is also contested.[23] Even if preserving investor expectations is a discrete component of FET, very few categories of contract-based expectations are likely to qualify as protected expectations. One category is specific commitments made by the host State to the investor and which induced the investor to invest.[24] Another category is investor expectations pertaining to the transparency and stability of the legal framework.[25] While investor expectations often feature in discussions on the content of FET, they do not inform the character of protection conferred by umbrella clauses on investment contracts. Whichever one of the three available interpretive approaches to umbrella clauses one prefers,

---

[19] *Joy Mining Machinery Ltd.* v. *Egypt,* ICSID Case No. ARB/03/11, Award on Jurisdiction, 6 August 2004 (Orrego Vicuña, Craig, Weeramantry), para. 79, also 72, 75 and 81. See discussion at Chapter 5, Section 5.3.3.2.

[20] Contrast this with how a breach of contract *iure imperii,* unaccompanied by aggravating circumstances, is unlikely to constitute a violation of FET, see discussion at Chapter 3, Section 3.4.3.

[21] *Noble Ventures* v. *Romania,* ICSID Case No. ARB/01/11, Award, 12 October 2005 (Böckstiegel, Lever, Dupuy), paras. 53–4. See discussion at Chapter 5, Section 5.3.3.3.

[22] See Chapter 3, Sections 3.3.1.1 and 3.3.1.3.

[23] Schreuer, 'Fair and Equitable Treatment (FET)', pp. 63, 93.

[24] See for instance *Duke Energy Electroquil Partners and Anor* v. *Ecuador,* ICSID Case No. ARB/04/19, Award, 18 August 2008 (Kaufmann-Kohler, Pinzón, van den Berg), para. 340: '[S]uch expectations must arise from the conditions that the State offered the investor and the latter must have relied upon them when deciding to invest.'

[25] Schreuer, 'Fair and Equitable Treatment (FET)', p. 93.

a breach of contract need not frustrate investor expectations for there to be a violation of an umbrella clause.

Third and finally, if FET and umbrella clauses are interchangeable, then FET clauses, just like umbrella clauses, potentially internationalise investment contracts. Full umbrella clause internationalisation, where every contractual obligation is converted into an international obligation, was analysed in Chapter 5, Section 5.3.3.3. For the arbitral tribunal in *Noble Ventures* v. *Romania*, full internationalisation may be justified by the wording of the umbrella clause. It found that Article II(2)(c) of the US-Romania investment treaty internationalised Romania's contractual obligations:[26]

> [T]he question for the Tribunal is whether Art. II(2)(c) BIT is an 'umbrella clause' that transforms contractual undertakings into international law obligations and accordingly makes it a breach of the BIT by the Respondent if it breaches a contractual obligation that it has entered into with the Claimant. Art. II(2)(c) reads as follows: 'Each Party shall observe any obligation it may have entered into with regard to investments.' ... Considering that Art. II(2)(c) BIT uses the term 'shall' and that it forms part of the Article which provides for the major substantial obligations undertaken by the parties, there can be no doubt that the Article was intended to create obligations, and obviously obligations beyond those specified in other provisions of the BIT itself ... Against this background, and considering the wording of Art. II(2)(c) which speaks of 'any obligation [a party] may have entered into with regard to investments', it is difficult not to regard this as a clear reference to investment contracts ... Accordingly, the wording of Article II(2)(c) provides substantial support for an interpretation of Art. II(2)(c) as a real umbrella clause.

The same cannot be said for FET clauses where expansive terms like 'any obligation' are absent. For example, Article II(2)(a) of the US-Romania investment treaty – the FET clause – provides that '[i]nvestment shall at all times be accorded fair and equitable treatment, shall enjoy full protection and security and shall in no case be accorded treatment less than that required by international law.' For the arbitral tribunal in *Noble Ventures* v. *Romania*, the dissimilarity between the FET and umbrella clauses in the US-Romania investment treaty is evident:[27]

> Considering the place of the fair and equitable treatment standard at the very beginning of Art. II(2), one can consider this to be a more general standard which finds its specific application in inter alia the duty to provide full protection and security [Article II(2)(a)], the prohibition of arbitrary

---

[26] *Noble Ventures, Inc.* v. *Romania*, ICSID Case No. ARB/01/11, Award, 12 October 2005 (Böckstiegel, Lever, Dupuy), paras. 46 and 51.

[27] Ibid., para. 182.

and discriminatory measures [Article II(2)(b)] and the obligation to observe contractual obligations towards the investor [Article II(2)(c)].

The generality of FET clauses inhibits their use as tools of internationalisation. As the arbitral tribunal in *Noble Ventures* v. *Romania* had already determined that Article II(2)(c) was a 'real umbrella clause' which internationalised Romania's contractual obligations before interpreting the FET clause, the reference to 'the obligation to observe contractual obligations towards the investor' is not an endorsement of the interchangeability of FET and umbrella clauses. The possibility of full internationalisation can only be realised through the umbrella clause because this is the clause which 'create[s] obligations, and obviously obligations beyond those specified in other provisions of the BIT itself ... [making it] difficult not to regard this as a clear reference to investment contracts'. Without Article II(2)(c), the tribunal lacked textual support for claiming that FET encompassed 'the obligation to observe contractual obligations'.

7.3   The Prospects of Contract-based FET Claims

When the purpose of FET clauses is understood as one of 'fill[ing] gaps which may be left by the more specific standards, in order to obtain the level of investor protection intended by the treaties',[28] it is tempting to regard FET claims as catch-all claims which are more likely to experience success than failure. The array of components which establish the content of FET,[29] as well as the array of contractual breaches that can be construed as a denial of FET,[30] seem to multiply an investor's chances of prevailing on a contract-based FET claim.

Reasoning *ex post* that contract-based FET claims succeed where other contract-based treaty claims fail because FET is such a flexible standard may be unduly hasty. It was argued at Chapter 6, Section 6.2.1.1 that the general international law on contractual protection has a stabilising influence on the content of FET, making it unlikely that current content will undergo radical expansion or revision. Moreover, the notable success rate of contract-based FET claims is largely due to the fact that most investors had a strong case. Claims that recount the arbitrary treatment (*Gemplus* v. *Mexico, Anatolie Stati, Gabriel Stati and Ors* v. *Kazakhstan*),[31] due process

---

[28] Dolzer and Schreuer, *Principles of International Investment Law*, p. 132.
[29] See Chapter 3, Section 3.3.1.2.
[30] See Chapter 3, Section 3.4.
[31] SCC Arbitration V (116/2010), Award, 19 December 2013 (Böckstiegel, Haigh, Lebedev).

violations (*Rumeli v. Kazakhstan, Biwater Gauff v. Tanzania*) and coercion and/or harassment (*Desert Line Projects LLC v. The Republic of Yemen*,[32] *Suez, Sociedad General de Aguas de Barcelona, S.A. and Vivendi Universal, S.A. v. Argentine Republic*),[33] flouted widely recognised components of FET. Those investors who were unable to match the host State conduct complained of at least one recognised component of FET had their contract-based FET claims dismissed (*Bayindir v. Pakistan, Toto Costruzioni Generali S.p.A. v. The Republic of Lebanon*).[34]

Whether an investor is more likely to engage a State's international responsibility for a breach of contract by presenting an FET claim than an expropriation or an umbrella clause claim cannot be settled by first impressions. It is the tribunals' final decision on the merits of these claims that explains their relative rates of success, and which therefore demand scrutiny. This section critically evaluates the prospects of State responsibility being engaged for a breach of contract under an FET claim and an expropriation claim (7.3.1), and those prospects under an FET claim and an umbrella clause claim (7.3.2).

7.3.1   FET and Expropriation Claims Compared

In contract-based FET claims, so long as the breach of contract, be it in the form of non-payment, cumulative acts and omissions, a breach *iure imperii*, coerced renegotiation or cancellation, flouts one of the components of FET like non-arbitrariness or due process, it will amount to a violation of FET. In contrast, for contract-based expropriation claims, usually only cancellations are construed as expropriatory contractual breaches. Moreover, the burden of proof, which falls on the investor, for two out of three conditions of unlawfulness – the absence of public purpose and the absence of due process – is rarely discharged.[35] This is likely to lower the success rate of contract-based unlawful expropriation claims because only investors who prove the cancellation of an investment contract and the absence of compensation will prevail. The better prospects of an FET claim

---

[32] *Desert Line Projects LLC v. The Republic of Yemen*, ICSID Case No. ARB/05/17, Award, 6 February 2008 (Tercier, Paulsson, El-Kosheri).

[33] *Suez, Sociedad General de Aguas de Barcelona, S.A. and Vivendi Universal, S.A. v. The Republic of Yemen*, ICSID Case No. ARB/03/17, Decision on Liability, 30 July 2010 (Salacuse, Kaufmann-Kohler, Nikken).

[34] *Toto Costruzioni Generali S.p.A. v. The Republic of Lebanon*, ICSID Case No. ARB/07/12, Award, 7 June 2012 (van Houtte, Schwebel, Moghaizel).

[35] See Chapter 4, Sections 4.4.2 and 4.4.3.

in comparison to an expropriation claim in general are reflected in the observation that 'the FET standard may offer redress where the facts do not support a claim for expropriation'.[36] The remainder of this section considers if this observation also applies to contract-based FET and expropriation claims.

In twenty-eight awards rendered between 2000 and 2012, investors presented contract-based FET and expropriation claims in twenty-two cases. In the other six cases, investors based their expropriation claim, but not their FET claim, on host State interference with contractual rights.[37] Among the twenty-two awards where both the FET and expropriation claims were based on a breach of contract, the tribunal found for the investor on both claims on eleven occasions[38] and dismissed both claims on four occasions.[39] One investor failed to show that the conduct purportedly in violation of the FET and expropriation clauses in the applicable investment treaty was attributable to the host State.[40] On six occasions, the investor succeeded on its contract-based FET claim but not its contract-based expropriation claim. As these six awards attest to how the same facts can substantiate an FET claim but not an expropriation claim, it is appropriate to take a closer look at them.

---

[36] Dolzer and Schreuer, *Principles of International Investment Law,* p. 132.

[37] *Ronald S. Lauder* v. *Czech Republic,* UNCITRAL, Final Award, 3 September 2001 (Briner, Cutler, Klein), para. 202; *Nykomb Synergetics Technology Holding AB* v. *Latvia,* SCC-ECT, Award, 16 December 2003 (Haug, Schütze, Gernandt), para. 4.3.1; *Azurix Corp.* v. *The Argentine Republic,* ICSID Case No. ARB/01/12, Award, 14 July 2006 (Rigo Sureda, Lalonde, Martins), para. 322; *LG & E Energy Corp.* v. *Argentina,* ICSID Case No. ARB/02/1, Decision on Liability, 3 October 2006 (de Maekelt, Rezek, van den Berg), paras. 198 and 200; *Enron Creditors Recovery Corp. and Anor* v. *Argentina,* ICSID Case No. ARB/01/3, Award, 22 May 2007 (Orrego Vicuña, van den Berg, Tschanz), paras. 245–6; also *Ioannis Kardassopoulos and Ron Fuchs* v. *Georgia,* ICSID Case Nos. ARB/05/18 and ARB/07/15, Award, 3 March 2010 (Fortier, Orrego Vicuña, Lowe), paras. 387 and 389. Within this cluster, the FET claims brought against Argentina challenged the legislative changes implemented by Argentina in relation to the broader regulatory framework, without discussing the impact of these changes on specific contractual rights.

[38] *Metalclad* v. *Mexico* Award, paras. 89, 99 and 103–4; *Wena Hotels* v. *Egypt* Award, paras. 84 and 98; *Inmaris* v. *Ukraine* Award, paras. 273–5 and 304–5; *Vivendi* v. *Argentina* Award, paras. 7.4.19 and 7.5.8; *Rumeli* v. *Kazakhstan* Award, paras. 15–18 and 705–8; *Biwater Gauff* v. *Tanzania* Award, paras. 519 and 622–8; *Gemplus* v. *Mexico* Award, paras. 7–76 and 8–25; *Occidental Petroleum* v. *Ecuador* Award, paras. 450 and 455; *Deutsche Bank* v. *Sri Lanka* Award, paras. 491 and 520–4; *SAUR* v. *Argentina* Decision, paras. 381–2 and 506–7.

[39] *Waste Management (No. 2)* v. *Mexico* Award, paras. 115, 175; *Parkerings* v. *Lithuania* Award, paras. 337–8 and 445–7; *Continental Casualty* v. *Argentina* Award, paras. 259 and 284; *Bayindir* v. *Pakistan* Award, paras. 193–9 and 461.

[40] *Gustav F. W. Hamester GmbH and Co. KG* v. *Republic of Ghana,* ICSID Case No. ARB/07/24, Award, 18 June 2010 (Stern, Cremades, Landau).

The first is *CMS* v. *Argentina*, where the arbitral tribunal dismissed the unlawful expropriation claim because there was no substantial deprivation of the claimant's investment[41] but upheld the FET claim because the emergency economic measures taken by Argentina interfered with contractual rights by refuting assurances given to investors which induced them to invest.[42] The second is *Sempra Energy* v. *Argentina*, where the arbitral tribunal dismissed the unlawful expropriation claim because the claimant still retained management and control of a gas distribution and transport license[43] but found that the destabilisation of the regulatory framework and of the original contractual bargain wrought by Argentina's economic recovery plan was a violation of FET.[44] The third is *Impregilo S.p.A.* v. *Argentine Republic*, where Argentina's decision to terminate a water and sewage services concession because the investor has 'grossly failed' in performing its contractual obligations was not, in the view of the tribunal, an act of expropriation,[45] but its refusal to renegotiate the concession was a violation of FET.[46] The fourth is *EDF* v. *Argentina*, where the unlawful expropriation claim failed and the FET claim succeeded for the same reasons as those given by the tribunals in *CMS* v. *Argentina* and *Impregilo S.p.A.* v. *Argentina*.[47] The fifth is *Suez* v. *Argentina*, where the tribunal found that Argentina behaved like a 'private contracting party' in terminating the water concession and dismissed the expropriation claim[48] but whose coercive renegotiation tactics prior to termination evinced a violation of FET.[49] The sixth is *Walter Bau* v. *Thailand*, where the tribunal held that the extent of host State interference with contractual rights did not amount to an expropriation because the highway was still in operation, but the taking of measures which frustrated investor expectations for a reasonable rate of return on the investment fell short of FET.[50]

From the foregoing, there are three indicia which permit the deduction that contract-based FET claims do not necessarily fare better than contract-based unlawful expropriation claims.

---

[41] *CMS Gas Transmission Company* v. *The Argentine Republic*, ICSID Case No. ARB/01/8, Award, 12 May 2005 (Orrego Vicuña, Lalonde, Rezek), para. 263.
[42] *Sempra Energy* v. *Argentina* Award, paras. 273–81.
[43] Ibid., paras. 280–1.
[44] Ibid., paras. 303–4.
[45] Ibid., para. 283.
[46] Ibid., paras. 315–31.
[47] Award, 21 June 2011 (Danelius, Brower, Stern), paras. 1113 and 1004–5.
[48] *Suez* v. *Argentina* Decision on Liability, para. 154.
[49] Ibid., paras. 241–2.
[50] UNCITRAL, Award, 1 July 2009 (Barker, Lalonde, Bunnag), paras. 10.17–10.18 and 12.43.

First, statistics show that around half of the investors prevail on both claims, while less than a third prevail on the FET claim but not on the unlawful expropriation claim.

Second, five out of the total of six awards where the tribunal upheld the FET claim but not the expropriation claim involved challenges to the compatibility of Argentina's emergency economic recovery measures with the FET standard. It is not surprising that different tribunals assessing Argentina's conduct in what is broadly the same factual matrix agree that the conduct in question violated FET.[51] That said, these findings support the narrower proposition that contractual breaches brought about by Argentina's emergency economic recovery measures amount to a violation of FET, rather than the broader proposition that contract-based FET claims are on the whole more likely to succeed than contract-based unlawful expropriation claims.

Third and finally, some investors choose to bring a contract-based expropriation claim but base the FET claim on other grounds.[52] For example, in *Lauder* v. *Czech Republic*, the factual grounds listed by the investor for its FET claim were the 'reversal of critical prior approvals ... [and] hostile conduct'.[53] Unlike the unlawful expropriation claim, which focused on host State interference with contractual rights arising from a broadcasting license,[54] the FET claim was framed like a catch-all claim since it referred to 'the totality of other actions and inactions' by the broadcasting authority of the Czech Republic.[55] As expropriation and FET clauses regulate different aspects of host State treatment of protected investments,[56] the use of different facts to support an unlawful expropriation claim and an FET claim is understandable. As pointed out in Section 7.2.1 earlier, a treaty claim for unlawful expropriation requires a showing that there has been a deprivation of a protected investment; an FET claim does not. Therefore, when the source of investor grievance is a breached investment contract, it is conceivable for the unlawful expropriation claim to be based on, for instance, the cancellation of the contract without compensation, while the FET claim refers to host State conduct that is arbitrary or disregards

---

[51] Cf. *Continental Casualty* v. *Argentina* Award, para. 259.
[52] See *Lauder* v. *Czech Republic* Final Award; *Nykomb Synergetics* v. *Latvia* Award; *Azurix Corp.* v. *Argentina* Award; *LG & E* v. *Argentina* Decision on Liability; *Enron* v. *Argentina* Award; also *Kardassopoulos* and *Fuchs* v. *Georgia* Award.'
[53] *Lauder* v. *Czech Republic*, Final Award, para. 212.
[54] Ibid., paras. 196–7.
[55] Ibid., para. 212.
[56] *Emmis International Holding BV and Ors* v. *Hungary*, ICSID Case No. ARB/12/2, Award, 16 April 2014 (McLachlan, Lalonde, Thomas), para. 167(a) (footnote omitted).

due process but not strictly related to the cancellation. As tribunals have not applied the FET standard to let any and every breach of contract violate FET, some investors may, in an excess of caution, hesitate to ground both the unlawful expropriation and FET claims on a breach of contract, which might overplay the capacity of a contractual breach to engage State responsibility.

7.3.2   FET and Umbrella Clause Claims Compared

While arbitral tribunals interpreting FET clauses may not accord the same importance to a particular component of FET, they nonetheless appear to gravitate towards non-arbitrariness and respect for due process as core components of FET.[57] Arbitral tribunals also agree that in a contract-based FET claim, a breach of contract violates FET so long as the investor manages to show that the breach infringed a discrete component of FET. Conversely, arbitral tribunals disagree fundamentally on how umbrella clauses protect contractual rights.[58] Tribunals are divided between viewing an umbrella clause as securing contractual rights under the proper law of the investment contract (the *SGS* v. *Philippines* approach), elevating only those breaches committed in a host State's sovereign capacity to a breach of treaty (the *Joy Mining* v. *Egypt* approach), and as a tool of internationalisation whereby every breach of contract amounts to a violation of international law (the *Noble Ventures* v. *Romania* approach). Therefore, how readily State responsibility is engaged in a contract-based umbrella clause claim depends on where a tribunal stands on umbrella clause internationalisation. This in turn affects how contract-based FET claims will fare alongside contract-based umbrella clause claims.

If the *SGS* v. *Philippines* approach is adopted, then it is unlikely, though not impossible, for State responsibility to be engaged in a contract-based umbrella clause claim. This is because the *SGS* v. *Philippines* approach stands for the enforcement of contractual rights in accordance with the proper law of the investment contract, and not international law. Should, for instance, the host State resist or thwart enforcement, the umbrella clause will be violated and State responsibility engaged. However, a breach of contract will not, as a general rule, violate the umbrella clause. In comparison, a breach of contract can violate FET so long as it flouts one component in a relatively stable list of components of FET. These components

---

[57] See discussion at Chapter 3, Section 3.3.1.2.
[58] See discussion at Chapter 5, Section 5.3.3.

cover a wide range of host State conduct, and not only conduct pertaining to the enforcement of contractual rights. Aside from cases where the breach of contract involved simple non-payment, most investors persuaded the tribunal that the contractual breach implicated one or several of the components of FET. Therefore, when a tribunal interprets an umbrella clause according to the *SGS v. Philippines* approach, an investor entertains better prospects for engaging State responsibility for a breach of contract with an FET claim than with an umbrella clause claim.

If the *Joy Mining v. Egypt* approach is adopted, then State responsibility in a contract-based umbrella clause claim is engaged only if the breach of contract is committed in the host State's sovereign capacity. As explained in Chapter 3, Section 3.4.3, not many tribunals hearing contract-based FET claims choose to classify a breach of contract as a sovereign or non-sovereign act. But, unlike in an umbrella clause claim, the classification alone does not determine if the breach of contract violates FET. Tribunals proceed to consider if the breach of contract *iure imperii* implicates a component of FET. In *Inmaris v. Ukraine*, the tribunal found that Ukraine acted in a sovereign capacity to coerce the investor into accepting new contractual terms,[59] while in *Duke Energy v. Ecuador*, the tribunal found that Ecuador acted in a sovereign capacity to frustrate protected investor expectations.[60] Therefore, in contract-based FET claims, whether or not a breach of contract is committed in a sovereign capacity is not the decisive factor for the engagement of State responsibility.[61] The breach must still flout a discrete component of FET before the tribunal can find that there has been a violation of FET. There is a possible parallel between the *Joy Mining v. Egypt* approach, and awards like *Impregilo v. Argentina* and *SAUR v. Argentina*, where the misuse of public power underscored a finding of the violation of FET. However, the *Joy Mining v. Egypt* approach requires the contractual breach only to reflect the use, not *misuse*, of sovereign power, for State responsibility to be engaged in an umbrella clause claim. In contrast, the *Impregilo v. Argentina* and *SAUR v. Argentina* tribunals either articulated or alluded to a certain component or components of FET that a misuse of public power implicated. Therefore, even if tribunals in contract-based FET claims highlight the use of public power when a State breaches a contract, this alone is not indicative of a violation of FET. By the mere fact that an investor only has to show to a tribunal applying the *Joy Mining v.*

---

[59] *Inmaris v. Ukarine* Award para. 273.
[60] *Duke Energy v. Ecuador* Award, para. 364.
[61] See also *Bayindir v. Pakistan* Award, paras. 184–90.

Egypt approach the use of sovereign power in a contract-based umbrella clause claim, and not the misuse of sovereign power in a contract-based FET claim, it is more likely to prevail in the former. That said, the unpredictability of acts being classified as sovereign or non-sovereign renders uncertain the actual prospects of success for either claim.

If the *Noble Ventures* v. *Romania* approach, where an umbrella clause furnishes the basis for internationalising contractual obligations, is adopted, then the prospects of State responsibility being engaged in a contract-based umbrella clause claim are far more promising than in a contract-based FET claim. If an umbrella clause transforms every contractual obligation into an international obligation, then every breach of contract engages State responsibility. No matter how protective of contractual rights FET clauses may be, the way FET clauses have been interpreted thus far makes it extremely unlikely that every breach of contract violates FET. According to the prevailing interpretive approach,[62] contractual breaches must infringe at least one of the components of FET for there to be a violation of FET. Even if, for the sake of argument, FET is reducible to a single component such as investor expectations, it is doubtful if every expectation arising from an investment contract, such as the expectation to be paid, qualifies as an expectation protected by an FET clause. Either way, a finding of State responsibility is not assured in contract-based FET claims. That said, very few tribunals to date endorse full umbrella clause internationalisation. Therefore, only in a minority of cases will the prospects of success on a contract-based umbrella clause claim far outweigh that of a contract-based FET claim.

7.4   Investment Contract Protection under Investment Treaties and Beyond

Given the different requirements for satisfying FET, expropriation and umbrella clause claims, it is unsurprising that current statistics on the relative success rate of contract-based FET claims are inconclusive. That said, impressions of FET clauses being more investor-friendly than other treaty clauses are not entirely unfounded. By recapping and comparing all the principal options available to an investor seeking to engage a host State's international responsibility for breaching an investment contract, this section demonstrates that FET claims, while not necessarily catch-all claims, accommodate a wider variety of contractual disputes and spare the investor from hurdles associated with other claims. Investment contract

---

[62] See discussion at Chapter 3, Sections 3.3.1.2 and 3.3.1.3.

protection may or may not involve an investment treaty. When there is no applicable investment treaty, a claimant seeking to engage the host State's international responsibility for breaching an investment contract has to bring a cause of action cognisable under general international law. One possibility is the violation of the core standard of treatment (7.4.1); another is unlawful expropriation (7.4.2). When there is an applicable investment treaty, the claimant's cause of action will be for a violation of the investment treaty. As discussed in preceding sections, the three leading causes of action here are the violation of FET (7.4.3), unlawful expropriation (7.4.4) and violation of an umbrella clause (7.4.5).

7.4.1 Protection via the Core Standard of Treatment

As set out in Chapter 3, Section 3.2, the core standard of treatment for contracts is derivative of the minimum standard of treatment for aliens. It is violated if the breach of contract by the host State is either arbitrary or *acta iure imperii* without compensation for injury suffered or opportunity of redress. The hitherto unexplored and therefore low visibility of a core standard of treatment specific to contracts makes its violation an in-principle cogent, but in-practice novel cause of action. Claimant investors who prefer to bring tried-and-tested causes of action may find this option for engaging a host State's international responsibility less reassuring.

7.4.2 Protection via the Expropriation of Alien Property

As set out in Chapter 4, Section 4.2.1.2.2, unlawful expropriation is a tried-and-tested cause of action for engaging a host State's responsibility for breaching an investment contract under general international law. So long as the claimant investor establishes that there has been substantial deprivation of its right to property, such deprivation unmatched by compensation, or the fulfilment of public purpose, or compliance with due process, State responsibility will be engaged. Some arbitral tribunal appears to regard satisfaction of the contract-as-property equation as a formality, while others will insist on verifying that the affected contract or contractual rights in question possess proprietary features before allowing a claim for unlawful expropriation to proceed.

While many investment contracts will satisfy a narrow definition of property,[63] which requires attachment of a monetary value, enforceability

---

[63] See Chapter 4, Section 4.2.1.1.1.

against the world at large, and alienability, a number of contracts will still fall on the borderline. It is not clear if rights arising from an investment project derailed at its inception by an open tender process gone awry, as well as contractual rights foiled or suspended midway by legislative change, are property. In the former scenario, an investor may have expended resources and entered into relevant transactions after being announced as the winning bidder for a public service contract or concession, only for the host State to proclaim the earlier tender process void and invite further tenders for the same contract or concession.[64] Although the right of a winning bidder to operate the public service is one to which a monetary value for expenditures can be attached, the timing and circumstances of its conferral and subsequent revocation question if it was ever enforceable against or transferable to third parties. In the latter scenario, a host State may rig a tender process to block an existing licensee from renewing its license,[65] or indefinitely suspend a concessionaire's right to performance of the concession.[66] It is debatable if a jeopardised right to renewal, which is usually personal to the licensee, can be transferred to third parties, or if an indefinitely suspended right of performance, whose legal effects are disputed, is enforceable against the world at large.

While a claim for unlawful expropriation under general international law does not carry the risk of novelty of a claim for the violation of the core standard of treatment, the imposition of the contract-as-property equation may, depending on the type of investment contract breached and the factual circumstances of its breach, erect a hurdle unaccompanied by instructions on how to clear it.

7.4.3   Protection via an FET Clause in an Investment Treaty

As set out in Chapter 3, Section 3.3 and in Chapter 6, Section 6.2.1.1, the content of FET on contractual protection preserves the core standard of treatment for contracts under general international law. In turn, the core standard of treatment stabilises the content of FET, relegating transgressions that lack the gravitas of arbitrariness and disregard for due process, such as the frustration of self-induced investor expectations, to the outer limits of acceptability. It bears repeating that FET preserves the

---

[64] See for instance *Robert R. Brown* (*USA* v. *Great Britain*) (1923) 6 RIAA 120, pp. 122–9.

[65] See for instance *Accession Mezzanine* v. *Hungary* Award, paras. 38–49.

[66] See for instance *Himpurna* v. *PT (Persero)*, Award, 4 May 1999 (Paulsson, de Fina, Setiawan) in van den Berg (ed.), *Yearbook Commercial Arbitration*, vol. 15, p. 11, para. 309.

core standard of treatment without necessarily being the core standard of treatment. Unless the applicable investment treaty provides otherwise,[67] FET can comprise components other than those that populate the core standard of treatment. The less controversial among them include bad faith and abuse, while the more controversial is the frustration of investor expectations.

Notwithstanding the stabilising effect of the core standard of treatment on FET, the list of components that define FET is not closed. Claimant investors are not constrained to a showing of arbitrariness or disregard for due process, although the strength of a claim is arguably enhanced if the core components of FET are infringed. International investment contract claims showing coercive or abusive conduct on the part of the host State,[68] or the frustration of expectations arising from specific undertakings given by the host State to induce the investor to invest,[69] or relating to a reasonable rate of return on the investment,[70] have succeeded in engaging a host State's international responsibility for violating FET.

---

[67] See for instance Agreement between the Government of Japan and the Government of the Republic of Kenya for the Promotion and Protection of Investment, signed 28 August 2016, entered into force 14 September 2017, Art. 5(1):

> Each Contracting Party shall in its Area accord to investments of investors of the other Contracting Party fair and equitable treatment and full protection and security in accordance with customary international law. Note: This paragraph prescribes the customary international law minimum standard of treatment of aliens as the minimum standard of treatment to be afforded to investments of investors of the other Contracting Party. The concepts of "fair and equitable treatment" and "full protection and security" do not require treatment in addition to or beyond that which is required by the customary international law minimum standard of treatment of aliens and do not create additional substantive rights. A determination that there has been a breach of another provision of this Agreement, or of a separate international agreement, does not establish that there has been a breach of this paragraph.

Note also in this regard the FET clause in the Association of South East Asian Nations (ASEAN) Comprehensive Investment Agreement, signed 26 February 2009, entered into force 24 February 2012, which identifies FET claims with denial of justice claims. ACIA Art. 11(2)(a) provides: 'For greater certainty: fair and equitable treatment requires each Member State not to deny justice in any legal or administrative proceedings in accordance with the principle of due process'.

[68] *Desert Line* v. *Yemen* Award, paras. 179–94; *Suez,* v. *Argentina* Decision on Liability, paras. 241–2.

[69] *CMS* v. *Argentina* Award, paras. 273–81; *Sempra Energy* v. *Argentina* Award, paras. 303–4; *EDF* v. *Argentina* Award, paras. 1004–5.

[70] *Walter Bau* v. *Thailand* Award, para. 12.1.

Furthermore, as set out in Chapter 3, Section 3.4, there is a variety of contractual breaches that implicate a discrete component of FET, giving rise to a finding of State responsibility. Unlike in a claim for unlawful expropriation under general international law, an investor need not show a substantial deprivation of rights, which is usually only brought about by a cancelled contract. Cancelled investment contracts form a segment of contract-based FET claims, but the bulk of contract-based FET claims consist of contractual interference not amounting to cancellation. Protection via an FET clause in an investment treaty is therefore capable of accommodating more configurations of contractual disputes than in a claim for unlawful expropriation.

7.4.4 *Protection via an Expropriation Clause in an Investment Treaty*

As set out in Chapter 4, Section 4.2.2, an investment contract can be an object of expropriation if it falls within the treaty definition of a protected investment. It is therefore possible that contractual rights that do not qualify as property and are unable to substantiate an unlawful expropriation claim under general international law are expropriable under investment treaty law. Yet, as demonstrated in Chapter 6, Section 6.2.1.2, there are occasions where the contract-as-property equation is introduced to investment treaty arbitrations, subjecting investment contract protection to the expropriation regime under general international law. When full stabilisation of investment treaty law by general international law occurs, seeking investment contract protection by establishing the expropriation of alien property or by invoking an expropriation clause in an investment treaty yields the same result. Moreover, even if the contract-as-property equation is satisfied, usually only cancelled contracts evince the existence of an expropriation. The more promising contract-based expropriation claims in investment treaty arbitrations are those involving cancelled contracts bearing proprietary features. In comparison, promising contract-based FET claims come in more shapes and sizes, since there is no need to satisfy any precondition for the infringement of a discrete component of FET, or assimilate the effects of various degrees of contractual interference to cancellation.

7.4.5 *Protection via an Umbrella Clause in an Investment Treaty*

Unlike FET and expropriation clauses, umbrella clauses are not ubiquitous investment treaty clauses. Moreover, their omission from newer investment treaties suggests that they are in the process of being phased out. Investment contract protection through the invocation of an archetypal umbrella clause may be on course for gradual demise.

At present though and as set out in Chapter 5, Section 5.3, archetypal umbrella clauses are believed to protect investment contracts in one of three ways. Arbitral *jurisprudence* is divided over protection through the enforcement of the proper law of the investment contract on the host State (no internationalisation), protection through the elevation of contractual breaches *iure imperii* to treaty breaches (partial internationalisation) and protection through the conversion of all contractual breaches into treaty breaches (full internationalisation). Given the strong and enduring resistance among most arbitral tribunals towards full umbrella clause internationalisation, claimant investors are likelier to face arbitral rulings that an umbrella does not internationalise, or only partially internationalises an investment contract. The engagement of State responsibility for breaching an investment contract will be highly exceptional in the former scenario, and only possible in the latter scenario if the breach is deemed to have been carried out in the host State's sovereign capacity. In comparison to contract-based umbrella clause claims, contract-based FET claims have the benefit of an evolving but stabilised, rather than a deeply divided, body of legal content. And although the future possibility of arbitral tribunals adopting an adventurous interpretation of FET cannot be ruled out, arbitral activism is minimised by greater recognition of the rules of treaty interpretation and greater precision in treaty drafting.[71]

The ongoing uncertainty over the character of protection conferred on investment contracts by umbrella clauses is compounded by the difficulty that arbitral tribunals in favour of partial internationalisation experience when applying the *iure gestionis–iure imperii* distinction to contract-based umbrella clause claims.[72] This distinction was developed in the context of defining the jurisdictional immunities of States in foreign courts. Legislation in many countries provide that the commercial activities or transactions of States do not benefit from jurisdictional immunity.[73] But national courts find it difficult to distinguish commercial acts from sovereign acts for the purpose of denying or awarding jurisdictional

---

[71] See discussion at Chapter 6, Section 6.3.
[72] *Sempra* v. *Argentina* Award, para. 311.
[73] See for instance UK State Immunity Act 1978, Section 3; US Federal Sovereign Immunities Act 1978, Section 1603; Australia Foreign States Immunities Act 1985, Section 11; Singapore State Immunity Act, Section 5.

immunity.[74] The *iure gestionis–iure imperii* distinction has also been heavily criticised as a poor analytical tool for State immunity.[75] While this distinction has been adopted by some tribunals for contract-based FET claims, it has never been considered pivotal to a finding of FET violation.[76] Seeking investment contract protection under an FET clause instead of an umbrella clause avoids the contrived application of the *iure gestionis–iure imperii* distinction to contractual breaches, many categories of which can be undertaken by both sovereign and private contracting parties.

7.5   Conclusion

Regardless of their relative success rates, FET claims are better suited to investment contract protection than other avenues for engaging host State responsibility. This chapter discerned three reasons that give FET claims an edge. First, FET clauses, unlike recourse to the general or treaty regime on expropriation, do not oblige or invite the prioritisation of certain types of investment contracts or contractual rights (property-like) over others (non-property-like). They focus the inquiry on the conduct of the host State when breaching the contract, and by doing do, give investment contracts situated in the grey expanse between property and non-property the benefit of the doubt of protection. Second, FET clauses, unlike umbrella clauses interpreted as tools of partial internationalisation, do not call for the prioritisation of contractual breaches committed in a sovereign capacity over those committed in a non-sovereign capacity. Although expropriations can only be carried out by a State acting in its sovereign capacity, hence a need to establish *acta iure imperii* unlawful expropriation claims,[77] most contractual breaches, even cancellations, do not fall within the exclusive competence of the investor or the host State. Distinguishing *acta iure*

---

[74] See for instance *Playa Larga* v. *I Congreso del Partido* [1981] 1 AC 244, p. 264; for a detailed critique of the case, see Crawford, 'International Law and Foreign Sovereigns', p. 74 at 98–102; see also J. P. Grant and J. C. Barker (eds.), 'Harvard Research in International Law' (1932) 26 AJIL Supplement Part III, 609–31; and S. Sucharitkul, 'Fourth Report on Jurisdictional Immunities of States and Their Property' (31 March 1982), UN Doc. A/CN4/357, pp. 208–22.

[75] Lauterpacht, 'The Problem of Jurisdictional Immunities of Foreign States', p. 220 at 222 and 224; Koskenniemi, *From Apology to Utopia*, pp. 488–9; see also Dissenting Opinions of Judges Yusuf, para. 25 and Trindade, para. 171, 177 in *Jurisdictional Immunities of the State (Germany* v. *Italy: Greece intervening)* (Judgment) [2012] ICJ Rep 99; cf. ILC, 'Draft Articles on Jurisdictional Immunities of States and Their Property, with Commentaries' (1991), *Yearbook of the International Law Commission*, vol. II, Part Two, p. 20.

[76] See discussion at Chapter 3, Section 3.4.3.

[77] See discussion at Chapter 4, Section 3.4.3.

gestionis from *acta iure imperii* in this context is not only difficult but also artificial. Although there is support for applying the *iure gestionis–iure imperii* distinction to ascertain the engagement of State responsibility in contractual disputes,[78] FET clauses, both old and new, do not limit the violation of a component of FET to contractual breaches committed in a sovereign capacity. Third and finally, the content of FET is neither bound by a closed list of conditions for illegality unlike the content of expropriation, nor beset by conflicting schools of thought unlike the content on contractual protection under umbrella clauses. Its capacity for incremental evolution, while staying grounded to the core standard of treatment, allows it to adapt to sanction newer ways of interfering with contractual rights.

The future of international investment contract claims is one where contract-based FET claims will feature prominently, if not take centre stage. Development in the content of FET is likely to contribute significantly to further development of the law of State responsibility for breaches of investment contracts.

---

[78] See discussion at Chapter 1, Section 1.3.3.3.

Conclusion

The law of State responsibility for breaches of investment contracts is the product of power, of adaptation, of innovation and of policy. Its origins can be traced back to the era of diplomatic protection, where States delegated the power to decide contractual disputes between nationals and host States to independent arbitral tribunals known as Mixed Claims Commissions. Legal content generated by the Commissions' arbitral awards became an early source of general principles on contractual protection, paving the way for arbitral awards rendered by other tribunals tasked with impartial adjudication to become the principal source of international law on investment contract protection. Absent guidance from State practice coalescing into a bespoke body of international law, pinpointing when and where State responsibility can be engaged for a breach of contract, arbitral tribunals turned to the rules governing alien and alien property protection, adapting them for contractual protection. When guidance appeared in investment treaties, arbitral tribunals became innovative treaty interpreters, spinning laconic treaty provisions into a detailed and variegated body of investment treaty law. The advancement made on imparting substance to an emerging international law on investment contract protection is nonetheless subject to fluctuations in State policy, which can vacillate from greater to lesser protection for investment contracts from host State interference and back, altering existing legal content. Investment contract protection is a unique branch of the law of State responsibility, whose journey to identifiable content merits an extended study.

In the course of narrating this journey, three characteristics of the law of State responsibility for breaches of investment contracts stood out. The first characteristic, as indicated in the opening paragraph, is the prominence of arbitral awards as a source of international law. The potential disorderliness of a source of law, untouched by any formal or informal system of binding precedent, was tempered by the higher persuasive value of arbitral awards boasting superior authors and reasoning, as well as the tendency of arbitral tribunals to gravitate towards a prevailing legal solution for their legal problem. It was therefore possible to distil shared content of an international law on investment contract protection from arbitral *jurisprudence*, albeit *jurisprudence* sporting a margin of differentiation and possibly never converging towards perfect uniformity. The second characteristic is its interconnected two-part structure, with the general international law on investment contract protection supplying the foundational content of and stabilising investment treaty law. This structure is evident in the broad but not necessarily exact alignment between general and specific law on the expropriation and objective treatment of investment contracts. It explains why the absence of foundational content on absolute contractual protection leaves attempts at full umbrella clause internationalisation scrabbling for purchase and acceptance. And it embraces the reality that both the enterprise and the foundational content of investment contract protection will endure beyond the availability of treaty safeguards. The third characteristic is the spectre of internationalisation that hovers at the outer limits of the international law on investment contract protection. At odds with the foundational content of investment contract protection which strongly recommends qualified protection, and propped up by obsolete or flawed theories, the assimilation of contractual obligations to international obligations survives through sheer conviction that absolute protection, being the best form of protection for investment contracts, is achievable.

The resulting law is undoubtedly distinctive but also fraught with tension. Tension over arbitral awards supplanting more familiar sources of international law as the main content supplier for investment contract protection, casting a pall over the legitimacy of a body of international law authored by arbitrators, not States. Tension over the gravitational pull of general international law on investment treaty law which appears stronger in some respects and weaker in others, complicating the duty of arbitral tribunals to interpret investment treaty provisions in light of relevant rules of international law on investment contract protection. Tension between the majority proponents of qualified contractual protection under both general international law and investment treaty law, and the minority proponents of absolute contractual protection, compelling the constant reanimation of a stale debate that has long depleted its intellectual capital. These tensions underscore what the law of State responsibility says about investment contract protection.

The law at present tells us that there are discrete causes of action for engaging a host State's international responsibility for breaching an investment contract, each with its own identifiable legal content. This monograph identified five main causes of action and their content: two under general international law and three under investment treaty law.

The first cause of action is violation of the core standard for contractual protection. This standard is derived from the minimum standard of treatment of aliens pegged at a denial of justice. The core standard for contractual protection is not an exact replica of the minimum standard for alien protection. This is because their respective components for a denial of justice are different, with the components of MST for aliens articulated in the *Neer Claim*, and those of the core standard of treatment for contracts distilled from other arbitral awards. To violate the core standard, contractual breaches have to evince arbitrariness, or, when committed in a sovereign capacity, evince disrespect for due process.

The second cause of action is unlawful expropriation under general international law. Developed to protect alien property, this head of protection required alien contracts to be assimilated to alien property. A breach of contract is internationally wrongful if the breach involved or amounted to a cancelled contract possessing proprietary features, and was unaccompanied by the payment of compensation, or the pursuit of a public purpose, or compliance with due process by the host State.

The third cause of action is violation of the fair and equitable treatment standard, which is ubiquitous in investment treaties. FET clauses assume one of three main forms. They can be laconic and promise FET without defining FET, or they can expressly equate FET with MST, or they can contain an enumerative list of components that trigger FET violation and which typically include the components or arbitrariness and unmet due process that trigger core standard violation. Clauses that bind FET to MST reflect the core standard of treatment established by *Neer*'s contract-oriented affiliates, since *Neer*'s MST components were articulated with alien protection, not contractual protection, in mind. Other types of FET clauses preserve the core standard of treatment, without necessarily limiting FET violations to core standard violations. Depending on the form of the applicable FET clause, a breach of contract falls short of FET if its commission was arbitrary, a snub at due process, an act of bad faith, abusive, and may fall short if it is a frustration of investor expectations induced by specific undertakings given by the host State.

The fourth cause of action is unlawful expropriation under investment treaty law. Investment treaties often define rights arising from contracts as protected investments which can form the object of an expropriation. Therefore, a breach of contract can form the basis of an unlawful expropriation treaty claim so long as the contract is a protected investment, the investor has been substantially deprived of its contractual rights or benefits, and cumulative treaty conditions for a lawful expropriation, which mirror the conditions under general international law, have not been satisfied.

The fifth and final cause of action is violation of an umbrella clause. Arbitral *jurisprudence* is deeply divided on how umbrella clauses protect investment contracts. One interpretive approach obtains permission from umbrella clauses to judge liability for the breach in accordance with the proper law of the contract; another elevates contractual breaches *iure imperii* to umbrella clause violations; and yet another elevates all contractual breaches to umbrella clause violations. The last approach internationalises investment contracts, turning umbrella clauses into symbols of absolute contractual protection. The likelihood of engagement of State responsibility for the violation of an umbrella clause depends on whether treaty interpreters perceive umbrella clauses as enabling full internationalisation, partial internationalisation or no internationalisation whatsoever.

The law at present also tells us that although the engagement of State responsibility is unconcerned with whether the act complained of was committed in the injuring State's sovereign or non-sovereign capacity, the *iure gestionis–iure imperii* distinction is pervasive in investment contract protection.

Contractual breaches *iure imperii* complement the due process component of the core standard of treatment, are a precondition to the validity of unlawful expropriation claims, are deemed relevant to a finding of FET violation, and, for those in favour of partial umbrella clause internationalisation, are the only genre of breach that amounts to a treaty violation. In a simple scenario where States govern and the governed trade, distinguishing acts committed in a State's sovereign capacity from those committed in a non-sovereign capacity can be straightforward. The termination of a concession by legislation, a sovereign prerogative which no private individual trader can exercise, for example, is indisputably *acta iure imperii*. In modern-day reality, States are not solely preoccupied with the business of governing. States also participate in commercial life in myriad forms ranging from sovereign wealth funds to State-owned and State-linked companies. A State contracting party seeking the expulsion of the foreign investor for the latter's inadequate contractual performance, and enforcing the expulsion with a military presence, does not appear to have acted in a purely non-sovereign or purely sovereign capacity, but a mix of both. The *iure gestionis–iure imperii* distinction is easy enough to understand, but with modern realities, is becoming increasingly difficult to apply.

Apart from the difficulty of its application, the distinction is only helpful to unlawful expropriation claims. As expropriation is by definition a sovereign act, a breach of contract can only qualify as expropriatory if it could not have been committed within the contractual framework. The distinction is at best supplementary to determinations of violations of the core standard of treatment, because it is the absence of due process, not *acta iure imperii*, that is the aggravating circumstance tipping conduct into internationally wrongful territory. The distinction is not a recognised component of FET, rendering its appearance in determinations on FET violations superfluous. So long as a breach of contract implicates a recognised component of FET like non-arbitrariness or due process, State responsibility can be engaged for a violation of FET. Finally, the distinction limits umbrella clause protection to breaches *iure imperii* when such clauses, wherever one stands on internationalisation, address all breaches. Applying the distinction to umbrella clause claims rewrites the scope of umbrella clause protection for investment contracts. Path dependency may prolong reliance on the *iure gestionis–iure imperii* distinction in the context of investment contract protection, but reason urges reconsideration.

The law of State responsibility for breaches of investment contracts has been hidden from view for far too long. This monograph is a first attempt at coaxing this unique branch of international law into the open, with the hope that exposure will augur informed reflection, application and development.

BIBLIOGRAPHY

Books

Ackerman, B., *Private Property and the Constitution* (New Haven, CT: Yale University Press, 1977).

Allot, P., *State Responsibility: A Dangerous Fiction* (London: British Institute of International and Comparative Law, 1987).

Alvik, I., *Contracting with Sovereignty* (Oxford: Hart Publishing, 2011).

Bernstein, D., *Rehabilitating Lochner: Defending Individual Rights against Progressive Reform* (Chicago, IL: University of Chicago Press, 2011).

Bjorklund, A. (ed.), *Yearbook on International Investment Law and Policy 2012–2013* (Oxford: Oxford University Press, 2013).

Borchard, E. M., *The Diplomatic Protection of Citizens Abroad; or, The Law of International Claims* (Cleveland, OH: Banks Law Publishing, 1915).

Breitenmoser, S., B. Ehrenzeller, and M. Sassoli (eds.), *Human Rights, Democracy and the Rule of Law: Liber Amicorum Luzius Wildhaber* (Baden-Baden: Nomos, 2007).

Brown, C., *A Common Law of International Adjudication* (Oxford: Oxford University Press, 2007).

  (ed.), *Oxford Commentaries on International Law: Commentaries on Selected Model Investment Treaties* (Oxford: Oxford University Press, 2013).

Cameron, P., *International Energy Investment Law: The Pursuit of Stability* (Oxford: Oxford University Press, 2010).

Cassese, A. (ed.), *Realizing Utopia: The Future of International Law* (Oxford: Oxford University Press, 2012).

Ch'en, J., *Yuan Shih-k'ai*, 2nd revd edn (Stanford, CA: Stanford University Press, 1972).

Cheng, B., *General Principles of Law as Applied by International Courts and Tribunals* (Cambridge: Grotius Publications, 1953).

Corten, O., and P. Klein, *The Vienna Convention on the Law of Treaties: A Commentary* (Oxford: Oxford University Press, 2011), vol. I.

Crawford, J., *Brownlie's Principles of Public International Law* (Oxford: Oxford University Press, 2012).

Crawford, J., A. Pellet, and S. Olleson (eds.), *The Law of International Responsibility* (Oxford: Oxford University Press, 2010).

D'Amato, A. (ed.), *International Law Anthology* (Cincinnati, OH: Anderson Publishing, 1994).

d'Aspremont, J., *Formalism and the Sources of International Law: A Theory of the Ascertainment of Legal Rules* (Oxford: Oxford University Press, 2011).

De Lapradelle, A., and N. Politis, *Recueil des Arbitrages Internationaux* (Paris: Pedone, 1905).

Diehl, A., *The Core Standard of International Investment Protection: Fair and Equitable Treatment* (The Hague: Kluwer Law International, 2012).

Diehl, P. F., and G. Goertz, *War and Peace in International Rivalry* (Ann Arbor, MI: University of Michigan Press, 2000).

Dolzer, R., and C. Schreuer, *Principles of International Investment Law*, 2nd edn (Oxford: Oxford University Press, 2012).

Dornbusch, R., *Keys to Prosperity: Free Markets, Sound Money, and a Bit of Luck* (Cambridge, MA: MIT Press, 2000).

Douglas, Z., *The International Law on Investment Claims* (Cambridge: Cambridge University Press, 2012).

Douglas, Z., J. Pauwelyn, and J. E. Viñuales (eds.), *The Foundations of International Investment Law: Bringing Theory into Practice* (Oxford: Oxford University Press, 2014).

Dugan, C. F., Wallace, D. Jr., Rubins, N., and Sabahi, B., *Investor-State Arbitration* (Oxford: Oxford University Press, 2008).

Dunn, P. S., *The Protection of Nationals: A Study in the Application of International Law* (Baltimore, MD: The Johns Hopkins Press, 1932).

   The Diplomatic Protection of Americans in Mexico (New York, NY: Columbia University Press, 1933).

Eagleton, C., *The Responsibility of States in International Law* (New York, NY: New York University Press, 1928).

Echandi, R., and P. Sauvé (eds.), *Prospects in International Investment Law and Policy* (Cambridge: Cambridge University Press, 2013).

Fabre-Magnan, M., *Droit des Obligations 2: Responsabilité Civile et Quasi-Contrats*, 3rd edn (Paris: Presses Universitaires de France, 2013).

   Droit des Obligations 1: Contrat et Engagement Unilatéral, 4th edn (Paris: Presses Universitaires de France, 2016).

Feis, H., *Europe, The World's Banker, 1870–1914* (New Haven, CT: Yale University Press, 1930).

Finnemore, M., *The Purpose of Intervention: Changing Beliefs about the Use of Force* (Ithaca, NY: Cornell University Press, 2004).

Franck, T. M., *The Power of Legitimacy among Nations* (Oxford: Oxford University Press, 2010).

Friedmann, S., *Expropriation in International Law* (translated by I. C. Jackson) (London: Stevens & Sons, 1953).

Friedmann, W., *The Changing Structure of International Law* (London: Stevens & Sons, 1964).

Fukuyama, F., *State-Building: Governance and the World Order in the 21st Century* (Ithaca, NY: Cornell University Press, 2004).

Gaillard, E., *La Jurisprudence du CIRDI* (Paris: Pedone, 2004), vols. I and II.

Gaillard, E., and Y. Banifatemi (eds.), *Precedent in International Arbitration* (New York, NY: Juris Publishing, 2007).

Glenn, P. H., *Legal Traditions of the World: Sustainable Diversity in Law*, 5th edn (Oxford: Oxford University Press, 2014).

Guinchard, S., and T. Debard, *Lexique des Termes Juridiques 2017–2018* (Paris: Broché, 2017).

Guzman, A. T., *How International Law Works* (Oxford: Oxford University Press, 2008).

Hackworth, G. H., *Digest of International Law* (Washington, DC: Government Printing Office, 1943), vol. 5.

Hale, T., *Between Interests and Law: The Politics of Transnational Commercial Disputes* (Cambridge: Cambridge University Press, 2015).

Harding, A., *Law, Government and the Constitution in Malaysia* (The Hague: Kluwer Law International, 1996).

Hart, H. L. A., *The Concept of Law* (Oxford: Clarendon Press, 1983).

Hidayatullah, M. (Mohammed), *Right to Property and the Indian Constitution* (Calcutta: Calcutta University Press, 1983).

Hilaire, M., *International Law and the United States Military Intervention in the Western Hemisphere* (Boston, MA: Kluwer Law International, 1997).

Hobson, C. K., *The Export of Capital* (New York, NY: Macmillan, 1914).

Hoffman, A. K. (ed.), *Protection of Foreign Investments through Modern Treaty Arbitration: Diversity and Harmonisation* (Geneva: Association Suisse de l'arbitrage, 2010).

Hogan, W., and F. Sturzenegger (eds.), *The Natural Resources Trap: Private Investment without Public Commitment* (Cambridge, MA: MIT Press 2010).

Hoover, H., *1929: Containing the Public Messages, Speeches, and Statements of the President, March 4 to December 31, 1929* (Ann Arbor, MI: University of Michigan Library Press, 2005).

Horn, N., and S. M. Kröll (eds.), *Arbitrating Foreign Investment Disputes – Procedural and Substantive Legal Aspects* (The Hague: Kluwer Law International, 2004).

Huber, M., *Réclamations britanniques dans la zone espagnole du Maroc* (The Hague: Publisher not identified, 1925).

Hudson, M., *International Tribunals Past and Future* (New Haven, CT: Rumford, 1944).

Hyde, C. C., *International Law Chiefly as Interpreted and Applied by the United States*, 2nd revd edn (Boston, MA: Little, Brown and Company, 1945).

Ingram, G., *Expropriation of US Property in South America* (Santa Barbara, CA: Praeger, 1974).

Jennings, R. Y., *Collected Writings of Sir Robert Jennings* (The Hague: Kluwer Law International, 1998).

Johnston, D., *International Exploration Economics, Risk and Contract Analysis* (Tulsa, OK: PennWell Corporation, 2003).

Kahn, P., and T. Wälde (eds.), *New Aspects of International Investment Law* (The Hague: Martinus Nijhoff, 2007).

Kelsen, H., *Principles of International Law*, 2nd edn (New York, NY: Holt, Rinehart and Winston, 1967).

Kjos, H. E., *Applicable Law in Investor-State Arbitration: The Interplay between National and International Law* (Oxford: Oxford University Press, 2013).

Kläger, R., *Fair and Equitable Treatment International Investment Law* (Cambridge: Cambridge University Press, 2011).

Koskenniemi, M., *From Apology to Utopia* (Cambridge: Cambridge University Press, 2005).

Kulick, A., *Global Public Interest in International Investment Law* (Cambridge: Cambridge University Press, 2012).

Kuusi, J., *The Host State and the Transnational Corporation* (London: Saxon House, 1976).

La Fontaine, H. (ed.), *Pasicrisie Internationale: Histoire Documentaire des Arbitrages Internationaux* (Paris: Stampfli & Cie, 1902).

Lauterpacht, H., *Private Law Sources and Analogies of International Law* (London: Longmans, 1927).

   The Development of International Law by the International Court (London: Stevens & Sons, 1958).

Law, J. (ed.), *A Dictionary of Law*, 8th edn (Oxford: Oxford University Press, 2015).

Lawson, F. H., and B. Rudden, *The Law of Property*, 3rd edn, (Oxford: Clarendon, 2002).

Leben, C., *The Advancement of International Law* (Oxford: Hart, 2010).

Lehoucq, F., *The Politics of Modern Central America: Civil War, Democratization, and Underdevelopment* (New York, NY: Cambridge University Press, 2012).

Lillich, R. B. (ed.), *International Law of State Responsibility for Injuries to Aliens* (Virginia: University Press of Virginia, 1983).

Lillich, R. B., and D. B. Magraw (eds.), *The Iran-United States Claims Tribunal: Its Contribution to the Law of State Responsibility* (New York, NY: Transnational Publishers, 1998).

Lim, C. L., J. Ho, and M. Paparinskis, *International Investment Law and Arbitration: Commentary, Awards and Other Materials* (Cambridge: Cambridge University Press, 2018).

Lipson, C., *Standing Guard: Protecting Foreign Capital in the Nineteenth and Twentieth Centuries* (Berkeley, CA: University of California Press, 1985).

Long, M., Weil, P., Braibant, G., Delvolvé, P. and Genevois, B. (eds.), *Les Grands Arrêts de la Jurisprudence Administrative*, 21st edn (Paris: Dalloz, 2017).

Lorca, A. B., *Mestizo International Law: A Global Intellectual History 1842–1933* (Cambridge: Cambridge University Press, 2014).

Loveman, B., *No Higher Law: American Foreign Policy and the Western Hemisphere since 1776* (Chapel Hill, NC: University of North Carolina, 2010).

Lyttleton, A., A. M. Ashmore, and R. K. Loveday, *Report of the Transvaal Concessions Commission (19 April 1901)* (London: Wyman & Sons, 1901).

Malatesta, A., and R. Sali (eds.), *The Rise of Transparency in International Arbitration* (New York, NY: Juris Publishing, 2013).

Marichal, C., *A Century of Debt Crises in Latin America: From Independence to the Great Depression, 1820–1930* (Princeton, NJ: Princeton University Press, 1989).

Maurer, N., *The Empire Trap* (Princeton, NJ: Princeton University Press, 2013).

McLachlan, C., L. Shore, and M. Weiniger, *International Investment Arbitration – Substantive Principles* (Oxford: Oxford University Press, 2007).

McNair, A., *International Law Opinions* (Cambridge: Cambridge University Press, 1956).

Merryman, J. H., and R. Pérez-Perdomo, *The Civil Law Tradition: An Introduction to the Legal Systems of Europe and Latin America*, 3rd edn (Stanford, CA: Stanford University Press, 2007).

Montt, S., *State Liability in Investment Treaty Arbitration: Global Constitutional and Administrative Law in the BIT Generation* (Oxford: Hart, 2009).

Moore, J. B., *A Digest of International Law in Six Volumes* (Washington, DC: Government Printing Press, 1906).

Morgenthau, H., *Politics among Nations: The Struggle for Power and Peace*, 1st edn (New York, NY: A. A. Knopf, 1948).

Politics among Nations: The Struggle for Power and Peace (revised by K. W. Thompson and W. D. Clinton), 7th edn (New York, NY: McGraw-Hill, 2006).

Muchlinski, P., *Multinational Enterprises and the Law* (Oxford: Blackwell, 1995).

Nijman, J., and A. Nollkaemper (eds.), *New Perspectives on the Divide between National and International Law* (Oxford: Oxford University Press, 2007).

O'Keeffe, D., and H. G. Schermers (eds.), *Essays in European Law and Integration* (Deventer: Kluwer, 1982).

Paparinskis, M., *The International Minimum Standard and Fair and Equitable Treatment* (Oxford: Oxford University Press, 2013).

Paulsson, J., *Denial of Justice in International Law* (Cambridge: Cambridge University Press, 2005).

Pausanias, *Description of Greece* (translated by W. H. S. Jones), revd edn (Cambridge, MA: Harvard University Press, 1918).

Penner, J., *The Idea of Property in Law* (Oxford: Oxford University Press, 2000).

Peter, W., *Arbitration and Renegotiation of International Investment Agreements* (The Hague: Kluwer Law International, 1995).

Picker, C. B., I. D. Bunn, and D. W. Arner (eds.), *International Economic Law: The State and Future of the Discipline* (Oxford and Portland, OR: Hart, 2008).

Platt, D. C. M., *Finance, Trade, and Politics in British Foreign Policy 1815–1914* (Gloucestershire: Clarendon Press, 1968).

Posner, R., *Economic Analysis of Law*, 9th edn (The Hague: Wolters Kluwer, 2014).

Radin, M. J., *Reinterpreting Property* (Chicago, IL: University of Chicago Press, 1993).

Ragazzi, M. (ed.), *International Responsibility Today: Essays in Honour of Oscar Schachter* (Leiden: Martinus Nijhoff, 2005).

Ralston, J. H., *Venezuelan Arbitrations of 1903* (Washington, DC: Government Printing Office, 1904).

  Report of French-Venezuelan Mixed Claims Commission of 1902 (Washington, DC: Government Printing Press, 1906).

Rogers, C. A., and R. P. Alford, *The Future of Investment Arbitration* (Oxford: Oxford University Press, 2009).

Rosenne, S. (ed.), *Conference for the Codification of International Law [1930]* (New York, NY: Oceana Publications, 1975).

Rousseau, C. E. (ed.), *Méelanges Offerts à Charles Rousseau* (Paris: Pedone, 1974).

Sabahi, B., *Compensation and Restitution in Investor-State Arbitration: Principles and Practice* (Oxford: Oxford University Press, 2011).

Salacuse, J. W., *The Law of Investment Treaties* (Oxford: Oxford University Press, 2010).

  The Three Laws of International Investment – National, Contractual, and International Frameworks for Foreign Capital (Oxford: Oxford University Press, 2013).

Sasson, M., *Substantive Law in Investment Treaty Arbitration – The Unsettled Relationship between International and Municipal Law* (The Hague: Kluwer, 2010).

Schill, S. (ed.), *International Investment Law and Comparative Public Law* (Oxford: Oxford University Press, 2010).

Schwebel, S. M. (ed.), *Justice in International Law: Selected Writings of Stephen M. Schwebel* (Cambridge: Grotius, 1994).

Shahabuddeen, M., *Precedent in the World Court* (Cambridge: Cambridge University Press, 1996).

Shaw, M. N., *International Law*, 6th edn (Cambridge: Cambridge University Press, 2008).

Shea, D. R., *The Calvo Clause: A Problem of Inter-American and International Law and Diplomacy* (Minneapolis, MN: University of Minnesota Press, 1955).

Shihata, I. F. (ed.), *The World Bank in a Changing World* (Dordrecht: Martinus Nijhoff, 1995), vol. 2.

Sidak, J. G., and D. F. Spulber, *Deregulatory Takings and the Regulatory Contract* (Cambridge: Cambridge University Press, 1997).

Silvestre, R., and J. Martha, *The Financial Obligation in International Law* (Oxford: Oxford University Press, 2015).

Simpson, A. W. B., *A History of the Land Law*, 2nd edn (Oxford: Oxford University Press, 1986).

Sørensen, M. (ed.), *Manual of Public International Law* (London: Macmillan, 1968).

Sornarajah, M., *International Commercial Arbitration: The Problem of State Contracts* (Singapore: Longman, 1990).

The International Law on Foreign Investment, 4th edn (Cambridge: Cambridge University Press, 2017).

Southwestern Legal Foundation, International and Comparative Law Center, *Rights and Duties of Private Investors Abroad* (Albany, NY: Matthew Bender, 1965).

Sureda, A. R., *Investment Treaty Arbitration – Judging under Uncertainty* (Cambridge: Cambridge University Press, 2012).

Thirlway, H., *The Sources of International Law* (Oxford: Oxford University Press, 2014).

Tomz, M., *Reputation and International Cooperation: Sovereign Debt across Three Centuries* (Princeton, NJ: Princeton University Press, 2007).

Torres-Rivas, E., *History and Society in Central America* (translated by D. Sullivan-González) (Austin, TX: University of Texas Press, 1993).

Trinh, H. Y., *The Interpretation of Investment Treaties* (The Hague: Brill, 2014).

Tudor, I., *The Fair and Equitable Treatment Standard in the International Law of Foreign Investment* (Oxford: Oxford University Press, 2008).

Twining, W. (ed.), *Legal Theory and Common Law* (Oxford: Basil Blackwell, 1986).

UNCTAD, *Bilateral Investment Treaties 1995–2006: Trends in Investment Rulemaking* (New York, NY and Geneva: United Nations, 2007).

Van den Berg, A. J. (ed.), *International Arbitration 2006: Back to Basics? ICCA Congress Series* (The Hague: Kluwer Law International, 2007), vol. 13.

(ed.), *50 Years of the New York Convention: ICCA International Arbitration Conference* (The Hague: Kluwer Law International, 2009).

Van der Walt, A. J., *Constitutional Property Clauses – A Comparative Analysis* (South Africa: Juta & Co., 1999).

Property and Constitution (Pretoria: Pretoria University Law Press, 2012).

Van Harten, G., *Investment Treaty Arbitration and Public Law* (Oxford: Oxford University Press, 2007).

Veeser, C., *A World Safe for Capitalism* (New York, NY: Columbia University Press, 2007).

Venzke, I., *How Interpretation Makes International Law – On Semantic Change and Normative Twists* (Oxford: Oxford University Press, 2012).

Von Bernstorff, J., *The Public International Law Theory of Hans Kelsen* (Cambridge: Cambridge University Press, 2010).

Waibel, M., *Sovereign Defaults before International Courts and Tribunals* (Cambridge: Cambridge University Press, 2011).

Waibel, M., Kaushal, A., Chung, K.-H. and Balchin, C. (eds.), *The Backlash against Investment Arbitration* (Alphen aan den Rijn: Kluwer Law International, 2010).

Weil, P., *Mélanges Offerts A Paul Reuter – Le Droit International: Unité Et Diversité* (Paris: Pedone, 1981).

Weiler, T. (ed.), *International Investment Law and Arbitration: Leading Cases from the ICSID, NAFTA, Bilateral Treaties and Customary International Law* (London: Cameron May, 2005).

Wells, L. T., and R. Ahmed, *Making Foreign Investment Safe: Property Rights and National Sovereignty* (Oxford: Oxford University Press, 2007).

Wharton, F., *A Digest of the International Law of the United States in Three Volumes* (Washington, DC: Government Printing Press, 1886).

White, G., *Nationalisation of Foreign Property* (London: Stevens & Sons, 1961).

Wistrich, R. S., *Who's Who in Nazi Germany* (London: Routledge, 2002).

Wortley, B. A., *Expropriation in Public International Law* (Cambridge: Cambridge University Press, 1959).

Zimmerman, A., Zimmermann, A., Oellers-Frahm, K., Tomuschat, C. and Tams, C. J. (eds.), *The Statute of the International Court of Justice: A Commentary*, 2nd edn (Oxford: Oxford University Press, 2012).

Book Chapters

Alexandrov, S., 'Breaches of Contract and Breaches of Treaty – The Jurisdiction of Treaty-based Arbitration Tribunals to Decide Breach of Contract Claims in *SGS* v. *Pakistan* and *SGS* v. *Philippines*' in T. Weiler (ed.), *International Investment Law and Arbitration: Leading Cases from the ICSID, NAFTA, Bilateral Treaties and Customary International Law* (London: Cameron May, 2005), p. 555.

Bjorklund, A., 'Investment Treaty Arbitral Decisions as Jurisprudence Constante' in C. B. Picker, I. D. Bunn, and D. W. Arner (eds.), *International Economic Law: The State and Future of the Discipline* (Oxford and Portland, OR: Hart, 2008), p. 265.

Cassin, R., and M. Waline, 'Préface' in M. Long, P. Weil, G. Braibant, P. Delvolvé and B. Genevois (eds.), *Les Grands Arrêts de la Jurisprudence Administrative*, 21st edn (Paris: Dalloz, 2017), pp. VI–VII.

Chinkin, C., 'Monism and Dualism: The Impact of Private Authority on the Dichotomy between National and International Law' in J. Nijman and A. Nollkaemper (eds.), *New Perspectives on the Divide between National and International Law* (Oxford: Oxford University Press, 2007), p. 135.

Cotterrell, R., 'The Law of Property and Legal Theory' in W. Twining (ed.), *Legal Theory and Common Law* (Oxford: Basil Blackwell, 1986), p. 81.

Crawford, J., 'Similarity of Issues in Disputes Arising under the Same or Similarly Drafted Investment Treaties' in E. Gaillard and Y. Banifatemi (eds.), *Precedent in International Arbitration* (New York, NY: Juris Publishing, 2007), p. 97.

D'Amato, A., 'Treaty-Based Rules of Custom' in A. D'Amato (ed.), *International Law Anthology* (Cincinnati, OH: Anderson Publishing, 1994).

Douglas, Z., 'Property, Investment and the Scope of Investment Protection Obligations' in Z. Douglas, J. Pauwelyn, and J. E. Viñuales (eds.), *The Foundations of International Investment Law: Bringing Theory into Practice* (Oxford: Oxford University Press, 2014), p. 363.

Douglas, Z., and J. Paulsson, 'Indirect Expropriation in Investment Treaty Arbitrations' in H. Horn and S. M. Kröll (eds.), *Arbitrating Foreign Investment Disputes – Procedural and Substantive Legal Aspects* (The Hague: Kluwer Law International, 2004), p. 145.

Engel, E., and R. Fischer, 'Optimal Resource Extraction Contracts under Threat of Expropriation' in W. Hogan and F. Sturzenegger (eds.), *The Natural Resources Trap – Private Investment without Public Commitment* (Cambridge, MA: MIT Press, 2010), p. 161.

Ho, J., 'Investment Contracts and Internationalisation' in C. L. Lim, J. Ho, and M. Paparinskis (eds.), *International Investment Law and Arbitration: Commentary, Awards and Other Materials* (Cambridge: Cambridge University Press, 2018), p. 37.

Jennings, R. Y., 'Rules Governing Contracts between States and Foreign Nationals' in Southwestern Legal Foundation. International and Comparative Law Center, *Rights and Duties of Private Investors Abroad* (Albany, NY: Matthew Bender, 1965), p. 123.

Johnson, L., and L. Sachs, 'International Investment Agreements, 2011–2012: A Review of Trends and New Approaches' in A. Bjorklund (ed.), *Yearbook on International Investment Law and Policy 2012–2013* (Oxford: Oxford University Press, 2013), p. 219.

Kessedjian, C., 'To Give or Not to Give Precedential Value to Investment Arbitration Awards?' in C. A. Rogers and R. P. Alford (eds.), *The Future of Investment Arbitration* (Oxford: Oxford University Press, 2009), p. 43.

Kingsbury, B., and S. Schill, 'Investor-State Arbitration as Governance: Fair and Equitable Treatment, Proportionality and the Emerging Global Administrative Law' in A. J. van den Berg (ed.), *50 Years of the New York Convention: ICCA International Arbitration Conference* (The Hague: Kluwer Law International, 2009), p. 5.

Koopmans, T., 'Stare Decisis in European Law' in D. O'Keeffe and H. G. Schermers (eds.), *Essays in European Law and Integration* (Deventer: Kluwer, 1982), p. 11.

Koskenniemi, M., 'Doctrines of State Responsibility' in J. Crawford, A. Pellet, and S. Olleson (eds.), *The Law of International Responsibility* (Oxford: Oxford University Press, 2010), p. 45.

Kreindler, R., 'The Law Applicable to International Investment Disputes' in N. Horn and S. M. Kröll (eds.), *Arbitrating Foreign Investment Disputes, Procedural and Substantive Legal Aspects* (The Hague: Kluwer Law International, 2004), p. 401.

Kriebaum, U., and C. Schreuer, 'The Concept of Property in Human Rights Law and International Investment Law' in S. Breitenmoser, B. Ehrenzeller, and

M. Sassoli (eds.), *Human Rights, Democracy and the Rule of Law: Liber Amicorum Luzius Wildhaber* (Baden-Baden: Nomos, 2007), p. 1.

Kröll, S. M., 'The Renegotiation and Adaptation of Investment Contracts' in N. Horn and S. M. Kröll (eds.), *Arbitrating Foreign Investment Disputes – Procedural and Substantive Legal Aspects* (The Hague: Kluwer Law International, 2004), p. 425.

Lalive, P., 'The Doctrine of Acquired Rights' in Southwestern Legal Foundation. International and Comparative Law Center, *Rights and Duties of Private Investors Abroad* (Albany, NY: Matthew Bender, 1965), p. 145.

Mourre, A., 'The Case for the Publication of Arbitral Awards' in A. Malatesta and R. Sali (eds.), *The Rise of Transparency in International Arbitration* (New York, NY: Juris Publishing, 2013), p. 53.

Nelson, T. G., '"History Ain't Changed": Why Investor-State Arbitration Will Survive the "New Revolution"' in M. Waibel, A. Kaushal, K.-H. Chung, and C. Balchin (eds.), *The Backlash against Investment Arbitration* (Alphen aan den Rijn: Kluwer Law International, 2010), p. 555.

Paulsson, J., 'International Arbitration and the Generation of Legal Norms: Treaty Arbitration and International Law' in A. J. van den Berg (ed.), *International Arbitration 2006: Back to Basics? ICCA Congress Series* (The Hague: Kluwer Law International, 2007) vol. 13, p. 879.

Pechota, V., 'The Limits of International Responsibility in the Protection of Foreign Investments' in M. Ragazzi (ed.), *International Responsibility Today: Essays in Honour of Oscar Schachter* (Leiden: Martinus Nijhoff, 2005), p. 171.

Pellet, A., 'Article 38' in A. Zimmerman, K. Oellers-Frahm, C. Tomuschat, and C. J. Tams (eds.), *The Statute of the International Court of Justice: A Commentary*, 2nd edn (Oxford: Oxford University Press, 2012), p. 731.

Penner, J., 'Basic Obligations' in P. Birks (ed.), *The Classification of Obligations* (Oxford: Clarendon, 1997), p. 91.

Reisman, W. M., 'The Future of International Investment Law and Arbitration' in A. Cassese (ed.), *Realizing Utopia the Future of International Law* (Oxford: Oxford University Press, 2012), p. 275.

Renault, L., 'Préface' in A. De Lapradelle and N. Politis (eds.), *Recueil des Arbitrages Internationaux* (Paris: Pedone, 1905).

Schill, S., 'International Investment Law and Comparative Public Law – An Introduction' in S. Schill (ed.), *International Investment Law and Comparative Public Law* (Oxford: Oxford University Press, 2010), p. 3.

Schreuer, C., 'Investment Treaty Arbitration and Jurisdiction over Contract Claims – The *Vivendi I* Case Considered' in T. Weiler (ed.), *International Investment Law and Arbitration: Leading Cases from the ICSID, NAFTA, Bilateral Treaties and Customary International Law* (London: Cameron May, 2005), p. 281.

'Fair and Equitable Treatment (FET): Interactions with Other Standards' in G. Coop and C. Ribeiro (eds.), *Investment Protection and the Energy Charter Treaty* (New York, NY: JurisNet, 2008), p. 63.

'Protection against Arbitrary or Discriminatory Measures' in C. A. Rogers and R. P. Alford (eds.), *The Future of Investment Arbitration* (Oxford: Oxford University Press, 2009).

'Fair and Equitable Treatment' in A. K. Hoffman (ed.), *Protection of Foreign Investments through Modern Treaty Arbitration – Diversity and Harmonisation* (Geneva: Association Suisse de l'arbitrage, 2010), p. 125.

'Coherence and Consistency in International Investment Law' in R. Echandi and P. Sauvé (eds.), *Prospects in International Investment Law and Policy* (Cambridge: Cambridge University Press, 2013), p. 391.

Schwebel, S. M., 'On Whether the Breach by a State of a Contract with an Alien is a Breach of International Law' in S. M. Schwebel (ed.), *Justice in International Law: Selected Writings of Stephen M. Schwebel* (Cambridge: Grotius, 1994), p. 425.

Shihata, I. F., 'Applicable Law in International Arbitration: Specific Aspects in the Case of the Involvement of State Parties' in I. F. Shihata (ed.), *The World Bank in a Changing World* (Dordrecht: Martinus Nijhoff, 1995), vol. 2, p. 595.

Sorel, J.-M., 'Article 31' in O. Corten and P. Klein, *The Vienna Convention on the Law of Treaties: A Commentary* (Oxford: Oxford University Press, 2011), vol. I, p. 804.

Villiger, M. E., *Customary International Law and Treaties: A Manual on the Theory and Practice of the Interrelation of Sources*, 2nd edn (The Hague: Kluwer Law International, 1997).

Virally, M., 'The Sources of International Law' in M. Sørensen (ed.), *Manual of Public International Law* (London: Macmillan, 1968), p. 116.

Wälde, T., 'Comments and Discussion' in Gaillard, E. and Y. Banifatemi (eds.), *Precedent in International Arbitration* (New York, NY: Juris Publishing, 2007), p. 149.

'The Specific Nature of Investment Arbitration' in P. Kahn and T. Wälde (eds.), *New Aspects of International Investment Law* (The Hague: Martinus Nijhoff, 2007), p. 118.

Weil, P., 'Les Clauses de Stabilisation ou d'Intangibilité Insérée Dans Les Accords de Development Economique' in C. E. Rousseau (ed.), *Méelanges Offerts à Charles Rousseau* (Paris: Pedone, 1974), p. 301.

'Droit International Et Contrats d'Etat' in P. Weil, *Mélanges Offerts A Paul Reuter – Le Droit International: Unité Et Diversité* (Paris: Pedone, 1981), p. 549.

White, G., 'Wealth Deprivation: Creditor and Contract Claims' in R. B. Lillich (ed.), *International Law of State Responsibility for Injuries to Aliens* (Virginia: University Press of Virginia, 1983), p. 149.

Journal Articles

Abs, H., and Lord H. Shawcross, 'The Proposed Convention to Protect Private Foreign Investment' (1960) 9 *Journal of Public Law* 115.

Adaralegbe, B., 'Stabilizing Fiscal Regimes in Long-Term Contracts: Recent Developments from Nigeria' (2008) 1(3) *Journal of World Energy Law & Business* 239.

Adelman, M. A., 'Economics of Exploration for Petroleum and Other Minerals' (1970) 8 *Geoexploration* 131.

Akinsanya, A., 'Host Government's Responses to Foreign Economic Control: The Experience of Selected African Countries' (1981) 30(4) ICLQ 769.

Al-Jumah, K. M., 'Arab State Contract Disputes: Lessons from the Past' (2002) 17(3) *Arab Law Quarterly* 215.

Al Qurashi, Z. A., 'Renegotiation of International Petroleum Agreements' (2005) 22(4) *Journal of International Arbitration* 261.

Allen, T., 'Commonwealth Constitutions and the Right Not to be Deprived of Property' (1993) 42 ICLQ 523.

Alvarez, J. E., 'The Public International Law Regime Governing International Investment' (2009) 344 *Recueil des Cours* 193.

Amerasinghe, C. F., 'State Breaches of Contracts with Aliens and International Law' (1964) 58 AJIL 881.

Antony, J., 'Umbrella Clauses since *SGS* v *Pakistan* and *SGS* v *Philippines* – A Developing Consensus' (2013) 29(4) *Arbitration International* 607.

Asante, S. B., 'International Law and Foreign Investment: A Reappraisal' (1988) 37 ICLQ 588.

   'Stability of Contractual Relations in the Transnational Investment Process' (1979) 28 ICLQ 401.

Bantekas, I., 'Corporate Social Responsibility in International Law' (2004) 22 *Boston University International Law Journal* 309.

Baxter, R. R., 'Treaties and Custom' (1970) 129 *Recueil des Cours* 25.

Berger, K. P., 'Renegotiation and Adaptation of International Investment Contracts: The Role of Contract Drafters and Arbitrators' (2003) 36 *Vanderbilt Journal of Transnational Law* 1347.

Bindschedler, R. L., 'La Protection de la Propriété Privée en Droit International Public' (1959) 90 *Recueil des Cours* 174.

Borchard, E. M., 'Contractual Claims in International Law' (1913) 13(6) *Columbia Law Review* 457.

   'The Mavrommatis Concessions Cases' (1925) 19 AJIL 728.

Bowett, D. W., 'State Contracts with Aliens: Contemporary Developments on Compensation for Termination or Breach' (1988) 58 BYIL 49.

Brower, C. N., 'The Charter of Economic Rights and Duties of States' (24–6 April 1975) *American Society of International Law Proceedings* 225.

Brown, R., 'The Relationship between the State and the Multinational Corporation in the Exploitation of Resources' (1984) 33 ICLQ 218.

Brownlie, I., 'Causes of Action in the Law of Nations' (1979) 50(1) BYIL 13.

   'International Law at the Fiftieth Anniversary of the United Nations: General Course on Public International Law' (1995) 25 *Recueil des Cours* 9.

Calamita, N.J., 'The British Bank Nationalizations: An International Law Perspective' (2009) 58(1) ICLQ 119.

Cantergreil, J., 'The Audacity of the Texaco/Calasiatic Award: René-Jean Dupuy and the Internationalization of Foreign Investment Law' (2011) 22(2) EJIL 441.

Cavaglieri, A., 'La Notion Des Droits Acquis Et Son Application En Droit International Public' (translated by R. Genet) (1931) Revue Générale de Droit International Public 257.

Chinkin, C., 'A Critique of the Public/Private Dimension' (1999) 10 EJIL 387.

Commission, J. P., 'Precedent in Investment Treaty Arbitration – A Citation Analysis of a Developing Jurisprudence' (2007) 24(2) Journal of International Arbitration 129.

Crawford, J., 'International Law and Foreign Sovereigns: Distinguishing Immune Transactions' (1983) 54 BYIL 74.

'Revising the Draft Articles on State Responsibility' (1999) 10 EJIL 435.

'The ILC's Articles on Responsibility of States for Internationally Wrongful Acts: A Retrospect' (2002) 96 AJIL 874.

'Multilateral Rights and Obligations in International Law' (2006) 319 Recueil des Cours 325.

'Treaty and Contract in Investment Arbitration' (2008) 24(3) Arbitration International 351.

Curtis, C. T., 'The Legal Security of Economic Development Agreements' (1988) 29 Harvard International Law Journal 317.

De Aréchaga, E. J., 'International Law in the Past Third of a Century' (1978) 159 Recueil des Cour 267.

de Szászy, S., 'The Protection of Acquired Private Rights of Foreigners in International Law' (1930) 36 International Law Association Reports of Conferences 583.

Delaume, G. R., 'State Contracts and Transnational Arbitration' (1981) 75 AJIL 784.

Dinstein, Y., 'The Interaction between Customary International Law and Treaties' (2007) 322 Recueil des Cours 243.

Douglas, Z., 'The Hybrid Foundations of Investment Treaty Arbitration' (2003) 74(1) BYIL 151.

'The MFN Clause in Investment Arbitration: Treaty Interpretation Off the Rails' (2011) 2(1) Journal of International Dispute Settlement 97.

Dragiuev, D., 'Bad Faith Conduct of States in Violation of the 'Fair and Equitable Treatment' Standard in International Investment Law and Arbitration' (2014) 5(2) Journal of International Dispute Settlement 273.

Dumberry, P., 'The Protection of Investors' Legitimate Expectations and the Fair and Equitable Treatment Standard under NAFTA Article 1105' (2014) 31(1) Journal of International Arbitration 47.

El-Kosheri, A. S., and T. F. Riad, 'The Law Governing a New Generation of Petroleum Agreements: Changes in the Arbitral Process' (1986) 1 ICSID Review: Foreign Investment Law Journal 257.

Fachiri, A., 'Expropriation and International Law' (1925) 6 BYIL 159.
  'International Law and the Property of Aliens' (1929) 10 BYIL 32.
Fatouros, A. A., 'International Law and the Internationalized Contract' (1980) 74
  AJIL 134.
Fietta, S., 'Expropriation and the "Fair and Equitable" Standard: The Developing
  Role of Investors' "Expectations" in International Investment Arbitration'
  (2006) 23(5) *Journal of International Arbitration* 375.
Fitzmaurice, G., 'The General Principles of International Law Considered from the
  Standpoint of the Rule of Law' (1957) 92 *Recueil des Cours* 1.
Franck, S. D., and L. E. Wylie, 'Predicting Outcomes in Investment Treaty Arbitration'
  (2015) 65 *Duke Law Journal* 459.
Friedmann, W., 'Half a Century of International Law' (1964) 50(8) *Virginia Law
  Review* 1333.
Geiger, R., 'The Unilateral Change of Economic Development Agreements' (1974)
  23 ICLQ 73.
Grant, J. P., and J. C. Barker, 'Harvard Research in International Law' (1932) 26 AJIL
  Supplement Part III.
Gray, K., 'Property in Thin Air' (1991) 50(2) *Cambridge Law Journal* 252.
Guillaume, G., 'The Use of Precedent by International Judges and Arbitrators' (2011)
  2(1) *Journal of International Dispute Settlement* 5.
Herz, J. J., 'Expropriation of Foreign Property' (1941) 35 AJIL 243.
Higgins, R., 'The Taking of Property by the State' (1982) 176 *Recueil des Cours* 263.
Ho, J., 'The Meaning of "Investment" in ICSID Arbitrations' (2010) 26(4) *Arbitration
  International* 633.
  'Circumstantial Indicia in Treaty Interpretation' (2017) 33(1) *ICSID Review –
  Foreign Investment Law Journal* (advance access), online: https://doi.org/
  10.1093/icsidreview/six011 (accessed 31 December 2017).
Holsti, K. J., 'The Concept of Power in the Study of International Relations' (1964)
  7(4) *International Studies Quarterly* 179.
Hughes, Hon. C. E., 'Observations on the Monroe Doctrine' (1923) 17 AJIL 611.
Jenks, W., 'Economic and Social Change and the Law of Nations' (1973) 138 *Recueil
  des Cours* 455.
Jennings, R. Y., 'State Contracts in International Law' (1961) 37 BYIL 156.
  'What Is International Law and How Do We Tell It When We See It?' (1981) 37
  Swiss Yearbook of International Law 59 reprinted in R. Y. Jennings, *Collected
  Writings of Sir Robert Jennings* (The Hague: Kluwer Law International, 1998),
  p. 730.
Jones, O. R., and C. Dunn, 'Consent, Forced Renegotiation and Expropriation in
  International Law' (2010) 26(3) *Arbitration International* 391.
Kahn, P., 'Contrats d'Etat et Nationalisation. Les Apports de la Sentence Arbitrale du
  24 mars 1982' (1982) 109 *Journal de Droit International* 844.
Karckenbeeck, G., 'La Protection Internationale Des Droits Acquis' (1937) 5 *Recueil
  des Cours* 317.

Kaufmann-Kohler, G., 'Arbitral Precedent: Dream, Necessity or Excuse?' (2006) 23(3) *Arbitration International* 357.

Kennedy, D., and F. Michelman, 'Are Property and Contract Efficient?' (1980) 8 *Hofstra Law Review* 711.

Kmiec, D. W., and J. O. McGinnis, 'The Contract Clause: A Return to the Original Understanding' (1986–7) 14 *Hastings Constitutional Law Quarterly* 525.

Ko, S. S., 'The Concept of Acquired Rights in International Law: A Survey' (1977) 24(1–2) *Netherlands International Law Review* 120.

Kobrin, S. J., 'Expropriation as an Attempt to Control Foreign Firms in LDCs: Trends from 1960 to 1979' (1984) 28(3) *International Studies Quarterly* 329.

Kuhn, A. K., 'Nationalization of Foreign-Owned Property in Its Impact on International Law' (1951) 45 AJIL 709.

Kunz, J., 'La Primauté du Droit des Gens' (1925) 6 *Revue de Droit International et de Législation Comparée* 556.

Kurtz, J., 'Adjudging the Exceptional at International Investment Law: Security, Public Order and Financial Crisis' (2010) 59(2) ICLQ 325.

Lalive, J. F., 'Les Contrats d'Etat: Développements Récents et Perspectives d'Avenir' (1983) 181 *Recueil des Cours* 163.

Lauterpacht, E., 'Anglo-Iranian Oil Company Ltd Persian Settlement – Opinion (20 January 1954)' in A. Sinclair, 'The Origins of the Umbrella Clause in the International Law of Investment Protection' (2004) 20(4) *Arbitration International* 411.

Leland, E. H., 'Optimal Risk Sharing and the Leasing of Natural Resources with Application to Oil and Gas Leasing of the OCS' (1978) 92(3) *Quarterly Journal of Economics* 413.

Lipstein, K., 'Conflict of Laws before International Tribunals (ii)' (1943) 29 *Transactions of the Grotius Society* 51.

Lauterpacht, H., 'The Problem of Jurisdictional Immunities of Foreign States' (1951) 28 BYIL 220.

Lowe, V., 'Regulation or Expropriation?' (2002) 55 *Current Legal Problems* 447.

MacGibbon, I. C., 'Estoppel in International Law' (1958) 7 ICLQ 468.

Maniruzzaman, A. F. M., 'Expropriation of Alien Property and the Principle of Non-Discrimination in International Law of Foreign Investment: An Overview' (1998–9) 8 *Journal of Transnational Law & Policy* 57.

Mann, F. A., 'The Law Governing State Contracts' (1944) 21 BYIL 11.

'The Proper Law of Contracts Concluded by International Persons' (1959) 35 BYIL 34.

'State Contracts and State Responsibility' (1960) 54 AJIL 572.

'British Treaties for the Promotion and Protection of Foreign Investment' (1981) BYIL 241.

McConnell, M. W., 'Contract Rights and Property Rights: A Case Study in The Relationship between Individual Liberties and Constitutional Structure' (1988) 76(2) *California Law Review* 267.

McDougal, M. S., L.-C. Chen, and H. D. Laswell, 'The Protection of Aliens from Discrimination and World Public Order: Responsibility of States Conjoined with Human Rights' (1976) 70 AJIL 432.

McLachlan, C., 'Investment Treaties and General International Law' (2008) 57(2) ICLQ 361.

McNair, A., 'The Legality of the Occupation of the Ruhr' (1924) 5 BYIL 17.
'The General Principles of Law Recognized by Civilized Nations' (1957) 33 BYIL 1.
'The Seizure of Property and Enterprises in Indonesia' (1959) 6(3) *Netherlands International Law Review* 218.

Meron, T., 'Repudiation of Ultra Vires State Contracts and the International Responsibility of States' (1957) 6 ICLQ 273.

Merrill, T. W. 'The Landscape of Constitutional Property' (2000) 86 *Virginia Law Review* 885.

Merrill, T. W., and H. E. Smith, 'Optimal Standardization in the Law of Property: The Numerus Clausus Principle' (2000) 110 *Yale Law Journal* 1.

Metzger, S. D., 'Multilateral Conventions for the Protection of Private Foreign Investment' (1960) 9 *Journal of Public Law* 133.

Miller, A. S., 'Protection of Private Foreign Investment by Multilateral Convention' (1959) 53 AJIL 371.

Muchlinski, P., 'The Rise and Fall of the Multilateral Agreement on Investment: Where Now?' (2000) 34 *International Lawyer* 1033.

Münch, F., 'Les Effets d'Une Nationalisation à l'Etranger' (1959) 89 *Recueil des Cours* 411.

Newcombe, A., 'The Boundaries of Regulatory Expropriation in International Law' (2005) 20(1) *ICSID Review – Foreign Investment Law Journal* 1.

Nwogugu, E., 'Legal Problems of Foreign Investments' (1976) 153 *Recueil des Cours* 167.

Palmeter, D., and P. C. Mavroidis, 'The WTO Legal System: Sources of Law' (1998) 92 AJIL 398.

Paparinskis, M., 'MFN Clauses and International Dispute Settlement: Moving beyond *Maffezini* and *Plama*?' (2011) 26(2) *ICSID Review – Foreign Investment Law Journal* 14.

Paulsson, J., 'Third World Participation in International Investment Arbitration' (1987) 2 *ICSID Review – Foreign Investment Law Journal* 19.

Pazarci, H., 'La Responsabilité Internationale des Etats à l'Occasion des Contrats Conclus Entre Etats et Personnes Privées Etrangères' (1975) 79 *Revue Générale de Droit International Public* 354.

Penner, J., 'Misled by Property' (2005) 18 *Canadian Journal of Law & Jurisprudence* 75.

Penrose, E., G. Joffé, and P. Stevens, 'Nationalisation of Foreign-Owned Property for a Public Purpose: An Economic Perspective on Appropriate Compensation' (1992) 55 *Modern Law Review* 351.

Poulsen, L., and E. Aisbett, 'When the Claim Hits: Bilateral Investment Treaties and Bounded Rational Learning' (2013) 65(2) *World Politics* 273.

Radi, Y., 'The Application of the Most-Favoured-Nation Clause to the Dispute Settlement Provisions of Bilateral Investment Treaties: Domesticating the "Trojan Horse"' (2007) 18(4) EJIL 757.

Reich, C. A., 'The New Property' (1964) 73 *Yale Law Journal* 733.

Reinisch, A., 'The Role of Precedent in ICSID Arbitration' (2008) 2 *Austrian Arbitration Yearbook* 495.

Reisman, W. M., 'The Cult of Custom in the Late 20th Century' (1987) 17 *Canadian Western International Law Journal* 133.

Reuter, P., 'Principes de Droit International Public' (1961) 103 *Recueil des Cours* 425.

Rigaux, F., 'Les Situations Juridiques Individuelles Dans un Système de Relativité Générale de Droit International Privé' (1989) 213 *Recueil des Cours* 154.

Roberts, A., 'Power and Persuasion in Investment Treaty Interpretation: The Dual Role of States' (2010) 104(2) AJIL 179.

Ryan, C. M., 'Discerning the Compliance Calculus: Why States Comply with International Investment Law' (2009) 38 *Georgia Journal of International and Comparative Law* 63.

Sacerdoti, G., 'State Contracts and International Law: A Reappraisal' (1986–7) 7 *Italian Yearbook of International Law* 26.

Salomon, M., 'From NIEO to Now and the Unfinishable Story of Economic Justice' (2013) 62(1) ICLQ 31.

Sampliner, G. H., 'Arbitration of Expropriation Cases Under US Investment Treaties – A Threat to Democracy or the Dog that Didn't Bark?' (2003) 18(1) *ICSID Review – Foreign Investment Law Journal* 1.

Schachter, O., 'Private Foreign Investment and International Organization' (1959–60) 45 *Cornell Law Quarterly* 415.

'International Law in Theory and Practice: General Course in Public International Law' (1982) 178 *Recueil des Cours* 1.

Schnitzer, M., 'Expropriation and Control Rights: A Dynamic Model of Foreign Direct Investment' (1999) 17 *International Journal of Industrial Organization* 1113.

Schreuer, C., 'Travelling the BIT Route: Of Waiting Periods, Umbrella Clauses and Forks in the Road' (2004) 5 *Journal of World Investment and Trade* 231.

'Fair and Equitable Treatment in Arbitral Practice' (2005) 6(3) *Journal of World Investment and Trade* 357.

Schwarzenberger, G., 'The Protection of British Property Abroad' (1952) 5 *Current Legal Problems* 295.

'The Abs-Shawcross Draft Convention on Investments Abroad: A Critical Commentary' (1960) 9 *Journal of Public Law* 147.

Schwebel, S. M., 'International Protection of Contractual Arrangements' (1959) 53 *American Society of International Law Proceedings* 266.

'The Kingdom of Saudi Arabia and Aramco Arbitrate the Onassis Agreement' (2010) 20(20) *Journal of World Energy Law and Business* 1.

Seidl-Hohenveldern, I., 'The Abs-Shawcross Draft Convention to Protect Private Foreign Investment: Comments on the Round Table' (1961) 10 *Journal of Public Law* 100.

'International Economic Law – General Course on Public International Law' (1986) 198 *Recueil des Cours* 9.

Sharp, M. P., 'Pacta Sunt Servanda' (1941) 41 *Columbia Law Review* 783.

Shawcross, Lord H., 'The Problems of Foreign Investment in International Law' (1961) 102 *Recueil des Cours* 335.

Sinclair, A., 'The Origins of the Umbrella Clause in the International Law of Investment Protection' (2004) 20(4) *Arbitration International* 411.

Snodgrass, E., 'Protecting Investors' Legitimate Expectations: Recognizing and Delimiting a General Principle' (2006) 21(1) *ICSID Review – Foreign Investment Law Journal* 1.

Sohn, L. B., and R. R. Baxter, 'Responsibility of States for Injuries to the Economic Interests of Aliens' (1961) 55 AJIL 545.

Sornarajah, M., 'Compensation for Expropriation: The Emergence of New Standards' (1979) 13 *Journal of World Trade Law* 108.

'The Myth of International Contract Law' (1981) 15 *Journal of World Trade Law* 187.

Sturzaker, D., and C. Cawood, 'The Sandline Affair: Illegality and International Law' (1999) *Australian International Law Journal* 214.

Sunstein, C., 'On Property and Constitutionalism' (1993) 14 *Cardozo Law Review* 907.

Thomas, J. C., 'Reflections on Article 1105 of NAFTA: History, State Practice and the Influence of Commentators' (2002) 17(1) *ICSID Review – Foreign Investment Law Journal* 21.

Titi, C., 'Les Clauses de Stabilisation dans les Contrats d'Investissement: Une Entrave au Pouvoir Normatif de l'Etat d'Accueil' (2014) 2 *Journal de Droit International* 541.

Tunkin, G., 'International Law in the International System' (1975) 147 *Recueil des Cours* 1.

'Is General International Law Customary Law Only?' (1993) 4 EJIL 534.

Vagts, D., 'Coercion and Foreign Investment Rearrangements' (1978) 72 AJIL 17.

Van Harten, G., 'Arbitrator Behaviour in Asymmetrical Adjudication: An Empirical Study of Investment Treaty Arbitration' (2012) 50(1) *Osgoode Hall Law Journal* 211.

Vasciannie, S., 'The Fair and Equitable Treatment Standard in International Investment Law and Practice' (1999) 70(1) BYIL 99.

Veeder, V. V., 'The Lena Goldfields Arbitration: The Historical Roots of Three Ideas' (1998) 47 ICLQ 747.

Verdross, A., 'La Primauté du Droit des Gens et La Conception Unitaire du Droit' (1927) 16 *Recueil des Cours* 287.

'Quasi-International Agreements and International Economic Transactions' (1964) 18 *Yearbook of World Affairs* 230.

Vesel, S., 'A "Creeping" Violation of the Fair and Equitable Treatment Standard?' (2014) 30(3) *Arbitration International* 553.

Wälde, T., 'The "Umbrella" Clause in Investment Arbitration – A Comment on Original Intentions and Recent Cases' (2005) 6 *Journal of World Investment & Trade* 183.

Wälde, T., and A. Kolo, 'Environmental Regulation, Investment Protection and "Regulatory Taking" in International Law' (2001) 50 ICLQ 811.

Wälde, T., and G. Ndi, 'Stabilizing International Investment Commitments: International Law versus Contract Interpretation' (1996) 31 *Texas International Law Journal* 215.

Wehberg, H., 'Pacta Sunt Servanda' (1959) 53 AJIL 775.

Weil, P., 'Problèmes Relatifs aux Contrats Passés entre un Etat et un Particulier' (1969) 128(3) *Recueil des Cours* 95.

'Towards Relative Normativity in International Law' (1983) 77 AJIL 413.

Wengler, W., 'Les accords entre Etats et entreprises étrangères sont-ils des traités de droit international?' (1972) 76 *Revue Geneérale de Droit International Public* 313.

Westermann, W. L., 'Interstate Arbitration in Antiquity' (1907) 2(5) *The Classical Journal* 197.

Weston, B., '"Constructive Takings" Under International Law: A Modest Foray into the Problem of "Creeping Expropriation"' (1975–6) 16 *Vanderbilt Journal of International Law* 103.

Whitehead, L., 'Latin American Debt: An International Bargaining Perspective' (1989) 15(3) *Review of International Studies* 231.

Williams, J. F., 'International Law and the Property of Aliens' (1928) 9 BYIL 1.

Witenberg, J. C., 'Protection of Private Property' (1930) 36 *International Law Association Reports of Conferences* 301.

Official Documents

Ago, R., 'First Report on State Responsibility' (7 May 1969–20 January 1970), UN Doc. A/CN.4/217.

Ago, R., 'Fifth Report on State Responsibility to the ILC' (22 March 1976), UN Doc. A/CN.4/291.

Dietring, 'Tientsin Trade Report for the Year 1902', Nationaal Archief Den Haag, 2.05.90/483.

Financial Times, 'India Overhauls Its Investment Treaty Regime (16 July 2016)', online: www.ft.com/content/53bd355c-8203-34af-9c27-7bf990a447dc (accessed 31 December 2017).

'South Africa: BITs in Pieces (19 October 2012)', online: www.ft.com/content/b0eec497-5123-3939-92f7-a5fbcb73dd33 (accessed 26 January 2018).

'US Trade Problems Begin at Home Not Abroad (20 November 2017)', online: www.ft.com/content/14b4ef1e-cbab-11e7-ab18-7a9fb7d6163e (accessed 26 January 2018).

García-Amador, F. V., 'Responsibility of the State for Injuries Caused in Its Territory to the Person or Property of Aliens (Part I: Acts and Omissions)' (15 February 1957), UN Doc. A/CN.4/106.

'State Responsibility' (20 January 1956), UN Doc. A/CN.4/96.

ILC, 'Diplomatic Intercourse and Immunities – Memrandum Prepared by the Secretariat' (21 February 1956), UN Doc. A/CN.4/98.

'Draft Articles on Responsibility of States for Internationally Wrongful Acts, with Commentaries' (2001), Yearbook of the International Law Commission, vol. II, Part Two.

Letter from the Swiss Secretariat for Economic Affairs to the ICSID Secretary-General, 'Umbrella Clauses in Bilateral Investment Agreements', 1 October 2003, 19 Mealey's International Arbitration Reports E1.

Netherlands Department of Foreign Affairs, Conference at the Hague (June 26–July 20, 1922) – Minutes and Documents (The Hague: Government Printing Office, 1922).

Sucharitkul, S., 'Fourth Report on Jurisdictional Immunities of States and Their Property' (31 March 1982), UN Doc. A/CN4/357.

UNCTAD, 'Proceedings of the United Nations Conference on Trade and Development – Third Session, Santiago de Chile' (13 April to 21 May 1972), UN Doc. A/PV.2315.

'Report of the Working Party of the Trade and Development Board', TD/B/AC.12/4, partially reproduced in J. Kuusi, The Host State and the Transnational Corporation (Michigan: Saxon House, 1976).

UNHRC, 'First Intergovernmental Working Group Session Report' (5 February 2016), UN Doc. A/HRC/31/50.

'Second Intergovernmental Working Group Session Report' (4 January 2017), UN Doc. A/HRC/34/47.

US Department of State, Papers Relating to the Foreign Relations of the United States (Washington, DC: Government Printing Office, 1861).

Papers Relating to the Foreign Relations of the United States (Washington, DC: Government Printing Office, 1900).

'US Withdrawal from the Proceedings Initiated by Nicaragua in the ICJ', Department Statement, 18 January 1985, Department State Bulletin, No. 2096 (March 1985).

US Senate, Treaties, Conventions, International Acts, Protocols, and Agreements between the USA and Other Powers (Washington, DC: Government Printing Office, 1938).

Occasional Papers and PhD Theses

Draper, P., S. Lacey, and Y. Ramkolowan, 'Mega-Regional Trade Agreements: Implications for the African, Caribbean, and Pacific Countries', ECIPE Occasional Paper No. 2/2014, online: www.ecipe.org (accessed 31 December 2017).

International Law Association Committee on Formation of Customary (General) International Law, 'Statement of Principles Applicable to the Formation of General Customary International Law', Final Report of the Committee (2000).

Nissel, T. A., 'A History of State Responsibility: The Struggle for International Standards (1870–1960)', PhD thesis, University of Helsinki (2016).

Shemberg, A., 'Stabilization Clauses and Human Rights', Research Project Conducted for International Finance Corporation and the United Nations Special Representative of the Secretary-General on Business and Human Rights (27 May 2009), online: www.ifc.org (accessed 7 June 2015).

Sinclair, A., 'State Contracts in Investment Treaty Arbitration', PhD thesis, University of Cambridge (2013).

Websites

ABC, 'ISDS: The Devil in the Trade Deal (26 July 2015)', online: www.abc.net.au/radionational/programs/backgroundbriefing/isds-the-devil-in-the-trade-deal/6634538 (accessed 31 December 2017).

Assembleé Nationale, 'Projet de loi no 3258, texte adopté no 785', online: www.assemblee-nationale.fr/11/pdf/ta/ta0785.pdf (accessed 31 December 2017).

BBC News, 'PNG Pays Up to Mercenaries (1 May 1999)', online: http://news.bbc.co.uk/2/hi/asia-pacific/333234.stm (accessed 17 January 2018).

Bureau of Labor Statistics, 'CPI Inflation Calculator', online: https://data.bls.gov/cgi-bin/cpicalc.pl (accessed 31 December 2017).

Dingle, L., 'Conversations with Professor Sir Elihu Lauterpacht, Second Interview (7 March 2008): USA (1940–44) and Career to 1962', online: www.squire.law.cam.ac.uk/eminent-scholars-archiveprofessor-sir-elihu-lauterpacht/conversations-professor-sir-eli-lauterpacht (accessed 31 December 2017).

German Federal Ministry of Justice, 'Gesetze im Internet', online: www.gesetze-im-internet.de (accessed 31 December 2017).

HeinOnline, 'Harvard Research in International Law', online: heinonline.org/HeinDocs/HarvardResearchbrochure.pdf (accessed 1 December 2017).

Historical Statistics, 'Historical Currency Converter', online: www.historicalstatistics.org/Currencyconverter.html (accessed 31 December 2017).

ICSID, 'The ICSID Caseload – Statistics (Issue 2017-2)', online: https://icsid.worldbank.org/en/Documents/resources/ICSID%20Web%20Stats%202017-2%20(English)%20Final.pdf (accessed 31 December 2017).

Investment Policy Hub, 'Model Text for the Indian Bilateral Investment Treaty (2016)', online: investmentpolicyhub.unctad.org/Download/TreatyFile/3560 (accessed 31 December 2017).

ITALaw, 'Indian Model Text of Bilateral Investment Protection and Promotion Agreement (BIPA) (2003)' online: www.italaw.com/sites/default/files/archive/ita1026.pdf (accessed 31 December 2017).

Life on TERRA, 'Life on TERRA: The Curse of Copper – Part 1', online: lifeonterra .com/terra-318-the-curse-of-copper-part-one/ (accessed 31 December 2017).

Kriebaum, U., and A. Reinisch, 'Property, Right to, International Protection' in R. Wolfrum (ed.), 'The Max Planck Encyclopedia of Public International Law (Oxford: Oxford University Press 2008)', online: www.mpepil.com/home (accessed 31 December 2017).

NAFTA Law, 'Interpretive Note of the NAFTA Free Trade Commission on Article 1105 – Minimum Standard of Treatment in Accordance with International Law (31 July 2001)', online: www.naftalaw.org/commission.htm (accessed 31 December 2017).

OANDA, 'Venezuelan Bolivar', online: www.oanda.com/currency/iso-currency-codes/VEF (accessed 31 December 2017).

OECD, 'Guidelines for Multinational Enterprises', online: www.oecd.org/corporate/mne/1922428.pdf (accessed 31 December 2017).

'Members and Partners', online: www.oecd.org/about/membersandpartners (accessed 31 December 2017).

'Multilateral Agreement on Investment', online: www.oecd.org/investment/internationalinvestmentagreements/multilateralagreementoninvestment .htm (accessed 31 December 2017).

'The Multilateral Agreement on Investment Draft Consolidated Text, 22 April 1998, DAFFE/MAI(98)7/REV1', online: www.oecd.org/daf/mai/pdf/ng/ng987r1e.pdf (accessed 15 January 2018).

Office of the UN High Commissioner for Human Rights, 'Guiding Principles on Business and Human Rights', online: www.ohchr.org/Documents/Publications/GuidingPrinciplesBusinessHR_EN.pdf (accessed 31 December 2017).

PCA Press Release, 'Arbitration between Limited Liability Company Lugzor and Four Others as Claimants and the Russian Federation as Respondent (13 December 2017)', online: www.pcacases.com/web/sendAttach/2262 (accessed 31 December 2017).

Stanford Law School, 'The Jackson H. Ralston Prize in International Law', online: https://law.stanford.edu/about/history/the-ralston-prize/ (accessed 31 December 2017).

The New York Times, 'NAFTA's Powerful Little Secret; Obscure Tribunals Settle Disputes, but Go too Far, Critics Say (11 March 2001)', online: www .nytimes.com/2001/03/11/business/nafta-s-powerful-little-secret-obscure-tribunals-settle-disputes-but-go-too-far.html (accessed 24 January 2018).

The White House Office of the Press Secretary, 'Presidential Proclamation – To Modify Duty-Free Treatment under the Generalized System of Preferences and for Other Purposes (26 March 2012)', online: obamawhitehouse.archives.gov/the-press-office/2012/03/26/presidential-proclamation-modify-duty-free-treatment-under-generalized-s (accessed 31 December 2017)

This Is Money, 'Historic Inflation Calculator: How the Value of Money Has Changed since 1900', online: www.thisismoney.co.uk/money/bills/article-1633409/Historic-inflation-calculator-value-money-changed-1900.html (accessed 31 December 2017).

Transnational Institute, 'Ecuador Terminates 16 Investment Treaties (18 May 2017)', online: www.tni.org/en/article/ecuador-terminates-16-investment-treaties (accessed 31 December 2017).

UN Global Compact, 'The Ten Principles of the UN Global Compact', online: www.unglobalcompact.org/what-is-gc/mission/principles (accessed 1 December 2017).

UN Office of Legal Affairs (Codification Division), 'Reports of International Arbitral Awards', online: https://legal.un.org/riaa/(accessed 31 December 2017).

UNCITRAL, 'UNCITRAL Rules on Transparency in Treaty-Based Investor-State Arbitration (Effective Date: 1 April 2014)', online: www.uncitral.org/uncitral/en/uncitral_texts/arbitration/2014Transparency.html (accessed 31 December 2017).

UNCTAD, 'Improving Investment Dispute Settlement: UNCTAD Policy Tools (IIA Issues Note – International Investment Agreements, November 2017)', online: investmentpolicyhub.unctad.org/Upload/Documents/IMPROVING%20INVESTMENT%20DISPUTE%20SETTLEMENT-%20UNCTAD%20POLICY%20TOOLS.pdf (accessed 31 December 2017).

'International Investment Agreements Navigator', online: https://investmentpolicyhub.unctad.org/IIA (accessed 1 December 2017).

'International Investment Instruments: A Compendium, Volume III (Regional Integration, Bilateral and Non-governmental Instruments)', online: http://unctad.org/en/Docs/dtci30vol3_en.pdf (accessed 24 January 2018).

'International Investment Instruments: A Compendium, Volume V (Regional Integration, Bilateral and Non-governmental Instruments)', online: http://unctad.org/en/Docs/dite2vol5_en.pdf (accessed 15 January 2018).

'Most-Favoured-Nation Treatment – Series on Issues in International Investment Agreements II (2010)', online: http://unctad.org/en/Docs/diaeia20101_en.pdf (accessed 24 January 2018).

'World Investment Report 2015', online: unctad.org/en/PublicationsLibrary/wir2015_en.pdf (accessed 31 December 2017).

'World Investment Report 2016', online: unctad.org/en/PublicationsLibrary/wir2016_en.pdf (accessed 31 December 2017).

'World Investment Report 2017', online: unctad.org/en/PublicationsLibrary/wir2017_en.pdf (accessed 31 December 2017).

Under Rich Earth, online: underrichearth.ryecinema.com/ (accessed 31 December 2017).

University of Wisconsin-Madison Libraries, 'Foreign Relations of the United States', online: https://digital.library.wisc.edu/1711.dl/FRUS (accessed 31 December 2017).

US Department of State, '2012 U.S. Model Bilateral Investment Treaty', online: www.state.gov/documents/organization/188371.pdf (accessed 24 January 2018).

'Interpretation of Certain Chapter 11 Provisions'; 'Statement on Non-Disputing Party Participation'; and 'Statement on Notices of Intent to Submit a Claim to Arbitration', online: www.state.gov/s/l/c3439.htm (accessed 31 December 2017).

Yannaca-Small, C., '"Indirect Expropriation" and the "Right to Regulate" in International Investment Law (2004)', online: www.oecd-library.org (accessed 31 December 2017).

INDEX

absolute contractual protection, 5, 9,
10, 46, 48, 51, 52, 54, 55, 57, 58,
60, 89, 202, 221, 228, 239, 280
Abs-Shawcross Draft Convention,
45, 46, 52, 54, 55, 56, 57, 58, 60,
214, 239
Abs-Shawcross Draft Convention on
Investments Abroad, 45,
214, 239
acquired rights, 101, 183, 189, 190, 191,
192
acta iure imperii, 127, 129, 130, 162,
277, 282
adherence, 22, 63, 72, 75, 78, 79, 81, 83,
85, 88, 89
adjudication, 9, 21, 24, 28, 59, 77, 84,
87, 121, 245, 279
adjudicatory proceedings, 117, 118
administrative proceedings, 116, 117,
118, 273
Africa, 146, 149, 177, 243
Agency for International Development.
See AID
aggravating circumstances, 94, 95, 96,
97, 98, 99, 100, 105, 106, 108, 114,
117, 118, 120, 121, 122, 123, 127,
261, 283
agreements, 1, 37, 48, 51, 55, 56, 65,
115, 149, 187, 188, 227, 259
AID, 156
Alabama Claims, 80
alien contracts, 139, 281
alien property, 2, 3, 4, 89, 139, 140, 180,
192, 220, 224, 231, 237, 245, 271,
274, 279, 281
alien protection, 91, 92, 93, 105, 109,
115, 137, 245, 281

aliens, 2, 3, 4, 31, 55, 57, 89, 90, 91, 93,
99, 111, 115, 116, 117, 153, 214,
220, 224, 231, 271, 273, 281
allegations, 60, 121, 249
Allied, 21
Allied blockade, 21
ambiguity, 64, 67, 69, 72, 103, 184, 204
American and English Encyclopedia of
Law, 29
American Independent Oil Company,
169, 179, 194, 230
Amity, Economic Relations, and
Consular Rights, 70, 155
analogy, 73, 75, 76, 79, 141
Anglo-Iranian Oil Company, 53, 54, 237
annulment, 78, 79, 81, 85, 87, 107, 124,
258, 197, 201, 208, 223, 232, 249, 258
applicability, 8, 37, 42, 44, 67, 148, 203,
226
Arab Republic of Egypt, 157, 165, 166,
209, 233, 260
arbitral awards, 3, 4, 5, 11, 36, 37, 43,
60, 61, 62, 63, 64, 65, 67, 69, 70,
71, 72, 73, 74, 75, 76, 77, 78, 79,
80, 81, 83, 84, 85, 86, 88, 89, 93,
96, 97, 99, 102, 109, 113, 115, 117,
118, 119, 121, 123, 127, 128, 130,
161, 186, 187, 208, 209, 210, 223,
227, 232, 237, 252, 279, 280, 281
arbitral tribunals, 4, 11, 35, 38, 41, 59,
60, 61, 62, 63, 64, 65, 67, 68, 69, 70,
72, 73, 74, 75, 76, 79, 81, 84, 85, 86,
88, 89, 91, 92, 101, 102, 104, 107,
114, 119, 120, 127, 135, 138, 163,
185, 190, 201, 210, 226, 228, 229,
232, 233, 236, 238, 240, 241, 242,
243, 247, 250, 268, 275, 279, 280

BOOKS IN THE SERIES

Lightning Source UK Ltd.
Milton Keynes UK
UKHW020852141121
393833UK00015B/510